ROYAL JUSTICE AND THE MAKING OF THE TUDOR COMMONWEALTH, 1485–1547

The dawn of the Tudor regime is one of most recognisable periods of English history. Yet the focus on its monarchs' private lives and ministers' constitutional reforms creates the impression that this age's major developments were isolated to halls of power, far removed from the wider populace. This book presents a more holistic vision of politics and society in late medieval and early modern England. Delving into the rich but little-studied archive of the royal Court of Requests, it reconstructs collaborations between sovereigns and subjects on the formulation of an important governmental ideal: justice. Examining the institutional and social dimensions of this point of contact, this study places ordinary people, their knowledge, and their demands at the heart of a judicial revolution unfolding within the governments of Henry VII and Henry VIII. Yet it also demonstrates that directing extraordinary royal justice into ordinary procedures created as many problems as it solved.

LAURA FLANNIGAN is a researcher at the University of Oxford. She has published several articles in *Law and History Review* and *Historical Research*, and was awarded the Sir John Neale Essay Prize in 2020. 'Her calendar of the early Court of Requests archive was published with the List and Index Society in 2023.'

CAMBRIDGE STUDIES IN EARLY MODERN BRITISH HISTORY

Series editors

MICHAEL BRADDICK, *Professor of History, University of Sheffield*
KRISTA KESSELRING, *Professor of History, Dalhousie University*
ALEXANDRA WALSHAM, *Professor of Modern History,*
University of Cambridge, and Fellow of Emmanuel College

This is a series of monographs and studies covering many aspects of the history of the British Isles between the late fifteenth century and the early eighteenth century. It includes the work of established scholars and pioneering work by a new generation of scholars. It includes both reviews and revisions of major topics and books which open up new historical terrain or which reveal startling new perspectives on familiar subjects. All the volumes set detailed research within broader perspectives, and the books are intended for the use of students as well as of their teachers.

For a list of titles in the series go to www.cambridge.org/earlymodernbritishhistory

ROYAL JUSTICE AND THE MAKING OF THE TUDOR COMMONWEALTH, 1485–1547

LAURA FLANNIGAN
University of Oxford

CAMBRIDGE
UNIVERSITY PRESS

Shaftesbury Road, Cambridge CB2 8EA, United Kingdom

One Liberty Plaza, 20th Floor, New York, NY 10006, USA

477 Williamstown Road, Port Melbourne, VIC 3207, Australia

314–321, 3rd Floor, Plot 3, Splendor Forum, Jasola District Centre,
New Delhi – 110025, India

103 Penang Road, #05–06/07, Visioncrest Commercial, Singapore 238467

Cambridge University Press is part of Cambridge University Press & Assessment,
a department of the University of Cambridge.

We share the University's mission to contribute to society through the pursuit of
education, learning and research at the highest international levels of excellence.

www.cambridge.org
Information on this title: www.cambridge.org/9781009371360
DOI: 10.1017/9781009371346

© Laura Flannigan 2024

This publication is in copyright. Subject to statutory exception and to the provisions
of relevant collective licensing agreements, no reproduction of any part may take
place without the written permission of Cambridge University Press & Assessment.

First published 2024

A catalogue record for this publication is available from the British Library.

A Cataloging-in-Publication data record is available from the Library of Congress.

ISBN 978-1-009-37136-0 Hardback

Cambridge University Press & Assessment has no responsibility for the persistence
or accuracy of URLs for external or third-party internet websites referred to in this
publication and does not guarantee that any content on such websites is, or will remain,
accurate or appropriate.

For Harry

Contents

List of Figures and Tables	*page* ix
Acknowledgements	x
Note on the Text	xiii
List of Abbreviations	xiv
Introduction	1

PART I THE NEW JUSTICE SYSTEM

1	The Principle and Problem of Justice	23
2	Conciliar Justice at Centre and Periphery	43
3	'Travailing between the Prince and Petitioners': The Court of Requests	62

PART II SEEKING AND REQUESTING JUSTICE

4	Geography and Demography	95
5	Disputes and Dispute Resolution	117
6	'Your Poor Orator': Petitioning the King	142

PART III DELIVERING AND CONTESTING JUSTICE

7	Before the King's Most Honourable Council	173
8	Answers and Arguments	203
9	'A Final Peax': Passing Judgment	224
	Conclusion: Justice and the Tudor Commonwealth	254

viii   *Contents*

Appendix   Personnel in the Court of Requests, 1493–1547   266
Bibliography   275
Index   297

Figures and Tables

Figures

4.1 Origins of litigants and their disputes in the Court of   *page* 97
     Requests, *c.* 1495–1547 (total: 4,023)
6.1 Petition of *Thomas May* v. *John Battel*, submitted to the king   155
     and Council in the Henrician period. © The National
     Archives, ref. REQ2/12/14
7.1 Writ for commission signed by Henry VIII, countersigned by   191
     William Atwater, and issued from Woking by the Court of
     Requests, August 1509. © The National Archives, ref. REQ2/
     5/379
7.2 The 'wet stamp' of Henry VIII's sign manual on a commission   193
     writ issued from the Court of Requests, June 1523.
     © The National Archives, ref. REQ3/5 *Slack* v *Colinson*

Table

4.1 Statuses of plaintiffs and defendants in the Court of Requests,   104
     c. 1495–1547

ix

Acknowledgements

As individualised a pursuit as academic history can be, no book in this field – let alone a first one – is a solo endeavour. First and foremost, this book emerges from several rewarding institutional associations that I have been lucky to hold down the years. Its initial ideas were planted just under a decade ago at the University of York, where I encountered both the Tudors and legal history for the first time. The text itself started life as a PhD project generously supported by the Cambridge Trust and hosted by the ever-inspiring Newnham College. It has grown further over the last few years in Oxford; initially during a year teaching early modern history at Christ Church, and more recently following my election to a Junior Research Fellowship at St John's College. A great deal of thanks is owed also to Cambridge University Press. I am especially grateful to the editors of this series for their support and comments on various versions of the manuscript, and to Liz Friend-Smith, the commissioning editor, for guiding me through the publishing process so seamlessly and patiently.

This study would not have taken its particular form, nor would it have its institutional and archival focus, without the supervision of Paul Cavill. Across three years of fortnightly meetings at Pembroke, Paul was unfailingly supportive, whether explaining the complexities of Tudor law, advising on early conference papers, or reading just about everything I ever wrote. Where there is precision within the following pages it is most likely thanks to his insights. Further thanks go to Steve Gunn and John Guy, who served as examiners for the thesis and who have both been instrumental in its reframing as a monograph. Tim Stretton, whose work on the Court of Requests was such an inspiration as I started my own research, gave his time generously to commenting on the thesis and the book proposals that followed. I will also be forever indebted to Tom Johnson at York for the suggestion of studying the Court of Requests in the first place, and for insightful discussions on law and legalism every time we've crossed paths since. The entirety of Requests' surviving paperwork is held

Acknowledgements xi

at The National Archives, and so I owe its teams of archivists a special thanks for their support on many visits to Kew. Daniel Gosling facilitated research with the miscellaneous collection of REQ3 and kept my spirits up during long days in the underground research room. Meanwhile, I have benefitted immensely from the extensive knowledge of English legal archives generously shared by Amanda Bevan, Sean Cunningham, and Euan Roger over coffees and at conferences. I am also grateful to The National Archives' Image Library for providing high-quality images and permissions for all the pictures printed in this book. Further thanks go as ever to a range of archive specialists – at the Staffordshire, North Yorkshire, Dorset, Birmingham, and Hereford Cathedral record offices, and also at the Huntington Library – for their assistance in providing scans from their respective collections.

The footnotes to this book testify to the influence of conversations with many scholars and colleagues that I greatly admire: Rowena Archer, Jess Ayres, Sir John Baker, George Bernard, John Guy, Neil Jones, Krista Kesselring, Hannes Kleineke, Harriet Lyon, James Ross, Fred Smith, Hillary Taylor, Penny Tucker, Brodie Waddell, John Watts, Ian Williams, Andy Wood, and Deborah Youngs, to name a few. For sharing their research findings, asking thought-provoking questions, or simply offering some encouraging words at crucial junctures in the writing-up process, I am very grateful. To the same end, audiences at the Late Medieval and the Tudor and Stuart seminars at the Institute of Historical Research, at the British Legal History Conference, and at the legal history seminars in Cambridge and Oxford heard snippets of this research and raised many valuable questions and qualifications that improved the text. Outside of writing, putting the world to rights with Mobeen Hussain and Laura Achtelstetter in the Iris Café and further afield since has provided some much-needed energy and encouragement. At Christ Church, an academic year overshadowed by the pandemic was eased by the camaraderie of Marcus Colla, Rowena Archer, Brian Young, Sarah Mortimer, and Kate Lebow. Most recently, the Senior Common Room community at St John's have dutifully listened to me vent about research, writing, and editing: to my fellow historians Aled Davies, Alice Raw, Teresa Witcombe, William Whyte, and Hannah Skoda, and to my college mentor, Katherine Southwood, I am particularly grateful. The wider community of early modern British historians at both Oxford and Cambridge, and the students I've taught in the subject over the last few years, have also been a regular source of inspiration and cheer.

xii   *Acknowledgements*

Many back home in Lincoln have provided constant moral support, whether they knew it or not. The Le Santo family at the Old Vicarage have always generously offered sanctuary, full of food and music, away from the academic world. My parents, Paul and Sharon Flannigan, have not only been life-long models of work ethic but also encouraged me to write ever since I was first taught to use a word processor. In many ways this book represents the culmination of that path. My grandma, Margaret Allen, has been one of my keenest readers – even working her way through the PhD thesis – and I dearly hope that she enjoys this book too. The most constant support through all the highs and lows of academia has come from Harry Le Santo. Whether collecting me from the train station at the end of a long day in the archive, providing near-constant tech assistance, or listening to an impromptu chapter reading, he has lived with Requests and Tudor England as much as I have. The least I could do is dedicate the finished work to him.

Note on the Text

Original spelling, punctuation, and capitalisation have been retained in transcriptions from primary source material. Exceptions include changing 'u' to 'v' and 'i' to 'j', and modernising 'y' (where it is used in a manner equivalent to þ, thorn) to 'th' for the sake of clarity. Abbreviations have been expanded in square brackets, text in superscript retained, and inter-lineations marked at beginning and end with ^. Dates are given in the Old Style, with the year taken to have started on 1 January.

Abbreviations

BL	British Library, London
Bodl.	The Bodleian Library, Oxford
Caesar, *The Ancient State*	Sir Julius Caesar, *The Ancient State, Authoritie, and Proceedings of the Court of Requests* (London, 1597)
CPR	*Calendar of the Patent Rolls*
EHR	*English Historical Review*
HL	Huntington Library, San Marino, California
HMSO	Her Majesty's Stationery Office
JBS	*Journal of British Studies*
JHC	*Journals of the House of Commons, 1547–1699*
JHL	*Journals of the House of Lords, 1509–1793*
LMA	London Metropolitan Archives
LP	*Letters and Papers, Foreign and Domestic, of the Reign of Henry VIII*, eds. J. S. Brewer, J. Gairdner, and R. H. Brodie (21 vols., London, 1862–1932)
ODNB	*Oxford Dictionary of National Biography*, www.oxforddnb.com
OHLE	*The Oxford History of the Laws of England: Volume VI 1483–1558* (Oxford University Press, 2003)
P&P	*Past & Present*
PROME	*The Parliament Rolls of Medieval England 1275–1504*, eds. Chris Given-Wilson et al. (16 vols., Woodbridge, 2005)
REQ	TNA REQ: Records of the Court of Requests

List of Abbreviations

SP	TNA SP: State Papers
The Narrative of Robert Pilkington	'The narrative of Robert Pilkington', printed in *Report on Manuscripts in Various Collections* (HMSO, 1901–14), vol. II, 28–56
TNA	The National Archives, Kew
TRHS	*Transactions of the Royal Historical Society*
YB	Year Books: *Les Reports des Cases*, ed. J. Maynard (11 vols., London, 1678–80). Cited by regnal year, term, plea number, and folio.

References to items in the miscellaneous part of the Court of Requests archive, TNA REQ3, are cited by box, part (where a box is split in half), and by the parties' names (e.g. REQ3/1/1 *Dible* v *Kirkham*). This reflects the listing of the first thirty boxes of this archive completed in 2022. Folio numbers for the REQ1 order books normally follow those printed in the top corners in black ink by the Public Record Office. Fragmentary order books filed as REQ1/104 and REQ1/105 and pages scattered in REQ3/14, 3/22, 3/29, and 3/30 have no modern foliation, and so the given numbers refer to the original brown ink figures written in the corners by Sir Julius Caesar.

Introduction

Justice was central to conceptions of good governance in Tudor England. Yet it was difficult to put into practice without attracting scrutiny about the proper remit of a government over its subjects. This book demonstrates how and why, despite the potential for controversy, the first two Tudor monarchs started to dispense justice more regularly from their own hands. A determined expansion of powerful conciliar and equitable courts in the early sixteenth century has been identified in the ascent of provincial councils, where disruptive subjects were kept in check, and in the delineation of the Court of Star Chamber, where ministerial careers were made. This book seeks to understand why so many people readily accepted and even invited the judicial intervention of courts like these into their lives. Its analytical focus is the lesser-studied but furthest reaching of the new royal tribunals of this age, known as the Court of Requests. From the 1480s onwards, this small and fluid court provided a channel for ordinary people from across the realm to petition their king for aid in resolving disputes between neighbours, friends, and kin. Yet it is the social depth of Requests' activities that has caused it to be overlooked by historians of this once heavily studied period.

Most importantly, Requests was reputed contemporarily to be the 'poor man's court'. Theoretically, then, it excluded the great men of the realm with whom scholars of governmental reform and court politics have traditionally been preoccupied. In fact, among its abundant paperwork we find everyone from 'paupers' and 'the porist prior of Englond' to Henry VIII himself, the ink of his signature smudged as his sleeve moved across the page. It therefore mobilised perhaps the largest social range of any lawcourt in the enterprise of justice-seeking and justice-making – and of defining one of the key tenets of the commonwealth. Moreover, its casefiles may tell us little about the machinations of monarchs and ministers in matters of state, but they do record some of the Crown's more quotidian business: its involvement in run-of-the-mill disagreements in far-flung

Introduction

parts of the realm about relatively small amounts of land, money, and property. These matters had little direct relevance to the king's estates or interests and nor, it has been supposed, to our narratives of the early Tudor regime's grasp for legitimacy and power. Yet they were life-and-death to the people who suffered the great costs of litigation to seek royal aid. Taking up their perspective reveals common experiences of dearth, plague, poverty, war, and religious transformation under the auspices of a new governing dynasty; a real belief that the king could and would step in to relieve his subjects of their troubles; and how far faith in the fount of royal justice might pay off. In the analysis that follows, this Court's supposed ordinariness proves a virtue, expanding our vision of who shaped the very principles and practices of government, and to what end. This has obvious implications for our conceptualisation of a period that is still associated principally with the lens of high politics and central government, and which has remained peculiarly sealed off from the advent of sociopolitical history besides studies of the reception of certain policies and rebellions against them.

The new tribunals of royal justice represented a responsive, sensitive, and possibly quite popular means of governing the realm. At the same time, offering fair and impartial justice on a regular basis arguably legitim-ised the monarchical regimes of early modern England in the eyes of their subjects. And yet this book checks the temptation to trace a simple and untroubled evolution in this sphere into early modernity, on two grounds. Firstly, no obvious moment of modernisation presents itself here. Contrary to any lingering perception of early modern novelty, the judicial institu-tions formulated in the early Tudor period prove to have been less an innovation of hands-on monarchs or efficiency-minded bureaucrats than a late-medieval principle of rule simply given fresh life through further routinisation. Requests received no definitive moment of foundation: no statute, proclamation, or commission established it as a fully fledged court. Instead, it gradually formalised in response to demand for better judicial procedures from subjects themselves. Such was its apparent social utility that one eighteenth-century lawyer memorialised this royal court as having 'descended from above, to still the passions', checking mischiefs and ending contests with little cost to litigants.[1] Secondly, and just as import-antly, improved access to the king's grace and mercy was not always warmly received. Curiously, the 150-year history of Requests is bookended

---

[1] William Hutton, *Courts of requests: their nature, utility, and powers described, with a variety of cases, determined in that of Birmingham* (Birmingham, 1787), 17–18.

Introduction

by attempts to remove it from the political and legal landscape. Its debut in the historical record is in reference to a bill at the 1485 parliament calling for the annulment of the 'C[ow]rt of Requests'; and one of its last is in another parliamentary bill calling for its 'suppressing and abolishing' in 1641.[2] Encapsulated in this tribunal's history is the rise and fall of a royal justice system that put long-standing principles of governance into practice and brought sovereign and subjects together in the process.

It is to the conditions shaping the *rise* of royal justice that this book primarily attends. Focusing for this purpose on the early Tudor period represents a significant point of departure from existing scholarship. Histories of society, law, and politics have drawn almost entirely from the material surviving from the Tudor royal courts – from Star Chamber and from Chancery, predominantly – at their peak, in the later reign of Elizabeth I. By that time, these institutions had become more differentiated and had evolved into fully fledged equity tribunals. Litigation was at an all-time high, and so the petitions and depositions surviving to us are plentiful. Yet often left unexamined is *how* seeking civil justice from the state at this time or any other actually unfolded; what sorts of structures, personnel, and procedures litigants encountered after petitioning; and what an accumulation of litigation towards central institutions meant for the function, reputation, and authority of those institutions in turn. In fact, the rationale behind the early modern tribunals for royal justice is most apparent not at their height but in their formative years. For that, we must look further back in time, to the political crucible of the late fifteenth and early sixteenth centuries. There, despite dynastic vulnerability, the meticulous Henry VII and the self-absorbed Henry VIII presided over a whole host of major political and social transformations. Their regimes centralised governmental processes, revised the relationship between monarchy and the landed nobility, established a more professional and bureaucratic system around the Crown, introduced a host of new laws and punishments, and installed a royal supremacy over Church and state. Judicial expansion was just one part of their governmental agenda, but one that has received noticeably less articulation and contextualisation than others.

Scepticism justifiably remains about the precise scope and speed of any so-called 'revolution in government' encompassing these changes, as set out by Geoffrey Elton nearly seventy-five years ago. Elton's characterisation of a shift in the 1530s from medieval household government, entirely

---

[2] W. Gurney Benham ed., *The Red Paper Book of Colchester* (Colchester, 1902), 64; *JHC* II, 184.

4   Introduction

determined by the personal whim of the king and flexible to a fault, to a bureaucracy centred around permanent 'out-of-court' offices and professionalised departments receives particular scrutiny in the analysis that follows here.[3] Yet this book joins other recent contributions to the field of Tudor government in maintaining that the early sixteenth century did mark an advancement in the 'pretensions of the state', with the creation of centralised archives and a nation-wide 'information revolution' just one element given recent attention.[4] Indeed, after decades of debate about the exact terms of the developments of this time having lain largely dormant, we are presently witnessing renewed engagement with the archives of early Tudor government. For example, one recent project has published and analysed the chamber account books of Henry VII and Henry VIII with an eye for the insights they can provide about how kingship worked on a daily basis.[5] Here the traditional sources of financial administration are examined with fresh eyes, and with emphasis once again on the personality of the ruler, the rhythms of the court, and the networks around the Crown.

This rekindling of interest and refreshing of the agenda does not diminish the 'liminality' once ascribed to the years around the turn of the sixteenth century.[6] The precise paths of this debate over periodisation are worn enough that they hardly require rehashing in detail here; in short, the organisation of university courses and subject groups either side of a dividing line around the year 1500 (though sometimes 1485 or 1529, depending on which aspect of English history is emphasised) means that anyone taking this as their centre-point finds themselves drawn into the intellectual currents of both late-medieval and early modern studies. In particular, scholars of the early Tudor period remain subject to a clash between different interpretive frameworks for characterising political society, its bounds, and its relative importance in governing the realm. At odds in this divide – once represented by K. B. McFarlane and Elton, respectively – is whether we look to the centre or the localities for the real power in the realm; whether the early sixteenth century was marked by continuity with the past or by a deliberate, rapid reform of governmental structures; and

---

[3] G. R. Elton, *The Tudor Revolution in Government: Administrative Changes in the Reign of Henry VIII* (Cambridge University Press, 1953); G. W. Bernard, *Who Ruled Tudor England: An Essay in the Paradoxes of Power* (Bloomsbury, 2021).

[4] K. J. Kesselring, *Mercy and Authority in the Tudor State* (Cambridge University Press, 2003), 16; M. McGlynn, 'From Written Record to Bureaucratic Mind: Imagining a Criminal Record', *P&P* 250:1 (2021), 55–86.

[5] 'Tudor Chamber Books: Kingship, Court and Society: The Chamber Books of Henry VII and Henry VIII, 1485–1521' (2017), www.tudorchamberbooks.org (accessed Jan. 2023).

[6] S. Gunn, 'Henry VII in Context: Problems and Possibilities', *History* 92:3 (2007), 301.

Introduction 5

whether our primary sources are family papers and chronicles or the fledgling archives of the state.[7] Although specific points of chronology may always be open to debate, the reception of both social and political outlooks by those working in these in-between years has already proven an advantage as much as a challenge. Combining these approaches has revealed the 'multidimensional nature' of certain central institutions overseen by the early Tudor kings, such as Parliament. Here the potential of the 'point of contact' between Crown and subjects has been fully realised, particularly for keeping the institutional, the interpersonal, and the ideological dimensions of personal monarchy in careful balance.[8]

Nowadays, the firmer border is that between the early Tudor period and the rest of the early modern age. Steven Gunn's observation in 1995 that there has been little social history of government for early Tudor England, of the kind produced even for later decades of the sixteenth century, still rings true today.[9] Some sociopolitical history on a smaller scale *has* been advanced for this period in recent years, including focused studies of popular politics and the exercise of authority in England's cities; the concerns and ideologies shaping riots and rebellions, and government responses to them; and areas of law and justice in which the Tudor government took care of the poor, the disadvantaged, and the needy.[10] Yet, noticeably, much of this work has been undertaken by historians otherwise interested in the long fifteenth century, the civil disturbances of which are increasingly seen to have encompassed the reign of Henry VII, too – that is, by medievalists. Meanwhile, this same period forms only a prelude to many early modern histories. Much of the defining work on state formation has cut the sixteenth century down the middle, with only

---

[7] For a summary of this historiographical positioning see S. J. Gunn, *Early Tudor Government 1485–1558* (Macmillan, 1995), 2–8.

[8] E.g., P. R. Cavill, *The English Parliaments of Henry VII 1485–1504* (Oxford University Press, 2009), 5–8. This builds on Elton's conception of the Tudor parliament, council, and court as 'points of contact' between government and the wider realm: 'Tudor Government: The Points of Contact' in Elton ed., *Studies in Tudor and Stuart Politics and Government* (Cambridge University Press, 1974–92), vol. III.

[9] Gunn, *Early Tudor Government*, 7–8.

[10] E.g., C. D. Liddy, *Contesting the City: The Politics of Citizenship in English Towns, 1250–1530* (Oxford University Press, 2017); M. L. Bush, *The Pilgrims' Complaint: A Study of Popular Thought in the Early Tudor North* (Routledge, 2009); M. McGlynn, 'Idiots, Lunatics and the Royal Prerogative in early Tudor England', *The Journal of Legal History* 26:1 (2005), 1–24; S. McSheffrey, *Seeking Sanctuary: Crime, Mercy and Politics in English Courts, 1400–1500* (Oxford University Press, 2017). Early modernists doing similar work in this field include A. Wood, *Faith, Hope and Charity: English Neighbourhoods, 1500–1640* (Cambridge University Press, 2020); J. Healey, 'The Fray on the Meadow: Violence and a Moment of Government in Early Tudor England', *History Workshop Journal* 85 (2018), 5–25.

6   Introduction

the second half taken to have been of longer-term significance even if the 1530s are accepted, from a distance, to have represented an earlier phase in the intensification of government.[11] Admittedly, variables such as population growth, continuing religious reformation, and improving literacy provide some rationale for erecting another boundary line at 1550. But a consequence of this divide is that while we possess models for a more socially inclined study of government, they have yet to form a 'ready bridge' through the fifteenth, sixteenth, and seventeenth centuries.[12]

At stake in this longer-term picture is our capacity to reconcile the moralistic 'commonwealth' attributed to the late-medieval polity with the bureaucratic 'state' described by early modernists. In classifying such concepts, historians of both fields have often circled similar points of discussion, particularly regarding the make-up and constitution of any 'political society', 'public', or 'commons' capable of making itself heard and felt in these visions of the realm. In the most generous interpretation, an emerging late-medieval 'political society' comprising 'all ranks' (though mostly husbandmen and upwards) was capable of exerting real 'pressure' on Crown and government. One implication of this interpretation is that the politicised public came into being *only* when central government acknowledged it, addressed it, and capitulated to its interests.[13] John Watts contributed some cultural-history colour to this general outline, suggesting that a more politicised society was facilitated by improved literacy and modes of communication but also, theoretically, by a 'common stock of political expectations and language' shared across the realm and, in turn, written with this public in mind. He suggested that the public's 'pressure' was thus felt not only in policymaking but also in 'demonstrating to [rulers] what principles . . . were most widely accepted at any given time' and flagging up gaps between expectations and action in governance.[14] This exploration of a discursive 'imagined community' emerging at either end of the social scale, evident in terminology such as 'commons' and 'public', found an echo in work undertaken around the same time by Andy Wood, John Walter, and others on the political languages and identities taken up by (and imposed upon) early modern

---

[11] M. J. Braddick, *State Formation in Early Modern England, c. 1550–1700* (Cambridge University Press, 2000), 4–5, 22, 436.

[12] To quote Gunn, *Early Tudor Government*, 7.

[13] G. Harriss, 'Political Society and the Growth of Government in Late Medieval England', *P&P* 138 (1993), 28–57.

[14] J. L. Watts, 'The Pressure of the Public on Later Medieval Politics' in L. Clark and C. Carpenter eds., *The Fifteenth Century IV: Political Culture in Late Medieval Britain* (Boydell, 2004), 173.

Introduction

peasants.[15] Questions of *who* we might reasonably include in our visions of political society, how the lines between 'popular' and 'elite' cultures were imagined, and when 'culture' became 'politics' have driven scholarship on either side of this historiographical divide, then.

What tends to differ between these two fields is the emphasis placed by its respective historians on any *agency* identifiable among the wider populace of England, especially in its head-to-head engagement with the governing elite. The potential for 'negotiation' in managing political relations is apparent across the expanse of these several centuries, but it has been given greater practical definition by those working on early modern contexts.[16] Putting the politics back into social history, scholars of the later sixteenth century in particular have unearthed from legal and local archives stories of class struggle manifested in constant (re)negotiations with the state for social regulation and financial aid.[17] Micro-political studies by Wood, Walter, and Steve Hindle have identified an active 'popular politics' at the level of the parish, the neighbourhood, and the city. Here people were mobilised by conflict over resources, which manifested in rioting, assembling, hedge-breaking, and other actions designed to bring the 'politics of subsistence' to the attention of the Crown.[18] Whether this pointed sort of 'popular politics' existed in the late medieval period has been doubted by its own historians, though this may reflect a lack of parity in evidence across the historical divide, the level of detail in early modernists' accounts being made possible by the much greater array of surviving sources for everyday lives, legal and otherwise, available for Elizabethan England.[19] Nevertheless, this vision of localised conflict touching

---

[15] Watts, 'The Pressure of the Public'; J. Watts, 'Public or Plebs: The Changing Meaning of "The Commons", 1381–1549', in H. Pryce and J. Watts eds., *Power and Identity in the Middle Ages* (Oxford University Press, 2007), 242–60; A. Wood, *The 1549 Rebellions and the Making of Early Modern England* (Cambridge University Press, 2007); J. Walter ed., *Crowds and Popular Politics in Early Modern England* (Manchester University Press, 2006).

[16] E.g., it appears throughout T. Johnson, *Law in Common: Legal Cultures in Late Medieval England* (Oxford University Press, 2019); and more prominently in M. J. Braddick and J. Walter eds., *Negotiating Power in Early Modern Society: Order, Hierarchy and Subordination in Britain and Ireland* (Cambridge University Press, 2001). The concept has received scrutiny most recently in Kesselring, *Mercy and Authority*, 200–8.

[17] See, for example, A. Wood, *The Politics of Social Conflict: The Peak Country, 1520–1770* (Cambridge University Press, 2009); and his 'Subordination, Solidarity and the Limits of Popular Agency in a Yorkshire Valley, c.1596–1615', *P&P* 193 (2006), 41–72; Steve Hindle, *On the Parish? The Micro-Politics of Poor Relief in Rural England c.1550–1750* (Oxford University Press, 2004).

[18] See, for example, the essays collected in Walter ed., *Crowds and Popular Politics in Early Modern England*; P. Griffiths, A. Fox, and S. Hindle eds., *The Experience of Authority in Early Modern England* (Macmillan, 1996).

[19] I. M. W. Harvey, 'Was There Popular Politics in Fifteenth-Century England?', in R. H. Britnell and A. J. Pollard eds., *The McFarlane Legacy: Studies in Late Medieval Politics and Society* (Alan Sutton, 1995), 155–74.

8   Introduction

on various spheres of authority is yet to be reconciled with the emphasis on commonality and culture in the 'commonwealth' stressed by late medievalists.

With more pragmatic and pessimistic conceptions of popular politics and its 'negotiations' now prevailing, the old claim that central government itself could have been 'moulded more by pressures within political society than by efforts of kings or officials to direct it from above' may seem overstated.[20] Yet establishing the extent to which wider society had *any* discernible impact on the centre of power has been demoted from the scholarly agenda for some time now, especially since politics itself has increasingly been located outside of formal institutions, offices, procedures of the Crown and in the localities, in social networks, and in culture instead. The new set of evidence examined in this book – the archives of the Court of Requests – returns our gaze to central government and lends support to the contention that such structures of governance were given shape by subjects. Here the aforementioned debates about the relative weight of political society and high politics are drawn into the early Tudor period, and into dialogue with the administrative-history methods traditionally associated with its study. Indeed, this book once again synthesises the dual historiographical framework of scholarship on these liminal years, looking both inwards to the preoccupations of central government and outwards to the people it reached. It also takes a step further, by situating the very development of government within the social realm.

While the detailed reconstructions at the heart of the following study are concentrated on the years before 1547, a much longer lifespan for the royal justice system also comes into view – one that brings minutiae and micro-studies to bear on the broader arc of litigation from the fifteenth to seventeenth centuries. The importance of justice-giving to the emergent early modern 'state' is hardly a new contention. In histories of the later sixteenth century and beyond, litigation to the Crown for justice (as opposed to prosecution *by* it) was promoted from a symptom to a primary cause of a more joined-up polity some twenty years ago. Michael Braddick located some of the participatory qualities of the emerging English state in both criminal *and* civil justice procedures. Ordinary people were engaged in reporting and testifying against their deviant neighbours before local and national authorities, but increasingly they used the same avenues to initiate lawsuits on their own behalf. By invoking

---

[20] Harriss, 'Political Society', 33.

Introduction 9

traditional notions of hierarchy and order in their own causes, petitioners contributed to the maintenance of the 'patriarchal state'.[21] Steve Hindle similarly identified 'popular legalism' as a cornerstone of the 'increase in governance' underway in the sixteenth and seventeenth centuries, manifested most clearly in the growth of the Court of Star Chamber.[22] Both historians concluded that law became 'an important social resource' for English subjects by the Elizabethan era, used as much to pursue individual interests and 'secure collective ends' as to impose state power.[23] The correlation between an expanded administration of royal justice, particularly in a form characterised as equitable, and the growth of centralised 'state' apparatus has been identified by historians in a range of contexts in Europe and beyond – in Scotland, France, the Iberian peninsula, the Netherlands, Sweden, and overseas in the colonies of 'New Spain' and Virginia – within the centuries up to *c.* 1700.[24] This phenomenon was so widespread from the late Middle Ages onwards that Richard Kagan called it a 'legal revolution ... in which the formal adjudication of disputes was sharply and dramatically on the rise'.[25]

In searching for the originating impulses of this 'revolution', this book demonstrates that people 'invited the state in' to their lives through pleas for justice much earlier than the emphasis in the English-focused literature on the period after 1550 suggests. This revision is not only chronological but contextual. It was in the political turmoil of the early Tudor years that a more formal *system* of royal justice, built on existing procedures and principles, took shape. After all, how better for the new regime taking the throne in 1485 to demonstrate good governance of the realm and its people than to show a care for subjects' troubles, and (conveniently) for the distribution of power and resources in local communities? And how better for the country's politicised society to exploit this vulnerability and lay claim to the reciprocity inherent to the commonwealth ideal by invoking royal aid in their personal disputes? The evidence uncovered in this book of constant petitioning to the king in the early Tudor period and long before

---

[21] Braddick, *State Formation*.

[22] S. Hindle, *The State and Social Change in Early Modern England, c.1550–1640* (Palgrave Macmillan, 2000).

[23] *Ibid.*, x, 13, 68; Braddick, *State Formation*, 162.

[24] A. M. Godfrey and C. H. van Rhee eds., *Central Courts in Early Modern Europe and the Americas* (Duncker & Humblot, 2020); S. Kellogg, *Law and the Transformation of Aztec Culture, 1500–1700* (University of Oklahoma Press, 1995); G. Vermeesch, 'Reflections on the Relative Accessibility of Law Courts in Early Modern Europe', *Crime, Histoire & Sociétés* 19:2 (2015), 53–76.

[25] R. L. Kagan, *Lawsuits and Litigants in Castile, 1500–1700* (University of North Carolina Press, 1981), xx–xxi.

10   Introduction

contradicts depictions of the years prior to the 1530s as being marked by a 'decline' in litigation, limited notions of the state, and minimal judicial sophistication around the Crown.[26] By examining the initial shaping of royal justice in these formative years, it becomes possible to address some of the vaguer claims made about the cause and effect of litigation in Elizabethan state formation; to set out more sharply the relationship between the 'massive growth in business' in royal lawcourts and the 'increase of governance', other than the fact that they occurred simultaneously.[27] Did justice-giving give order to society and legitimacy to authority?

The apparent popularity of royal justice certainly has ramifications for our understandings of why, and on what terms, the far-reaching changes unfolding in early Tudor England and beyond were accepted by its wider populace. Inhabitants of cities, towns, and villages were suffering from the consequences first of economic stagnation and then of a rapidly rising population: vagrancy, poverty, and crime, worsened by regular outbreaks of plague, the enclosure of land for pasture, the depopulation of rural settlements, and price and rent inflation. Within the first few decades of the early sixteenth century alone, they were subjected to unprecedented programmes of taxation and an extraordinary requirement to pledge public allegiance to monarchical supremacy. And yet, no matter how personally powerful the sixteenth-century monarchs became, they lacked the force and infrastructure necessary to communicate with or physically coerce their subjects. At the same time, those subjects were hardly ignorant or blithely accepting of profound changes to traditional political and religious structures around them; though nor were they as given to rebellion as we might have once presumed.[28] The binary between outright resistance and simple acquiescence in popular responses to rule is beginning to dissolve. In studies of the Henrician regime's contentious religious policies, in particular, conformity to the state in such life-changing circumstances has been reconceived as collaboration *with* it, with certain 'points of contact' between Crown and society – courts, commissions, churches – making government more visible and encouraging changes in practice to take hold.[29] This is one field in which

---

[26] C. W. Brooks, *Pettyfoggers and Vipers of the Commonwealth* (Cambridge University Press, 1986), 84, 93–4; Hindle, *The State and Social Change*, 14, 32, 89.

[27] *Ibid.*, 15, 32.

[28] G. R. Elton, *Policy and Police: The Enforcement of the Reformation in the Age of Thomas Cromwell* (Cambridge University Press, 1972), 2–3.

[29] *Ibid.*, 424–5; E. Duffy, *The Voices of Morebath: Reformation and Rebellion in an English Village* (Yale University Press, 2001); E. H. Shagan, *Popular Politics and the English Reformation* (Cambridge

Introduction

it has been possible to show how policy proceeded in practice and how, where, and among whom acquiescence (however grudging) was at least outwardly achieved. And if the Reformation was one area of royal policy that 'was not done *to* people' but 'done *with* them', so too was the administration of justice, surely?[30]

For answers this book turns to the Court of Requests, an institutional body more directly responsive to subjects than most within Tudor government, more socially collaborative than many of its fellow central lawcourts, and more regularly operational than other modes for dispensing royal mercy. As we have seen already, this tribunal was of little interest to Tudor administrative historians of previous generations largely because its remit was perceived to be somewhat 'trivial'.[31] It has also been left effectively unstudied by lawyers undertaking legal histories except insofar as it might tell us more about Chancery, the more important equity court, and has been largely overlooked by sociolegal scholars of the early modern period who, when interested in state–society relations, tend to prefer the dramatic disruptions handled by Star Chamber. Requests is therefore ripe for re-examination. The abundant archives of this national tribunal have rarely been the subject of book-length analysis. Tim Stretton's study of women's use of this Court is the major exception, situating it within the Elizabethan 'boom' in litigation and standing as a model of sociolegal history undertaken with reference to both theory and practice.[32] Elsewhere, an unpublished PhD thesis written by D. A. Knox in 1974 provides a detailed account of the administration of Requests in the short reign of Edward VI and shows the value of building up a full picture of its work from all available records (though his conclusion defers, disappointingly, to the question of Requests' similarity to Chancery).[33] The only study of the Court's history from its inception to the end of Henry VIII's reign remains I. S. Leadam's 1898 volume for the Selden Society, which contains selected cases and a brief history of the Court. This work rightly remains

---

University Press, 2003); J. P. D. Cooper, *Propaganda and the Tudor State: Political Culture in the Westcountry* (Oxford University Press, 2003).

[30] Shagan, *Popular Politics and the English Reformation*, 25 (emphasis in original).

[31] As, for example, in J. A. Guy, *The Cardinal's Court: The Impact of Thomas Wolsey in Star Chamber* (Harvester Press, 1977), 71.

[32] T. Stretton, *Women Waging Law in Elizabethan England* (Cambridge University Press, 1998). Another smaller but rich study of Requests' Jacobean pleadings is L. J. Meyer, '"Humblewise": Deference and Complaint in the Court of Requests', *Journal of Early Modern Studies* 4 (2015), 261–85.

[33] D. A. Knox, 'The Court of Requests in the Reign of Edward VI' (unpublished PhD thesis, University of Cambridge, 1974), 30–2.

12   Introduction

influential, especially for characterising the potential social significance of
Requests, but while it has long been superseded by further archival discov-
eries it has yet to be replaced.[34] This is despite the fact that the evident
potential of Requests to contribute to our picture of law and politics in
early Tudor England has been well recognised. As Elton himself acknowledged in 1964, a full study of this Court's proceedings was essential 'if the
history of the early-Tudor Council is ever to rest on knowledge as full as it
can be made'.[35] Much more recently, the pre-eminent legal historian of this
period, Sir John Baker, remarked that though Requests is 'one of the best
documented of the English bill jurisdictions', 'the material still awaits its
historian'.[36]

This book takes up this challenge, presenting the first comprehensive
history of Requests in its evolutionary phase, from the accession of Henry
VII in 1485 to the death of Henry VIII in 1547. While 'early Tudor' is used
throughout as a shorthand for the period in question, it deliberately does
not include Edward VI's reign. A minor king and an offshoot 'court of
requests' overseen by his protector, the Duke of Somerset, means that this
period presents a different set of enquiries about monarchical government
and justice – ones that have been well served in Knox's thesis.[37] A more
concentrated timeframe has made it possible to examine all the surviving
documentation from this period: 3,300 catalogued and 2,500 uncatalogued
casefiles containing litigants' stories and arguments, and evidence from the
ten books of orders and decrees covering these years.[38] This is a mere
fragment of what is available for later years in this Court's lifespan; by 1600,
active cases in Requests and its fellow equity tribunals numbered in the
hundreds of thousands each year. But examining the entirety of the much
smaller but no less colourful volume of suits surviving from Requests

---

[34] I. S. Leadam ed., *Select Cases in the Court of Requests, A.D. 1496–1569*, Selden Society 12 (Bernard
Quaritch, 1898). A reference to a 'C[ow]rt of Requests' in 1485 (mentioned above, n. 2) in the
Colchester archives was published four years after Leadam's work and so was missed from his
account, for example.

[35] G. R. Elton, 'Why the History of the Early Tudor Council Remains Unwritten', in Elton ed., *Studies*
vol. I., 328. The following year he advocated again for more study of the Tudor lawcourts, especially
Star Chamber and Requests, as 'the common way in which government appeared to the people':
'The Problems and Significance of Administrative History in the Tudor Period', in Elton ed., *Studies*
vol. I., 254–5.

[36] J. Baker, *OHLE*, 203–4.   [37] Knox, 'The Court of Requests in the Reign of Edward VI'.

[38] The surviving archive of the Court of Requests at The National Archives, Kew, is divided into four
classes: TNA REQ1 (books of orders and decrees), REQ2 (pleadings), REQ3 ('miscellaneous' and
unsorted pleadings), and REQ4 (documents related to William Shakespeare). Research for the
present study has focused on REQ1/1–8, 1/104, 1/105, fragments of an order book from the early 1520s
now found in REQ3/14, 3/22, 3/29 and 3/30, and on all the documents in REQ2/1–13 and REQ3/
1–30.

Introduction

between 1485 and 1547 allows for analysis unlimited by geographical boundary, case type, or strata of litigant. Instead, the following study charts an overarching trajectory of curial evolution while also reconstructing the day-to-day processes of litigation that shaped it; identifies every party involved in the creation of justice in Requests; and characterises both the mechanisms of justice-*seeking* and the outcomes of justice-*giving*. This ambition for comprehensiveness puts a more connected study of political society, shaped through the ideals of the commonwealth and their shaping in institutional contexts, within reach.

The first of three themes woven through this book is the institutionalisation of royal justice within early Tudor government and the various factors at play in this process. To begin with this means, in a sense, bringing politics back to its traditional home of the central institution; even accepting Elton's argument that 'no one can hope to write about any aspect of Tudor history without the solid grasp of the realities and probabilities, without the deep understanding of the records before him [*sic*], which administrative history . . . alone can supply'.[39] We begin, then, in the structured and seemingly static world of govern*ment*; with a reconstruction of the routine, personnel, and curial identity of the early Tudor Requests, informed by examination of its entire archive. Yet by exploring the varying interfaces between these recognised components of courthood over time and considering some others, a more dynamic picture emerges – one inspired by a new strand of administrative history, emerging at present, that looks to revise our understandings of who or what constitutes an institution.[40] The combined influences of digital methods and intradisciplinary connections – of comprehensive, data-based studies and of cultural and spatial examinations, for example – are informing a reconceptualisation of representative institutions as entities that lived not only in the records that happen to survive to us but in the minds of those who used and ran them.[41] In short, any lingering contrast between 'examining the minutiae of government administration' and 'analysing the government['s] attempts at self-representation' presents a false dichotomy.[42] Administration

---

[39] Elton, 'The Problems and Significance of Administrative History', 259.

[40] For further examples see Johnson, *Law in Common*; J. McGovern, *The Tudor Sheriff: A Study in Early Modern Administration* (Oxford University Press, 2022); 'Recovering Europe's Parliamentary Culture, 1500–1700: A New Approach to Representative Institutions', Oxford University: https://earlymodern.web.ox.ac.uk/recovering-europes-parliamentary-culture-1500-1700-new-approach-representative-institutions (accessed Jan. 2023).

[41] P. Seaward, 'Why the History of Parliament Is Not Written', in D. Hayton and L. Clark eds., *Historians and Parliament, Parliamentary History* Special Issue 40:1 (2021), 21.

[42] E. H. Shagan, 'Protector Somerset and the 1549 Rebellions: New Sources and New Perspectives', *EHR* 115:455 (1999), 47.

14 Introduction

was a means of representation; it could be both procedure and event. This was especially true of the dispensation of extraordinary justice from the king's own hand.

Echoing more contemporary models of curial development, this study foregrounds the currents of supply and demand from which this paradoxically intimate *and* outward-facing strand of government flowed. Late sixteenth-century writers spoke of three main ways by which 'All courtes in England have their beginning': royal grant, Act of Parliament, or just 'use and custome'.[43] In the absence of any official moment of creation, it was the notion of 'use and custome' to which defenders of the new system of royal justice turned to justify its existence. One of the chief proponents of Requests – and someone with whom we will become familiar in the analysis that follows – was Sir Julius Caesar, an Elizabethan master of that Court. In the early 1590s, he produced and published his own history of his institution, entitled *The Ancient State, Authoritie and Proceedings of the Court of Requests.* Built around a calendar of all the Court's registers up to that point, its central contention was that a close connection to the monarch and the royal Council had bequeathed to Requests an essentially social remit. It served plaintiffs of 'mean estate' who were without remedy at common law, and who appealed directly to the king for aid according to his ancient jurisdiction over private causes.[44] Other commentators on the legal system around the same time similarly allowed that the monarch had a special responsibility for seeing civil justice done, in courts – or even in entities as fluid as a 'commission' or 'company' – that mediated 'between the prince and petitioners'.[45] These accounts evoke two qualities that prove especially resonant in the study undertaken in this book: the role and capacity of petitioners, who instigated all cases, in communicating with the sovereign about the proper application of justice; and the continual value of fluid, even informal, modes of operation in facilitating access for these petitioners. Both are not only at odds with administrative historians' traditional concerns for identifying ministerial influence and modernising trends in Tudor government but paint a more vivid picture than the passive model of 'pressure' or 'participation'

---

[43] BL Lansdowne MS 125, fols. 184v–185.

[44] Caesar, *The Ancient State*, v. See also the edition of the text edited and published by L. M. Hill, which includes additional notes from Caesar's annotated copy of his work (BL Lansdowne MS 125): *The Ancient State, Authoritie, and Proceedings of the Court of Requests by Sir Julius Caesar* (Cambridge University Press, 1975).

[45] William Lambarde, *Archeion or, a Discourse upon the High Courts of Justice in England* (London, 1635), 227.

Introduction 15

in law sketched out within sociopolitical histories on either side of the historiographical divide.

The second theme developed in this book concerns the implications that this perceptibly social origin of royal justice might have for our view of the wider polity and its cohesion. Here we must mediate the space between the behemoth of centralised govern*ment* and the active and more localised practice of govern*ance*.[46] Of course, given that we have rightly witnessed a retreat from the state papers to the archives of the county and the manor to establish a discrete 'local agenda' in studies of politics, it may seem strange to return our gaze to the centre in search of this perspective.[47] That vantage point is taken up again here in order to add nuance to our visions of what, exactly, 'prerogative' justice had to offer. The simple availability of such justice, enumerable in the stacks of surviving pleadings and perceptible in statistics on case type and litigant status they can yield, has been taken in and of itself as proof that law-mindedness was pervasive by the late sixteenth century. Yet the intangible, ideological elements of litigation – the role it had in the lives of those who pursued it – cannot simply be counted. The central archives of these processes have much more to tell us about what they entailed than has hitherto been considered.

Most obviously, the well-studied petition, as a demotic genre of complaint and form of communication with authorities, is only a starting point here for illuminating the interests that shaped royal justice. Certainly, the power of petitions lay, for their writers and makers, in the opportunity to raise grievances, to define themselves in relation to authorities, and to seek aid; and remains, for historians, in the recording of subaltern voices and hard-to-reach details of everyday life. They are as key to this study as to any other examination of litigation. Yet in order to fully appreciate the social depth and geographical breadth of the 'co-creation of "justice"' we must range beyond these instigating documents and examine the raft of procedures that followed them.[48] After all, when we talk about the 'power of petitioning' or the 'participatory state' that justice-seeking formulated we refer to the capacity of litigants to open up a set of judicial procedures in which justice might be accordingly dispensed. And yet, because court registers, orders, and decrees survive far more rarely than do the bills that commenced them, there is often little we can say definitively about post-petition outcomes. It therefore

[46] Hindle, *The State and Social Change*, 17–20, 23.
[47] *Ibid.*, 10; a point made also in Johnson, *Law in Common*, 13–14.
[48] Concepts and terminologies developed in Braddick and Walter eds., *Negotiating Power*, 1–42; K. J. Kesselring and N. Mears eds., *Star Chamber Matters: An Early Modern Court and Its Records* (University of London Press, 2021), 17.

16　　　　　　　　　　Introduction

becomes easy to take for granted that the submission of a petition meant that justice was done. The present study takes advantage of Requests' archive of pleadings *and* registers of decisions to reconstruct its procedures from beginning to end. In line with the latest sociolegal research, it takes into account not only the formal conventions of petitions and court rolls but also the ephemeral notes that moved intermediary processes – writs, drafts, and incidental memoranda – and explores the lives of and meanings attributed (and attributable) to such a wide range of constructed and costly documents.[49] Indeed, a smaller body of scholarship has even started to reflect critically on what this document-mill and its consumption of money and time might have meant for what, exactly, petitioning could realistically achieve.[50] What happens to our model of litigation as state–society cooperation when the full process of justice-seeking and justice-giving is factored in?

The appearance of cracks in the metanarrative of royal justice as an extraordinary, benevolent force points us to the third theme of this book: the controversies surrounding judicial procedures like those on offer in Requests, even in the early sixteenth century. We know already that participation in justice-giving did not mean consensus about its terms, but the archives of Tudor litigation comprise a hitherto untapped spring of voices and perspectives on this topic. One of the most overlooked but important parties in play here is the defendant, summoned into court under mechanisms already deemed controversial by the late fifteenth century and who remained (by design) on the back foot once litigation commenced. Again, this oversight is in part predicated on the great abundance of petitions versus the relative absence or inaccessibility of defendants' answers, interrogatories, and exceptions. The need for this alternative perspective is becoming ever more apparent, however: in some of his most recent work, Hindle has acknowledged the evident reluctance of all parties to enter into litigation.[51] Indeed, the demands placed on royal

---

[49] E.g., T. Johnson, 'Legal Ephemera in the Ecclesiastical Courts of Late Medieval England', *Open Library of Humanities* 5:1 (2019), 1–27; F. Dabhoiwala, 'Writing Petitions in Early Modern England', in M. J. Braddick and J. Innes eds., *Suffering and Happiness in England, 1500–1850* (Oxford Scholarship, 2017), 127–48; J. Bailey, 'Voices in Court: Lawyers' or Litigants'?', *Historical Research* 74:186 (2001), 392–408; S. McSheffrey, 'Detective Fiction in the Archives: Court Records and the Uses of the Law in Late Medieval England', *History Workshop Journal* 65 (2008), 65–78; C. Beattie, 'A Piece of the Puzzle: Women and the Law as Viewed from the Late Medieval Court of Chancery', *JBS* 58:4 (2019), 751–67.

[50] E.g., M. Almbjär, 'The Problem with Early-Modern Petitions: Safety Valve or Powder Keg?', *European Review of History* 26:6 (2019), 1013–39.

[51] S. Hindle, 'The Micro-Spatial Dynamics of Litigation: The Chilvers Coton Tithe Dispute, *Barrows* vs. *Archer* (1657)', in M. Lobban, J. Begiato, and A. Green eds., *Law, Lawyers and Litigants in Early Modern England* (Cambridge University Press, 2019), 142. The same ideas were present in his *State*

Introduction

justice-giving were not restricted to the pleas of plaintiffs for mercy and pity. They also included defendants' legitimate concerns about the bluntness of this forum and its overt preference for petitioners. Without this more critical angle, we risk interpreting the trend for subjects 'inviting the state in' through the same simplistic framework of popular reception and acquiescence that we have so long sought to break down.

In these concerns we are reminded again of the crux at the junction of late-medieval and early modern histories: the potential pointedness of popular politics when balanced against an increasingly centralised government. One reading underpinning the analysis that follows is that the new justice system, while it existed, represented a 'discursive space' in which ideals about governance were expressed and enacted. Yet the strain of conflict proved ever-present. Justice may have been a key tenet of the 'commonwealth' and its literature, but there was no truly commonplace view of its meaning. If even 'law', with all of its associated codes and rules, has been a 'diabolically ambiguous term' for both sixteenth-century observers and for historians, so too is 'justice'.[52] Crucially, law and justice were not synonymous in the period under consideration here. Law was patently felt to not always result in justice, producing demand for more flexible procedures; meanwhile, processes operating on the broader notion of justice were often criticised for not living up to the standards enshrined in a hard-won series of statutes protecting due process. Arguments made in the intimate environs of Requests' courtroom drew from this wider discourse on the justness of law and the unlawfulness of justice-giving. Through these debates the longer lifespan of this system, between the Wars of the Roses in the fifteenth century and the Civil Wars in the seventeenth, comes into view. In the long term, recurring criticism of royal justice from legal theorists and disgruntled defendants runs contrary to the largely positive assessment of the role played by litigation in early modern state formation. Contestation in the early Tudor period provides a prologue to the more high-profile clashes between equity and the common law in the run-up to the former jurisdiction's dissolution in the 1640s – but was also, this book argues, part of the conception of royal justice in the first place.

The analysis that follows sets out the structural and cultural frameworks inherent to the early Tudor government's growing remit over

---

and Social Change, 92–3. See also H. Taylor, 'Labourers, Legal Aid and the Limits of Popular Legalism in Star Chamber', in Kesselring and Mears eds., *Star Chamber Matters*, 115–34.

[52] C. W. Brooks, *Law, Politics and Society in Early Modern England* (Cambridge University Press, 2009), 5.

extraordinary justice, charts the process litigants undertook to sue to their monarch, and explores the ramifications of this activity for all involved. Part I, 'The New Justice System', lays the foundation of administrative history upon which the rest of this study builds. It explores the theory behind monarchy as the fount of justice in a healthy commonwealth and the perceived potential and paradoxes of this ideal, before outlining the evolution of a new set of conciliar courts offering royal justice in the late fifteenth and early sixteenth centuries. It ends with the first history of the early Court of Requests, considered as one of those conciliar courts but also as an element of the itinerant royal household and a manifestation of the king's own justice. Part II, 'Seeking and Requesting Justice', commences a study of litigation to the early Tudor kings from the beginning of a dispute through to its end. It undertakes a sociopolitical analysis of royal justice, charting the movement of cases from villages, towns, and cities to the king's new courts. The logistics and expenses required to litigate to the Crown lead us to question whether royal justice could feasibly serve the poor. The final part of the book, 'Delivering and Contesting Justice', explores an aspect of litigation not often considered by historians of law in society: the ends of judicial processes overseen at the heart of government, and their significance for the local communities they touched upon. Characterising the process of pleading before the Crown as furthering a continual debate over subjects' rights at law ongoing in Council and Parliament, these chapters consider how far royal judges met petitioners' expectations – or why they might choose not to. The closing chapters also explore the means by which agents of this justice started to regulate their activities, in response to criticisms from lawyers and defendants about the unjustness of conciliar procedures and preference for the poor.

In all, this study both reconstructs and recontextualises the rise of royal justice. At the dawn of Tudor England, justice was widely heralded as a binding force in political society, most appropriately wielded both in principle and – increasingly – in practice by the king himself. All the people introduced across the following chapters – complainants, defendants, witnesses, lawyers, commissioners, and judges alike – held a sincere belief in the power invested in the Crown to mediate whenever and wherever justice was required. Taking a step back from the minutiae of the procedures involved, we might assume that this amounted to an opportunity for the new regime to usurp the traditional authority of local governors in dispute resolution. Yet this study rejects such a unidirectional account of these developments. Responsiveness, flexibility, and ideological imprecision – *not* determined

Introduction

reform and targeted intervention – were the defining features of justice in Requests. Through it, king and Council offered decision-making processes that were almost consciously vague, and which contained several paradoxes: applying extraordinary principles to everyday cases, being supposedly 'indifferent' but preferential to the poor, and working to maintain the *status quo* while arguably disrupting legal and social hierarchies to do so. This pillar of good governance may have remained standing for some time, but it was not as sturdy as it appeared. Even in its formative years, royal justice became more concrete *and* more challengeable.

PART I

The New Justice System

CHAPTER I

The Principle and Problem of Justice

In late medieval and early modern England, justice was ascribed many roles. It was a moral and legal facet of good rule, according to the realm's governors; a justification and an expectation raised by the period's successive rebels; and, all agreed, a right and a responsibility of everyone engaged in the enterprise of the commonwealth. Traversing this conceptual landscape takes us some way from Elton's dismissal of the 'pompously pointless' virtuous theorising of the 'medieval' mindset that supposedly came crashing down in the face of Cromwellian rationality under early Tudor government.[1] Authority figures from the monarch downwards were continually informed and inspired by the standards of chivalry and piety, by ever-present bonds of neighbourliness and duty, and by the new intellectual currents of Christian humanism and the commonwealth. Such ideals were far from being fixed and inflexible. Before we can turn to the emerging practices of royal justice, this chapter will grapple with its theoretical complexities.

Principles outside of constitutional ideologies were once neglected as real political motivations by historians because it was presumed that they were wielded only as covers for other intentions, justifying actions without necessarily carrying any real meaning.[2] As definitions of 'politics' have broadened, researchers of this and other periods are now far more accepting of the earnestness and importance of the political nation's aspirations. Yet we continue to be faced with interpretive problems when attempting to explain the origins and application of ideals. The first of these problems is social: how do we reconcile historians' careful anatomisations of the social order, and all its overlapping hierarchies, networks, and 'grids of power',

---

[1] G. R. Elton, 'Review: *The Foundations of Political Economy: Some Early Tudor Views on State and Society* by Neal Wood', *EHR* III:444 (1996), 1265; G. R. Elton, *Reform and Reformation: England 1509–1558* (Edward Arnold, 1979), 1.

[2] J. L. Watts, 'Ideas, Principles and Politics', in A. J. Pollard ed., *The Wars of the Roses* (Macmillan, 1995), 112–18.

24   The New Justice System

with the lingering notion of a 'commonplace' ideal binding it all together? Even within one stratum of society there were disagreements over the exercise of the most obvious of governmental aspirations. So, it was possible for Thomas Wolsey and other high-ranking clerics to opine that 'this noble Realme [was] in suche goode order tranquyllite and peax as never was seen within memorye of man' thanks to the expansion of the royal Council's provision of justice in the 1510s, while the chronicler and common lawyer Edward Hall argued that the same innovations had brought 'many an honest man to trouble and vexacion'.[3] Such disagreements only multiply when we take in the wider range of viewpoints present in courtrooms.

The second problem is intellectual. Andy Wood recently defined 'the fundamental contradiction in the history of [a] concept': that we might find it to be 'discursively dominant' and yet considered to be under existential threat at the same time.[4] Just as we observe in discussions of counsel in high-political circles, or of neighbourliness in ordinary lives and communities, justice was at once so banal a sentiment that it was frequently evoked in the literature of the late medieval and early modern periods without clear definition *and* declared as being in terminal decline.[5] The root of this contradiction is a contrast between principles and realities being made in the minds of contemporaries. As we will see, justice *was* dispensed with greater fervour over the course of the sixteenth and seventeenth centuries. Yet it was also continually felt to be endangered by what were vaguely referred to as the 'enormities' ongoing within the realm: crime, corruption, carelessness. Elsewhere, procedures purportedly designed to deliver justice became noticeably more controversial, and the fear that justice was not being properly and lawfully done only grew over time.

This chapter explores the meanings of justice for the wider political nation of fifteenth- and sixteenth-century England. To do so, it steps away from the often-obscure writings of this period's best-known theorists – the moralistic Edmund Dudley and the more progressive thinking of Thomas More, Thomas Elyot, and Thomas Starkey – to examine a range of elite and non-elite sources. These include coronation oaths and proclamations

---

[3] SP1/16 fol. 16v (*LP* II. 38), SP1/29 fol. 299 (*LP* III. App. 21); Edward Hall, *Hall's Chronicle: Containing the History of England, During the Reign of Henry the Fourth and the Succeeding Monarchs to the End of the Reign of Henry the Eighth* (London, 1809), 585.

[4] Wood, *Faith, Hope and Charity*, 43, 260.

[5] J. Rose ed., *The Politics of Counsel in England and Scotland 1286–1707* (Oxford University Press, 2016); Wood, *Faith, Hope, and Charity*.

The Principle and Problem of Justice

issuing from the monarchy; depictions of the sovereign and government in treatises, sermons, law readings, and legal reports by contemporary commentators; and bills of complaint, popular poetry, rebel petitions, and commonplace books produced by more ordinary folk. The following pages delve into this material to chart the origins and trajectory of a guiding principle of government, but also the fractures that had started to emerge within it by the time the Tudors came to the throne.

Fundamentals

From the top to the bottom of the social hierarchy, justice was considered a cornerstone of good kingship. Since at least the early fourteenth century, English monarchs had commenced their reigns by publicly swearing to administer 'rightfull Justice ... and Jugements, and discrecion w[ith] mercie and trowthe' or some variation thereof.[6] By the time of the early Tudors, this oath was taken before the king's anointment, making his accession contingent upon a promise to dispense justice. In theoretical literature, too, this duty of monarchy gained potency, refracted through analogies of the realm as 'body politic', 'ship of state', or 'tree of commonwealth' – as a corporation, sustained by reciprocity and headed by the king. More pointedly, Sir John Fortescue advised Edward IV that while kingship was the 'highest temporal estate on earth', it was still an office, which had as one of its primary duties the defence 'of his subjects against wrongdoers, through justice'.[7] As chief justice of the realm, Fortescue was likely thinking of institutionalised judicial procedures. But justice also emanated out of the arcane and divine qualities of personal monarchy. In France, it had been most clearly embodied by (Saint) Louis IX in the thirteenth century; Jean de Joinville, the biographer of the famed ruler, witnessed Louis sitting under an oak tree at Vincennes and walking in the public gardens of Paris, personally hearing and judging the suits of his subjects.[8] The centrality of the monarch to the dispensation of justice in the realm was writ into the records and structures of English government: symbolised in the depiction of the seated king, surrounded by advisors of state and Church, on the

---

[6] This is the version delivered at Henry VII's coronation, based on the script in place since Edward I's coronation in 1309: printed in L. G. Wickham Legg, *English Coronation Records* (A. Constable & Co. Ltd., 1901), 230. See also C. Stephenson and F. G. Marcham eds., *Sources of English Constitutional History* (Harper Brothers, 1937), vol. I, 192; A. Hunt, *The Drama of Coronation: Medieval Ceremony in Early Modern England* (Cambridge University Press, 2009), 27.

[7] Sir John Fortescue, *On the Laws and Governance of England*, ed. S. Lockwood (Cambridge University Press, 1997), 90, 100.

[8] M. R. B. Shaw trans., *Joinville and Villehardouin: Chronicles of the Crusades* (Penguin, 1974), 186–7.

26   The New Justice System

opening membranes of some of the period's common-law court rolls, and in the very naming of the Court of King's Bench and description of its work as taking place 'before the king' (*coram rege*).

For the mentalities that bolstered this belief in monarchical justice, we naturally turn first to the perceptions of those people involved in the act of justice-giving and law-making on the king's behalf. As the chief court of the realm, Parliament was one especially well-recorded forum for invocations of justice and its benefits to the commonwealth.[9] At the session of 1467, Robert Stillington, the Bishop of Bath and Wells and Lord Chancellor to Edward IV, asked 'what is justice?' and supplied his own answer. 'Justice is every person to do his office that he is put in according to his estate and degree', he declared, 'and as for this land it is understood that it standeth by three estates and above that one principal: that is to wit Lords Spiritual, Lords Temporal and Commons, and over that Estate Royal above'.[10] This definition, with its trust in the power of the governing classes and its reference to hierarchy, duty, and status, would be echoed across the following several decades in sermons delivered at the opening of parliamentary sessions. The parliament of 1489 opened with a lengthy sermon by John Morton, Archbishop of Canterbury, on the theme of righteousness. God was the emanative origin of justice and eternal law, he noted, but the 'imperative origin of justice' in the realm was the prince.[11] In 1504, Morton's successor as archbishop and Lord Chancellor, William Warham, delivered a more detailed speech on the same subject, reminding listeners that 'justice was of all things the single most valuable' means of ensuring the 'common welfare' of the realm. It was also 'not just any virtue, but a major and principal one, lighting the way for the other virtues with its glory like the evening star'.[12] Such generalised pronouncements, delivered by the ecclesiastical heads of the realm in the context of legislative proceedings, blended the divine, moral, and legal qualities of government.[13]

---

[9] See, for example, the draft sermons written by Bishop John Russell of Lincoln for the planned parliaments of 1483 and 1484: printed in S. B. Chrimes, *English Constitutional Ideas in the Fifteenth Century* (Cambridge University Press, 1936), 167–91; and that delivered by John Alcock, Bishop of Worcester, in 1485: *PROME* xv, 90–1 (1485 parliament, item 1).

[10] *PROME* xiiii, 362 (1467 parliament, items 24–7); discussed in E. Powell, 'Law and Justice', in R. Horrox ed., *Fifteenth-Century Attitudes: Perceptions of Society in Late Medieval England* (Cambridge University Press, 1994), 31.

[11] *PROME* xvi, 8–9 (1489 parliament, item 1).

[12] *PROME* xvi, 319–21 (1504 parliament, item 1). He reprised this theme at Westminster in 1515 for Henry VIII, whom he exhorted to restore the state through the administration of justice: *LP* II. 119.

[13] For the purpose and contexts of these sermons, see J. Watts, '*The Policie in Christen Remes*: Bishop Russell's Parliamentary Sermons of 1483–84' in G. W. Bernard and S. J. Gunn eds., *Authority and Consent in Tudor England* (Ashgate, 2002), 33–59; D. E. Seward, 'Bishop John Alcock and the

The Principle and Problem of Justice 27

A less abstract version of the same discourse was contained in a sermon delivered by Cuthbert Tunstall before king and parliament at Blackfriars in spring 1523, for which a full draft survives. Coming shortly after the heavy-handed financial policies of the previous year, Tunstall's speech espoused the rather traditional form of social stratification common to political treatises and advice books for princes produced in the preceding decades. Framed first by the vision of the celestial city and then by the late-medieval 'body politic', Tunstall picked up on the standard refrain of the king's ultimate duty to set 'all hys citesauns … yn moste convenient order accordyne to there decreys and merytes'. To achieve this end, it was crucial that 'a kynge schle [shall] order hys subgettes by hys lawes by justice and equite', since 'justice ys chyve [chief] morale vertue[,] sche ys the goodlyest vertue and garment for a kynge'.[14] Sermons like this one rehearsed 'sound-bites' summarising the direction of government before the very men who were about to direct policy.[15] As Cromwell reported, the three parliamentary sessions that followed Tunstall's sermon 'communyd of … pease, Stryffe, contencyon, debate, murmure, grudge, Riches, poverte, penury, trowth, falshode, Justyce, equyte, discayte [disceit], opprescyon, Magnanymyte … and also how a commune welth myght be edifyed and a[lso] contenewid within our Realme'.[16] In this context, justice was central to a Christian, patriarchal interpretation of the realm's estates and their natural duties.

By this logic, the absence of justice meant disorder. Many parliamentary sermons lamented a decaying body politic, pointing to specific ills experienced by its members.[17] Warham evoked Augustine to underline this point: 'When justice has been taken away, what are kingdoms but great bands of robbers?'[18] While any implied offences could be hypothetical, the remedy was certain. Tunstall spoke generally of miscreants who 'corrupted and infectythe' the commonwealth, making it necessary to 'separate or cute [them] off'.[19] Wolsey was more precise in his speech before the gathered Council in May 1516, identifying various 'enormities' committed by the king's subjects, including 'mayntenaunce, supportacion, imbrasrye' and

---

Roman Invasion of Parliament: Introducing Renaissance Civic Humanism to Tudor Parliamentary Proceedings', in L. Clark ed., *The Fifteenth Century XV: Writing, Records and Rhetoric* (Boydell & Brewer, 2017), 145–68; Cavill, *The English Parliaments of Henry VII*, 22–3.

[14] SP6/13 fols. 2–10. [15] Watts, '*The Policie in Christen Remes*', 43.

[16] SP1/28 fol. 153 (*LP* III. ii. 3249). Printed in J. Guy, 'Wolsey and the Parliament of 1523', in C. Cross, D. Loades, and J. J. Scarisbrick eds., *Law and Government under the Tudors* (Cambridge University Press, 1988), 1.

[17] As in one of Bishop Russell's draft sermons for 1484: Chrimes, *English Constitutional Ideas*, 181.

[18] *PROME* xvi, 320 (1504 parliament, item 1). [19] SP6/13 fol. 5v.

28 The New Justice System

other 'sinister' activities, that had upended the 'restfull tranquillite of [the king's] subjectes'. To restore peace, Wolsey publicly reminded Henry VIII of 'his oathe taken at the tyme of his moste triumphant coronaccion' and called upon him to undertake 'thindifferent ministracion of Justice to all personnes aswell heighe as lower'.[20] This belief in the power of the Crown to restore and instil order fed into the orders and Acts it issued in this period. For example, an Act passed in 1533 to regulate clothing according to yearly income directly addressed the 'utter impoverysshement and undoing of many inexpert and light p[er]sones inclined to pride moder [mother] of all vices', which the Crown aimed patriarchally to protect and curtail.[21] These and many other Acts on the early Tudor books reflect a concern for social and moral control enacted through punitive legislation.

In both the abstract sentiments delivered in the chambers of Parliament and the prefaces to the legislation they issued, the remit for this kind of control was typically the proper distribution of goods and property – justice ensuring 'to each his own'. Fortescue, after all, had argued that 'when [subjects] lack goods they will arise, saying they lack justice', and so if the prince wanted to ensure that his subjects would not rise up against him, he needed to see that they were not poor, just as he should keep himself wealthy enough to withstand the ambitions of his nobility.[22] Thereafter, the early Tudor period witnessed further developments in concepts of possession, and particularly landholding. Tenants increasingly sought more flexibility in passing their property on to their heirs and turned to new forms of contract to lease and transfer lands. And in imagining more progressive channels through which to pursue these rights, they began to turn to the extraordinary powers of their king. Among the several 'fitting means' by which the king could administer justice, listed by Morton in 1489, were the obvious routes of overseeing laws and statutes, distributing offices, rewarding good and punishing offenders, but also, seemingly, hearing cases himself – remaining 'calm in discussing and determining cases' and delivering 'equity in judgment'.[23] Edmund Dudley later advised the recently crowned Henry VIII that administering justice 'betwene subiectes and subiectes' was the 'chief charge' of the king.[24] Tunstall, too, suggested that if any member of the body politic 'for his private lucre . . . do wronge or injurye to hys neghbure' it would be

---

[20] HL Ellesmere MS 2655 fols. 10–10v.   [21] 1 Hen. VIII c. 14; 24 Hen. VIII c. 13.
[22] Fortescue, *On the Laws and Governance of England*, 110.
[23] *PROME* xvi, 8–9 (1489 parliament, item 1).
[24] Edmund Dudley, *The Tree of Commonwealth*, ed. D. M. Brodie (Cambridge University Press, 1948), 34–6.

The Principle and Problem of Justice

against 'the order of justice', requiring remedy from 'hyme whiche hath auctorite' – often the king himself.[25] These comments voiced the expectation, long-standing by the late fifteenth century and gathering pace in the sixteenth, that the monarch would deliver justice to subjects in their private quarrels over rights and assets. Anarchy was as much about downward social mobility and dispossession as it was about riots and rebellions, and royal justice was the primary cure.

Did the rest of the realm have faith in this cure? Its availability, at least, was openly publicised. At the pronouncement of a 1532 proclamation ordering local officers to better enforce statutes, listeners would have heard that the king 'nothing more earnestly desireth than the advancement of the realm [and] the due execution and equal administration of justice' to all – a common refrain of the royal proclamations and statutes read out in marketplaces and public spaces up and down the country.[26] Whether or not such declarations were widely heard and taken seriously, the ideal of the king as a fount for justice in ordinary suits does appear in the snippets of popular sentiment that survive to us. When Henry VII's first progress reached Bristol in 1487, he was greeted by pageants laid on by the citizenry. At St John's Gate, a figure portraying 'Justicia' welcomed the king and praised him for 'Minisshing justice duly in every place / Thorough this region where ye ride or goo / Indifferently both to frende and foo'. Tellingly, she also declared that 'Justice defende possessions / And kepe people from oppressions'.[27] Late-medieval vernacular literature, coming down to us through chance survival in manuscript collections and administrative archives, is more critical in tone but redolent with the same expectations. The anonymous complaint poetry contained in the Digby MS, dated to the early fifteenth century, contains commentary on the importance of truth, right, and justice as gifts from God – along with the notion that, should disputes break out, 'The king shulde both partyes here [hear]'.[28] On this evidence the notion of justice emanating from the king, and trained towards defending and sustaining people as much as punishing them, seems to have been part of popular conceptualisations too.

---

[25] SP6/13 fol. 4v.

[26] P. L. Hughes and J. F. Larkin eds., *Tudor Royal Proclamations* (Yale University Press, 1964–9), vol. I, 19, 143, 206, 263. For examples of the same sentiments in statute preambles, see 11 Hen. VII c. 12; 3 Hen. VII c. 1; 11 Hen. VII c. 25; 19 Hen. VII c. 12.

[27] E. Cavell ed., *The Heralds' Memoir, 1486–1490* (Shaun Tyas, 2009), 95.

[28] J. Kail ed., *Twenty-Six Political and Other Poems*, Early English Text Society Original Series 124 (Trübner & Co., 1904), 9–10. For the wider political thought expressed in this collection, see J. Coleman, *English Literature in History, 1350–1400: Medieval Readers and Writers* (Hutchinson, 1981), 98–111.

30   The New Justice System

It was not, however, so readily assumed that these expectations were being met. Indeed, what often marks vernacular complaint literature of the period apart from the contemporaneous sermons and treatises of the elites, aside from the anonymity of its authors, is its specificity about abuses and absences of justice. For example, a set of 'seducious billes' that were 'sette upon [th]e Mynster' in Coventry in the summer of 1496 decried recent events that had seen their nearby common lands 'closed in & hegged full fast' and hailed a guildsman who had been imprisoned for speaking against the town's mayor and corporation. These rulers were warned: 'luff [love] with our hertes shull ye have non'.[29] Whereas Bishop Stillington had declared before Parliament the utmost importance of the three highest estates – the lords temporal and spiritual, and above them the king himself – bill culture and popular poetry treated the Commons (that is, the commoners) as the pre-eminent estate. Another of the Digby poems, taking on the typical common voice of this genre, warned landlords to listen to '[y]oure tenauntes playntes ... ffor [th]ey kepen all [y]oure tresour'.[30] The abstract rhetoric of justice and the commonwealth was largely absent from these more direct statements, though it does not necessarily follow that such ideals were absent in wider society. After all, it was these broader expectations about good governance that the Earl of Warwick and the Duke of Clarence played into in 1470, when they promised on their return to England to 'sett righte and iustice in theire places to se theim egally mynistred and indeferently withoute mede or drede as they ought to be'. These were the sentiments that they displayed in open letters, posted up in marketplaces, on bridges, and on church doors across various English cities.[31]

Regardless of any promises made by rulers, prospective or otherwise, it was a common refrain among authors of both popular and elite laments in this period that Justice – often personified – had left the realm, lay dormant, or was dead.[32] Only occasionally were individual governors

---

[29] Printed in M. Dormer Harris ed., *The Coventry Leet Book, or Mayor's Register*, Early English Text Society Original Series 134–5, 138, 146 (Trübner & Co., 1907–13), vol. IV, 577–8. For more on this dispute, see M. Dormer Harris, 'Laurence Saunders, Citizen of Coventry', *EHR* 9:36 (1894), 633–51; C, Liddy, 'Urban Enclosure Riots: Risings of the Commons in English Towns, 1480–1525', *P&P* 226:1 (2015), 67.

[30] H. Barr, *The Digby Poems: A New Edition of the Lyrics* (Liverpool University Press, 2009), 208.

[31] M. L. Kekewich, C. Richmond, A. F. Sutton, L. Visser-Fuchs, and J. L. Watts eds., *The Politics of Fifteenth Century England: John Vale's Book* (Alan Sutton, 1995), 219.

[32] Hall, *Hall's Chronicle*, 7; W. Scase, '"Strange and Wonderful Bills": Bill-Casting and Political Discourse in Late Medieval England', in R. Copeland, D. Lawton, and W. Scase eds., *New Medieval Literatures* (Clarendon Press, 1998), vol. II, 244–5; E. Powell, *Kingship, Law, and Society: Criminal Justice in the Reign of Henry V* (Clarendon Press, 1989), 38–44. See, for example, John Skelton's translated poem, which opened 'Justyce now is dede', printed in D. R. Carlson, 'The Latin

The Principle and Problem of Justice

singled out for blame, however. In the early 1520s, the common lawyer and administrator Edward North, imprisoned for writing poetry critical of Wolsey, composed an anti-clerical ballad entitled 'The Ruyn of a Ream [Realm]' in which he took aim at the leading ecclesiastical figures of the day for their empty words. 'Where be the Rulers & mynesters of Justyce / That sum[m]tyme spake for the comon wele', he asked; 'Now they be gon'.[33] As intriguing as this criticism appears, much more commonly the realm was said to be not only lawless but chronically loveless. A carol noted down in a manuscript compiled at the Benedictine abbey of Bury St Edmunds at the beginning of the fifteenth century had vividly depicted 'Trewthe' being unable to find succour with the great lords, the elite ladies, the men of law, or even 'in holy cherche' – indeed, anyone aspiring to truth must seek exile from the realm.[34] Such characterisations persisted through the years and across social boundaries. In the late fifteenth century, Robert Reynes of Acle in Norfolk – a church reeve, alderman, and general literate neighbour – recorded into his commonplace book a short poem that began 'Lex is leyd adown / Amor is full small / Caritas is owte of [t]own / Veritas is go withal'.[35] Again, it was law that was crowned chief virtue here. And where it fell into abeyance, others soon followed.

This rift in social relations was perceived well into the sixteenth century, despite improving economic and social conditions. A general decline in justice was depicted in one early Tudor interlude called '*Albion, Knight*', in which 'Injury' – said to be 'supported in such suffrency / From the lowest unto the highest degree' – sought to sabotage 'Albion' (England) by setting 'Justice' and 'Principality' (the king, or the royal prerogative) against one another.[36] As the play progressed, the authority of 'Principality' proved to be easily undermined by deeply ingrained ill-feeling in his realm. Similarly, in the preface to his translation and adaptation of Brant's *Das Narrenschiff* – also known as the *Ship of Fools* – the poet Alexander Barclay lamented in 1509 that 'the stony hartys of pepyl ar so harde' that

---

Writings of John Skelton', *Studies in Philology* 88:4 (1991), 94–5. Alexander Barclay had claimed that 'Justyce and right is in captyvyte' and that 'the lady Justyce lyeth bounde': *The Ship of Fools*, ed. T. H. Jamieson (London, 1874), 26, 28.

[33] This appears in the commonplace book of John Colyns, dating to the 1520s and 1530s: BL Harley MS 2252 fol. 25.

[34] R. H. Robbins, *Historical Poems of the XIVth and XVth Centuries* (Columbia University Press, 1959), 146–7.

[35] Bodl. Tanner MS 407 fol. 18; printed in C. Louis ed., *The Commonplace Book of Robert Reynes of Acle* (Garland Publishing, 1980), 181.

[36] This play survives only in a partial manuscript, and so we never find out whether Injury's plan to set estate against estate succeeds: J. S. Farmer ed., *Six Anonymous Plays (Second Series)* (Early English Drama Society, 1906), 117–32.

32   The New Justice System

neighbours now turn against one another in pursuit of their ambitions.[37] This was in contradiction to the expectation, as expressed in one of the Digby complaint poems, that 'If a man do a-nother [a]mys, Neighbores should [t]hem a[d]vyse' and 'Do bothe parties evene assise'. In other words, while the king might provide justice in a broad sense, dispute resolution often naturally rested with neighbours in the first instance (as we will see further in Chapter 5). Yet this amiable arbitration was not happening as it should, and 'old horded hate' was hindering social stability.[38] Consequently, justice in the sense of both social ideal *and* practical relief mechanism was visibly diminished.

Fragmentations

Given this perceptibly unsettled state of affairs, how might anyone, even the king, hope to maintain peace and order in the commonwealth? To many commentators the means to administer justice to that end already existed in the law, and especially in the distinctive English legal tradition of common law enshrined in statutes, maxims, and case precedents. As John Spelman pronounced at a reading before Gray's Inn in 1519, if justice was a 'spring' to nourish the commonwealth then one of its main channels was 'law and custom'.[39] To Fortescue, too, justice and law were explicitly intertwined: 'Human laws are none other than rules by which perfect justice is taught', and 'legal justice' is the 'perfect virtue'. English common law offered the pre-eminent set of rules, of course. Fortescue found the increasingly popular civil-law codes taught at the universities to be 'deficient in rendering justice to injured parties' because they could not guarantee each his own.[40] Meanwhile, as chief justice he expressed the view that the relative newness of the canon law used in church courts meant that it could not supersede the ancient common law.[41] As we shall see later, questions of jurisdictional and juridical hierarchy were much debated across the sixteenth century.[42]

In more popular sources these distinctions were not drawn so markedly, however. From the 'public debate' engaged in by the Duke of York about

---

[37] Barclay, *The Ship of Fools*, 13.   [38] Kail ed., *Twenty-Six Political and Other Poems*, 6.
[39] J. H. Baker ed., *John Spelman's Reading on Quo Warranto, delivered in Gray's Inn (Lent 1519)*, Selden Society 113 (Selden Society, 1997), 76.
[40] Fortescue, *On the Laws and Governance of England*, 9, 34.
[41] M. Hemmant ed., *Select Cases in the Exchequer Chamber 1377–1461*, Selden Society 51 (Selden Society, 1933), 108–9.
[42] For a discussion of legal developments in this period, see the introduction to Baker's *OHLE*.

The Principle and Problem of Justice

the duties of rulership on the eve of the Wars of the Roses emerged the memorable line that 'a king or alorde lawlesse ys as afisshe watirless'.[43] This tapped directly into a general sentiment, and even a sense of nostalgia, for upholding the ancient laws of the land – that is, those contained within common law. Rebel manifestos produced and circulated across our period evoked centuries-old legislation as the benchmark for good rule. Robin of Redesdale, the talisman of the 1469 northern revolts against Edward IV, demanded that statutes be properly observed in order to keep the 'trewe commons' and the 'commonwele' in peace.[44] Later, the rebellion led by the pretender Perkin Warbeck in 1497 promised to restore 'remembrance [of] the good Laws and Customes heretofore made by our noble progenitors' and to administer them as they had been originally intended.[45] The same argument emerged again in response to Henry VIII's Reformation policies. The prophetic, seditious text known as 'The Cock of the North', the origins of which was investigated intensively by the royal Council in the later 1530s, mused simply that 'We shall have plentye and pease whan law hath not [been] lett.'[46] The articles and petitions produced in the rebellion year of 1536 and submitted to the Council complained specifically about the overriding of the law by local officials and the introduction of legislation that harmed the rights of subjects and the liberties of the Church. In the style of their fifteenth-century forbears, these rebels and the lawyers and gentlemen who led them pled to the king that 'the common lawes ma[y] have place as was usid in the beginning of your grace['s] Reign'.[47]

Other, more learned commentators of the time, especially humanist writers, were unconvinced that following law of any kind inevitably imparted justice. Quite the opposite, in fact: in Erasmus's satirical *In Praise of Folly*, written in *c.* 1509 during a spell in England, the personified Folly criticised kings who evoke 'appropriate forms and suitably contrived pretexts' to dispossess their own subjects, 'so that their practices preserve a façade of justice however iniquitous they are'.[48] Erasmus's friend and fellow humanist (and namesake of the *Moriae Encomium*), Thomas More,

---

[43] Kekewich et al. eds., *The Politics of Fifteenth Century England*, 12–14, 188.

[44] J. O. Halliwell ed., *A Chronicle of the first thirteen years of the reign of King Edward the Fourth, by John Warkworth* (Nichols and Son, 1839), 51.

[45] Printed in A. F. Pollard ed. *The Reign of Henry VII from Contemporary Sources* (AMS Press, 1967) vol. I, 154. I am grateful to Dr James Ross for bringing this and the previous source to my attention.

[46] S. L. Jansen, *Political Protest and Prophecy Under Henry VIII* (Boydell, 1991), 98–101, 103.

[47] See many of the documents printed in A. Fletcher and D. MacCulloch eds., *Tudor Rebellions* (5th ed., Routledge, 2014), 142, 144, 148, 151.

[48] Desiderius Erasmus, *Praise of Folly*, trans. and ed. B. Radice (Penguin, 1971), 174–5.

34   The New Justice System

similarly put into the mouth of his Utopian explorer Hythloday the complaint that any royal councillor 'calls to mind some old moth eaten laws' to impose fines on his king's subjects, craftily gaining the king some 'credit for upholding law and order, since the whole procedure can be made to look like justice'.[49] Given the timing of both their publications, More and Erasmus undoubtedly alluded here to the financial exactions wrought through bonds and recognisances on the knights, lords, and bishops of the realm in Henry VII's later years, it being the 'mynde of the kinges grace . . . to have many persons in his danger at his pleasure'.[50] Indeed, the formal institutions of law and justice were typically deemed open to illegal and immoral subversion. In the '*Albion, Knight*' interlude, the villainous 'Injury' seemed to echo real-life truths when he insisted that 'Albion's' parliament had a reputation for dismissing legislation that disadvantaged the prince, the lords, or the merchants.[51] The letter of the law was a potential source of justice, then, but it could just as easily be abused and corrupted. As an adage of the time had it, 'the extremitie of justice, is extreme injurie'.[52]

Consequently, perhaps, those individuals to whom the king delegated his justice-giving on a day-to-day basis perceived their authority to emanate from sources outside of written law. Certainly it descended from God, as did all justice, but also from something closer to the 'special virtue' that Morton spoke of in 1489.[53] In 1516, More wrote personally to Wolsey, the Lord Chancellor and judge in Star Chamber and Chancery, and reminded him that it was 'the law of Christ . . . [that] provides you with the prudence and authority which enable you to administer justice'.[54] While such spiritual origins for justice were widely acknowledged, not everyone at court shared such a positive outlook on its application. To more critical onlookers, judges in such new and experimental tribunals undermined written laws of which they were largely ignorant. The vivid verses of the laureate John Skelton sniped about how, as a mere 'poore maister of arte', Wolsey showed little care 'for lawe canon, or for the lawe common, or for law cyvyll' when dealing with the many 'sutys and supplycacyons' furthered in his courts.[55] In fact, on one occasion in 1517 Wolsey himself spoke

---

[49] Thomas More, *Utopia*, ed. G. M. Logan (3rd ed., Cambridge University Press, 2016), 32.

[50] C. J. Harrison, 'The petition of Edmund Dudley', *EHR* 87:342 (1972), 86–87.

[51] Farmer ed., *Six Anonymous Plays*, 121–2.   [52] Hall, *Hall's Chronicle*, 499.

[53] *PROME* xvi, 8–9 (1489 parliament, item 1).

[54] Printed in Thomas More, *Latin Poems*, ed. C. H. Miller, L. Bradner, C. A. Lynch, and R. P. Oliver, *Complete Works of St Thomas More* (Yale University Press, 1984), vol. 3, pt. II, 269, 409.

[55] John Skelton, 'Why Come Ye Not to Court?', in A. Dyce ed., *The Poetical Works of John Skelton* (Little Brown and Company, 1970), vol. II, 39.

The Principle and Problem of Justice 35

of administering a 'new law of the Star Chamber', albeit to complement the temporal law with which the king's more belligerent courtiers were familiar.[56] This was a considerable exaggeration; there was nothing codified about the application of justice in the conciliar courts in this period. But these comments together reflect that the Crown's civil justice was taken to represent something extraordinary and distinctive.

These lines of discussion also illustrate how justice was far more nebulous than codified law could fully capture. We need only look to adverbs associated with justice to see the range of hopes and aspirations pinned to its execution. Alexander Barclay claimed similarly that Henry VII had evinced 'mercy and pitie / The love of concorde, Justice and equitie' (though not all his contemporaries would have been so praising of the late king).[57] In such mixtures of virtues it can be difficult to separate differing concepts out from one another, yet they were clearly not taken to be synonymous. This is especially apparent in an attainder declared in parliament in 1475, in which it was remarked that Edward IV had already been moved by 'benygnitie and pitie' to lay 'aparte the grete rigour of the law' and pardon some of those involved – law was softened by pity. Yet his lords were at pains to ensure 'that benignite and pite be not so exalted that Justice be not sett apart . . . nor that Justice so procede that benignite and pite have no place'.[58] In an entirely different context, the proper balance between Justice as the principal virtue and her sister concepts of Mercy, Truth, and Peace was tackled in fifteenth- and sixteenth-century morality plays performed at the royal court and further afield. Of these 'Four Daughters of God' it would be Justice who retained her central role throughout the sixteenth century; the character appeared in at least eleven plays between 1400 and 1600, initially as a harbinger of divine judgement but later as something more akin to a judge in a lawcourt.[59] Proclamations and plays therefore illuminate the mental association of justice with states like peace and tranquillity, and with qualities such as truth, mercy, charity, constancy, pity – while, at the same time, implying some hierarchical relationship between them by the early Tudor years.

Of particular relevance to the growth of the Crown's own judicial processes at this time was the invocation of justice as 'indifferent'. Where this promise appeared within proclamations and statutes it meant, in the

---

[56] SP1/16 fol. 16v (*LP* II. 38).   [57] Barclay, *The Ship of Fools*, lvii.

[58] *PROME* xiv, 298–9 (1472 parliament, third roll, item 34).

[59] J. Wilson McCutchan, 'Justice and Equity in the English Morality Play', *Journal of the History of Ideas* 19:3 (1958), 405–10; P. McCune, 'Order and Justice in Early Tudor Drama', *Renaissance Drama* 25 (1994), 171–96.

36 The New Justice System

first instance, the pursuit and resolution of legal issues with impartiality: that 'indifferent persons' should be chosen to act as local officials or as commissioners and that the king would enforce justice even against his favoured courtiers and powerful noblemen.[60] By extension, it also entailed that justice would be accessible for all the king's subjects in equal measure. In an Act passed in 1495 to ensure that the destitute could sue at law, it was said that the king 'entendith indiffrent Justice to be had and mynystred according to his comen lawes to all his true subgettis as well to pou[r] as riche'.[61] This common principle was reiterated when judges of the royal common-law courts of King's Bench and Common Pleas swore on their appointment to 'administer justice indifferently, as well to the poor as to the rich'.[62] Not everyone believed this ideal to be practicable in reality, of course. When the constable of the Tower of London, William Kingston, tried to convince an imprisoned Anne Boleyn in 1536 that even 'the porest sugett the Kyng hath, hath justice', Anne is said to have laughed out loud.[63] The supposed impartiality of the prince was also clearly in contradiction with his duty to prioritise his poorer subjects, as well as 'strangers and orphans and widows, who are more likely to be oppressed by potentates'.[64] In meeting this expectation of rule, royal justice would surely be preoccupied with examining abuses of power and widening social disparities – hardly convenient to those benefitting from such arrangements.

Another concept encapsulating the notion of socially sensitive justice was that of equity. The term itself, descending from the Latin *aequitas*, turns up in all the sources already discussed here – parliamentary sermons, treatises on kingship, popular poetry and verse, and drama – but usually without reference to the complex coalescence of inward conscience, moral reasoning, and divine intuition that it would come to represent in legal circles. As Baker has outlined, equity had several overlapping meanings in late fifteenth-century England. According to more ancient and continental traditions, it referred to an overarching and near-objective sense of right and wrong, as well as to the righteous intentions perceived to have

---

[60] See, for examples, A. Luders, T. E. Tomlins, John France, W. E. Taunton, and John Raithby eds., *The Statutes of the Realm* (London, 1810–28), vol. II, 551, 584, vol. III, 437, 775; and Dudley, *The Tree of Commonwealth*, 34.

[61] 11 Hen. VII c. 12.

[62] See, for example, the Chancellor's declaration at Anthony Fitzherbert's swearing-in as justice of Common Pleas in 1522: J. H. Baker ed., *The Reports of Sir John Spelman*, Selden Society 93–4 (Selden Society, 1976–7), vol. I, 159.

[63] *LP* X. 793.

[64] Stephen Baron, *De Regimine Principum (1509)*, ed. P. J. Mroczkowski (Peter Lang Publishing, 1990), 79.

The Principle and Problem of Justice 37

underpinned all legislation. Within the English legal system, it was also coming to refer to 'the relaxation of known but unwritten general rules of law to meet the exigencies of justice or conscience'. It was generally accepted that it was better to allow occasional 'mischiefs' to befall an individual in order to avoid greater 'inconveniences' to the rule of law through discrepancies in verdicts, but the application of equity might relieve the individual *and* leave the law untouched.[65] By the later sixteenth century, this more defined notion of equity sat at the heart of a distinct jurisdiction running parallel to the common-law courts. But it was hardly so concrete in the early Tudor period. In judicial contexts, the term 'equity' was not much used at this time; legal commentators and petitioners alike turned instead to the language of 'conscience' to evoke the same sense of reason and fairness in the judgment of disputes. Still, the positive effect of such righteousness on society was evident; as in in More's *Utopia*, where the superior equity of the natives was set against the justice of real-world 'nations'.[66] There was even a concurrent sense, going all the way back to Aquinas, that equity or *epieikeia* could ultimately displace the more nebulous ideal of justice by offering specific, sensitive applications of law.[67] Indeed, in the realm of morality plays it was the personification of Equity that eventually came to represent the qualities of fairness and righteousness, with Justice associated with formal legal processes.[68]

On the tongues of commoners and councillors alike the equity of the early Tudors was simply a tempering force to government, once again in the gift of their king. A rhyme composed as an 'exhortation to the nobles and commons of the North' by the friar Dr John Pickering in the later 1530s, and said to be 'in every man's mouth' in Bridlington and Pontefract, contrasted the lawfulness of the Pilgrimage with the lawlessness of the exactions placed upon them by 'naughty Cromwell and the Chancellors'. Of the king, to whom the pilgrims remained resolutely loyal, it was hoped that 'God send him long time to reign with equity'.[69] So, despite its classical origins, this was not an unfamiliar concept among the wider populace, even if its meaning for them remains somewhat indecipherable. Some clearer sense is gained from Injury's scheme in '*Albion, Knight*',

---

[65] Baker, *OHLE*, 40–1.   [66] More, *Utopia*, 110.
[67] J. Guy, 'Law, Equity and Conscience in Henrician Juristic Thought', in A. Fox and J. Guy eds., *Reassessing the Henrician Age: Humanism, Politics, and Reform, 1500–1550* (Blackwell, 1986), 186–7.
[68] McCutchan, 'Justice and Equity in the English Morality Play', 407–10.
[69] *LP* XII. i. 1019; SP1/118 fols. 282–293v; printed in S. E. James, 'Against Them All for to Fight: Friar John Pickering and the Pilgrimage of Grace', *Bulletin of the John Rylands University Library of Manchester* 85:1 (2003), 61–4.

38   The New Justice System

which involved an attempt to convince Albion that 'Principality in no wise / His will with equity will grant to exercise / But that the law should be but after his liking / And every writ after his entitling'. Most straightforwardly, then, the result of a prince acting *in*equitably was a heavy-handed abuse of law and its processes.[70] Conversely, the literature, oaths, and sermons of the period emphasised the role that equity – or righteousness – ought to play in mitigating the judgments, laws, and will of the monarch.[71] This was closer to the conception of equity shaped in the 1520s and 1530s by Christopher St German, a lawyer and the early Tudor period's strongest proponent of equity, who stressed its potential as a positive force *within* the common law and not just outside of it, in the chancellor's own conscience.[72] Yet it is also suggestive of a *non*-legal meaning for the term, used in reference more to good governance than to judicial standards.

A more abstract and potentially problematic facet of royal justice in particular at this early time was mercy. This was a universal virtue that was not exclusive to commentary on justice and judicial proceedings but which was widely expected to underpin their practice nonetheless. Like equity, it was thought to be especially evinced by the monarch himself, though in several different ways. As we saw at the outset of this chapter, the English king swore at the very start of his reign to administer justice with mercy, with the implication being that the latter mediated the former. So, the various figures supposed to speak at the entry pageant at Worcester for Henry VII's visit in 1486 – including Henry VI, St Wulfstan, and St Oswald – were to preach mercy above all other qualities, begging the new king to have 'pytie with mercy' in his heart following the town's recent support for Stafford's rebellion.[73] For the most part, mercy as practice was defined as a mechanism for relieving subjects from the full force of the law. When Henry VIII pardoned Scottish prisoners in 1511, they were supposedly told that 'you shall find the kinges mercy above his justice ... where you were ded by the law, yet by his mercy he will revive you'.[74] It was this aspect of royal grace that was evoked to relieve men and women accused or already indicted of serious crimes through the monarch's general and special pardons, as Kesselring's study of royal pardons

---

[70] Farmer ed., *Six Anonymous Plays*, 121–2, 131.
[71] Legg, *English Coronation Records*, 241; *PROME* xvi, 8–9 (1489 parliament, item 1); SP6/13 fol. 5v.
[72] Christopher St German, *Doctor and Student*, eds. T. F. T. Plucknett and J. L. Barton, Selden Society 91 (Selden Society, 1974).
[73] In the end, this pageant does not seem to have been performed, though Henry VII's herald recorded the plans: Cavell ed., *The Herald's Memoir*, 83.
[74] Hall, *Hall's Chronicle*, 525.

The Principle and Problem of Justice

has demonstrated at length.[75] In these heady circumstances, mercy encapsulated the sovereign's divine oversight of life, death, and salvation, for the good of the commonwealth and the celestial realm.

As we will see in the hearings of Requests, the king's mercy came to be conceptualised in a slightly different way within a more regular judicial setting. Blended with equity and conscience, it often referred to allowing the poor fairer access to justice in the first place, on the basis of their disadvantages – figured, therefore, as something closer to charity or pity for the complainant, *not* the accused. Along these lines, Barclay's panegyric for Henry VIII (perhaps initially intended for Henry VII) upheld the ideal of a king who sought 'By iustice and pitie his realme to maynteyne.'[76] In a very different context, a list of articles prepared by Sir Thomas Tempest for the rebels gathered at Pontefract in 1536 declared that a king should 'rewle his subjetes vertuus[ly] be jutece myxyd with mercy and pyty' – which, in the context of this rebellion, he again referred to as relief from 'rygore to [p]u[t] men to de[the]'.[77] Here any conceptual differentiation between justice and the mitigating forces of mercy and pity was non-existent, put aside in favour of the insistence that any and all people placed in a position of judicial authority should behave with a merciful temperament. Widely circulated maxims of the age ran that 'the judge's decision must follow clemency' ('*Judicis sentencia oportet sequum clemenciam*') and 'justice follows the compassion (or pity) of judges' ('*Justicia judicum sequatur pietas*').[78] As to the performance of kingship, there was more debate to be had about this balance of qualities. To some theorists of the time, pity was always an excess of monarchical mercy; a sign of weakness and overwrought emotion. It could not be offered at 'all tymes to all them that nedith it lest Justice wold seasse', even if 'it besemith a christen king rather to gyve to mutche then to lytle'.[79] Nonetheless, the very assertion in the coronation oath that justice was to be administered *with* mercy, truth, and equity and *according to* conscience makes plain that this was a baseline ideal qualifiable by other concerns.

Overall, in this hotly contested area of rule it seems that problems stemmed from disagreements about *practice* rather than with the general principle. On the one hand, as we have already seen, Hall and Robert

---

[75] Kesselring, *Mercy and Authority*. See also McSheffrey, *Seeking Sanctuary*.
[76] A. Fox, *Politics and Literature in the Reigns of Henry VII and Henry VIII* (Basil Blackwell, 1989), 41–2.
[77] Printed in Fletcher and MacCulloch eds., *Tudor Rebellions*, 146.
[78] Cambridge, Trinity College MS O.2.53, fols. 7–7v.
[79] Thomas Elyot, *The Book Named the Governor*, ed. S. E. Lehmberg (J. M. Dent & Sons, 1962), 119; Dudley, *The Tree of Commonwealth*, 61.

40   The New Justice System

Fabyan, the chronicler of London, complained openly about courts in the capital city that favoured the poor 'more somtyme than Justice & good lawe Requyrid', ultimately harming the more powerful men of the city.[80] But their view of the accessibility of the legal system seems exaggerated when compared with more popular accounts of litigation. A poem about husbandry recorded in commonplace books across the fifteenth century contained a brief passage bemoaning the reality that 'yf we woll plete [plea] / We shalnot be spared good chepe nor dere / Our man of lawe may not be for gete / But he most have money every quarte'.[81] A stronger indictment of the central administration was instilled within the popular poem 'London Lickpenny' (possibly by John Lydgate, the monk of Bury), which told the vivid and amusing tale of a prospective litigant who ventured from Kent to Westminster to complain of being defrauded out of his goods, only to receive cold shoulders at every turn and find that 'they that lacked money mowght [might] not spede'.[82] Even if procedures could be initiated, other pithy complaints found in commonplace books and elite treatises alike ran that 'Better is a frende in courte than a peny in [your] purse' and that 'the law was ended as a man was friended' – that justice mattered less than well-connected friends in gaining a favourable judicial remedy.[83] Troublingly, many of these verses indicated that the heartlessness of the realm reached all the way into Westminster, into the king's own courts of King's Bench, Common Pleas, and Chancery.[84]

Conclusion

The history of justice in the early Tudor period is characterised by blurred conceptual lines and by differences in precision of views, though not in strength of feeling, from the top to the bottom of society. Clearly justice could go astray. And yet, the hope and expectation that the king *would* provide justice of an extraordinary kind directly to his subjects

---

[80] A. H. Thomas and I. D. Thornley eds., *The Great Chronicle of London* (London, 1938), 320; Hall, *Hall's Chronicle*, 585.

[81] BL Lansdowne MS 762 fol. 5. See also Barclay, *The Ship of Fools*, 12.

[82] Printed in Robbins, *Historical Poems*, 130–4.

[83] Barclay, *The Ship of Fools*, 70; figured in Latin as '*melius est habet amicum in curia quam denarium in bursa*' in the commonplace book of the Ramston family of Essex: Cambridge, Trinity College MS O.2.53 fol. 8v; Henry Brinklow, *Complaynt of Roderyk Mors*, ed. J. Meadows Cowper, Early English Text Society Extra Series 22 (N. Trübner & Co., 1874), 25; Thomas Starkey, *A Dialogue Between Reginald Pole & Thomas Lupset*, ed. K. M. Burton (Chatto & Windus, 1948), 86.

[84] For a summary of the criticisms of lawyers and courts in this period, see E. W. Ives, 'The Reputation of the Common Lawyers in English Society 1450-1550', *University of Birmingham Historical Journal* 7 (1961).

The Principle and Problem of Justice

only intensified within the early Tudor period. It had become so self-evident by the mid-1530s that Sir Adrian Fortescue daringly complained 'in the kinges presence, that the kyng had done hym wronge' in his suit, while another man, John Snowe, said 'to the king that no Justice could be had' in his cause. Both men were swiftly imprisoned for questioning this evident quality of Henry VIII's benevolence.[85] Around the same time, that king amended the text of the coronation oath so that the promise to 'do in his judgementes equytee and right justice with discression and mercye' became 'he shall *according to his conscience* in all his judgementes mynystere equytee right Justice *shewyng where is to be shewyd* mercy', adding further emphasis to the personal discretion in justice associated with the royal prerogative.[86] Although we might think immediately here of a leaning towards royal authority bolstered by law – of the royal supremacy, the use of Parliament as a legislative body to reset the political agenda, and the ascent of lawyers into the ministerial class – this top-down vision of law and power alone does not provide us with a full picture. There was also a bottom-up *demand* driving the expansion of the king's civil justice for his subjects, influenced by sharply attuned criticisms of existing avenues for redress. To facilitate its supervision of justice, the Crown relied on the private accuser to present offences and misdemeanours for attention. In turn, through its heavy association with equity and mercy, royal justice was perceived as a remedy to the ills of the legal system and, perhaps, of society at large.

What this chapter has demonstrated, however, is how unlikely it is that the rebels of the north, the ordinary litigant, the common lawyer, the landlord, the royal councillor, or Henry VIII himself would have agreed on exactly *how* the Tudor government ought to fulfil its obligation to provide due justice to all, much less how it was to balance calls for conscientiousness, righteousness, charity, mercy, equity, and pity under that general responsibility. Justice in its broadest terms was a buzzword, a soundbite, an 'atmospheric' of late fifteenth and early sixteenth-century England.[87] But it could quickly become a weapon: its absence a line of criticism that legitimised resistance. The very existence of so many cognate concepts, even if they lacked firm definition, is enough to show the potential cracks in justice's construction, despite its deep foundations. The longer sweep of the sixteenth century encompassed an unfolding clash between universally appealing ideals like mercy and charity and

---

[85] HL Ellesmere MS 2652 fol. 14.   [86] Legg, *English Coronation Records*, 241 (my emphasis).
[87] Watts, '*The Policie in Christen Remes*', 44.

the precision of the 'law of the land' – a debate that determined what the Crown could reasonably do in the name of the commonwealth. As we turn now to the *practice* of royal justice from the late fifteenth century onwards, it will become apparent that the challenge facing the early Tudor authorities was how to encompass such elastic principles within the ordered space of the courtroom.

CHAPTER 2

Conciliar Justice at Centre and Periphery

In late medieval England, all formal processes for the dispensation of justice technically ran in the king's name, no matter how close to him they were in reality. What changed under the early Tudors was how often this business was delegated to members of the royal Council, and so kept within the central administration. As pleas for justice proliferated, the same councillors were organised into a set of authoritative tribunals around the Crown, with independent power to hear and determine subjects' suits. The distinguishing feature of this jurisdiction was its relative fluidity and mobility. Overseen by a rotating circle of men in the king's service, these tribunals acted in a more ad-hoc manner than did the more ancient and fixed common-law courts. Much to the dismay of many of the period's common lawyers, these new courts quickly joined the ranks of the more ancient and austere forums settled within the legal marketplace of Westminster Hall: the royal common-law courts of King's Bench and Common Pleas, the revenue Court of Exchequer, and the primary conscience Court of Chancery. In a sense they also supplemented Parliament as avenues for appealing to the king as the ultimate judge and lawmaker.[1] Although the conciliar courts were popular with litigants unsatisfied with the broader judicial system, the once-accepted narrative that they drained business from the existing courts has been proven false by legal scholars. In fact, the common-law and conciliar systems ran as parallel, if sometimes conflicting, jurisdictions that litigants could use in tandem to secure the most advantageous end to their case.[2] Still, that there *was* something qualitatively and structurally different about the extraordinary courts that came into being under the early Tudors and survived through to the mid-seventeenth century seems undeniable.

[1] For Parliament's function as judicial forum, see G. Dodd, *Justice and Grace: Private Petitioning and the English Parliament in the Late Middle Ages* (Oxford University Press, 2007).
[2] Baker ed., *The Reports of Sir John Spelman*, vol. II, 38–9; Baker, *OHLE*, 40–2; Brooks, *Pettyfoggers and Vipers*, 82–8.

44   The New Justice System

This chapter charts the development of conciliar justice throughout the late fifteenth and early sixteenth centuries – its formative years. That Henry VII and then Henry VIII oversaw a 'rapid expansion of conciliar justice' and of their judicial reach is well known to historians of this period and is demonstrated most obviously in the available statistics for caseloads across all the central courts of the early sixteenth century.[3] What remains to be understood is the process by which conciliar justice was diversified in the first place; how and why it came to be represented in several differentiated tribunals, some settled within the centre of government at Westminster and some in the troublesome provinces of the north and the Welsh marches, with others working across the spaces in between. This last group included the itinerant Court of Requests, which we will come on to in the next chapter. For now, the survey of the greater span of the tribunals staffed out of the royal Council in the following discussion helps explain how they became popular, effective, and efficient, in contrast with the existing common-law processes of which people so often complained in the fifteenth century. An understanding of their institutional qualities also lends itself to an investigation of why a population broadly supportive of the (common) law, and mostly hostile to innovation, would welcome a new and controversial jurisdiction into their government, communities, and lives.

Late Medieval Origins

The Council's ancient remit for justice descended from the responsibilities of its master, the king. As per the contemporary ideal of the monarch as fount of all justice, subjects with complaints about injustices had long been able to approach him personally for aid, wherever he happened to be. In 1420, one Ralph atte Ree travelled all the way from Essex to Normandy to seek out 'o[u]r lyge lord the Kyng', Henry V, 'at the Castel of Monterell', recently besieged and captured by the English Crown. Ree desired the king's help in restoring him to a tenement back home in the royal manor of Ramsden Hall, from which Ree claimed to have been ousted. His request apparently found some favour, since a letter from Henry to his Lord Chancellor furthering this suit, dated 4 July that year at Montereau-Fault-Yonne, still survives.[4] The same

---

[3] M. M. Condon, 'Ruling Elites in the Reign of Henry VII', in C. Ross ed., *Patronage, Pedigree and Power in Later Medieval England* (Alan Sutton, 1979), 132; Gunn, *Early Tudor Government*, 77; J. A. Guy, 'Wolsey, the Council, and the Council Courts', *EHR* 91:360 (1976), 481–505.

[4] J. Caley and J. Bayley eds., *Calendar of Proceedings in Chancery in the Reign of Queen Elizabeth* (1827–32), vol. I, xvi–xviii.

Conciliar Justice at Centre and Periphery

route of access followed by intervention was available under the Yorkist kings, too. Documents transcribed by John Vale in the fifteenth century illustrate Edward IV's practice of forwarding petitions for justice on to local judges, with orders to expedite their hearing. His covering writs proclaimed a care for seeing justice done 'aswele to the poure as to the riche', 'withoute hede, socour or supportacion'.[5] Eventually, any and all complainants were openly invited to pursue a royal route for redress. A narrative account of litigation undertaken by Warwickshire gentleman Nicholas Catesby in the latter half of the fifteenth century included the recollection that 'kynge Richard the iijde made a p[ro]clamacion gen[er] all that ev[er]y man wronged that wolde c[om]pleyn shuld have hasty remedye . . . no man except[ed]'.[6]

This opened up a wide remit for the king to right many perceived wrongs, presented to him and handled through increasingly formal mechanisms. The artificial archival repository of late-medieval bills known as the 'Ancient Petitions' (TNA SC 8) contains a mix of complaints submitted to Parliament, the Chancellor, and to the king for grants of offices, pardons, and letters of safe conduct – requests for grace or favour. There are also plenty from the later fifteenth century addressed directly to the king and asking for judicial remedies in disputes between two private parties. Some petitioners complained of felonious offences, such as murder and robbery, but more sought restitution for damages to or loss of property, withheld wages, and the restoration of disseised lands. Many simply requested that orders be sent to gather local gentlemen to arbitrate between them and their opponents.[7] Yet many others asked that the king and Council hear these matters themselves, as an act of 'mercyfull petie . . . att the rev[er]ens of god and the wey of charite'. Plaintiffs of this sort also stressed their inability to access legal remedy elsewhere, because of various disadvantages: for example, in the case of Elizabeth Strelley in *c.* 1471, because she and her husband 'for lak of goodes' were not able to make suit.[8] As Mark Ormrod once wrote, these petitions 'represented the "demand" rather than the "supply" side of later medieval royal government'.[9]

---

[5] Kekewich et al. eds., *The Politics of Fifteenth Century England*, 164.

[6] TNA E163/29/11 m. 9. I am grateful to Dr Euan Roger for his help in identifying and locating this document. It could refer to several different proclamations made in 1483 and 1484: C. Ross, *Richard III* (Eyre Methuen, 1981), 173–4.

[7] For examples from the latter half of the fifteenth century, see TNA SC8/132/6576, 8/138/6864, 8/176/8788, 8/289/14448, 8/336/14900.

[8] SC8/176/8788.

[9] W. M. Ormrod, 'Introduction: Medieval Petitions in Context', in W. M. Ormrod, G. Dodd, and A. Musson eds., *Medieval Petitions: Grace and Grievance* (York Medieval Press, 2009), 3.

The New Justice System

Part of this demand was a growing expectation that the king would be interested in his subjects' rents, lands, inheritances, and marriages – matters which touched neither his own estates nor the peace of the realm at large. Determining the truth of interpersonal disputes placed a very different claim on the Crown's time and resources than did granting a reward or an office. And so, although petitions for favour and for justice were at first bundled together, they came to be sifted to dedicated attendants working in discrete institutions.[10] Indeed, by the middle of the fifteenth century, petitioners knowledgeably applied for adversaries to be summoned with a writ under the royal privy seal ordering them to appear and answer to set complaints, and perhaps also to 'other wronges by [them] don as ... shalbe declared and shewed'.[11] Evidently, it was understood by complainants and the legal professionals increasingly on hand to advise them that there existed a mechanism not only for petitioning but for *litigating* before the king's Council. This involved some means of accessing the royal court to submit a complaint, the receipt of a written petition by the Council and/or its clerks, the production of a paper trail to have the matter investigated, and a formal hearing before royal councillors.[12] Furthermore, in their rhetoric these earlier petitions imply that subjects anticipated – and the king accepted – an emphasis on especial protection for the poor and vulnerable.

Such were the expectations placed on rulers as the English Crown came into the hands of the Tudors in 1485. Various chronicles of the following decades make passing reference to the new monarchs being inundated by complaints as they traversed their dominions, just like their predecessors. After Henry VII had been treated to the pageants at Bristol in 1487, he reportedly spent time after evensong listening to the mayor and burgesses of the town explain the 'cause of ther povertie', the 'great losse of shippes and goodes' in recent years; supposedly 'they harde not this hundred yeres of noo king so good a comfort'.[13] During his first progress, in 1510, Henry

---

[10] For this distinction between justice and grace, or complaints and requests, see R. W. Hoyle, D. Tankard and S. R. Neal eds., *Heard Before the King: Registers of Petitions to James I, 1603–1616*, List and Index Society Special Series 38–39 (List and Index Society, 2006), vol. I, xiii–xv; Dodd, *Justice and Grace*, 1–2.

[11] TNA SC8/176/8788.

[12] For examples of these processes taking place, see Kekewich et al. eds., *The Politics of Fifteenth Century England*, 164. Even in the early fifteenth century, petitioners might receive a written response from the Council once the matter had been examined by them, as is suggested by the fragmentary response to Edmund Spayne's petition of *c.* 1427: SC8/141/7017. Dr James Ross is currently examining evidence of the Lancastrian council's procedures for summoning litigants, particularly in the wake of the 1454 statute concerning writs of proclamation, as evidenced among various writs in TNA C 255.

[13] Cavell ed., *The Heralds' Memoir*, 97.

VIII heard a raft of grievances against Richard Empson and Edmund Dudley – possibly remaining from the *oyer and terminer* commissions that had convened for a few months in the previous year – while in 1515 he 'visited his towns [and] castles . . . & heard the complaints of his poor commonality'.[14] Later on, the plans for reorganising the Council contained in the Eltham ordinances of the mid-1520s were motivated partly by concerns that many 'matters of justice and complaints' were 'made, brought, and presented unto his Highnesse . . . in his demurre or passing from place to place' and had to be 'debated, digested and resolved' by the king himself.[15] The monarch could hardly *avoid* his duty as justice-giver. Petitions would come, whether invited or not. To handle an increasing volume of requests for royal redress, the early Tudors presided over a shift from a flow of informal, oral complaint and resolution to a system of documented petitioning, pleading, and judgment.

Facilitating this expanding judicial provision was a reliance on the Council as a curial body in its own right, both as a place to appeal decisions made elsewhere but also to bring cases in the first instance. As Stephen Baron explained to the young Henry VIII in 1509, since a king 'is not able to do [justice] by himself in all places, he must needs appoint ministers of justice' to dispense it efficiently on his behalf.[16] Baron likely referred literally to official ministers of state – the Lord Chancellor, the Treasurer, the chief justices. Yet, in reality, the same sort of business was routinely delegated to regular councillors and even to coun*sellors*; the distinction being important since, for this period, we might talk of members of the royal Council, listed as attending its meetings, and other men who were part of the king's entourage and provided a diverse range of services, spiritual and secular. Moreover, when discussing the Council as an institution, we refer to several concentric, overlapping circles in which its members moved: including a 'main' or 'central' Council concerned with all aspects of the realm's administration, an inner ring of the most favoured and trusted men, and an outer circle of conciliar committees undertaking specific tasks.[17] Increasingly across the early sixteenth century there was also a split between the Council in operation within the chambers of

---

[14] Hall, *Hall's Chronicle*, 513, 582–3. Complaints raised against ministers at the *oyer and terminer* commissions held between July and October 1509 are filed in TNA KB9/453. The commissions were closed by the Council on 11 October 1509: HL Ellesmere MS 2655 fol. 7v.

[15] John Nichols ed., *A collection of ordinances and regulations for the government of the royal household* (London, 1790), 159.

[16] Baron, *De Regimine Principum*, 79.

[17] See, for example, S. B. Chrimes's description of Henry VII's Council, which comprised at least 227 members: *Henry VII* (Eyre Methuen, 1972), 97–100, 102, 129, 150, 152.

48 The New Justice System

Westminster Palace and that part attendant on the king's person as he itinerated between houses on a seasonal rotation, on grand progresses for diplomacy and display, and on hunting trips and pilgrimages. This ambulant portion comprised those most trusted counsellors as well as the men of the household clergy, tasked with the spiritual wellbeing of the sovereign (sometimes, but not always, also members of the Council). By the later 1530s, the more concentrated 'privy' Council based at Westminster started to emerge as the principal conciliar body, with the peripheral functions of its 'parent stem' – like justice-giving – 'hived off' into separate courts and committees.[18]

All the while, though, discrete groups of councillors could be drawn out from the main body and reabsorbed back into it whenever necessary. This 'adhoccery' in conciliar government meant that justice could move in and out of frame as a matter of concern, too.[19] The kings of the fourteenth and fifteenth centuries had occasionally passed down orders to their councils to set aside time in their weekly or even daily schedule to read bills of complaint, with some order of priority established. In 1390, an ordinance for the organisation of Richard II's Council declared that each day its members should first dispense with the business of the realm and that, turning to justice, it should refer matters of common law to the justices and retain only the bills of 'people of small charge' ('*poeple du meindre charge*') to be examined by the Keeper of the Privy Seal and other councillors.[20] The parliament of 1429 decreed that the clerk of the Council of the seven-year-old Henry VI – not yet crowned – should 'be sworn, that every day that the counseill sitteth on any billes betwixt partie and partie, that he shal . . . loke which is the poverest suitours bille, that furst to be r[e]ad and answerd'.[21] According to the Commons at the parliament of 1453, the Lord Chancellor had promised them at the session's opening in Reading that an entire 'learned and wise council should be ordained and established . . . to whom all people might have recourse for the administration of justice, equity and

---

[18] The main scholarship on the late-medieval and Tudor Council includes Elton's 'Why the History of the Early Tudor Council Remains Unwritten'; and, ten years later, his 'Tudor Government: The Points of Contact', 21–38; J. Guy, 'The Privy Council: Revolution or Evolution?', in C. Coleman and D. Starkey eds., *Revolution Reassessed: Revisions in the History of Tudor Government and Administration* (Clarendon Press, 1986), 59–86.

[19] J. Watts, 'Counsel and the King's Council, *c.*1340–1540', in J. Rose ed., *The Politics of Counsel in England and Scotland 1286–1707* (Oxford University Press, 2016), 63–87.

[20] Sir Nicholas Harris Nicolas ed., *Proceedings and Ordinances of the Privy Council of England* (Eyre & Spottiswoode, 1834–7), vol. I, 18b. This perhaps advanced on a previous agreement by the young Richard, in his first year as king, that his Council would not itself determine suits between subjects: *PROME* vi, 46 (1377 parliament, item 87).

[21] *PROME* x, 393–94 (1429 parliament, item 27, no. XV).

Conciliar Justice at Centre and Periphery

wisdom'. They lamented that nothing had ever come of this proposal.[22] Since at least the mid-fifteenth century, then, there had existed some desire – and expectation, perhaps, on petitioners' parts – to build on existing elements of organisation for royal justice-giving with a more permanent, substantive avenue for that work within the Council.

Procedural Models

The trend towards justice by committee continued apace under the Tudors. Henry VII turned 'naturally to a conciliar solution for every administrative problem', so much that he is said to have ushered in an age of 'conciliar omnipotence'.[23] His regime benefitted from several delineations within the channels of communication between Crown and subjects that had been established over the preceding century. These included, firstly, a distinction between petitioning for *grace* (for an office, an estate, a wardship, or other reward in the king's gift) and for *justice*; then a gradual transition away from treating justice as a subsidiary part of administration undertaken by the main Council and towards the use of tribunals and committees for which it was the *primary*, and sometimes *only*, purpose; and the separation out of serious matters touching the king and his magnates (both civil and criminal) and the interpersonal disputes of ordinary subjects, furthered through litigation to the Crown. This last and latest change was especially important, since it represented a dividing line between the truly 'prerogative' tribunals emerging in the decades after 1485, including Henry VII's notorious Council Learned in the Law, Henry VIII's Court of Wards and Liveries, and the Exchequer of Pleas, which pursued royal revenues and interests, and those emerging forums through which supplicants could pursue their own causes against and between one another.[24] In light of the usual characterisation of all royal conciliar courts as prerogative and authoritarian by the late sixteenth century, this distinction deserves further articulation.[25]

Of course, while the result of these adjustments was a more systematised, centralised provision for justice, it was not wholly new. Echoing earlier

---

[22] *PROME* xii, 256–7 (1453 parliament, item 30).
[23] Condon, 'Ruling Elites in the Reign of Henry VII', 131–4.
[24] See, for example, W. H. Bryson, 'The Court of Exchequer Comes of Age', in D. J. Guth and J. W. McKenna eds., *Tudor Rule and Revolution: Essays for G.R. Elton* (Cambridge University Press, 1982), 152.
[25] Hindle has referred to the later Star Chamber as a tool of 'prerogative justice', but that term is less useful for the early Tudor years: *The State and Social Change*, 66–86.

50   The New Justice System

mandates on the Council's schedule, an ordinance of 1492, establishing a regency council under Prince Arthur during a short royal campaign into France, ordered that one day a week be set aside to read the 'billes' of any 'partie suying', with decisions to be endorsed on the bills. Another article repeated verbatim the 1429 ordinance for prioritising the 'poverest suitours bille'.[26] Elsewhere, plans were afoot to increase the independent authority of certain ministers and councillors to dispense justice outside of the main Council. The so-called 'Star Chamber Act' of 1487 did *not* found a court in that space, but it did strengthen the remit of the Chancellor, the Keeper of the Privy Seal, and the Treasurer, alongside temporal and spiritual lords and the common-law justices, to examine and punish cases of mainten-ance, retaining, empanelling of corrupt juries, making false verdicts, and riots – notably, all offences which diverted lawful proceedings.[27] The prominent role given in this crusade to the Chancellor reflected the existing connection between the office of the Chancellery, which oversaw the production of governmental writs and orders, and the judicial *Court* of Chancery, already fully fledged by the time the Tudors came to the throne.[28] Still, statutes like this only temporarily delegated the Council's own authority to determine criminal matters considered to be especially pressing – they did not establish discrete courts.

The step from conciliar oversight of country-wide judicial processes to the institution of its *own* procedures was a short one. Various procedural models were readily available for adaptation: the most obvious being those used in Chancery, which had come into its own as a settled civil jurisdic-tion in the early fifteenth century and had experienced a substantial period of growth in business from the 1470s onwards.[29] Like Chancery, all the conciliar courts accepted bills of complaint written in English and initiated a series of back-and-forth pleadings intended to uncover the truth of the dispute at hand, including the defendant's answer and possibly also the complainant's replication, the defendant's rejoinder, and so on. Within

---

[26] This ordinance is printed in full in M. M. Condon, 'An Anachronism with Intent? Henry VII's Council Ordinance of 1491/2', in R. A. Griffiths and J. Sherborne eds., *Kings and Nobles in the Later Middle Ages* (Alan Sutton, 1986), 245. Incidentally, the procedure of endorsing orders on the reverse side of bills was later followed in Requests.

[27] 3 Hen. VII c. 1. Preceding Acts include 13 Hen. IV c. 7 and 31 Hen. VI c. 2. See also 11 Hen. VII c. 25, and the 1529 Act to update the 1487 'Star Chamber' Act by authorising the President of the Council to summon and hear causes alongside the Chancellor and Lord Privy Seal: 21 Hen. VIII c. 20.

[28] N. Pronay, 'The Chancellor, the Chancery and the Council at the End of the 15th Century', in H. Hearder and H. R. Lyon eds., *British Government and Administration* (University of Wales Press, 1974), 87–103.

[29] *Ibid.*, 88–9.

Conciliar Justice at Centre and Periphery

this flexible pleadings system, Chancery allowed the law of the land to be weighed up against the more nebulous concept of 'good conscience', with the Chancellor (usually trained in canon and/or civil law) sitting in judgment alongside the realm's chief justices and serjeants-at-law. The classic example of a case determinable in this forum, explicated by Christopher St German in the later 1520s, was that of the foolish debtor who failed to acquire or had misplaced the written acquittance proving that they had paid off a debt. In such instances, the debtee arguably acted legally, if not morally, in suing the debtor to pay up again. Some late-medieval judges, especially clerics, thought it preferable to save the plaintiff's money – and the defendant's conscience – than to allow abuses of legal technicalities and documents.[30] As Tim Haskett's analysis of the late-medieval Chancery has shown, suits concerning 'instruments' like acquittals made up the majority of its workload by the early sixteenth century.[31]

Perhaps because of this narrowing jurisdiction, by the middle of the fifteenth century Chancery's own shortcomings were becoming apparent to some keen observers. One proclamation from the rebel leader Jack Cade in 1450 lamented how 'the law servyth of nowght ellys in thes days but for to do wrong', with no remedy to be had even in 'ye cowrt of conscience' – surely a reference to Chancery, though he did not elaborate.[32] The narrator of the 'London Lickpenny' poem also condemned the 'Clarkes of the Chauncerye' in the same breath as the judges of King's Bench and Common Pleas for refusing to hear cases without payment up front.[33] Owing to its derivation out of the Chancellery and its leading minister, the Court of Chancery cannot truly be labelled a *conciliar* tribunal. As such, its perceived limitation did not preclude, and may even have necessitated, the enriching of a very similar jurisdiction under direct control of the sovereign. It bequeathed to the conciliar courts a role for equity and conscience in institutionalised dispute resolution – this was, at least initially, 'what Chancery did', even if such pigeon-holing has led to this court monopolising legal histories and

---

[30] St German, *Doctor and Student*, 79. The question of a plaintiff's right in conscience if not in law to possession of land on default of a statute merchant was debated in Chancery among the justices and serjeants in 1492: YB 7 Hen. 7, Pasch. Plea 2, fols. 10b–13b.

[31] T. S. Haskett, 'The Medieval English Court of Chancery', *Law and History Review* 14:2 (1996), 296–9, 305. In St German's classic case, the issue came down to whether a documented acquittance was required to void a bond for the debt. Elsewhere, in the mid-fifteenth century, Lord Chancellor Stillington argued that remedy could be had for breach of faith in Chancery regardless of the absence of a sealed deed proving the promise in the first place: YB 8 Ed. IV, Pasch. Plea 11, fol. 4b.

[32] 'A proclamation made by Jacke Cade, Capytayn of ye Rebelles in Kent', printed in J. Gairdner ed., *Three Fifteenth-Century Chronicles with Historical Memoranda by John Stowe*, Camden New Series 28 (Camden Society, 1880), 96.

[33] Robbins, *Historical Poems*, 131.

52   The New Justice System

obscuring what *other* tribunals contributed to these developments.[34] In the end, Chancery and the conciliar courts would come to be tarred with the same brush. Yet initially, and likely by design, the latter were functionally distinct from their procedural predecessor.

More personal, extraordinary qualities of the royal courts were borrowed from outside the central administration. The councils of the country's magnates offered one such standard. Documents scattered across the archival holdings of England's noble households reveal how often members of the baronage and upper echelons of the Church were called upon to determine disputes between their tenants and retainers, which often concerned possession of lands. The intervention of these leading men could start with informal conversations with warring factions, escalating to investigations that involved viewing written evidence, taking depositions, and hearing the disputants' arguments – in essence, the same procedures followed by Chancery. Although lawyers within a magnate's own 'council learned' might be called in to advise on these deliberations, the point was not to find the correct legal ruling.[35] Rather, this form of remedy has been characterised by Carole Rawcliffe as both a solution to the obvious shortcomings of the legal system, already evident by the late fourteenth century, and as a means of reaching a resolution with the flexibility required for stubborn disputants. The result was an agreement or a compromise rather than an award with a winner and loser, the classic example being the division of estates between claimants.[36] Ultimately this served as an extension of the usual practice of going to one's neighbours for 'a[d]vyse' and 'evene assise', with the added invocation of a local powerholder who could compel mediation *and* enforce its terms later down the line.[37] In taking on the mantle of the ultimate arbiter and embedding the required fact-finding within established bill procedure, then, the early Tudor kings oversaw an expansion of the Crown's judicial capacities in several dimensions at once: legally, socially, and geographically.

---

[34] See J. B. Post, 'Equitable Resorts before 1450', in E. W. Ives and A. H. Manchester eds., *Law, Litigants and the Legal Profession* (Royal Historical Society, 1983), 68–79.

[35] C. Rawcliffe, 'Baronial Councils in the Later Middle Ages', in C. Ross ed., *Patronage, Pedigree and Power in Later Medieval England* (Alan Sutton, 1979), 90–2.

[36] C. Rawcliffe, 'The Great Lord as Peacekeeper: Arbitration by English Noblemen and their Councils in the Later Middle Ages', in J. A. Guy and H. G. Beale eds., *Law and Social Change in British History* (Royal Historical Society, 1984), 34–54; J. B. Post, 'Courts, Councils and Arbitrators in the Ladbroke Manor Dispute', in R. F. Hunnisett and J. B. Post eds., *Medieval Legal Records Edited in Memory of C. A. F. Meekings* (HMSO, 1978); M. A. Hicks, 'Restraint, Mediation and Private Justice: George, Duke of Clarence as "Good Lord"', *The Journal of Legal History* 4:2 (1983), 56–71.

[37] Kail ed., *Twenty-Six Political and Other Poems*, 6.

The Marches, the North, and Westminster

The ultimate lord in the realm was the king, and organised conciliar justice was born from a need to keep royal estates and their tenants in check. Principal among the Crown holdings was the Duchy of Lancaster, which encompassed lands in thirty-two counties, including Lancashire, parts of Warwickshire, Leicestershire, Nottinghamshire and Yorkshire, swathes of the midlands and East Anglia, and certain areas of South Wales. Many of these territories were annexed to the Crown in 1399 as part of Henry IV's 'heritage of Lancaster' and were incorporated with a separate administration in the mid-fifteenth century. The chancellor and Council overseeing the Duchy were mostly preoccupied with prerogative and prosecutorial business, pursuing the tenants and lords within their remit for money owed to the Crown. Fifteenth-century ordinances were designed to manage revenues derivable from Duchy estates, right down to the employment of a 'swanne herde' to protect the waterfowl of the Lincolnshire fens for the king's use. Through to the sixteenth century this Council busied itself collecting fines from men who had not come forward to take up a knighthood on reaching the income threshold of £40 per year in lands or rents.[38] It was perhaps as a consequence of this revenue-raising function that the Duchy Council came to overlap so seamlessly with Henry VII's notorious Council Learned in the Law, the two tribunals sharing Richard Empson, chancellor of the Duchy, as their presiding judge and a set of order books under his purview.[39]

The administration of such a large estate also involved judicial work, with stewards and bailiffs employed to oversee leet, great, and fen courts and the Council itself tasked with hearing bills and supplications. To reach the estates within its jurisdiction, the Duchy Council regularly travelled into the countryside. Its first surviving order book, commenced in 1474, contains a memorandum from March 1476 laying out a planned 'progresse to bee made by the kings counsaill of his duchie of Lancastr[e]', to include stops at York, Pickering, Knaresborough, Leeds, Pontefract, and Tickhill, with several 'turnes' or court sessions planned to last for several days at each.[40] By the early sixteenth century it undertook the larger part of its business in a room 'on the left hand above the staire' leading up to

---

[38] R. Somerville, 'Ordinances for the Duchy of Lancaster', *Camden Miscellany* Fourth Series 14 (Royal Historical Society, 1975), 20. See, for example, the order-book entries for Hilary term 1503: TNA DL5/2 fols. 45v–50.

[39] DL5/4 is essentially a register of the Council Learned's business in the period 1505–9, contemporaneous with the Duchy's work recorded in DL5/3.

[40] TNA DL5/1 fol. 89v.

54   The New Justice System

Westminster Hall, at which point it was referred to as the Council or Court of the 'Duchy Chamber'.[41] Its surviving decree books document its determination of disputes very similar in nature to those presented to the king and main Council throughout the early Tudor period: variances over title to lands, the use of commons and woods, and riots and affrays. In procedure and in style of determination, the late-medieval Duchy Council was also operating as a 'conscience' court akin to Chancery, applying the spirit but not necessarily the letter of the law in private causes.[42]

Elsewhere, the earliest judicial bodies to diverge entirely from the parent stem of the royal Council were provincial councils, established to govern the further reaches of the realm. A royal Council in the Marches of Wales stemmed from the customary delegation of the governance of lands around and across the Welsh border – claimed in various late-medieval statutes to 'abound and increase in evil governance' and lawlessness – to the royal heir, the Prince of Wales.[43] It was Edward IV who utilised commissions and letters patent to establish a physical royal presence in the region, with a princely court and council based at Ludlow. From here various councillors were under orders to quell disorder and crime, including high levels of theft and violence, in the imprecisely defined marcher lordships, in lands under Crown rule in Snowdon and Flintshire, and in the adjoining English counties of Cheshire, Gloucestershire, Herefordshire, Shropshire, Worcestershire, and (notionally, at least) the city of Bristol.[44] After a resumption of this activity in *c.* 1490, the early Tudor government continued to appoint 'Lord Presidents of the Council in the Marches' to govern in the heir's name, first under Prince Arthur and later Princess Mary. This growth in the royal prerogative here culminated in the so-called 'Act of Union' in 1536 and the abolition of the marcher lordships.[45] A further Act in 1542 decreed 'that there shalbe and remaine a President and Counsaill in the said Dominion and Principalitie of Wales and the Marches'.[46] Although the various surviving instructions issued to this Council across the early Tudor period placed great emphasis on justice

---

[41] John Stow, *A Survay of London Contayning the originall, antiquity, increase, moderne estate, and description of that citie* (London, 1598), 391; DL5/3 fol. 46v.

[42] W. D. Shannon, '"On the Left Hand above the Staire": Accessing, Understanding and Using the Archives of the Early-Modern Court of Duchy Chamber', *Archives* 123 (2010), 23.

[43] C. A. J. Skeel, *The Council in the Marches: a study in local government during the sixteenth and seventeenth centuries* (Hugh Rees Ltd., 1904), 14.

[44] In reality, the jurisdiction of the Council over Bristol, technically a county of its own, was contested in the sixteenth century: see E. Ralph ed., *The Great White Book of Bristol* (Bristol Record Society, 1979), 5–6.

[45] 27 Hen. VIII, c. 26.   [46] 34 & 35 Hen. VIII, c. 26.

Conciliar Justice at Centre and Periphery 55

in a general sense, it often found itself preoccupied with the investigation of criminal behaviour – for example, the prosecution and execution of outlaws.[47] But this body was also expected to receive and act upon bills of complaints from subjects of the area, too. Petitions for justice submitted directly to this Council survive in regional archives, while instructions given to its iteration under Princess Mary included the mandate to see 'due Justice administered, [and] poor Men's causes rightfully redressed' just as in much older ordinances for the main Council.[48]

Analogous and contemporaneous to the Council in the Marches was the Council of the North, which oversaw the administration of justice in lands beyond the Trent, across the sprawling county of Yorkshire and up into the frontier regions around the border with Scotland. This Council evolved out of the major noble councils that had governed this remote and troubled landscape in the late medieval period: especially that presided over by Richard, Duke of Gloucester, who was made Lieutenant of the North by his brother, Edward IV, in 1482. On becoming King Richard III just one year later, the well-established ducal council at Middleham became the king's Council. Under an official commission issued in 1484, a separate Council of the North was settled at York and given its own remit. Compared to earlier iterations, this body stemmed more directly from the king's own Council rather than from a regional magnate; especially since, as R. R. Reid pointed out, the new lieutenant, the Earl of Lincoln, had no estates in the north.[49] During Henry VIII's reign this entity would, like the Council in the Marches, revert back into the hands of a direct royal heir instead of an official. For a short time, that king's illegitimate son Henry Fitzroy, made Duke of Richmond in 1525, was lodged at Middleham to administer justice. This proved largely ineffective, however, and within the following decade the Council was reinstituted with a president and commissioners, mirroring the set-up at Ludlow. Of the two, the reach of the northern Council experienced greater fluctuation across our period, temporarily including all the manors north of the Trent

---

[47] SP1/101 fol. 100 (*LP* X. 130).

[48] Cited in Skeel, *The Council in the Marches*, 50, 57–8. For a more recent account of the development of the Council of the Marches, see P. Roberts, 'The English Crown, the Principality of Wales and the Council in the Marches, 1534–1641', in B. Bradshaw and J. Morrill eds., *The British Problem, c.1534–1707: State Formation in the Atlantic Archipelago* (Macmillan Press, 1996), 118–30. For evidence of this Council's civil activities, see the orders from 1528–9 preserved in REQ3/9 *Plommer* v *Ward*.

[49] This account of the Council of the North's development is taken from R. R. Reid, *The King's Council in the North* (Longmans, Green and Co., 1921), 47–67; see also F. W. Brooks, *The Council of the North* (Historical Association, 1966), 1–32.

56   The New Justice System

except Durham though more usually being restricted to Yorkshire alone.[50] But its purpose, restated several times over the early sixteenth century, remained consistent. 'Instructions' issued in 1484 ordered the Earl of Lincoln and the Council to 'ordre all billes of compleyntes and other there before theym to be shewed' and also to restore peace in the face of 'alle riottes, forcible entres, distresse takinges variaunces, debates and other mysbehaviors', mostly by imprisoning the perpetrators in the nearest castle or common gaol. The same orders for a dual civil and criminal jurisdiction would be repeated again in ordinances issued to the respective lieutenants and presidents in 1525, 1538, and 1545.[51]

In all their iterations the councils of the North and Welsh Marches were spiritually and procedurally very similar. They executed a form of civil justice-giving in a fashion that was near identical to Chancery, including determination of a bill of complaint through examination of evidence, often through a commission, with an eye eventually to a decree or an order. As representatives of the king's person, they also applied the standard qualifications with regard to who, exactly, was especially deserving of the sovereign's merciful justice. The commission issued to the Council in the North in 1530 specified that it was to hear 'all actions of debts and demands whatsoever when both parties or one party is so burdened by poverty as to be unable to pursue his right according to the common law'.[52] As well as acting as courts of first instance, they were also avenues for appeals, offering a sympathetic ear to those who felt wronged by verdicts passed elsewhere. For example, in Coventry in 1480 a town chamberlain called Laurence Saunders – later the champion of the common people in their war against the corporation over common lands – asked for leave to 'ryde to Southaumpton', only to flee to Ludlow to complain to Prince Edward and his council that the city officials 'shulde denye hym Justice'. The prince immediately wrote to the mayor on the very same day to demand that 'some discrete persone'

---

[50] Reid, *The King's Council in the North*, 108–10.

[51] *Ibid.*, 502–5; *State Papers, published under the authority of His Majesty's Commission: King Henry the Eighth* (His Majesty's Commission for State Papers, 1830–52), vol. V, 406; SP1/133 fol. 211–221v. The Duke of Norfolk was ordered to investigate recent rebellions but also to hear cases relating to enclosures: SP1/114 fols. 103–23 (*LP* XII. i. 98). The orders given to the Duke of Richmond in 1525 do not now survive, but a letter from his Council to Wolsey mentions 'instruccions signed with the gracious hande of the Kinges Highnes' and the need to see a 'great nombre of the Kinges subjectes of thies parties . . . greatly eased, quyetid, and delyvered from the daunger of suche enormyties . . . as heretofore they have bene molestid and disturbid': printed in *State Papers, published under the authority of His Majesty's Commission*, vol. IV, 392.

[52] Reid, *The King's Council in the North*, 282, 502–3. Evidence of that Council's hearing of complex land disputes too survives in REQ3/9 *Fox* v *Vyncent*.

Conciliar Justice at Centre and Periphery

be sent to explain 'the trouth of the same'.[53] Otherwise, these councils were not simply subordinate to the 'main' Council of the king. Rather, they facilitated a two-way passage of information and deliberation between centre and peripheries. The king and Chancellor might 'remit' or send down causes considered more relevant to trusted advisors in situ, but those advisors also sent matters back the other way when a higher authority was required.[54] So, experimental as these councils undoubtedly were as supervisory bodies, as judicial tribunals they formed a bridge between local and central legal systems and provided another route to justice for supplicants.

Although we might reasonably assume that accessibility and authority made the provincial councils an attractive prospect to the poor and to the litigious, they were only intermittently active throughout the early Tudor period. They could ultimately ebb and flow according to governmental priorities; their members could be tasked with quelling rebellion rather than hearing complaints, and their business might lapse entirely if it so suited the Crown. Little evidence survives to suggest that a Council in the Marches operated during the reign of Richard III, in the early years of Henry VII's reign, or for about a decade after Prince Arthur's death in 1502.[55] The Council of the North similarly appears to have worked in phases under Henry VII, with some judicial business (mostly of a criminal nature) committed to the Earl of Surrey as lieutenant and a flurry of activity between 1502 and 1507 under Thomas Savage, Archbishop of York.[56] Some 'honorable counsell of Yorkshire', staffed by such regional stalwarts as the archdeacons Thomas Dalby and Thomas Magnus and by Sir Marmaduke Constable, may well have outlived Savage; admittedly, the absence of ordinances or instructions in this period may give a false impression of inactivity.[57] In Henry VIII's reign, only the backlash generated from the taxation policies of 1523 and 1525 followed by the rebellions of the mid-1530s forced that king to implement some more permanent means

---

[53] Dormer Harris ed., *Coventry Leet Book*, vol. II, 430–2.

[54] For example, a dispute between the Abbot of Shrewsbury and the bailiffs of the same town in 1495 was initially heard by Prince Arthur's Council in the Marches, where 'the said princes counseill awarded your said orators to shew unto your grace [the King] their grevis and complaint' instead: REQ2/9/107.

[55] Skeel, *The Council in the Marches*, 29, 31. See also REQ3/8 *Leighton v Leighton*.

[56] Reid, *The King's Council in the North*, 77–9.

[57] Letters between the Prior of Durham and this 'counsell' suggest that they were still determining civil disputes in spring 1509: Durham, Durham Cathedral Archive, Registrum Parvum IV fols. 171v–172. I am grateful to Professor Steven Gunn for bringing this reference to a post-Savage Council in the North to my attention.

58 The New Justice System

of keeping an eye on the region. This was notwithstanding reports that the situation on the ground was already dire by 1523, when the Earl of Surrey wrote to Wolsey to report that he had been 'at York with the justices iiij [w]hole days' hearing the 'infynyte complaints of the poore people'. Indeed, he noted, 'the Judges ... have seen somoche mysordre of thies parties that they have sayed to me that they think it x tymes more necessary too have suche a counsaill here as in the marches of walys'.[58]

Hence for much of our period conciliar justice – no matter how much it was needed – was so informal as to be almost transient. In addition to the tribunals just described, for a decade or so from 1499 onwards Margaret Beaufort, the king's mother, presided over a Council at her palace of Collyweston in Northamptonshire. This was not quite an 'equity court' in its own right, but it achieved enough administrative and judicial oversight of the surrounding area to have caused some historians to call it an 'unofficial council of the midlands' – though one not replaced after Beaufort's death in 1509.[59] A Council in the West, headed by Lord John Russell and tasked with governing the south-western counties of England, was even shorter-lived. This was explicitly established by a commission in 1539 to ensure the 'speedy and indifferent administration of justice between party and party' in sittings at Exeter, Dorchester, and Wells, but was apparently in abeyance by the time of Cromwell's fall in 1540.[60] Gaps in the conciliar justice provision may have been unavoidable given the considerable expenses it put on the Crown: each cost somewhere in the region of £1,000 in fees and diets per year in the late 1530s.[61] Even the great men tasked with sitting in council in the Marches, the North, or the Duchy estates were typically only expected to do so a few times each year; more like a quarter session than a regular court. In their absence, complainants seeking judicial remedy but unable to make the journey to Westminster would have had to rely on the very local courts they sought to circumvent or, if they could, wait for a more opportune moment to seek out their king directly.

---

[58] SP49/2 fols. 17–17v. For more on popular demand for this Council and its reinstitution in 1538, see L. Flannigan, 'New Evidence of Justice-Giving by the Early Tudor Council of the North, 1540–43', *Northern History* 49:2 (2022), 281–92.
[59] M. K. Jones and M. G. Underwood, *The King's Mother: Lady Margaret Beaufort Countess of Richmond and Derby* (Cambridge University Press, 1992), 88.
[60] C. A. J. Skeel, 'The Council of the West', *TRHS* Fourth Series 4 (1921), 63; J. A. Youings, 'The Council of the West', *TRHS* 10 (1960), 41–59. To the numerous anecdotal references to this Council discovered by Skeel, the Requests archive adds another, which mentions proceedings and a decree made before Lord Russell's Court just before the 'said Cort was by ye kynges maiestie ... dissolved': REQ2/4/394.
[61] Youings, 'The Council of the West', 44 n. 1. *LP* XII. ii. 914. For the wages granted to the Council of the North in 1538, see SP1/133 fols. 211–221v.

Conciliar Justice at Centre and Periphery

So great was the demand for justice from the hand of the king himself, partly as a means of appealing from the provincial councils, that it soon became necessary to establish more central tribunals for litigation. One remained at Westminster (Star Chamber) while the other travelled with the attendant household (Requests), mirroring the bifurcation of the royal Council itself by the very end of the fifteenth century. As surviving transcripts from the now-lost registers tell us, Henry VII's large main Council met to discuss matters of diplomacy, war, and finance alongside concerns about justice, often pertaining to serious riots and assemblies but also, on occasion, complex disputes between subjects.[62] For this work its members typically occupied the Star Chamber – the *Camera Stellata*, in fact comprising an inner and outer chamber with star-embossed ceilings, in the Palace of Westminster – as the king's Council had done since the construction of that space in 1347. Yet, in contrast with the provincial councils, the remit for litigation before this central body was relatively restricted. Perhaps following the spirit of an allowance made in 1377 that the royal Council might determine cases only if the accused was 'so great a person, that one might not expect to have justice elsewhere', the Council in the Star Chamber mostly heard disputes that had erupted between the great men of the nobility or even between its own members, which presumably could not be determined in any local or provincial forum, where one of the disputants might themselves be the lord.[63] Otherwise, this arm of the Council prosecuted individuals alleged to have spoken unfitting, seditious, and treasonous words against the king. And so, like the Duchy Council, it protected the Crown's interests.

Eventually, and certainly by the end of Henry VII's reign, where there had once been a *Council* in the Star Chamber, for which matters of justice were one part of a broader agenda, there was a discrete *Court of* Star Chamber sitting exclusively for justice-giving.[64] Chronologising this change is made difficult by the incompleteness of that Court's surviving archive, which mostly consists of loose pleadings dating from *c.* 1485 onwards, the order books now being lost.[65] Anecdotal evidence is

---

[62] Principally those produced in the 1590s by Thomas Egerton, Lord Ellesmere: HL Ellesmere MSS 2652, 2654, 2655. Some of these are printed in C. G. Bayne and W. H. Dunham eds., *Select Cases in the Council of Henry VII*, Selden Society 75 (Bernard Quaritch, 1958).

[63] *PROME* vi, 46 (1377 parliament, item 87); HL Ellesmere MS 2654 fols. 3v, 13v, 14v, 20, 22; Ellesmere MS 2655 fols. 12v, 13v.

[64] For a fuller account of this development, see Guy, *The Cardinal's Court*; Guy, 'The Council: Revolution or Evolution?'.

[65] D. Gosling, 'The Records of the Court of Star Chamber at The National Archives and Elsewhere', in Kesselring and Mears eds., *Star Chamber Matters*, 19–39.

60 The New Justice System

illuminating, however: intriguingly, the troublesome Laurence Saunders of Coventry, having failed to acquire a remedy at Ludlow, eventually appeared 'before ye kynges Counceil in ye Sterre Chambre' in 1496, where a series of pleadings were heard by John Morton (Archbishop of Canterbury and Chancellor), Thomas Savage (Bishop of London and President of the attendant Council), and John Fyneux (Chief Justice).[66] This suggests the operation of a Chancery-style pleadings process undertaken by a small quorum of the main Council in a dedicated space, at least. Indeed, the surviving pleadings for the early Star Chamber tells us that while it took on some cases initiated at the instigation of the attorney general or its own judges – essentially, criminal prosecutions brought on behalf of the Crown against 'heinous' riots and corrupt officials – the majority of its business was party versus party cases.[67] Later, in Henry VIII's reign, discussions in the main Council resulted in a further separation of centralised judicial functions. In 1517, Mondays, Tuesdays, Thursdays, and Saturdays were appointed as days for Star Chamber hearings, with Wednesdays and Fridays reserved for Chancery business, probably to make it more feasible for Wolsey, as head of both courts, to fulfil all of his duties.[68] And so, whether as Council in or Court of Star Chamber, this body encapsulated efforts to expand the provision for litigation moved by bill of complaint and to handle matters both civil and criminal in the Crown's immediate remit. As such, it epitomised and led a trend towards centralised royal justice-giving.

Conclusion

To summarise, the overtures being made about the need for due justice and order in Parliament, poetry, and plays in late medieval England were already being met with judicial structures and processes by 1485. The early Tudor kings further intensified and centralised these practices by forming more permanent offshoots of their main Council. Central to government policy in this sphere was a growing distinction drawn first between general administration of the realm and justice-giving as discrete processes, and, thereafter, between the investigatory activities of tribunals established explicitly to pursue the king's rights and a provision for litigation laid on in response to subjects' suits. The emerging forums of conciliar

[66] Dormer Harris ed., *Coventry Leet Book*, 579.
[67] Guy counts four attorney-general prosecutions under Henry VII before the Council in Star Chamber, and nine under Wolsey's chancellorship: Guy, *The Cardinal's Court*, 18, 72–8.
[68] BL Lansdowne MS 1 fol. 108; Guy, *The Cardinal's Court*, 492.

Conciliar Justice at Centre and Periphery

justice saw the king drawn in on the side of the plaintiff, while also being asked to step in as the main arbiter. Moreover, whereas the magnate councils and the Duchy Council essentially intervened in matters that touched the estates and properties of their respective leading judges, there was plainly a growing expectation that the king would entertain cases that did not interest him personally at all – that lay outside of lands he legally 'owned' or revenue streams he had rights to – but which he furthered in the name of charity or mercy. To that effect, the new royal justice system served to provide relief to the wider legal system in light of complaints against it, and to put many of the contemporary expectations about government, law, and justice into practice. From the perspective of litigants, the presumption that such royal conciliar justice would be routinely accessible quickly set in. By 1494, it was felt unusual enough to be noted by Sir John Paston that Chancellor Morton had 'kept not the Star Chawmber thys viij. days', and we have seen already that officials stationed in the further reaches of the realm called for provincialised royal justice, too.[69] We turn now to the branch of this system that was less clearly situated, and which existed between the centre and the localities: the Court of Requests.

[69] J. Gairdner ed., *The Paston Letters A.D. 1422–1509* (Cambridge University Press, 1904), vol. VI, 152.

CHAPTER 3

'Travailing between the Prince and Petitioners'
The Court of Requests

The creation of provincial councils and a settled tribunal in the Star Chamber represented another turn in the cycle of processes moving 'out of court', away from the 'constant wanderings in the train of an ever restless king', to become discrete, self-sufficient institutions of government.[1] Yet the king was not relieved of the expectation that he would receive complainants whenever and wherever they happened to find him. The peripatetic royal household required its own mechanisms for handling the clamours of prospective petitioners following in its wake. These too became more routinised under the conciliarist early Tudors. Indeed, the initial vulnerability of this ruling dynasty meant that there were perceptible benefits to bolstering both the institutionalised *and* the informal, personality-driven aspects of government.[2] As the judicial provision in closest proximity to the king, the Court of Requests possessed both these qualities. More than the other conciliar courts just discussed, this Court specialised in 'travailing between the prince and petitioners by direction from the mouth of the King', as legal antiquarian William Lambarde would later recall.[3]

As illuminating as this sounds, writing the early history of Requests poses as many challenges as it does possibilities. We have observed already that the provincial councils were largely founded by commissions coming down from the king, sent under his great seal. The Council in the Marches was even shored up by statutory legislation in the early 1540s. In contrast, so far as we know Requests was *not* created by any kind of order, ordinance, or Act. Its archives tell us that some discrete function existed, but that it ran for decades without name, routine, or identity as a court. Moreover, Requests and Star Chamber were both curiously absent from law students'

---

[1] T. F. Tout, *Chapters in the Administrative History of Mediaeval England* (Manchester University Press, 1920–33), vol. I, 12, 105, 179–80, 313, vol. II, 48–50, 291, 311, vol. III, 55, 176, vol. V, 3, 18–19, 30, 52.
[2] Gunn, *Early Tudor Government*, 13.   [3] Lambarde, *Archeion*, 227.

62

'Travailing between the Prince and Petitioners' 63

descriptions of the lawcourts of the realm in the early sixteenth century.[4] As conciliar offshoots, their curial identity was at times almost deliberately obscure, a fact turned creatively into a blessing by Sir Julius Caesar when he laid claim to the origin and authority of his Elizabethan Court of Requests in the monarch's own Council.[5] But how do we begin to interpret the significance and purpose of a tribunal that does not seem to have had much hold on the minds of its contemporaries? In the following discussion, as in Leadam's century-old analysis, 'Court of Requests' serves as an 'anachronistic but convenient' name for the nascent equity tribunal of the late fifteenth and early sixteenth centuries.[6] Yet putting inverted commas around this name does not have to mean searching for evidence that it *was* a court, nor pinning down *when* exactly it became so. The amorphousness of Requests was part of its design, not an inconvenience to be worked around in historical analysis.

Paying singular attention to Requests allows us to address mischaracterisations surrounding its place in the legal and administrative landscape, therefore improving our overall survey of that landscape. This Court has sometimes been treated as the 'poor man's Chancery', a phrase that refers to its supposed handling of poorer suitors than Chancery (often true) but which also, at times, encapsulates the belief that it was simply an identical but inferior jurisdiction to which Chancery delegated its business (less accurate, especially for this period).[7] So ingrained is the assumption that we can take these two courts together without distinction that entire research projects have been conducted on late sixteenth-century rulings about Requests with the intention only of telling us something about the more legally significant Chancery.[8] This approach elides the fact that one tribunal retained a connection to the royal Council and the other was part of its own governmental department, the result being that they were positioned differently in the legal hierarchy of the day and served different classes of plaintiff and different types of cases. In fact, Requests was more similar on these grounds to other conciliar tribunals – and especially to the provincial

---

[4] See, for example, the reading given on Chapter 29 of Magna Carta at Lincoln's Inn in *c.* 1491/1508: John H. Baker ed., *Selected Readings and Commentaries on Magna Carta 1400–1604*, Selden Society 132 (Selden Society, 2015), 252.

[5] Caesar, *The Ancient State*, v; Hill ed. *The Ancient State*, 23.

[6] Leadam ed., *Select Cases in the Court of Requests*, xviii.

[7] J. R. Lander, *Government and Community: England, 1450–1509* (Harvard University Press, 1980), 38; F. Metzger, 'The Last Phase of the Medieval Chancery', in A. Harding ed., *Law-Making and Law-Makers in British History* (Royal Historical Society, 1980), 82.

[8] C. M. Gray, 'The Boundaries of the Equitable Function', *The American Journal of Legal History* 20:3 (1976), 192–226.

64   The New Justice System

councils, occasionally referred to as local 'Courts of Requests' – than it was to Chancery or the central common-law courts.[9]

This chapter sets out the first comprehensive history of the early Court of Requests, with particular attention to its distinctive itinerancy. It will demonstrate that Requests was animated as much by its conciliar roots and extra-legal qualities as by its presence in the king's own household and role in the performative progresses of the early Tudor regime. The following discussion takes in the ordinances and organisational lists that have traditionally been seen as marking out Requests' development, but maps these onto details yielded by its whole archive – especially its caseload over time and the annotations made by its judges – to provide a more nuanced study of institutionalisation over time. We will observe changes in the routine and volume of business before Requests, in its archival practices, in the use of the name 'Court of Requests', and, eventually, in the regularity of its judiciary over time. Yet its proximity to the king's person and alignment with the principle of truly extraordinary justice was continually central to its operation and essential to its efficiency.

Displaying Good Governance

By the coming of the Tudor regime, itinerant justice in the king's name had a long heritage but was less prevalent than it had once been. The 'instrument *par excellence*' of the Angevin rulers, the general eyre, which had travelled along county circuits to hear civil, criminal, and Crown pleas, was long gone.[10] The royal courts of King's Bench and the Exchequer had once been part of the roving *curia regis*, attached to the monarch, but rarely sat anywhere other than Westminster by the fourteenth century. A delegated form of justice on the move continued to be offered by the six assize circuits undertaken by the chief justices, where criminal and civil cases pending before lower courts could be tried. In the meantime, as we have seen, the sovereign's role as the superior legal authority in the realm was represented by the arms of his Council in the west and north of England and within his Duchy of Lancaster. Still, in some cases there was simply nothing that could replace the king's own justice, especially when a matter could not be determined in the existing system. On at least one occasion in Edward IV's reign, the chancellor and Council of the Duchy of Lancaster had opined that the 'great stryfes variances controversies & debates' arising in Lancashire

---

[9] Reid, *The King's Council in the North*, 83, 97, 107; Youings, 'The Council of the West', 56.
[10] Powell, *Kingship, Law, and Society*, 9–13.

'Travailing between the Prince and Petitioners' 65

could be 'remedied by noo personne but oonly by ye king him self if it wold like his grace to comme into thoos parties'.[11] The expectation of *personal* royal justice remained alive.

It was therefore evident that some means to handle petitions presented to the monarch and his entourage on the move was once again required. All available evidence indicates that Richard III offered just that in the wake of his declaration that anyone 'grieved, oppressed, or unlawfully wronged, do make a bill of his complaint and put it to his highness, and he shall be heard and without delay have such convenient remedy'.[12] Although there is no central record of this business taking place, anecdotal accounts inform us that it did, and that it was well-received. Before he ever came before Henry VII's Council, Nicholas Catesby, having heard Richard III's proclamation, 'put abille to [the king] at Warr[wick] of the said injurie to hym don' and subsequently had his opponent 'arested by a s[er]jeant of armes and brought afore the lordes ... of [the king's] Counsell'.[13] This presumably refers to Richard's first progress in the summer of 1483, when he stayed at Warwick Castle for around a week in early August.[14] A week later he was in Nottingham, where he had his 'lords and juges in every place sittyng, determynyng the compleynts of pore folks with due punycion of offenders a yenst hys lawes'.[15] Further information about what this looked like is provided by an answer submitted in a Requests suit in *c*. 1497, which recounted how a dispute had been heard 'yn the tyme off King Richard the iijde late yn dede and nott of ryght Kinge off Yngeland' by the 'Bysshopp off Sentas [St Asaph]' and by 'other nobull lordys and men of honor ... off the conceyll'.[16] Perhaps owing to these hints of organised delegation and initiation of procedure, by late 1483 it was already apparent to Thomas Langton, Bishop of St David's, that the new king 'contents the people wher he goys best that ever did [a] prince; for many a poor man that hath suffred wrong many days [have been] relevyd and helpyd by hym and his commands in his progresse'.[17]

---

[11] TNA DL5/1 fol. 62.
[12] As proclaimed just after Buckingham's Rebellion, in late 1483: J. Gairdner ed., *History of the Life and Reign of Richard the Third* (Cambridge University Press, 1898), 343; and also in 1484: R. Horrox and P. W. Hammond eds., *British Library Harleian Manuscript 433* (Alan Sutton, 1979), vol. II, 48–9. See A. Sutton, 'The Administration of Justice Whereunto We Be Professed', *The Ricardian* 4:53 (1976), 4–15.
[13] TNA E163/29/11 m. 9.
[14] Rhoda Edwards, *The Itinerary of King Richard III 1483–1485* (Alan Sutton, 1995), 5–6.
[15] Angelo Raine ed., *York Civic Records* (Yorkshire Archaeological Society, 1939–78), vol. I, 78.
[16] REQ2/10/101.
[17] J. B. Sheppard ed., *Christ Church Letters: a volume of medieval letters relating to the affairs of the Priory of Christ Church Canterbury*, Camden New Series 19 (Camden Society, 1877), 46.

The New Justice System

As Hannes Kleineke has convincingly shown, it was around the same time, in December 1483, that we find the first known reference to a provision for petitioning the royal Council known by the shorthand 'Requests'.[18] Among the patent rolls of that month is recorded a royal grant to John Harrington, a civil lawyer and clerk of the common council of York, for an annuity of £20 and the office of the 'clerk of our council of requests and supplications' ('*clericus consilii nostri requisicionum ac supplicacionum*'), specifically those presented by 'poor persons'.[19] Since Harrington was a northerner and a clerk of Richard's ducal council, his appointment was characteristic of this over-anxious king's hopes to foster existing loyalties; the aforementioned Bishop of St Asaph, Richard Redman, had the same background. No record of Harrington's work for the main Council now survives, but he was clearly kept busy. In December 1484, Richard wrote personally to York's common council to excuse Harrington from his duties there, owing to unspecified 'urgent causes' at court.[20] Harrington remained in this position for the entirety of Richard's reign, and in a renewal of his grant in March 1485 was referred to as the 'clerk of our council of requests' ('*clericus consilii nostri de requisicionibus*').[21] The Latin is admittedly vague, but it indicates that there was part of the council *of* or *for* requests by this time.

What did 'requests' mean here? The diplomatic records of late-medieval Europe show that many royal and ducal households employed men titled as '*Master* of Requests', including those of the kings of France and Castile, the dukes of Burgundy and Brittany, and, in the early sixteenth century, of the Holy Roman Emperor and Scotland.[22] The duties of these officials appear to have primarily involved representing their rulers in formulating agreements and treaties with foreign powers. Occasionally, surviving dispatches provide a glimpse into their domestic work: in 1517, one French 'Master of Requests' was stationed in Brittany to quell 'remonstrances' against the king in the build-up to war with the papacy, which involved reading out a parliamentary speech before the troublemakers.[23] Conversely, that prolific ambassadors to England such as Eustace

---

[18] H. Kleineke, 'Richard III and the Origins of the Court of Requests', *The Ricardian* 11 (2007), 22–32.

[19] *CPR 1476–1485*, 413; Ross, *Richard III*, 57.

[20] L. C. Attreed ed., *The York House Books, 1461–1490* (Alan Sutton, 1991), vol. II, 347, 352.

[21] *CPR 1476–1485*, 296; TNA C66/449 m. 6.

[22] Thomas Rymer ed., *Foedera* (London, 1704–35), vol. X. 234, vol. XI. 97, 101, 103, 126; *CPR 1452–1461*, 19. Surviving commissions from the 1470s identify the 'Master of Requests' of the Dukes of Brittany and Burgundy, respectively: TNA E30/544, E30/562; *LP* I. i. 3053, II. 1119, 1414, III. 1460, 1637, 3018, IV. 2345, App. 41, 147, VII. 1436, XVI. 289, 350, 1238, XX. i. 22.

[23] *LP* II. 3702.

'Travailing between the Prince and Petitioners' 67

Chapuys and Charles de Marillac were also titled as Masters of Requests suggests that the representation of their rulers overseas made up the entirety of their agenda, far as they were from their home court.[24] The same title came into use in England in the early fifteenth century, apparently with the same emphasis on diplomacy. In August 1464, the Dean of Salisbury, James Goldwell, was described as the 'Master of Requests' in his role on a commission to treat for a truce with the Duke of Brittany; possibly this was intended to bestow upon Goldwell a rank analogous to the duke's own masters.[25] This association continued right to the end of Henry VIII's reign, when the doctor of canon and civil law John Tregonwell was described as a 'Master of Requests' on a commission to treat for peace with Francis I.[26]

That all of these references appear in relation to peacekeeping does not necessarily preclude the suggestion, implicit in the grant to Harrington, that 'requests' was synonymous with supplications, written or oral. In France, Jean de Joinville recounted how each day after mass, Louis IX had asked his councillors 'to go and hear the pleadings at the gate of the city which is now called the Gate of Requests'.[27] This route of access may have been connected with the judicial tribunal known as the *Chambre de Requêtes*, in operation within the royal palace in Paris to hear civil cases from the mid-fourteenth century onwards.[28] Alternatively, it may have been related to the *Requêtes l'Hôtel du Roi*, which handled causes presented to the king's household and disputes involving its own members, and kept its own engrossed decrees in the early sixteenth century.[29] Either way, given that the early Tudors kept a keen eye on their continental rivals it is plausible that they modelled their own household 'requests' provision on the French example – just as they borrowed the office of the *gentilshommes de la chambre* from 1518 onwards.[30] By the time that the English Crown employed Masters of Requests on a more regular basis, in the 1540s, they

---

[24] *LP* XV. 885, XVI. 1238.   [25] Rymer ed. *Foedera*, vol. XI, 695.
[26] SP1/208 fol. 190 (*LP* XX. 553).   [27] Shaw trans., *Joinville and Villehardouin*, 182.
[28] This tribunal was given some founding ordinances in November 1364: A. J. L. Jourdan, J. Decrusy, and F. A. Isambert eds., *Recueil general des anciennes lois françaises depuis l'an 420 jusqu'à la révolution de 1789* (Paris, 1822–33), vol. 5, 224–5.
[29] I am grateful to Professor Sir John Baker for providing me with information about one engrossed decree surviving from this court for July 1519, which is MS 30 in his own personal collection. For details see Baker, 'Migrations of Manuscripts', *Journal of Legal History* 9:2 (1988), 255.
[30] D. Starkey, 'Intimacy and Innovation: The Rise of the Privy Chamber, 1485–1547', in D. Starkey, D. A. L. Morgan, J. Murphy, P. Wright, N. Cuddy, and K. Sharpe eds., *The English Court: From the Wars of the Roses to the Civil War* (Longman, 1987), 81–2. A petition from Charles I's Masters of Requests to their king spoke of 'the state of France from whence it is thought the title of Mr of Requests hath been taken up in this kingdom', at least: Leadam ed., *Select Cases in the Court of Requests*, c.

68   The New Justice System

were predominantly tasked with channelling petitions too.[31] The afore-mentioned Tregonwell spent much of his time as an active member of the judiciary in the Court of Requests, as his signature on numerous of its petitions and pleadings confirms.[32]

As to the English *Court* of Requests, the earliest known reference appears in a peculiar place: not in the records of that tribunal, which were not commenced until 1493, but within the diary kept by the burgesses from Colchester during their attendance at Henry VII's first parliament in 1485. Here they recorded in passing that in the House of Commons 'there passed a bill for the C[ow]rt of Requests that it is annulled, and it shall be occupied no more'.[33] The word 'court' here would seem to attribute some curial formality to Requests at a much earlier point than we have been led to expect; earlier, even, than the supposed emergence of the *Court* of Star Chamber, contrary to the usual assertion that Requests was the lesser of the early sixteenth-century conciliar tribunals.[34] Given that it predates the earliest Requests order-book entry by almost seven years, this reference also complicates the automatic association that historians often draw between the creation of records and the foundation of an institution. There is no other known evidence pertaining to this bill; it does not appear on the relevant Parliament rolls, so it presumably neither reached the Lords nor received the king's assent. We cannot therefore rule out the possibility that the Coventry burgesses recorded word-for-word the terms they heard when the bill was discussed. Their report stands as 'astonishing' and apparently indisputable evidence that a 'Cowrt of Requests' of some description was imaginable by 1485.[35]

Historians have varied in how far they interpret this 'bill' as evidence of the existence of a 'Court of Requests' comparable to that in operation in later decades, however.[36] The argument made by A. F. Pollard, and more recently

---

[31] The earliest known use of this title in an English source and with reference to judicial capacity was at a Privy Council meeting in Jan. 1541, when Robert Southwell – who signed Requests pleadings – was named as 'one of the masters of the Requests': *LP* XVI. 447.

[32] For examples, see REQ2/1/101, 103, 117, 2/2/131, 185, 2/3/27, 47, 158, 270, 402, 2/4/106, 117, 299, 388, 391, 2/6/203, 2/7/69, 89, 2/8/28, 35, 2/9/21, 64, 145, 2/10/40, 62, 209, 223, 25. Incidentally, the other men named to the commission for peace with Francis I in 1545 were Thomas Thirlby, Bishop of Westminster, who also worked in Requests at this time: SP1/208 fol. 190.

[33] Benham ed., *The Red Paper Book of Colchester*, 64.

[34] Even Leadam described Star Chamber as 'the more important Court' compared to Requests: I. S. Leadam ed., *Select Cases before the King's Council in the Star Chamber, commonly called the Court of Star* Chamber, *A.D. 1477–1509*, Selden Society 16 (Spottiswoode and Co., 1903), xvii; Guy, 'The Privy Council: Revolution or Evolution?', 61.

[35] A. F. Pollard, 'The Growth of the Court of Requests', *EHR* 56:222 (1941), 301.

[36] Baker, *OHLE,* 203; Kleineke, 'Richard III and the Origins of the Court of Requests', 23; M. Hicks, 'King in Lords and Commons: Three Insights into Late-Fifteenth-Century Parliaments, 1461–85', in K. Dockray and P. Fleming eds., *People, Places, and Perspectives* (Nonsuch Publishing, 2005), 147.

and in greater detail by Kleineke, that the bill referred to a 'Cowrt' that had developed out of Harrington's clerkship, seems the most plausible explanation for the shared terminology between a grant and bill written just two years apart.[37] As to the fate of this tribunal in the years that followed, we are left with considerable space for speculation. By itself, the 1485 'bill' can be and has been interpreted in either direction. On the one hand, absence of any evidence for the bill's success and the emergence of a recorded Court in the 1490s could lead us to assume that this single 'Cowrt' survived its critics. On the other, since no such 'Cowrt' had ever been established by statute it would not technically have required statutory abolition, and so could have been dissolved without the bill being passed. After all, the overthrow of Richard III had seen Harrington lose his clerkship and annuity, with the new king recommending that he was to retain and personally fulfil his clerkship in York from November that same year.[38] The transition and displacement of personnel around the Crown in 1485 created the ideal atmosphere for grievances about the expanding scope of extraordinary justice to emerge and organise. Whatever grievances were raised in Parliament may have been enough for the king to subsume this business back into his Council at this point, to be re-established later.

Reaching a firmer conclusion on what happened next is helped by a hitherto unnoticed reference seemingly to the same 'Cowrt' in 1486, now found only within late sixteenth-century copies of early Tudor records. The lawyer Thomas Egerton, Lord Chancellor from 1596 onwards and later Baron Ellesmere, was a keen researcher of the government archives to which he had access. Among his surviving papers are various notes and abstracts drawn from the now-lost registers of the Henrician Council meetings.[39] Alongside his transcripts from these registers, Egerton compiled a rough digest or calendar of the contents he found most interesting, concerning everything from the men sworn in as councillors to specific instances of libel and slander that they heard. One item in particular caught Egerton's attention:

> Decree agaynst one for practisinge by fraud & covine, to avoyde a decree made in the Cort of Requestes . . . 6 Febr a[nno] 1 h 7 A cause hearde before the presulent of the Co[ur]t of Requestes & after in the Starrechamber and therupon an Injunccion agaynst Margery Becket to staye further sute.[40]

[37] Pollard, 'The Growth of the Court of Requests', 300–3; Kleineke, 'Richard III and the Origins of the Court of Requests', 24–42.

[38] Attreed ed., *The York House Books*, 388–9, 394, 399, 440, 474, 491, 505, 508, 510.

[39] HL Ellesmere MSS 2652, 2654, 2655; discussed in W. H. Dunham, 'The Ellesmere Extracts from the "Acta Consilii" of King Henry VIII', *EHR* 58:231 (1943), 301–18.

[40] Ellesmere MS 2652 fols. 2v, 5v (underline in original text).

70 The New Justice System

This case must have become somewhat well known by the end of the sixteenth century, because Lambarde made mention of it in his writings on the judicial powers of the Council, too. By his account and Egerton's, the case of Margery Becket and her sister Florence against one Alice Radley of Kent 'had been heard first before the Councell of King Edward 4. And after that, before the President of the Requests of that King Henry 7. And then lastly, before the Councell of the same King'. Lambarde further elaborated that by 'President of the Requests' he meant 'the Lord, or Bishop, which was the principall person of this Commission or Companie'.[41] In suing first before the main Council of Edward IV, then before the presiding judge of an entity that might have been known as the 'Co[ur]t of Requestes', and finally to Henry VII's Council in the Star Chamber, the sisters were presumably taking their chances with the royal justice provisions of different kings, hoping for a more favourable hearing. On 6 February 1486, the Star Chamber Council moved to restrict the plaintiffs' attempts to circumvent the Requests ruling by issuing an injunction ordering them to cease any further vexatious suits – the information recorded by Egerton.

Aside from the glimpse into the legal agency of three late fifteenth-century women that these accounts provide, they are also telling of the form that 'Requests' took at this time. Of course, we cannot rule out that Egerton and Lambarde both applied the name 'Court of Requests', well recognised by their day, to this less-distinct entity; though their differing accounts suggest at that they at least studied this case independently of one another. A further implication to be drawn from Lambarde's citation is that this 'Requests' belonged to Henry VII, and not to Richard III as we might have otherwise assumed. That Egerton copied out and underlined the term 'presulent', derived from the Latin *praesul* and often pertaining to a prelate or prominent cleric, might indicate that this function continued to have a bishop-councillor as its presiding judge, similar to the Bishop of St Asaph's role in 1483.[42] That said, since that president's decision was given no specific date in the transcribed accounts of this case, we cannot be certain that any tribunal he operated within survived the bill of December 1485. Still, that the main Council apparently moved to ensure the robustness of a determination made by the 'President' or 'Co[u]rt of Requests' in February 1486, *after* the bill's reading implies that its authority survived intact and separate from that of

---

[41] Lambarde, *Archeion*, 139–40, 227.

[42] R. E. Latham ed., *Revised Medieval Latin Word List from British and Irish Sources* (The British Academy, 1965) gives 'bishop', 'abbot', or 'pope'; R. K. Ashdowne, D. R. Howlett, and R. E. Latham eds., *The Dictionary of Medieval Latin from British Sources* (The British Academy, 2018) gives 'person in charge', 'protector', or 'bishop'.

'Travailing between the Prince and Petitioners' 71

the tribunal 'in the Starrechamber'. Such a ruling probably had the effect not of curtailing the authority of an expanding conciliar jurisdiction, as the proponents of the 1485 bill presumably wanted, but of bolstering it.

Justice on the Move

Vindication of this provision in 1486 makes the archival silence between the mention of this 'Cowrt' and the earliest evidence of a recorded tribunal seven years later even more difficult to explain, however. As with other institutions of law and government, it is this movement into written record in 1493 that has usually been perceived as marking the (re)birth of the Court of Requests – a chronology given even greater weight by Caesar's mythologising of the Court's 'Ancient State' through its books of orders and decrees.[43] In reality, its earliest registers hardly herald a firmer curial identity than before. They contain no sign of any name or title for the committee whose business they contain, alluding only to the royal Council as the motivating authority. We have only the passing references to a 'counsell of [the king's] requestes' in external records to confirm that such a name still applied to this judicial function in the 1490s.[44]

This conundrum notwithstanding, what we do have from this point onwards is a consistent set of books containing its orders, decrees, and memoranda, surviving in virtually the same form in which they appeared to Caesar and complete with the folio numbers that he added. The earliest entry in the very first book records a meeting at Sheen on 23 March 1493. There gathered a small group of councillors, their names recorded in the margins of the page: the Bishops Richard Foxe of Bath and Wells (also Keeper of the Privy Seal) and Thomas Savage of Rochester (elect); members of the royal household clergy including the Dean of the Chapel Royal, Thomas Janne, and a chaplain, John Bailey; and two lawyers, Robert Middleton and Robert Rede. These men made and recorded their decisions in two cases. In the first, concerning lands and tenements, the disputants were ordered to produce witnesses and the petitioner was enjoined not to make waste of these lands until the matter had been more fully discussed in the Council, with a penalty of £40 imposed if he failed to obey. In the second, the councillors agreed to give the defendant three weeks to produce examinations regarding a debt of four marks, apparently to be taken in King's Bench in the near future.[45]

[43] Caesar, *The Ancient State.*
[44] As described by Nicholas Catesby's opponents in *c.* 1498: TNA E163/29/11 m. 16. In 1504, the Duchy of Lancaster also referred to the 'kinges counsel of Requestes': TNA DL5/2 fol. 80; see also DL5/4 fol. 106.
[45] REQ1/1 fol. 77.

72   The New Justice System

This business is so mundane as to hardly suit the opening salvo of a new court, but it set the precedent for Requests' activities over the next few decades. This 23 March was a Saturday in the fourth week of Lent, the day before Passion Sunday. It fell between the normal legal terms of Hilary and Easter, and within a series of holy days during which lawyers and litigants otherwise observed a vacation. And yet the king's councillors sat together for judicial business on this day, at the favoured royal palace of Sheen (the site of the palace of Richmond from 1501 onwards), where Henry VII resided for that whole month. This visit was occasioned by the normal seasonal circulation of the household; the palace was not permanently occupied by the monarch or this arm of his Council. The entries for Requests' business in the next several years continue to be dated outside of terms, within the summer months, and recorded at a variety of locations along the king's itinerary: 6 April 1493 at Sheen again, and at Northampton on 25 and 29 September of the same year; then March and early April 1494 and throughout the summer of that year, when the royal entourage journeyed to Canterbury and then northwards to Woodstock via Sheen, Windsor, and Langley.[46] At first, then, Requests' register appears to have only recorded judicial process in suits brought to the Council *outside of term* and *beyond Westminster*. The contents of the councillors' discussion set the standard for what was to come, too, with the order books that followed mostly comprising short Latin memoranda recording the initial hearings of parties and their cases, and interlocutory orders to financially bind disputants to good behaviour until further decisions could be made. Far from constituting a brand-new tribunal, these records represent a more formalised practice of administering justice on the move, perhaps at Henry VII's instigation.

The year 1493 certainly marked an inauspicious moment for the king's fledgling regime, with lingering accusations that he had usurped the throne having already given rise to support for the pretender Lambert Simnel and then, in short order, the Perkin Warbeck rebellion unfurling from 1490 onwards. Preparations for the parliament of 1495 included the creation of a committee to investigate all the ills of the realm, demonstrating the king's concern for displaying good governance.[47] Aside from these interests of statecraft, certain administrative contingencies might have made recording the attendant Council's hearings especially necessary at this juncture. The Council in the Star Chamber sat within the legal terms, always at Westminster, and on entirely different days to the fluid committee that

---

[46] REQ1/1 fols. 83–91v.   [47] Cavill, *The English Parliaments of Henry VII, 1485–1504*, 74–7.

'Travailing between the Prince and Petitioners' 73

would eventually be known as 'Requests'.[48] Perhaps this practical separation engendered the creation of distinct record series for each arm of the Council; certainly, transcriptions taken from the now-lost Star Chamber registers indicate that they might have been kept as early as 1493, too.[49] The Requests committee also started to record hearings within the legal terms from Trinity term 1494, and to sit occasionally at Westminster after October 1495. But by that time its differentiation from the Star Chamber branch was jurisdictional as much as it was physical. Even in their early years the two tribunals heard different sorts of cases, with minor party-to-party suits heard in Requests and matters touching the king or civil suits between magnates still dominating the agenda in Star Chamber. That these twin tribunals were diverging from one another was already apparent in the allusions to their separate but supportive relationship to one another in the suit between the Becket sisters and Alice Radley in *c.* 1486. Furthermore, by 1500, Requests remitted cases *to* that Council at Westminster as an entirely distinct entity.[50]

The very first folio of Requests' earliest book confirms that, in its initial formulation, this tribunal was attached to the peripatetic arm of government. It comprises a list of seventeen lords and councillors appointed by Henry VII in February 1494 to attend on him for the duration of a summer '*iter*', or progress. Most of these men were assigned a timetable for their attendance: the Prior of St John's was to attend for fifteen days after Easter and then continuously until August, while the various knights and doctors on the list were to stay for the whole tour.[51] We should not take this as some founding ordinance of Requests, especially since the book's pages are filed out of order and so this is not its earliest-dated document. Moreover, not only was the work of justice-giving *not* specified as the main duty of the men named in this list, but going by the attendance registers in the pages that follow, many of those listed for the progress did not involve themselves in Requests' business thereafter anyway.[52] Meanwhile, others not initially named for that progress joined the entourage somewhere on the road and *were* enlisted as judges – including

---

[48] HL Ellesmere MSS 2654, 2655.

[49] It also had a book of at least 150 folios in Trinity term 1537: see K. J. Kesselring ed., *Star Chamber Reports: BL Harley MS 2143* (List and Index Society, 2018), 135–7.

[50] REQ1/2 fol. 120v; REQ1/3 fols. 105, 190v, 208, 209, 241.

[51] REQ1/1 fol. 1. The full list included the bishops of Bath, Exeter, and Rochester, the Prior of St John's, Lord Daubeney, Lord Broke, Sir William Hussey, Robert Rede, John Kingsmill, Sir Andrew Dymmock, Sir Reginald Bray, Sir Richard Guildford, Sir Thomas Lovell, the Keeper of the Rolls (Geoffrey Blythe), Thomas Janne, Henry Ainsworth, and William Warham.

[52] Of those named on the list, the Bishop of Exeter (Oliver King), the Prior of St John's (John Kendal), Lord Broke, Sir William Hussey, John Kingsmill, and Henry Ainsworth are never recorded as having sat in Requests.

74 The New Justice System

some, like Dr Robert Middleton, who were present for hearings more regularly than any of the men on the list.[53] Observed here is not any formal 'bench' of judges but an informal and variable group of men who happened to be available in the king's retinue and who were not apparently afforded any official judicial position. Putting their decisions on paper may have been about keeping track of business as it passed through so many hands. It may also have helped to bestow greater authority on their jurisdiction, in an age in which the quality and organisation of an archive was often pointed to as a measure of a court's constitution.[54]

The Requests committee operated as a part of the itinerant royal household in some capacity all the way through to the middle of the sixteenth century. This is evident first and foremost in the thousands of order-book entries attributed with locations, recording judicial deliberations taking place within the palaces, castles, and houses owned by the Crown and brought under its ownership in the early Tudor period. They are telling as to the Court's initial geographical range. While most of its hearings took place within the main London circuit, most often at Westminster, Sheen/Richmond, the Tower of London, and Windsor Castle, at least 114 sessions were held outside of the Thames Valley, with some as far north as Nottinghamshire and others beyond the bounds of England, in Wales and France. In this movement the Requests provision always orbited the king, with almost all recorded seats mapping directly onto the known itineraries of Henry VII and Henry VIII.[55] What this often meant was that justice-giving through this fluid tribunal was part of the royal progresses of this period. Progresses differed from the normal movement of the household from residence to residence with the seasons in that they were longer, lasting usually for several months across the summer, and

---

[53] The additional figures listed in REQ1/1 but not in the '*iter*' list are John Bailey (the king's chaplain), Dr Robert Middleton, John Arundell, Richard Empson, the Bishop of Salisbury (John Blythe), the Lord Steward (John Ratcliffe), William Sheffield, Richard Mayhew (President of Magdalen College, Oxford), and Henry Wyatt.

[54] In 1510, the main Council debated the integrity of courts without proper records of their judgments: HL Ellesmere MS 2655 fol. 8. In the late sixteenth century, Star Chamber was criticised for the lack of 'strictness and diligence' shown in its record-keeping: William Hudson, 'Treatise of the Court of Star Chamber', printed in F. Hargrave ed., *Collectanea Juridica: consisting of tracts relative to the law and constitution of England* (London, 1791–2), vol. II, 5–6.

[55] Lisa Ford utilised REQ1 for her itinerary, and corroborated many of its recorded locations with evidence from the warrants to the privy and great seals, the chamber books, and other Exchequer records: 'Conciliar Politics and Administration in the Reign of Henry VII' (unpublished PhD thesis, University of St Andrews, 2001), 209–93; Neil Samman used the accounts of the Cofferer and Comptroller alongside records from the privy and signet seals and ambassadorial reports: 'The Henrician Court during Cardinal Wolsey's Ascendancy, c.1514–1529' (unpublished PhD thesis, University of Wales, Bangor, 1988), 327–92.

'Travailing between the Prince and Petitioners' 75

ranged far beyond the cluster of royal homes in the Thames Valley.[56] Whereas the palaces around London might be visited for necessity, to facilitate the process of cleaning up after a bustling household, progresses were motivated by weightier matters: by a need to be seen in the cities and towns of the realm through diplomacy, pageantry, generosity, and (it has often been assumed) through the imposition of the majesty of monarchy on potentially unruly subjects.

Requests' archive reveals how far progresses also involved the visible, merciful dispensation of justice in response to subjects' personal complaints, revitalising the practice of peripatetic governance observed by earlier Lancastrian and Yorkist kings and putting royal aid within reach of the peoples and territories residing in between the provincial and central courts. So, in 1495, as Henry VII journeyed through the midlands to Nottingham, his attendant Council sat to hear cases on at least seven of his ten stops along the way, including at Collyweston. The same committee was active during the king's venture in 1499 southwards, to the Isle of Wight, where he looked to shore up support following the flight of Edmund de la Pole, the Earl of Suffolk, who had led the Blackheath rebellion and been indicted for murder.[57] Sitting in Newport and at Carisbrooke Castle, the Requests councillors passed a decree in a local dispute over rights to lands on the Isle, presumably presented to the king during his stay.[58] The same dedication to resolve controversies in towns treated to a rare royal visitation was apparent the following June in Calais, which Henry VII visited to avoid the threat of plague in London, to check on the garrison, and to meet with Archduke Philip of Burgundy.[59] There Thomas Savage, the Bishop of London and president of the attendant Council, sat for six days, heard at least thirteen different cases, and passed five final decrees.[60] He also received and appended his signature to a whole packet of petitions against Sir James Tyrell, the Lieutenant of the Castle of Guisnes, accusing him of withholding payments, lands, and crops from local men and women.[61] In each of these instances, the Requests committee on the move transformed into a temporary tribunal for the king's subjects in far-flung dominions. Whether this could always be the case

---

[56] N. Samman, 'The Progresses of Henry VIII, 1509–1529', in D. MacCulloch ed., *The Reign of Henry VIII: Politics, Policy, and Piety* (Macmillan, 1995), 61–2.

[57] REQ1/1 fol. 123v.   [58] REQ1/2 fol. 61.

[59] According to Polydore Vergil, *The Anglica Historia of Polydore Vergil, A.D. 1485–1537*, ed. Denys Hay, Camden Third Series 74 (Royal Historical Society, 1950), 119.

[60] REQ1/2 fols. 104–8.

[61] REQ2/2/158. Some of these complainants were heard by Savage: REQ1/2 fols. 104, 106v.

76 The New Justice System

depended on the purpose of an individual progress, however. So, when Henry VII and his mother, Margaret Beaufort, went on pilgrimage to Walsingham and Collyweston via various monastic houses in the summer of 1498, no Requests business was recorded; their choice of religious settings presumably limited the accessibility of the court for secular business.

This occasion aside, though, the default mode of the itinerant household was to entertain petitioners wherever they happened to appear. The performative function of justice in more typical progresses reached an apex in the summer of 1502, during the journey of Henry VII and Elizabeth of York to Raglan Castle in South Wales following the death of Prince Arthur. At almost every stage of this four-month journey, the attendant councillors working in Requests heard cases: at Woodstock, in Gloucester and the small border towns of Flaxley and Mitchel Troy, and at the castles of Raglan and Berkeley; then, on the return leg, at Fairford in Gloucestershire, the private royal residence at Langley, and East Hampstead in Berkshire before returning to Windsor and Westminster. This capacity for receiving petitioners and making deliberations, even in small villages where space must have been limited, saw the councillors record orders in sixty-three separate cases, including five decrees, during this single progress.[62] Yet in the years that followed, the frequency of this activity gradually declined. Requests sat much less regularly during the shorter and less ambitious tours of the mid-1500s: for just two days of a three-month tour of the Home Counties in 1504 and twelve days of a summer progress through Berkshire and Hampshire in 1505.[63] Thereafter, 1507 was the first year in which Requests registered no hearings between mid-July and the beginning of Michaelmas term in October, although Henry VII ventured to Woodstock and Langley via Cambridge that summer. Where justice-giving on progress had been reinvigorated by the need to display good kingship in the more precarious years of the reign, perhaps it was stifled by the long periods of illness suffered by the king in his final years.

Still, during those most important of progress times, the king's justice had been neither a bureaucratic process going on behind closed doors nor a one-off spectacle. Here procedure blended with statecraft, administration with event. Importantly, itinerancy did not prevent Requests' councillors and clerks from overseeing proceedings of comparable complexity to those offered in the other conciliar courts, including the receipt of a full set of

---

[62] REQ1/2 fols. 9v–16v.   [63] REQ1/3 fols. 133, 207v–209v.

'Travailing between the Prince and Petitioners' 77

pleadings, issuing authorised commissions, and holding final hearings where required. To keep up with this work, Henry VII's Requests established a flexible but efficient schedule. It functioned almost anywhere, on most days throughout the year, and without being confined exclusively to the four legal terms, like other courts of law. In 1495, the clerks of the Council recorded Requests business on Good Friday and into the Easter week, and across the 1490s the tribunal acted throughout Lent, between Hilary and Easter terms. It usually continued past the end of Michaelmas term, as late as 23 December in 1497. Likewise, on a weekly basis it did not keep set days or observe any defined pattern of activity, gathering for hearings, processing petitions, and issuing authorising writs on Sundays as much as on any weekday. It did follow a daily routine of sorts: just as the king's justices sat in court from 8am to 11am, and as Wolsey was said to have presided in Chancery 'til eleven of the clock' most days, in one instance a party was ordered to appear before Requests at 10am the following Monday, implying at least some pre-planning and timetabling.[64] But any such organisation as we can discern in this period was entirely subject to the rhythms of a changeable, peripatetic royal administration. For example, in April 1495 one defendant was told to appear before Henry VII and his Council when the king visited Worcester in July of that year.[65] A few years later, various parties were ordered to return for further hearings on the 'next juridical day after the arrival of the said lord king' (*proxime die juridico post adventum dicti domini regis*).[66] The very life of this Council's judicial functions depended on the king's presence.

Requests' attachment to the monarch's person is no more evident than during a handover between reigns, these brief interregnums initially having a noticeable impact on its functioning. When Robert Beale, a clerk of the Elizabethan Privy Council, consulted Requests' order books in the 1590s, he observed that 'the booke of kinge Henry the 7 desivit [ended] 25 April anno Regni 24' – that is, on 25 April 1509, shortly following the late king's death on 21 April – and that 'the booke of kinge Hen the 8 beginnethe 9 Julij followinge'.[67] This register no longer survives, but Beale's notes tell us that Requests ceased to record business for a couple of months after the old king's death was announced at court on 23 April. Among the uncatalogued

---

[64] Fortescue, *On the Laws and Governance of England*, 74; George Cavendish, *The Life and Death of Cardinal Wolsey* (Houghton Mifflin and Company, 1995), 24–5; REQ1/2 fol. 99.
[65] REQ1/1 fol. 102. For a similar request to appear before the king when he arrived at Windsor, see REQ1/1 fol. 33v.
[66] REQ1/2 fol. 96v.   [67] BL Additional MS 48025 fol. 51v.

78 The New Justice System

Requests material there is a single petition for justice from a royal servant dateable within this window, dated in an endorsement to 14 May 1509. Yet, unusually, this was addressed to the 'King our Sov[er]ain lord and his noble lord[es] of p[ar]liament both sp[irit]uall & temp[or]all' and not, as was standard, to the just king or to his Council.[68] Perhaps no such route perceptibly existed at that time; or perhaps there was confusion about where to send bills, since Parliament was not in session that year either. In the short period of minority kingship before Henry VIII turned eighteen on 28 June, the composition and constitution of the central administration, Council, and household was in flux.

Eventually Henry VIII would revive his father's attendant judicial provision almost wholesale. Yet for the few years immediately following the accession of 1509, his Council and all its judicial offshoots apparently deprioritised justice-giving.[69] Only seventy-five or so of Requests' surviving petitions can be dated definitively to the years 1509–15, compared to just over 400 for the period 1502–8. Levels of litigation across the board picked up once again by the end of the 1510s, encouraged by Wolsey's popularisation of conciliar justice and augmentation of its tribunals. A consequence of this sudden in-flow of business – and perhaps also of the delegation of all Requests' business to just two members of the household clergy, as we will see in Chapter 7 – was that Requests' work was increasingly confined to the entourage's seasonal rotation of the Thames Valley. In fact, across the later 1510s and 1520s the only locations recorded for Requests' hearings were Greenwich, Woodstock, Bridewell Palace, Windsor Castle, and Westminster.[70] This was hardly for lack of progresses: Henry VIII travelled beyond Westminster in almost every year of his reign up to 1529, to cultivate allegiance in cities, to avoid plague, to impress visiting diplomats, make pilgrimage, call in on his nobility, or to go hunting. Yet whereas Requests had been engaged in every stage of the extensive progress of 1502, the 'grand sweep' of Henry VIII through seven counties across 113 days in 1526 did not involve Requests at all. In fact, the Court recorded no business that summer.[71] The combination of growing business and limited resources at this time meant that Requests could no longer always sit for hearings wherever convenient and necessary while the king was on the move.

This is the picture gained from the order books, at least. Another place in which Requests' councillors and clerks made note of their activities was

---

[68] REQ3/15 *Dawtrey* v *Wotton and Charles*.
[69] A decline discussed further in Guy, 'Wolsey, the Council and the Council Courts', 481.
[70] REQ1/4 fols. 91–2, 95, 135v; REQ1/104 fol. 21; REQ1/5 fol. 21.
[71] Samman, 'The Progresses of Henry VIII', 61, 63–4; REQ1/5 fols. 28–33v.

'Travailing between the Prince and Petitioners'

within the loose pleadings – petitions, answers, and depositions – that formed the other half of their archive. Here we find evidence of their more immediate decision-making, in notes scrawled onto documents while on the road with the royal entourage, right through to the middle years of the sixteenth century. For example, a dispute between a husbandman and a gentleman from Hertfordshire over payment for possession of a tenement was, according to memoranda on the petition and answer, heard by Requests first at Bridewell on 8 March 1524, when a letter was sent to the defendant requesting his appearance, and then again at Croydon on 19 March, when the defendant attended and was ordered to pay compensation. The case never appeared in the order books; in fact, it falls within a period of time in which the books give the impression of business being at an all-time low, with only four entries for the whole year of 1524.[72] An apparent mid-1520s slump is further qualified by evidence of attendant justice-giving in the latter half of 1525, even as the king fled London to avoid plague.[73] One case from this time saw a defendant attend on Richard Wolman and William Sulyard for a week in early November at Reading Abbey, where they passed a final order that was again not recorded in the books.[74] Furthermore, writs ordering commissions in Requests' cases continued to be sent out on the move, from the palace of Beaulieu (previously New Hall, Essex) in April and from Enfield in July 1524, from Guildford in July 1525, and from Chertsey Abbey in July 1526, each signed off by attending judges and clerks.[75] These documents confirm a greater persistence and extent of attendance on the king than Requests' order books alone can reveal, and certainly suggest that any settlement at Westminster in the early 1520s was neither total nor irreversible.

The provision of royal orders in the itinerant household did not abate even into the 1530s and beyond, when Requests much more frequently occupied the White Hall at Westminster for its formal hearings. Privy-seal writs summoning defendants for hearings were sent out from Waltham Abbey in July, Langley in August, and Dover Castle in November of 1532; from Abingdon Abbey in July and the manor of Thornbury in August 1535; and from Sittingbourne, Dover, and Woking across the spring and summer of 1542.[76] Orders scrawled onto the backs of petitions and anecdotal accounts of Requests' business from these years suggests that it was still receiving defendants at Ampthill in September 1539 and at Grafton around

---

[72] REQ3/15 Long v Sankey; REQ1/5 fols. 22–3. [73] REQ2/9/61. [74] REQ3/6 Turnor v Smith.
[75] REQ3/5 Pope v Baskerville; REQ2/7/26, REQ2/9/61, REQ2/12/195, REQ2/7/149.
[76] REQ2/5/45, 2/6/166, 2/7/56, 2/8/119, 336, 2/11/30, 199.

80   The New Justice System

the same time.[77] There is evidence not only of parties being entertained spontaneously on the road, but also of pre-planned hearings designed for the convenience of the Court and its litigants. With the examination of the dispute between Thomas Russell and Thomas Sparke running on at the end of Trinity term 1540, it was suggested that they 'kepe ther day at Ampt[h]ill' – just five miles north of their homes in Pulloxhill, Bedfordshire – 'yf the kinges grace kepe his progresse'.[78]

That cases like this one continued to be received and processed on the road and eventually heard by Requests in more formal, term-time hearings – and vice versa – indicates that the ongoing itinerant activity fed into an increasingly sedentary Court and was not an altogether separate enterprise. In other words, Requests had not gone 'out of court' and been replaced by a provision for justice 'in court'. Instead, it continued to operate both centrally *and* itinerantly. In the old administrative-history mindset, the slowness with which Requests moved definitively to the centre would be seen as a failure of imagination or intention on the part of the early Tudors. But a fairer interpretation is that the attachment of this tribunal to the most personal, attendant part of the royal administration gave it an inherent flexibility that naturally eludes the clear definition sought by historians. That it continued to possess a dual personality is reflected in later self-identification within its own orders as 'the kinges honorable Counsaill attendaunte upon his person *and* comenly sitting in the kinges Ma[jes]ties Courte of White Hall at Westminster'.[79]

Reforms and Routinisation

As an arm of central government as much as a performance of statecraft or court of law, Requests was subject to early sixteenth-century reforms. That Requests would eventually join Chancery and Star Chamber at Westminster and would be known as the 'Court of the White Hall' by the end of the sixteenth century is undeniable.[80] But when, exactly, this settlement occurred is less definitive. The connection between court and space had come about at least by the end of the 1510s, when petitioners were already beginning to ask for hearings before the Council in the White Hall and were received by the men otherwise attached to the Court of Requests.[81] Conscious development in this direction was undertaken more readily in

---

[77] REQ3/8 *Gardefield* v *Alye*; REQ3/16/1 *Barret* v *Barnard*.   [78] REQ1/6 fol. 67, REQ2/4/9.

[79] As appears in an obligation from October 1546, recorded within the book fragments now in REQ3/14 fol. 285 (my emphasis).

[80] See Caesar's dedicatory epistle to Lord Burghley: Hill ed., *The Ancient State*, 3.

[81] REQ2/4/99, 2/5/184, 2/10/200, 2/12/28.

'Travailing between the Prince and Petitioners'   81

the middle years of Henry VIII's reign, and especially in the 1530s, such that we might presume it to be part of the 'revolution' long associated with that decade. Yet this apparently straightforward administrative trajectory belies the fact that the commission, Council, or Court of Requests was, for the most part, peripheral to the best-known reformist policies of the early Tudor period. It was not itself the subject of an ordinance or order for its foundation, but it was affected by the standards for administering justice that were taking shape in the early sixteenth century. Moreover, it did *not* generally experience a linear or speedy trajectory towards institutionalisation, as the dip in business just after 1509, the limitation of the Court's movements in the late 1510s and early 1520s, and the low point of the mid-1520s should have already indicated. With these caveats in mind, situating Requests within and against the reformist trends up to the end of Henry VIII's reign helps us to better understand the course of the expansion of royal, conciliar justice and the choices it offered litigants.

From the start, the diversification of the conciliar justice system discussed in the previous chapter – the initial firming up of provincial councils, followed by the stratification of a static (Star Chamber) and an attendant (Requests) committee for justice – saw its respective elements defined *against* one another. That Requests did not act in a vacuum is most clear in its relationship to other pre-existing and emerging tribunals within the conciliar justice system. To these other courts it might commit (temporarily defer for hearing and certification) and remit (dismiss and transfer) its cases. This movement of suits from one tribunal to another did not necessarily denote any hierarchy between them; rather, it depended on the nature of the case in hand. Most obviously, for reasons relating to the geographical origin of disputes, Requests might send cases on to the committees of the Duchy of Lancaster, the Marches of Wales, the North of England, and the transient Council in the West.[82] Where the text moving these deferrals survives, it appears that they took the form of committals or commissions, of the kind otherwise used to order local powerholders to investigate a case in its immediate vicinity, help find a 'fynall end and determinacion', and prevent the king (and Requests) from being 'further molested with anie pursuit to bee made unto us in this matter'.[83] Requests itself took on this same function

---

[82] REQ1/3 fol. 247; REQ2/3/16, 112, 2/10/51. For examples pertaining especially to the Council in the Marches, see REQ1/1 fol. 146; REQ1/2 fols. 6, 55v, 114, 148v; REQ1/3 fols. 173v, 223; REQ1/4 fol. 187v; REQ1/4 fol. 167v; REQ2/7/87, 143, 2/10/176, 186, 2/13/73; Caesar, *The Ancient State*, 52.

[83] As in a letter remitting a case from Requests to the Council in the Marches in Feb. 1521, printed in Skeel, *The Council in the Marches of Wales*, 32. See also REQ2/7/87, 143. For an example of Requests sending a Yorkshire case to the Council in the North, see REQ3/14 *Day* v *Malleverer*.

82 The New Justice System

at times as a means of relieving the heavy workloads of the other central courts, especially Star Chamber and Chancery. During a very busy spell in conciliar justice in the late 1510s and early 1520s, notations on petitions indicate that they were 'comittitur' to the Dean of the Chapel Royal and the rest of his conciliar colleagues on the order of the Chancellor. In these instances, there appears to have been no route to send these disputes back up the chain; they were to be finally determined by Requests.[84] Otherwise, Requests would only remit cases in the other direction occasionally, and under mitigating circumstances: such as in October 1505, when its judges transferred a case to Chancery at Westminster because one of the disputants was too infirm to travel after the itinerant household.[85]

All of this is to say that, notwithstanding its relative novelty, Requests quickly became a distinctive component of a busy network of judicial tribunals – a system which, like many others, underwent another phase of growth in the early sixteenth century. Administrative historians studying this phenomenon have made much of several orders recorded by the main Council in the late 1510s to establish more committees at Westminster for handling litigation to the king, in the wake of Wolsey's overtures about the importance of justice in 1516.[86] The first, in the minutes from a Council meeting presided over by Wolsey on 17 June 1518, ordered that the Abbot of Westminster (John Islip) and eight other men gather 'to heare poore mens causes', either in the Exchequer Chamber, the Lord Treasurer's Chamber, or the White Hall, all at Westminster.[87] The second, surviving now in the State Papers collection and dated by its compilers to sometime before or around 1519, is almost identical. Said to be explicitly issued by 'Thomas Lord Cardinale chanceler', it appointed the same abbot and a very similar group of eight men to sit in the White Hall for 'thexpedicion of poore mens causes'.[88] These two documents probably represent versions of the same initial order, and refer to the same committee.

---

[84] REQ2/2/4, 168, 2/3/90, 122, 166, 398, 2/4/364, 2/5/148, 403, 2/7/42.   [85] REQ1/3 fol. 211.

[86] HL Ellesmere MS 2655 fol. 10–10v.

[87] Ellesmere MS 2655 fol. 12. The full list of names included the Abbot of Westminster, the Dean of St Paul's Cathedral (John Colet), Sir Thomas Neville, Sir Andrew Windsor, Dr John Clerk, William Roper, and Robert Toneys, with the addition of the Bishop of Hereford (Charles Booth) and Sir Henry Wyatt.

[88] SP1/19 fol. 142. This may well in fact date to a few years earlier than usually suggested, as Leadam argued: Select Cases in the Court of Requests, xiii. It appoints six of the same men as the 1518 order, including the abbot, the Dean of St Paul's, Sir Thomas Neville, Sir Andrew Windsor, Dr John Clerk, and William Roper. Its added names are the Prior of St John's (Thomas Docwra) and Sir Richard Weston.

'Travailing between the Prince and Petitioners'   83

Importantly, that committee was *not* the Court of Requests, as has often been claimed based on the references here to poor men's causes and the White Hall.[89] Most obviously, that Requests had been keeping a consistent record of its own business for twenty-five years by this point surely contradicts the view that these Council orders founded that older tribunal. But for the avoidance of doubt, none of the men named to these committees for poor men's causes worked in Requests at this time, going by that Court's attendance registers and the signatories to its pleadings. An exception is John Clerk, who was named to the 1518 commission but would not work in Requests until the very end of 1519, when he became Dean of the Chapel Royal. Even more conclusive is the evidence that the Abbot of Westminster's tribunal, established in the order from June 1518, functioned simultaneously to and separately from the rest of the conciliar tribunals, Requests included. That this tribunal existed at all is confirmed by endorsements on Star Chamber bills mentioning commissions and other investigations established by the abbot and his colleagues.[90] It did not operate for very long, however. One particularly detailed petition to Wolsey as Chancellor in *c.* 1523 reported how a matter had been sent to 'my lord the Abbote of Westmynster and other commissioners sittyng in the Whight Halle' but that after a year and a half 'they sate no longer in the haule' and so the plaintiff had petitioned the king again, and been sent instead to 'Doctor [John] Stokysley', in Requests.[91] Elsewhere, annotations on the reverse side of several more petitions to Wolsey tell us that they were committed *from* the Abbot of Westminster and his committee *to* the Dean of the Chapel, by that time the head judge in Requests. One even stated that it had to be moved on specifically because the abbot's committee was no longer active.[92]

The reason for setting up this short-lived committee in the first place is implied by the terms set out in *another* order for a new conciliar tribunal, from October 1520. Appointing a different set of councillors, led by the Prior of St John's (Thomas Docwra), to hold meetings in the Treasurer's Chamber, the Council specified that this committee was to act 'for thexpedicion of poore mens causes *dependinge in the Starre*

---

[89] Leadam ed., *Select Cases in the Court of Requests*, xi, xiv; Guy, 'The Privy Council: Revolution or Evolution?', 66.

[90] See the commission made by the abbot and his colleagues recorded on the back of a Wolsey-era Star Chamber bill: TNA STAC2/17/389.

[91] REQ3/1 *Orgor* v *Hovill* et al.

[92] REQ3/5 *Broke* v *Bradbury*, the verso of which reads '*Coram domini Abbate West[monasterii] et aliis de consilio. Et quia non Agitur de causis commissis eisdem committantur domino decano capelle*'. See also REQ2/3/90.

84   The New Justice System

Chamber.[93] Fortunately we possess evidence confirming that this tribunal was active for at least a couple of years, too. It apparently kept its own registers, now unfortunately lost, but excerpts surviving in later transcriptions record that some of those men named in the 1520 order did sit to hear civil cases 'referred to them by the cardinall'.[94] This indicates that Wolsey and the main Council were concerned about the volume of litigation that had been invited to the centre of government over the past several years, and that by the mid-1520s were moving to remit much of it elsewhere – initially to these temporary subcommittees, and then back out to the counties.[95] As Hall and other commentators at Wolsey's fall in 1529 would have it, the Chancellor had founded as many as four different 'under courtes' for the purpose of relieving his Court of Star Chamber, and to meet the ancient responsibility for prioritising the most vulnerable.[96] Requests experienced a spike in caseload around this time: its rate of heard business doubled between 1515 and 1516 and the next regnal year, and it was examining just shy of 300 cases a year by 1520–1.[97] It was part of the relief effort, then – but it was *not* constituted by it.

Requests soon moved more clearly to the centre of political attention, however. Probably the earliest reference to it within Tudor policymaking – though, again, not by name – comes in Wolsey's aborted Eltham ordinances for reform of the royal household in 1526. As part of a host of suggestions about how to better organise the attendant administration, the canon and civil lawyer Richard Wolman was named to travel with the king for the 'ordering of poore mens complaintes and causes'.[98] Far from representing a formal appointment, this clause in fact confirmed a situation that had been ongoing for some time. Wolman had been active from at least early 1524 as a signatory to Requests' petitions and orders, and quickly became the overseer of all its business.[99] And notwithstanding the eventual foundering of Wolsey's plans on this front, Wolman continued to lead

---

[93] HL Ellesmere MS 2655 fol. 16 (my emphasis).   [94] BL Lansdowne MS 160 fols. 310v–311.

[95] Guy, 'Wolsey, the Council and the Council Courts', 501; Ellesmere MS 2655 fol. 18.

[96] SP1/54 fol. 213 (*LP* IV. 5750); Hall mentioned a court in the White Hall, one held before John Stokesley (which would appear to be Requests, in reality), another in the Treasurer's Chamber, and the fourth 'at the rolles at after noone': *Hall's Chronicle*, 585.

[97] This is according to the number of order book entries for these years in REQ1/4, REQ1/104, and REQ1/105.

[98] Nichols ed., *A collection of ordinances and regulations for the government of the royal household*, 160.

[99] The petition of Roger Orgor to Wolsey from sometime in late 1523 suggests that Wolman had taken over from Stokesley in Requests: REQ3/1 *Orgor* v *Hovill* et al.; see also REQ2/4/140, 2/6/129, 2/7/149, 2/12/195; REQ3/5 *Pope* v *Baskerfeld*; REQ1/5 fol. 24. A petition from *c.* 1528 was addressed 'To master doctor Wolman and other of the mooste honorabill Counceill of o[u]r sovereygne lord the kyng attending upon hys person': REQ2/11/122.

'Travailing between the Prince and Petitioners' 85

Requests' business into the later 1520s. Another apparently unsuccessful attempt to shore up the judicial procedures around the Crown came in a Council order of November 1526, which stated that 'The deane of the k[inge]s Chappelle & 7 others [be] deputed to heare causes for poore men.'[100] Presumably this too refers to Requests, where the dean had been the leading judge for more than two decades, but there is no other evidence to suggest that an eight-strong judiciary was thereby installed. Comparing such ordinances to the annotations and signatures in Requests' archive confirms the general ineffectiveness of change imposed from outside the Court.

In the years that followed, several so-called 'reconstitutions' recorded within Requests' own files indicate there was more concerted effort inside the central administration to reshape this tribunal, in a manner more directed and successful than before.[101] Just before the start of Hilary term 1529, an undated list of 'the names of suche Counsaillours as be appointed for the heryng of power mennes causes in the kynges Courte of Requestes' was recorded in that tribunal's order books.[102] The list is significant for several reasons: the implication of a formal appointment of members to this tribunal, the use of the name 'Court of Requests', and the clear jurisdictional statement on 'power mennes causes'. This combination of characteristics suggests some continuity between the conciliar 'Requests' function described in the 1483 grant to Harrington and this 'Court' of 1529 – a restatement, rather than some new conception, of Requests' purpose. It also likely represents an attempt to smooth the flow of judicial business within the royal household, motivated by the apparent slowdown of work in the later 1520s. No more than three hearings were recorded for each term between Michaelmas 1526 and Michaelmas 1528, and the relative rate of surviving petitions submitted in this window is low, too.[103]

The appearance of decline here does not signal a drop in numbers of petitioners but rather in the number of men on hand to handle and record their cases. Alongside Richard Turnor, the stalwart clerk of the privy seal and of 'the kynges honorable cort of requestes', attendant justice in the later 1520s was undertaken almost entirely by Wolman with only occasional support from Richard Sampson, Dean of the Chapel Royal, and the common lawyers Thomas Englefield and William Sulyard.[104] Consequently, by the

---

[100] HL Ellesmere MS 2652 fol. 4v.
[101] Guy, 'The Privy Council: Revolution or Evolution?', 71, 82.   [102] REQ1/5 fol. 43v.
[103] REQ1/5 fols. 33–42. There are, in fact, more catalogued petitions (in REQ2) dating to this time than there are order-book entries.
[104] LP IV. 1860 (5); REQ2/4/181.

86 The New Justice System

beginning of 1529 it had become necessary to employ a larger group of councillors, encompassing more varied areas of expertise, than had been seen in Requests since the beginning of the century. This included a host of clergymen, the bishops of Lincoln and St Asaph (John Longland and Henry Standish), the Abbot of Westminster (John Islip), the Prior of St John's (William Weston), and the Dean of the Chapel Royal (Sampson); the doctors of law Wolman, Rowland Philipps, Roger Lupton, 'Doctor Cromer', and Sulyard; and the knights Thomas Neville, John Hussey, William Fitzwilliam, and Roger Townsend. Curiously, the very last name on the list is one 'SaintJermyne' – most likely Christopher St German, the common lawyer, who had just published the first edition of his dialogue *Doctor and Student*, on the subject of equity and the law.

Why these men? Wolman, the dean, and others on the list were attendant upon the king; meanwhile, no singular place was appointed for Requests' meetings at this point. So, one possibility is that Henry VIII himself selected or confirmed this group, in a manner reminiscent of Henry VII's '*iter*' list from 1494. Yet some of those named were plainly not always expected to be on the road with the household. The bishops would have had duties within their dioceses; for example, if 'Doctor Cromer' was *George* Cromer, the Archbishop of Armagh, then he was presumably much too busy with events in Ireland to be present in England in 1529 or for much time thereafter.[105] As with many of the political goings-on of these years – especially where conciliar justice is concerned – we might look more promisingly to Wolsey as the driving force for reform. Although his orders for temporary committees in 1518 and 1520 did not found Requests itself, his oversight of the central administration means that he could have had a hand in choosing its personnel in 1529. Some on the list had also been named to Wolsey's commissions in the late 1510s, including Islip and Longland, while others had been part of the proposed 'council of twenty' in his Eltham ordinances of 1526.[106] A few were agents of Wolsey at some point or another: including Dr Rowland Philipps, the vicar of Croydon, who represented the Chancellor in his attempts to convince the Abbot of Wigmore to

---

[105] For Cromer's active primacy of Ireland, see L. P. Murray, 'Archbishop Cromer's Register', *Journal of the County Louth Archaeological Society* 8:4 (1936), 338–51. Leadam weighed up other possible candidates, but the archbishop was the most senior and had, as royal chaplain, been referred to as 'Dr Crowmer' in household account books previously: Leadam, *Select Cases in the Court of Requests*, cxv; TNA E36/216 fol. 27.

[106] HL Ellesmere MS 2655 fol. 12; SP1/19 fol. 152; for the compositions of the household ordinances see the charts in Guy, 'Wolsey, the Council and the Council Courts', 504–5.

'*Travailing between the Prince and Petitioners*' 87

resign later in 1529.[107] It is certainly plausible that Wolsey was personally interested in the composition of this tribunal, to which he had been committing cases for almost a decade. In any case, the 1529 list represents the first definitive, *internal* statement of Requests' formality, jurisdiction, and composition. It marked a turning point for the reinvigoration of the Court, too. In the Hilary term immediately following the recording of the list of new judges, there was a sharp rise in received and recorded cases, with the number of surviving bills doubling on the previous year and a healthy 122 cases heard in 1531 – totals not seen since the tenure of John Stokesley a decade earlier.

Yet, in the end, this reorganisation stalled in its one clear intention: in installing a larger cohort of judges in Requests. The strongest indicator that it *did*, at least initially, change the way the Court was staffed is a single petition from *c.* 1529 endorsed with the signatures of Neville, Fitzwilliam, Sulyard, and Philipps, an unusually high number of signatories listed in a manner suggesting that they sat together for this business.[108] But there is no evidence that all fifteen men on the list ever sat for hearings at the same time, and seven of them appear to have never worked in Requests at all. Those that did had generally already been involved in the Court prior to 1529. Wolman remained just as busy in Requests after this point as he had been before, and would serve there until his death in 1537 despite also holding numerous benefices, including the deanery of Wells. As Dean of the Chapel Royal, Sampson had technically been attached to the Court for several years, with many commission certificates addressed to him personally, though he had spent much of the later 1520s away on embassies. The 1529 order tied him more closely to judicial business for the years that followed, since he and Sulyard were the busiest and longest-serving staff in Requests through the 1530s. Longland, peculiarly, worked in Requests in the 1510s and mid-1520s but not at all after 1529, when he was likely kept busy with tracking down heresies within his sizeable and diverse diocese of Lincoln and with his duties as Henry VIII's confessor.[109] As for St German, while it is known that he had acted as legal counsel in Requests in his early career, and would go on to advise the government on the Bishops' Book in

---

[107] As detailed in J. P. D. Cooper, 'Philipps, Rowland (1467/8–1538?), college head', *ODNB*, Oxford University Press, Sept. 2004, www.doi.org/10.1093/ref:odnb/22132 (accessed Jan. 2023).

[108] The four men signed an order sending the case to a commission headed by the Abbot of Shropshire: REQ3/9 *Tong* v *Banaster*; the case appears in the Requests order books twice, in 1530, following that commission: REQ1/5 fols. 76v, 77v.

[109] See M. Bowker, *The Henrician Reformation: The Diocese of Lincoln under John Longland, 1521–1547* (Cambridge University Press, 1981).

88 The New Justice System

1537, there is nothing to suggest that he took up a place on any Requests bench after 1529. After all, he was almost seventy years old by this date and had been retired from legal practice for almost two decades.[110] That his was likely a notional appointment should alert us to the possibility that the same was true of others named on the list. It may have been intended to comprise a set of commissioners working as a quorum rather than an established bench. Either way, the result was only to slightly expand the circle of men attached to Requests for the time being.

Perhaps in recognition of this failure to institute a more permanent judiciary, in January 1538 another, more effective order with the same intent was put forward. The relevant order-book page is now missing and so we must rely on Caesar's transcription of it, which reads: '23 Januarii ... Heereafter followe the names of the Comissioners appointed to sit in the Court of Requests in the Whitehall at Westminster: First, the reverend father in God *Richard* the Bish. of Chichester, *Nicholas Hare, Tho[mas] Thirleby, Edmond Boner,* and *Edward Carne.*'[111] Here the White Hall was singled out as Requests' primary seat, confirming the many requests for process in, writs for return to, and draft orders taken by the Council in '*alba aula*' across the 1530s.[112] In the absence of the original pages we cannot be certain of the order's source, but we can perceive the machinations of the realm's chief ministers behind it nonetheless. The king was still being 'molested' by suitors as late as 1540, and so would have benefitted from a better-staffed attendant court for justice.[113] Of course, we might look also to that omnipresent reformist, Thomas Cromwell, for this reform as for many others at this time. Whereas Wolsey had worked in Requests as royal almoner in the early 1510s (incidentally, a detail usually omitted from accounts of his career, which tend to restrict assessment of his judicial duties to his chancellorship, beginning 1515), there is no evidence for Cromwell's purported involvement in this Court, whether as a young lawyer or as a minister of the state.[114] Still, at least one supplication to Cromwell as Lord Privy Seal was redirected to Requests' judges, and so he may have had a vested interested in streamlining this arm of the central administration's business too.[115]

---

[110] REQ1/3 fol. 215v; *LP* XII. ii. 1151; J. A. Guy, *Christopher St German on Chancery and Statute,* Selden Society Supplementary Series 6 (Selden Society, 1985), 3–5, 11.

[111] Caesar, *The Ancient State,* 91 (emphasis in original text).

[112] REQ2/8/119, 294, 2/9/164, 2/10/208, 234, 2/12/152.

[113] Nicolas ed., *Proceedings and Ordinances of the Privy Council of England,* vol. VII., 51–2.

[114] See, for example, Guy, *The Cardinal's Court;* and P. Gwyn, *The King's Cardinal: The Rise and Fall of Thomas Wolsey* (Barrie and Jenkins, 1990); M. Everett, *The Rise of Thomas Cromwell: Power and Politics in the Reign of Henry VIII, 1485–1534* (Yale University Press, 2015), 16.

[115] REQ2/2/47.

'Travailing between the Prince and Petitioners'   89

The smaller group appointed here, including canon, civil, and common lawyers, was comprised of men mostly fresh to Requests and marked a clearer break from its past than had the 1529 list. Only Richard Sampson, now Bishop of Chichester, was a returning figure; Hare, Thirlby, Bonner, and Carne were new. Moreover, the relationship of these men to the Court was more formal and, at times, more exclusive than that of their predecessors in the household. Among them was one of the first men to be referred to as a 'Master of Requests' in this petitionary and judicial context: Nicholas Hare, who attended on the Privy Council to discuss 'thaffayres of the suttours' and who was the most active judge in Requests for the entire early Tudor period, signing almost 300 pleadings in the two decades after 1538.[116] For his efforts he was granted an annuity of £100, which would later become the regular salary of the Masters.[117] Right through to Edward VI's reign Hare was accompanied consistently in Requests business by Carne and Thirlby, and sometimes by Bonner too, usually working in groups of three or four. In addition to the officialness bestowed on Hare, from this point onwards the judges in Requests could be formally replaced. So, when William Petre was sworn in by the Privy Council in October 1540 he was tasked specifically to take 'that place in the White Haull that Doctor Thirleby elect Bishop of Westm had before he was Bishopp', indicating some desire to retain the bench established a couple of years earlier.[118]

In contrast with the ad-hoc and at times improvised management of Requests in previous decades, after 1538 its personnel seem to have represented something approaching a regulated judiciary for the first time. It also had a marked impact on the Court's function: following another small dip in business in the middle years of the 1530s, where cases declined to around fifty bills a year according to a count of surviving casefiles, 1538 saw the start of a steep increase of work, with around 200 casefiles surviving for each of the next few years. Recovery is also reflected in, and may have been facilitated by, improved record-keeping. Around this time, Requests' clerks started to keep two books, to keep track of its more definitive orders and the appearances and continuations of cases separately.[119] Notably, this

---

[116] J. R. Dasent, E. G. Atkinson, J. V. Lyle, R. F. Monger, and P. A. Penfold eds., *Acts of the Privy Council of England* (HMSO, 1890–1964), vol. II, 355, 358, 410.

[117] TNA C66/675 m. 26, *LP* XII. ii. 1008 (38); J. H. Baker, 'Hare, Sir Nicholas (c.1495–1557), Lawyer and Speaker of the House of Commons', *ODNB*, Oxford University Press, Jan. 2008, www.doi.org /10.1093/ref:odnb/12305 (accessed Jan. 2023). This annuity was redirected to Robert Southwell, another Requests judge, after Hare's arrest in 1540: *LP* XV. 436 (56); TNA C82/764.

[118] Nicolas ed., *Proceedings and Ordinances of the Privy Council*, vol. VII, 50.

[119] Knox, 'The Court of Requests in the Reign of Edward VI', 30–2.

90 The New Justice System

'reconstitution' also coincided with the emergence of the compact Privy Council out of the old, nebulous main Council, a shift which generally saw certain people and processes 'hived off' to external institutions. And yet Requests was not so simply broken away from the king. By the mid-1540s, most of the men working in the Court – Thirlby, Petre, Robert Southwell, Nicholas Heath, and Robert Dacres – were either regular privy councillors or designated 'ordinary' councillors, attending when required.[120] As such, they could be as attendant upon the king as the Requests judges of previous decades had been, though they were now more exclusively tasked with justice-giving. This shoring up of Requests' structures kept it partly itinerant with the king, ensuring that it not only survived but thrived through the final years of Henry VIII's reign.

The orders for renewed and expanded judiciaries just described tell us something about Requests' form but little about how it worked or to what end. A final, more detailed set of ordinances for the Court in our period, written in *c.* 1543 by Robert Dacres, another Master of Requests, is more illustrative on this front.[121] It confirms the impression that where this had once been a fluid and mobile tribunal, setting up shop in royal residences, local churches, or just on the roadside, it had by the 1540s become a more settled court, with an established space for its business and a defined judiciary to oversee it. One article in Dacres's list complains of the 'exclamacion or interuptions of any persons standing, or being present at the hearing[s]' of the Court, and ordered that they 'doe keepe silence' to allow the Council to work in peace. This stands as one of the only eyewitness accounts we possess for hearings in the White Hall, confirming that they were bustling, noisy, and contentious. Besides bringing more reverence to proceedings, Dacres' primary intention was to regularise the Court's business – for example, by affirming that it would only hear cases submitted by parties worth under a certain value per year (that is, *not* gentlemen, as we will see more later). As with any of the orders already discussed, we cannot rule out that Dacres was essentially putting into writing some conditions that had already existed for some time. Yet his laments about the 'great hinderaunce and delaie' to justice that he must

---

[120] Nicolas ed., *Proceedings and Ordinances of the Privy Council*, vol. VII, xviii–xix, 49, 60, 74, 77; Dasent et al. eds., *Acts of the Privy Council of England*, vol. I, 8–568.

[121] The dating of these orders derives from the title given to them in transcriptions taken by Caesar and later antiquarians, which describe them as being 'found in an old paper booke written by Robert Dacres esquier Mr of Requests anno Regni domini Regis 35': BL Additional MS 25248 fol. 29, BL Lansdowne MS 125 fol. 169. In the absence of the original we cannot be certain of this dating to 1543–4, but if it is accurate, since Dacres died in November 1543 the date can be narrowed down to between April and November that year.

'Travailing between the Prince and Petitioners' 91

have observed first-hand suggests otherwise.[122] The Court was still a work in progress by the end of our period, then; making extraordinary justice-giving more ordinary did not prove an easy task.

Conclusion

To the broader story of the evolution of governmental functions out of principles under the early Tudors, Requests lends a hitherto overlooked perspective. This Court challenges the traditional accounts of institutionalisa-tion in this period. A set of significant dates in Requests' development emerged in previous scholarship: the incidental references to a 'requests' provision from 1483 and 1485, the commencement of the books in 1493, the expansion of conciliar justice in 1518–20, and attempts at reorganisation in 1529 and 1538. Requests had reached independent courthood by 1547, cer-tainly, even if there was more work to be done. It could be autonomous even from its master, the king. Whereas it had suspended all activity during the uncertain months of Henry VIII's brief minority rule in 1509, its business was entirely unaffected by that king's death on 28 January 1547. In fact, its order books reveal that there was no break in its business at all, with the entries for the day of Henry VIII's death and the first ones for Edward VI's reign on 1 February appearing on the very same page.[123] But taking any established set of milestones in sequence implies a straightforward line of development and simplifies the more complex story of demand and litigation that will become apparent in the following chapters. An evolutionary narrative is not entirely without value. The emphasis on change over time serves as an important corrective to the static vision of an ancient 'Court of Requests' projected backwards from the 1590s by Caesar, at least. Yet a more comprehensive and direct examination of Requests and its ample surviving archive demonstrates that this tribunal neither remained an unchanging and unchallenged branch of the royal Council *nor* transformed into an institutionalised 'Court' through successive top-down reorganisations. Instead, Requests' development was more convoluted and sporadic than either of these models can fully capture.

Indeed, as more recent histories of the evolution of English government and the 'state' have suggested, these were 'actions without designs, patterns without blueprints'.[124] Crucially, and contrary to the traditional vision of

---

[122] BL Add. MS 25248 fols. 29–33. This was transcribed in the later sixteenth century by Julius Caesar and printed in Leadam ed., *Select Cases in the Court of Requests*, lxxxv–lxxxvii.

[123] REQ1/8 fols. 56–7; see also the fragments filed under REQ1/105, separate from the 1520s material, which seem to represent the book of Latin appearances kept by 1547: fols. 294–296v.

[124] Braddick, *State Formation*, 427.

92 The New Justice System

household governance as inefficient and obsolete, Requests' fluidity made it responsive to petitioners and effective in its judicial processes. It bridged the space between petitioners and their prince. Notwithstanding the refinements made to its judiciary and jurisdiction in the early decades of the sixteenth century, Requests' attachment to the king's 'honourable council' remained the core of its identity. Hence litigants, lawyers, commissioners, and even its own clerks gave it many names: still the 'counsaill attendaunt upon [the king's] personne for requestes' throughout this period; increasingly the 'court of the white hall' or, more precisely, the 'court of conscience in the white hall'; and only occasionally the 'Court of Requests', even by 1547.[125] It is, after all, worth remembering that, compared to 'Chancery', whose name pertained to its authorising administrative office, and 'Star Chamber', named for the specific space at Westminster, the 'Requests' epithet had a much wider application. The full name 'Court of Requests' was used in reference to at least two temporary tribunals headed by the mayor and aldermen of London in the early sixteenth century, to a forum for redress supposedly held at Protector Somerset's home in the late 1540s, and to over 360 local courts for small debt cases that were founded by statute in towns and cities across England from the early seventeenth century onwards.[126]

All of this denotes a sense of 'Requests', or the receipt of subjects' supplications, as a *function* of governance rather than simply as an institution of government. As much a manifestation of statecraft as a standard lawcourt, Requests was small but ideologically rich. It put into regular practice the prevailing notions about the king's natural good grace, merciful countenance, and peaceable temperament. Above all, it brought the monarch's responsibilities and obligations towards his subjects, and not his rights to take from them, into the foreground.[127] Requests offers a lens through which to examine how the expectations surrounding royal justice worked in practice for all involved, and how far they could be pushed. That is the story that the rest of this book takes up.

---

[125] See REQ3/15 *Cokkes v Pate*; REQ3/11/2 *Herd v Estwood and Sone*; REQ2/7/101.

[126] Thomas and Thornley eds., *The Great Chronicle of London*, 320; P. Tucker, *Law Courts and Lawyers in the City of London 1300–1550* (Cambridge University Press, 2007), 87, 117–18; LMA COL/AD/01/013 fol. 72, LMA COL/CA/01/01/010 fol. 137; M. L. Bush, 'Protector Somerset and Requests', *The Historical Journal* 17:3 (1974), 451; John Tidd Pratt, *An Abstract of all the printed Acts of Parliament for the establishment of Courts of Requests in England and Wales with the cases decided thereon* (London, 1824).

[127] A trend also identified in McGlynn, 'Idiots, Lunatics and the Royal Prerogative in Early Tudor England'.

PART II

Seeking and Requesting Justice

CHAPTER 4

Geography and Demography

The deeply held principle of justice as an ordering force emanating from a divinely ordained monarch was realised in the expanding circle of Tudor conciliar tribunals. The second part of this book explores their potential utility by taking up the perspective of their petitioners, at whose behest all judicial procedures in Requests were initiated. In the first place, examining the documents produced by these litigants – petitions and pleadings – provides an overview of this Court's geographical reach and demographic spread. Petitions commonly open with a declaration that the author 'sheweth and complaineth' as a loyal 'bedeman', 'subjecte', or 'orator' to their sovereign lord. The handful of descriptors that might follow included the plaintiff's full name, and some combination of their status, occupation, or place in a hierarchy of land- or office-holding ('husbandman', 'cord-wainer', 'prioress'), their hometown, and sometimes their place in a familial lineage ('cousin and heir of John Smith, son of John Smith ...'). The clarity and regularity of these statements mean that the origins of individual cases and the identities of principal parties can be feasibly drawn out from most of the 5,133 casefiles firmly dateable to the early Tudor period.[1] Comparison can also be made with equivalent information presented in single-court studies of Star Chamber and Chancery – that is, to the other central conciliar court emerging in this period, and to that conscience court most usually grouped with Requests.[2] Was this *the* 'poore manes Courte', as late sixteenth-century treatises on the English legal system claimed and modern scholarship has repeated?[3] In drawing together

---

[1] That is, the documents and files dateable to *c.* 1495–1547 in REQ2/1–13 and REQ3/1–30. There are no surviving bills predating 1495.

[2] Especially Haskett, 'The Medieval English Court of Chancery'; Stanford E. Lehmberg, 'Star Chamber: 1485–1509', *Huntington Library Quarterly* 24:3 (1961), 189–214; Guy, *The Cardinal's Court.*

[3] Sir Thomas Ridley, *A View of the civile and ecclesiastical law and wherein the practise of them is streitned, and may be relieved within this land* (London, 1607), 228–9; Alexander Fisher, 'A Description of the Cortes of Justice in England' (1576), in SP 12/110 fol. 34; Lambarde, *Archeion*, 118; Richard Robinson, 'A Briefe Collection of the Queenes Most High and Most

95

96 Seeking and Requesting Justice

such data, this chapter scrutinises the supposedly social dimension of Requests' jurisdiction, while setting out a statistical backdrop against which more individual stories of litigating to the Crown might be better understood.

Indeed, Part II as a whole advances a more sociopolitical analysis of royal justice, charting the movement of cases from English villages, towns, and cities to the extraordinary royal courts. Taking a positive view of litigation as a benevolent problem-solving exercise on the part of the Crown – as does much of the existing scholarship on petitioning and the state – the benefits for supplicants and the central government seem obvious. Yet an unfolding examination of the physical and economic costs of litigation, even for complainants, should encourage us to be cautious of such a glowing assessment. We should rather ask what would push anyone to go to such lengths to seek out royal justice. That means also mapping these findings onto the administrative history of Requests set out in the previous chapter. Did a shift from itinerancy with the royal household to settlement at Westminster make its facility to care for the poor less feasible or, conversely, more easily regulatable from the top down? As we will see, the answer depends on how poverty was delineated and defined, with reference to a range of material and social realities.

Counties of Origin

Almost all bills surviving in the Requests archive specify a county, town, village, or even a street to which a dispute pertains – sometimes the home of the petitioner, sometimes the location of disputed properties and wares, though fortunately for the analysis that follows these were often the same. Indeed, the majority of the surviving pleadings files from the early Tudor Requests concern localised cases, with one clear county of origin (this being the case for 4,023 out of the total 5,133 casefiles for this period). Mapping this information out, as in Figure 4.1, illustrates that Requests was a properly national court, with litigants hailing from almost all the English-ruled territories.

There are some identifiable trends within this broader picture. Certainly, Middlesex dominates: at least 432 individual cases dateable to this period were brought by petitioners from London and the surrounding countryside, and/or primarily concerned property in that region,

Honourable Courtes of Recordes', ed. R. L. Rickard, *Camden Miscellany* 20, Camden Third Series 83 (Royal Historical Society, 1953), 24.

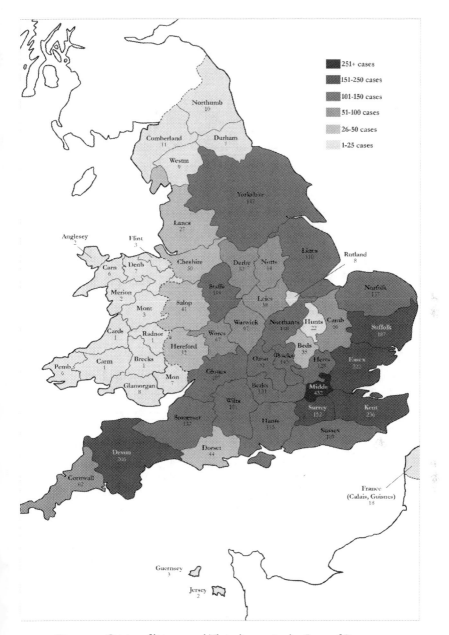

Figure 4.1 Origins of litigants and Their disputes in the Court of Requests, c. 1495–1547 (total: 4,023)[4]

[4] This number refers to the total number of casefiles that identify a *single* clear county of origin, suitable for mapping. The remaining 1,110 cases either have no identifiable place of origin at all – because they are fragmentary or contain only later pleadings – or, more occasionally, name several

representing almost 11 per cent of the total. This figure perhaps reflects Requests' usual location within the royal palaces somewhere in the Thames Valley. That said, the total number may be skewed somewhat by the much higher number of casefiles surviving from the later years of our period, *after* the Court had settled in the White Hall, at which point it presumably became particularly accessible to Middlesex-based litigants. The same explanation may apply to the home counties of Essex, Kent, Surrey, and Sussex, whose peoples benefitted from well-established routes to the capital (though Sussex could be harder to reach by road) and from Requests' circulation around the southern royal residences most years.

At the other end of the scale, it is hardly surprising that litigants from the small counties of Huntingdonshire and Rutland appear more occasionally in Requests, despite being in an otherwise well-served part of the country. Similarly, the distant counties of Cumberland, Northumberland, Westmorland, and Durham rarely show up in Requests' archives. Certain disputes in this part of the country were better suited to the growing equity jurisdictions of the exchequers of the Cheshire and Durham palatines, or to the palatinate Court or Duchy chamber of Lancaster, in the first instance. That any cases bypassed this route in favour of a suit to the Crown directly suggests that the hegemony of these tribunals was less total than was once thought – received down south no matter how much defendants dragged to Westminster might protest that their case lay within palatinate privilege.[5] Otherwise, we might suspect that subjects living closer to the Scottish border received more ready remedy from the powerful nobility in its marches, and were therefore spared the expense of a trip to the capital.

Disputants of the southern and midland counties of England certainly benefitted from the requisite social and physical connections for seeking out legal counsel and accessing the royal household. Yet proximity to Requests cannot have been the main determining factor in litigants' choice to sue there. After all, there are sixty-two files pertaining to Cornish litigants (1.5 per cent of the total) while the similarly distant counties of west Wales produced far fewer. Meanwhile, Yorkshire exceeded most of the southern counties in the number of petitions submitted to a tribunal that was almost always hundreds of miles away. The distribution of cases in Figure 4.1 generally maps onto population density, the socioeconomic

---

relevant counties. For discussion of those cases see below, Chapter 5, section 2: 'Relationships at Risk'.

[5] For a summary of these jurisdictions and their relationship to Westminster, see T. Thornton, 'Local Equity Jurisdictions in the Territories of the English Crown: The Palatinate of Chester, 1450–1540', in D. E. S. Dunn ed., *Courts, Counties and the Capital* (Sutton Publishing, 1996); REQ2/12/198.

Geography and Demography

condition of the realm, and the availability (or not) of other judicial authorities, too. These elements likely account for the prevalence of Devonshire litigants, who hailed from a county that had become populous and wealthy owing to its adaptable terrain and lucrative cloth industry. As a consequence of its prosperity, the county proved to have been a 'hotbed for lawsuits' and for lawyers in most jurisdictions across the early modern period, and so it contributed just over 5 per cent of cases to the early Tudor Requests.[6] Norfolk was notoriously litigious in the early modern period, as a result of its own role in the late-medieval wool trade, its encompassing of the country's second city, Norwich, and its healthy population of inn-trained lawyers.[7] A greater surprise in the data, perhaps, is the decent share of cases submitted from Lincolnshire, a large but isolated county that was only partially accessible from London by the Great North Road owing to its swathes of undrained fenlands. Ongoing drainage projects in the southern part of the county often instigated friction over land usage, and the region lacked a leading nobleman to act as mediator in the early Tudor period.[8] Such localised socioeconomic and political factors may explain Requests' relative popularity with this and other areas of the country.

Elsewhere, degrees of appetite for royal justice might also have shaped a region's relationship with Requests. The Council of the Marches seems to have had a strong hold on the subjects in its remit, going by the relatively low rate of twenty-five to fifty cases apiece from the belt of western counties, particularly Shropshire and Herefordshire, laying within its jurisdiction. A contrary case is provided by Yorkshire, its surprisingly high number of suits reflecting its great size, increasing wealth, and relatively large population of resident lawyers but also, perhaps, its growing demand for Crown remedies.[9] Not only was the intermittent royal Council in the North repeatedly called for by governors of the region, as we saw in Chapter 2. The steward of Kendal in Westmorland also complained of the many crafty litigants in his area who 'prosecute vex and sue to London suche poore men as bee not of substaunce to folowe theire right and causes' and who might be 'compelled by constraint of povertie to remyt and slak theire suetes and rightes at the pleasur of the appellant'.[10] Data from

---

[6] Brooks, *Pettyfoggers and Vipers*, 6, 33.

[7] *Ibid.*, 8, 113; C. Brooks, *Lawyers, Litigation and English Society Since 1450* (Hambledon Press, 1998), 21, 76.

[8] G. Dodd and A. K. McHardy eds., *Petitions from Lincolnshire c.1200–c.1500* (Lincoln Record Society, 2020), xliii–lvii. See also G. A. J. Hodgett, *Tudor Lincolnshire* (History of Lincolnshire Committee, 1975), 1–9.

[9] Brooks, *Pettyfoggers and Vipers*, 8, 113.   [10] SP1/69 fol. 323–4.

100 Seeking and Requesting Justice

Requests certainly undermines the notion that northern people could not or did not access central justice, whether in the absence of or alongside any conciliar body active there. On the contrary, and corroborating the steward of Kendal's grievance, it suggests that some parts of the Yorkshire population may have appreciated the potential vexatiousness of a suit lodged down south. As the pilgrims of 1536 complained, the practicalities of Westminster-based royal justice presented more problems for defendants summoned by writs of *sub poena* than for petitioners.[11] In essence, then, justice from the king himself was a recognised route for galvanising a dispute or ending it forever, even in regions otherwise served by provincial conciliar courts.

Similarly intriguing is the smaller number of litigants who apparently made their way from (or complained about) homelands in the further parts of the realm, a presence within Requests' archives that exemplifies the reach of royal justice. For the sake of analysis the Welsh cases have here been categorised according to the system of shires created by the 1535–6 'Act of Union'; before that time, the country was divided into the 'principality' in the west and the various marcher lordships around the border with England.[12] Not included in the mapped figures above are six additional cases that refer to origins and lands in just 'Wales' or 'South Wales'. In all, this makes fifty-four known casefiles concerning Welsh disputes, constituting 1.3 per cent of the total – more cases overall than some English counties, such as Bedfordshire (thirty-five cases/0.87 per cent). Coverage of the country was more uniform than we might expect, with thirty-five cases coming out of the marches and at least eighteen suits from the western reaches, including the peripheries of Pembroke and Anglesey. All these Welsh litigants sought extraordinary royal justice based on their (alleged) poverty and disadvantage but also, particularly in the marches, because the king's common-law writs held no authority over their opponents.[13]

Other disputants from further afield had a right to royal justice on the same basis. The combined five cases submitted from the Channel Islands reflect the early Tudor monarchy's ongoing concern for securing these territories against potential threats on the continent and, more generally, for severing any remaining constitutional connections with France. These isles also had their own dedicated receivers of petitions in the English Parliament, although this may have been more of an honorific role by the

---

[11] SP1/112 fol. 118.
[12] 27 Hen. VIII c. 26. The newly created counties were Denbighshire, Flintshire, Montgomeryshire, Radnorshire, Breconshire, Monmouthshire, Glamorganshire, and Pembrokeshire.
[13] See, for example, REQ2/4/28, 2/9/73.

Geography and Demography

early Tudor years. Nonetheless, as in Star Chamber and Chancery, in Requests it was possible for islanders to have their disputes about merchandise, debt, and property aired and remedied; at least one of the cases included here involved establishing customs of inheritance on Jersey.[14] Similarly, at a consistent rate across this period a trickle of cases came to Requests from the sliver of remaining English lands in France – primarily Calais and Guisnes. Some of these cases arose from moments of royal presence in the area, including the handful of suits against the Lieutenant of Guisnes submitted during Henry VII's visit there in spring 1500.[15] When Henry VIII went to France under less peaceful circumstances a decade or so later, he did not undertake justice-giving in situ, with Requests suspended until his return.[16] Regardless, the England-based Requests continued to occasionally receive cases about land and property and complaints about local officials in pale of Calais, often as an appellate jurisdiction following hearings and mediations made by its own authorities.

It is worth noting, too, that while litigants from the English pale in Ireland leave no trace within Requests' casefiles they *do* appear in the order books. Several Irish cases, all dating to the later years of Henry VII's reign, saw this committee determining the rights to ships seized in the port at Dublin and weighing up disputes over 'certain landes and tenements within the lordship or land of Irland'.[17] In at least one of these cases the defendants, two merchants from Dublin, had been bound to appear before the royal Council in England by Gerald Fitzgerald, eighth Earl of Kildare and the king's lieutenant in Ireland.[18] Since by the early sixteenth century the lordship of Ireland possessed its own system of common-law and equity courts under which this civil case might have been tried, Kildare was likely acting here more in his deputised capacity as governor than as justiciar in his own right – he had, he explained in a missive to Henry VII, imprisoned these defendants in Dublin Castle until they could find sureties to face their accusers, all merchants from Chester.[19] By itself this cross-jurisdictional

---

[14] REQ2/5/320. The other Channel Islands cases are REQ2/7/147, 2/8/250, REQ3/8 *Gangpam* v *Favor* and Favor, REQ3/23 *Morice* v *Cosyn*, REQ3/29/1 *Fashon* v *Grenefield*. On the judicial context, see T. Thornton, *The Channel Islands, 1370–1640: Between England and Normandy* (Boydell & Brewer, 2012), 62.

[15] REQ2/2/158.

[16] One bill submitted around this time has a note on the back suspending the case 'at the requeste of the complain[an]t whiche nowe ys appoynted to attende upon the kinges magiste over the see . . . unto the kinges retorne agayne': REQ3/25 *Morgan* v *Gilbanke*.

[17] REQ1/1 fol. 57v; REQ1/3 fols. 188v, 191, 193, 226.   [18] REQ1/3 fols. 194, 226.

[19] S. Ellis, *Reform and Revival: English Government in Ireland 1470–1534* (The Boydell Press, 1986), 106–64.

102   Seeking and Requesting Justice

suit does not, therefore, confirm the nature of Requests' remit in Ireland. But it does suggest that some (presumably English-born) plaintiffs living in the pale had the imagination and means to seek royal redress, while non-Irish defendants appealed to the reach of their king when trying property and people there.

What becomes apparent from this survey of litigation origins is that even in its earliest years people far and wide knew about this conciliar route for dispute resolution and understood how to access it. This, of course, has implications already for our understanding of Requests' clientele. It was not always the case that prospective petitioners travelled from faraway locales to the English court in search of justice. Certainly, in many cases a dispute and its principal parties *did* hail from specific, intimate communities, and subsequently relied on networks of people, communication, and travel to litigate. Yet many better-off or itinerant litigants likely had multiple homes and petitioned from one place about assets they claimed to hold elsewhere entirely. The eventual rulings of the king's Council on civil matters reached into all corners of the realm – but already caveats begin to emerge with regard to *whom* they could touch.

Litigants' Identities

Identifying litigants with any certainty from formulaic legal records is never a straightforward task. At common law, it had been a requirement that defendants' names be recorded alongside their 'Estate or Degree, or Mystery, and of the Towns or Hamlets, or Places and Counties, of which they were' on writs for personal actions since the early fifteenth century.[20] Elsewhere, in various ecclesiastical and civil courts, deponents called in to give testimony were asked to provide an estimation of their economic worth in moveable goods as a measure of their reliability, with the resulting data proving a goldmine for Alexandra Shepard's study on the distribution of wealth and cultural notions of status across the early modern period.[21] Real anxiety around the identity and credibility of the people called into court did not set in fully before the late sixteenth century, however. As such, the fragments of pleadings and perfunctory registers surviving for the new and emerging conciliar courts of the early Tudor period do not always offer us much besides the names of disputants. Still, self-identification in

[20] 1 Hen. V c. 5.
[21] A. Shepard, *Accounting for Oneself: Worth, Status and the Social Order in Early Modern England* (Oxford University Press, 2015).

Geography and Demography 103

the plaintiffs' own words frequently appears within their petitions. The volume of status and occupational labels – 'additions', to use the common-law terminology – appearing within Requests' early Tudor casefiles is not complete (only 1,700 plaintiffs are identified across the 5,133 relevant case-files), but it is enough to build up a rough statistical overview of this Court's complainants.

Petitioners also had the first opportunity to identify the people they complained against. For judicial proceedings to run smoothly, it was imperative that bills named all defendants precisely and fully, since only those clearly identified could be summoned to make answer. Whereas the plaintiff took great pains to set out their own background, and their right to whatever possession was in dispute, it often suited their narrative to treat the defendant as arriving entirely out of nowhere: to imply that everything was fine 'until such time that one John Smith' appeared on the scene and committed some offence. Defendants are therefore, by design, less fully realised than the protagonists of petitions. Still, complaints often supplied *some* status identifier and origin for defendants as well. In fact, much ink was spilled explaining the social disparities between the disputants in any given case, specifying the wealth, authority, or kinship of the accused party. Defendants themselves did not usually give any space in their formal answers to the Court to defining themselves in any way, instead attending to each accusation raised by the petitioner. So, to a certain extent, we must rely on petitioners' accounts of their own opponents.

Drawing together all the available social information about petitioners and defendants from the pleadings yields a rudimentary survey of who sued and was sued in Requests. In Table 4.1 the identifying terms present in its petitions have been arranged into categories that adhere to contemporary conceptions of the social order. These do not align with the simplistic 'three estates' model – of clergy, chivalry, and commonality – central to the period's theories of the commonwealth and body politic. Nor do they restrict us to the limited grouping of petitioners into ranks above or below that of 'gentleman' common to older surveys of common-law and equity tribunals.[22] Delineations between the better and poorer sorts fell along subtler lines, according to differences in livelihoods – especially between work with hands or with quills – as well as to possession of lands and moveable property, and to reliance on credit or on the charity of neigh-bours for survival. These stratifications were wrought into everyday life,

---

[22] Brooks, *Pettyfoggers and Vipers*, 61; Guy, *The Cardinal's Court*, 109; Stretton, *Women Waging Law*, 93.

Table 4.1 *Statuses of Plaintiffs and Defendants in the Court of Requests, c. 1495–1547*

	Plaintiffs (total: 1,700)		Defendants (total: 1,745)[23]	
	Number	*% of total*	Number	*% of total*
Civic and Administrative	60	*3.52*	208	*11.91*
Clergy	261	*15.35*	372	*21.31*
Crafts, Trades, and Services	389	*22.88*	282	*16.16*
Gentle Landed	156	*9.17*	572	*32.77*
Non-gentle Landed	214	*12.58*	116	*6.64*
Royal Servants	169	*9.94*	41	*2.34*
Professionals	26	*1.52*	49	*2.80*
Groups	72	*4.23*	15	*0.85*
Widows	345	*20.29*	90	*5.15*
Miscellaneous	8	*0.47*	0	*0*

even in the way people dressed and the food they consumed, and the most recent studies of contemporary social conceptions confirm that even the lower sorts were conscious of their status and possessed a complex vocabulary for describing it.[24] Many supplicants were therefore capable of defining themselves and their adversaries in petitions to their king.

Analysis of the social make-up of the Court's clientele must begin by recognising that litigation, here as elsewhere, was male dominated. Going by Christian names in petitions, around 20 per cent of all cases in this period were brought by female plaintiffs – some alone, some alongside other complainants to whom they were associated, related, or married. This overall figure compares quite favourably to Chancery in the late medieval and early Tudor period, where women made up 21 per cent of petitioners, and is higher than recent estimations of around 14 per cent of cases commenced by women in Star Chamber in the same period.[25] Whatever their numbers, the categorisation of women in society and at law was much narrower than that of men. Women were defined almost exclusively by their marital status or lack thereof; as either a spinster, a wife, or a widow, rather than by some occupation or trade, members of the

---

[23] Totals refer to numbers of individuals given identifiable status. Most litigants in the REQ2 casefiles (including 68 per cent of all plaintiffs) are not supplied any occupational or status label, as discussed in Chapter 6, section 2: 'The Substance of Petitioning'.

[24] Shepard, *Accounting for Oneself*; M. Hayward, *Rich Apparel: Clothing and the Law in Henry VIII's England* (Ashgate, 2009).

[25] Haskett, 'The Medieval English Court of Chancery', 286, 289; D. Youngs, '"A Besy Woman . . . and Full of Lawe": Female Litigants in Early Tudor Star Chamber', *JBS* 58:4 (2019), 740.

Geography and Demography 105

ecclesiastical hierarchy excepted. Consequently, in Table 4.1, a tabulation of litigants afforded some clear label of occupation or status (which, it should be reiterated, is less than half of all recorded clients of the Court in this period anyway), women are not given their own category. They do, nevertheless, make their mark in various ways across each of the others.

Most importantly, *not* reflected in the present dataset but significant in the broader picture of litigation patterns is the frequency with which women appeared as the 'wife of' the primary male plaintiff. This was true of about 14 per cent of all the cases in this study and – to put it another way – of around 60 per cent of the smaller number involving female petitioners. As Cordelia Beattie has recently described in reference to Chancery litigation, suits brought by husbands and wives often ultimately pursued the rights of the latter, the initiating petition taking up her voice – that of 'your oratrice' – as the protagonist to whom wrong had been done.[26] In the early Tudor Requests it was possible for a married woman to sue alone against individuals outside of her own household, with regard to lands, titles, and possessions to which she herself had some right. This was notwithstanding the prevalent common-law concept of 'covert baron' or coverture, which dictated that a married woman's identity and capacity to sue at law were subsumed into that of her husband. Generally this was a notional doctrine and not necessarily followed in the early equity tribunals – detached as they were from the letter of the law – especially where married women could make excuses for their husbands' absence.[27] For example, in 1517 one Margaret Burton litigated as the sole plaintiff in a case in Requests over ejection from her house expressly because her husband, a citizen and draper of London, was 'beyond the sea'.[28] Much later in Henry VIII's reign, Elizabeth Poncherton petitioned the Court about the loss of her house in Westminster while her husband was stationed in Boulogne in the king's service.[29] These married women had recourse to Requests as principal petitioners, but only under exceptional circumstances.

Turning back to the data tabulated in Table 4.1, it is immediately apparent that women referred to as widowed were prevalent in Requests. After wives, they make up around 6 per cent of the total female clientele of the Court. More importantly, widows represented a fifth of *all* the Court's 1,700 plaintiffs given identifying labels in this period, and the second-largest social category overall. Their apparent prevalence may reflect the

---

[26] C. Beattie, 'Your Oratrice: Women's Petitions to the Late Medieval Court of Chancery' in B. Kane and F. Williamson eds., *Women, Agency and the Law, 1300–1700* (Routledge, 2013), 17–29.
[27] See the discussion of this doctrine and practice in Stretton, *Women Waging Law*, 129–35.
[28] REQ2/6/190. [29] REQ3/16/2 *Poncherton v Davy*.

106   Seeking and Requesting Justice

very ubiquity of the term 'widow' in social and legal contexts as much as anything else, but we will explore their roles and motivations as litigants here in the coming chapters. A small number of women otherwise fall into the 'Miscellaneous' category in the table above, being described in terms that tell us little about their social status but something of their marital relations: including several 'maidens' and two women described as a 'spinster' and 'single woman', respectively.

All the other categories in Table 4.1 are largely comprised largely of men positioned within hierarchies and occupations which were relatively distinct from one another, if not altogether mutually exclusive: primarily those of the Church, the rural landed elite, and the urban trades. Contemporary assessments of subjects' wealth undertaken in advance of subsidies and the *self*-assessments offered by witnesses in church courts give us some means by which to establish rough economic parameters for these categories and their members, of use in our inquiry into the relative accessibility of royal justice.[30] The most predominant category in the dataset here is that containing disputants in 'Crafts, Trades, and Services', who typically lived and worked in England's growing towns and cities. This diverse group contains men attached to over seventy different occupations: mostly textile workers, such as drapers, tailors, and weavers, as well as fishermen and fishmongers, goldsmiths and ironmongers, and stationers and scriveners. Although none appear within the Requests data, women were engaged in these crafts, too; several suits in which widows and wives disputed the possession of brewhouses and their implements indicate their work in that industry, with one case from 1546 involving Dyonise Duffen of Winchester petitioning for her right to fulfil a commission directed to her to 'brewe for [the king's] Armye and flete' at Portsmouth.[31] Even without women represented among the figures here, this is the most diverse of all the occupational categories discernible in Requests, its sheer scope explaining its prevalence.

This diversity produced considerable variations in worth and status among the men of this category. Some were highly skilled artisans, while others were local traders; some had livery status, and belonged to lucrative and protective urban guilds, while others were unincorporated. Julian Cornwall's 'working model' of personal wealth distribution, modelled from taxation records of the

---

[30] The studies of society and wealth referred to in the following discussion are: J. C. K. Cornwall, *Wealth and Society in Early Sixteenth Century England* (Routledge & Kegan Paul, 1988); Shepard, *Accounting for Oneself.*

[31] REQ2/6/231. See also REQ3/14 *Smith* v *Porchion*, REQ3/15 *Perpoynt* v *Foxley*, REQ3/15 *Rede* v *Stockwood.*

Geography and Demography 107

early 1520s, found craftsmen and merchants at every level, from artificers assessed at £1 and under in goods and lands up to overseas traders at £100 or more.[32] Elsewhere, self-estimations of worth in goods expressed before church courts in the mid-sixteenth century suggest that maltmen and brewers existed at the poorer end of the scale of craftsmen, members of the booming textile trade were more middling, and innholders were among the wealthiest.[33] Yet it was the tradesmen, including merchants or mercers of all types, who represented the single most prominent occupation in this category appearing in Requests (with forty-five in total here). Some no doubt belonged to the richest urban companies of the time; they were, after all, followed closely in numbers by the tailors, grocers, and drapers who supplied them. But we also find more humble, rural traders such as chapmen and cattle drivers among the ranks represented in Requests. The petitioner James Acoyte of Farnell in Yorkshire was referred to as a 'chapman', a travelling trader, and also identified by the Court's judges and clerks as a 'pauper'.[34] This great economic range notwithstanding, this was a quarter of society that was in the ascendancy; by the late fifteenth century certain craftsmen and traders were on par with the lower landed gentry.[35] As such, men of this broad category appear in substantial numbers on both sides of Requests' disputes, though they were more likely to sue than to be sued. Much of the litigation involving members of this category was internal, so to speak, with craftsmen often complaining about the failure of their merchant suppliers to uphold sales of the materials they needed for their craft. The same merchants and artisans could find themselves in dispute with a much wider range of people – widows, clergymen, civic administrators – for defaults in providing services or keeping agreements.

Also featuring prominently in Requests as petitioners and as defendants was the clergy. This includes people titled as archbishops and bishops, abbots and abbesses, deans, deacons, and priests, canons and chaplains, parsons, vicars, and rectors. It also includes members of monastic orders: priors, prioresses, monks, and even a couple of hermits. Some of these labels were more definitive than others. In the lower ecclesiastical orders terms of description could be interchangeable, and the same person might be described as a clerk (or '*clericus*', in the Latin), a parson, and a chaplain in one document.[36] Others are immediately recognisable: the bishops of Norwich, Chichester, and London – Richard Nix, Richard Sampson, and

---

[32] Cornwall, *Wealth and Society*, 16–17, 29–30.   [33] Shepard, *Accounting for Oneself*, 68–9, 73–4.
[34] REQ2/7/148.
[35] C. Dyer, *Standards of Living in the Later Middle Ages: Social Change in England c.1200–1520* (Cambridge University Press, 1989), 20; Shepard, *Accounting for Oneself*, 102–3.
[36] As in REQ2/13/26.

108   Seeking and Requesting Justice

Edmund Bonner, all royal councillors and sometime judges in Requests –
brought cases in 1506, 1537, and 1541, respectively.[37] In numerical terms
those at the top of the ecclesiastical hierarchy – the archbishops and
bishops – acted almost exclusively as defendants, usually accused by
complainants of lower social or clerical rank in matters concerning grants
of offices and benefices. More middling figures, the priors and abbots, and
the lowlier priests appeared in similar proportions on either side of the
court, pursuing and defending rights to lands.

Attention solely to titles and hierarchies gives the illusion of stasis in an
arm of English government that underwent significant change in our
period, however. On the cusp of the rapid destruction of the Church's
authority under Henry VIII, the valuations of England's religious foundations in the *Valor Ecclesiasticus* of 1534–5 furnishes more precise information about the standards of living for some of the monastic petitioners
to Requests (assuming that they litigated in the name of their houses and
so not on the basis of any temporalities). By this measure, the poorest
prior to appear in Requests was that of Penwortham in Lancashire, who
petitioned for his right to eight acres of moorland in 1504 and whose
house was valued at £29 in temporalities thirty years later. Still, even he
may have been more stable than William Alston, the Prior of Canwell,
a house dissolved in the first wave of the dissolution to fund Wolsey's
Cardinal College, when it was worth only £15 in temporalities and its
buildings were decaying. On a commission writ issued from Requests for
Alston's case in 1516, it was noted that he was 'the porist prior of
Englond'.[38] On the other end of the scale, the Prior of Lewes, whose
case appeared before Requests in 1505, oversaw an estate eventually worth
£920 per annum.[39] Overall, the average institutional value represented by
petitioning priors was £292, and £142 for prioresses. This kind of money
surely put the costs of litigation on behalf of benefices and houses well
within reach, making the numbers of even the lower clergy here unsurprising. One caveat to this conclusion, posited by Haskett of the equivalent Chancery data, is that churchmen were more likely than most to
offer or be given definitive description, and that they may therefore be
over-represented in legal records; the same has been observed of last wills,
in which clergy stated their occupation more regularly than other

---

[37] REQ1/3 fol. 234; Caesar, *The Ancient State*, 91; REQ3/8 *Bonner v Smyth*.
[38] W. Dugdale, *Monasticon Anglicanum* (London, 1846), vol. IV, 108–9; REQ3/7 *Prior of Canwell v Aston*.
[39] REQ1/3 fols. 133, 213v; *Valor Ecclesiasticus Temp. Henr. VIII Auctoritate Regia Institutus* (London, 1810–34), vol. I, 332, vol. V, 233.

Geography and Demography 109

testators.[40] Yet their position as major landholders in England before the Reformation accounts both for their use of Crown litigation to affirm their rights and dues *and* for the number of allegations raised against them on the same grounds.

Conversely, it may surprise us that there were so many lay petitioners of 'landed status' in a tribunal supposedly reserved for poor suitors. Altogether they comprise around 21 per cent of the total number of identified petitioners, though this group is socially broad enough that it has been split into those of gentle (9 per cent) and non-gentle (12 per cent) ranks. The former includes members of the nobility: those entitled as earls, dames, ladies, lords, viscounts, and countesses. As historians have already pointed out in qualification of Requests' jurisdiction over the poor, some of its litigants sat within the upper echelons of society.[41] Margaret Beaufort herself was plaintiff in a suit in 1496, according to one entry in the order books.[42] Cases were also presented and pursued by Margaret Pole (Countess of Salisbury) and her aunt, Elizabeth de la Pole (Duchess of Suffolk), both Plantagenet descendants.[43] At the time of petitioning, all three of these aristocratic women were widows, a position acceptably vulnerable enough to potentially justify suit to the king regardless of their wealth. The recourse of any such high-ranking individuals to this attendant conciliar court may also have overlapped with its convenience for members of the royal household, as is examined below. Nonetheless, the presence of particularly elite plaintiffs tailed off after the end of Henry VII's reign, while their prevalence as defendants – at a rate three times higher than their proportion as petitioners and as the largest category of accused parties overall – was consistent across our period.

Otherwise, by far the most numerous individuals among the 'gentle landed' petitioners were men referred to as 'knights' and as 'gentlemen'. As social categorisations these were both notoriously vague, with evident points of economic overlap. The term 'gentleman' was assumed by a range of individuals, including professionals such as lawyers as well as those of gentle birth more generally. It therefore encapsulates a wide wealth distribution. In the lead-up to the early 1520s subsidies, the term was applied to men assessed at values ranging from £3 up to £100 and over, varying by region and levels of personal indebtedness.[44] The rank of

---

[40] Haskett, 'The Medieval English Court of Chancery', 291–2; Hayward, *Rich Apparel*, 58–60.
[41] See, for example, J. F. Baldwin, *The King's Council in England during the Middle Ages* (Clarendon Press, 1913), 444.
[42] REQ1/1 fol. 167.   [43] Caesar, *The Ancient State*, 52; REQ2/3/195.
[44] Cornwall, *Wealth and Society*, 16–17, 20–1.

110   Seeking and Requesting Justice

knighthood was more defined, claimable once a man reached an annual
income of £40 in lands or rents.[45] In fact, by the 1520s most knights were
assessed, in total, to be worth £100 or more.[46] This widening gap could
have left Requests more open to the lower gentry than we might have
expected. Certainly, at one point in 1517 the Requests judges referred to
a plaintiff 'possessed of landes and tenements to the yerely value of xl li' as
a 'gent', on which basis he was remitted to the common law.[47] An upper
limit set for petitioners' wealth as measured in lands, goods, and chattels
within Dacres's orders of *c.* 1543 – unfortunately left blank in surviving
copies, but most likely the common benchmark of £40 – was designed to
clear space for 'poore mens causes'.[48] Yet according to the values just cited
it would not necessarily have affected all those identifiable as 'gentlemen',
who even by the middle of the sixteenth century might themselves claim
a yearly worth – in goods, at least – more within the region of £20 to £24
when called as deponents to the church courts.[49] In other words, litigation
in the Requests committee was reasonably extended to those on the lower
end of this category throughout this period.

Although we might presume that a relative shortage of moveable wealth
and ready money negatively affected *non-*gentle landed people and their
access to justice, the data in Table 4.1 suggests otherwise. In fact, litigants of
this type sought out Requests more often than their gentle counterparts.
Both of the main descriptors in this category, 'husbandman' and 'yeoman',
referred traditionally to those holding small estates of land and with some
involvement in agricultural production. According to the sumptuary legislation of the early sixteenth century, 'husbandman' pertained to the
poorest sort of landholder, typically possessing goods below the value of
£10.[50] 'Yeoman', meanwhile, emerged in this period as a term referring to
a more affluent sort of husbandman, essentially, though might also have
been associated more closely with service. In traditional stratifications,
yeomen fitted in just above husbandmen but below the landed gentry, as
freeholders with perhaps no more than 80 acres of lands, goods worth
somewhere in the region of £6 to £15 (according to their own estimations),
and an overall income anywhere in the range of £10 to £99.[51] The potential

[45] H. Leonard, 'Knights and Knighthood in Tudor England' (unpublished PhD thesis, Queen Mary
    University of London, 1970), 43, 138.
[46] Cornwall, *Wealth and Society*, 16, 21.   [47] REQ2/3/137.   [48] BL Add. MS 25248 fol. 30.
[49] Shepard, *Accounting for Oneself*, 69.
[50] 1 Hen. VIII c. 14. This was supported by Shepard's analysis, which found that husbandmen
    estimated their worth to range from £3.62 to £8.03 per year in goods in the mid to late sixteenth
    century: *Accounting for Oneself*, 69, 74, 102; Hayward, *Rich Apparel*, 213.
[51] Shepard, *Accounting for Oneself*, 74; Cornwall, *Wealth and Society*, 16.

Geography and Demography

for these individuals to farm and lease large swathes of land and live off rents and profits complicates their classification among the 'peasantry', and so some historians have grouped them, along with better-off labourers, into the emerging 'middling sort' of the early sixteenth century instead.[52] Some such men appearing before Requests were likely more impoverished than such a categorisation would have us believe, however; a couple of husbandmen were identified as 'paupers' in annotations made by the Court's judges on their petitions.[53] Husbandmen also typically sued other, neighbouring husbandmen, and only sometimes those of marginally greater status than themselves, such as yeomen, squires, gentlemen, and local clergy – that is, not their greater lords. Yeomen, meanwhile, were more preoccupied with suing those slightly outranking them in the rural hierarchy – abbots, gentlemen, and knights – or the merchants, craftsmen, and fellow yeomen with whom they had dealings.

There are other groups with a smaller presence in Requests, perhaps owing to the imprecision and non-exclusivity of the descriptors therein contained for the people who used them. 'Civic and Administrative' comprises a variety of urban and rural officials: mayors and aldermen, bailiffs and stewards, escheators and rent collectors, churchwardens and parkers. Such positions were usually temporary, held for a certain term that might last no longer than a year or so, and therefore hardly represent the whole definition of the men to whom they were attributed. 'Professionals' includes any person identified by their education: mostly medical doctors and members of the legal profession, ranging from public notaries and attorneys to serjeants-at-law and justices. They appeared in roughly equal proportions on either side of the Court's clientele, though among the professional defendants we find more elite office holders such as university vice chancellors and the justices of the common-law benches. Litigants in both these categories were mostly occupied in urban locales, and they turned up in Requests in matters related to their offices and occupations: as petitioners, with complaints related to the privileges of their positions; as defendants, where they were generally more prevalent, to abuses of their authority.

A more itinerant group, and one more unique to Requests, were the royal servants who make up just under 10 per cent of its identifiable petitioners. This includes everyone from the below-stairs servants and officers of the Great Hall, pantry, kitchen, confectionary, and bakehouse

---

[52] Dyer, *Standards of Living in the Later Middle Ages*, 22–3; Hayward, *Rich Apparel*, 213–21.
[53] REQ2/5/58, 2/12/155.

to the gentlemen, yeomen, grooms, and pages of the king's private chambers. Their suits were similar in nature to those brought by all other types of plaintiff, concerning possession of lands and goods rather than their employment within the household. Since they worked in constant proximity to the king, they were usually unable to conveniently access justice at Westminster or elsewhere, particularly in the far-flung locale of their disputed properties. An especially vivid example is the plea of John Wrey, a gentleman of the ewery in Catherine of Aragon's household, who insisted that 'for fere of the plaag of pestilence that now reigneth in diverse parties of this yor royme', referring to the outbreak of 1517–18, he 'dare [not] goo a brode to pursue for his right by due course of yor comon lawes'.[54] Occasionally featured in this category too are royal councillors and even judges in the Court of Requests itself, who were apparently – without much internal consternation – permitted to sue before their colleagues. The councillor Sir Henry Wyatt, sometimes judge and bill signatory in Requests in the reigns of both Henry VII and Henry VIII, petitioned Requests because he 'in noo wise canne be absent' from court, and his matter was duly heard in 1522.[55] The same courtesy had been extended in 1506 to the active judge and common lawyer Richard Sutton, whose complaints were heard in the very same week that he was himself determining cases in Requests – despite the objection of his opponent that 'the said Richard is oon of the jugges in this Courte' and so it was 'nott resonable' for the case to proceed.[56] The understanding that Requests had a jurisdiction over royal servants was so prevalent that in one case a defendant tried to have himself dismissed on the basis that his accuser was 'nott servant to our suffren lorde the kyng' and so had no right to sue in this forum.[57] Perhaps Requests was here being confused with the Court of the Verge, which more closely meets this description.[58]

Overall, this focus on 'additions' confirms that a great swathe of people engaged with Requests, even if they can only tell us so much about them individually. Many descriptors are socially levelling. 'Widow', for example, may be the single most common term applied to any person in Requests but it yields little insight into the wealth or status of a woman so-called in the absence of any additional contextual information. Within the Requests records, 'widow' encompasses women who otherwise belonged to the

---

[54] REQ3/20 *Wrey* v *Nele*.   [55] REQ3/15 *Wyatt* v *Mercer*; REQ3/22 fol. 302.

[56] REQ3/30 *Sutton* v *Delves and Cudworth*; REQ1/3 fols. 230v, 240, 241v.

[57] REQ3/20 *More* v *Woodcock*.

[58] W. R. Jones, 'The Court of the Verge: The Jurisdiction of the Steward and Marshal of the Household in Later Medieval England', *JBS* 10:1 (1970), 1–29.

Geography and Demography

gentry, including Dame Jane Kidwelly, the widow of the prominent lawyer Sir Morgan Kidwelly, but also Joan Tolby, who was recognised by the Court's judges as *'paupericula'*.[59] Any such descriptor should not be taken as mutually exclusive, either; just as an ennobled woman with ample estates could also describe herself as a widow, so a man entitled as 'Sir' and holding the rank of knighthood might also be a royal servant with an official position in the household, and a seemingly humble draper from the capital city might also be an alderman and a prominent figure in his trade's guild with the landholdings of a yeoman or husbandman. Moreover, even where some sense of social hierarchy comes into play there are clear overlaps between categories. Wealthier churchmen had enough land and authority to be equivalent to lay lords, while the boundary between the 'peasantry' and the lower gentry is hardly fixed. In fact, all descriptors evoked before the law depended on the circumstances of a given case and reflect numerous coterminous, flexible social hierarchies rather than any single, static order.

A Poor Man's Court?

Were the true poor unrepresented in Requests? A few people who identified as servants on estates and in households emerge from its archives, and are included in the 'Crafts, Trades, and Services' category in Table 4.1. Twenty men in this group described themselves as labourers, though the nature of their labour is unclear. Most of their complaints pertained to their rights as tenants in houses or farms, though Harry Yolond went into greater detail, describing himself as a 'powre yong man ... havyng and yernyng always hys levyng by hys due labor as yn husbandrye and jorney laborer ... from the tyme of hys berth ... havyng no other handy crafte or scyens to leffe apon', with an alleged assault that had broken his arm keeping him from his crucial 'dayly labor'.[60] Still, another petitioner confused matters by defining himself as both a yeoman *and* a labourer in the same complaint – again demonstrating the instability of such categorisations.[61] More often, the poorer sorts appear among capacious collectives of petitioners referring to themselves only as 'inhabitants', 'tenants', or 'parishioners' of a village or parish, who make up the 'Groups' category in Table 4.1 and 4 per cent of all plaintiffs in this period. Such groups only occasionally identified their members or estimated their number; for their statuses we must rely instead on the

---

[59] REQ1/3 fol. 274; REQ3/6 *Tolby* v *Knighte*.   [60] REQ3/21 *Yolond* v *Sturre*.
[61] REQ3/7 *Rylands* v *Portwood*.

114   Seeking and Requesting Justice

impressions of the Court and its delegates. In 1517, the inhabitants of Nether Shuckburgh in Warwickshire were perceived by Requests' judges to be truly poor when they petitioned about their rights to common lands, as the annotation of '*paup[eres]*' on their petition indicates.[62] An even more colourful example of the same identification appears within the suit of one Richard Lacey and other inhabitants of the small parish of Abbotsham, Devonshire, against the Abbot of Tavistock, concerning their duty to set up butts for the regular practising of longbow shooting. The commissioners appointed to investigate the matter reported that these inhabitants were so 'undon in this worlde' that they had 'borowyde of the store of ther church vj li' to pay for their litigation; perhaps similar collaborative petitions were paid for with loans of this kind, or else through common purses.[63]

Very occasionally a plaintiff's status as a free man came into contention in Requests, and it is here that we probably see the greatest social depths reached by royal justice. The suit brought by men of the Snelgare family of Cranborne Chase in Wiltshire rested on the assertion by John Mounpesson, a local gentleman, that they were 'bonde of blodde' to him and his manor and ought of right to be put to 'streit and hard prison'. This was a label the Snelgares strongly protested, referring to themselves instead as husbandmen.[64] Later in Henry VIII's reign, John Burde and his son alleged that their goods had been seized on the basis that they were classed as 'villein regardant' to the manor of Holne in Devon, in the keeping of the Earl of Bath.[65] Although villeins or bondsmen were less easily ejected than a copyholder and are known to have litigated widely outside their manor, they were unlikely to have been able to amass the resources required to sue against their lords. Hence villeinage was, according to one commentator in 1523, 'the grettest inconvenience that nowe is suffred by the lawe'.[66] The Burdes contested their status, but Requests eventually found that they had shown nothing convincing 'for triall of theyr libertie', even in two years of pleading.[67] Still, that these cases were entertained at all suggests that even those in bondage could reach royal justice somehow, and that the Court was willing to scrutinise these social conditions.

---

[62] REQ2/8/339.   [63] REQ3/16/1 *Lacey v Abbot of Tavistock.*   [64] REQ2/4/327.
[65] REQ2/3/338, 2/5/145.
[66] John Fitzherbert, *Here begynneth a ryght frutefull mater: and hath to name the boke of surueyeng and improumentes* (London, 1523), fol. 26v; C. Briggs, 'Seigniorial Control of Villagers' Litigation beyond the Manor in Later Medieval England', *Historical Research* 81:213 (2008), 399–422.
[67] REQ3/14 fol. 274.

Geography and Demography 115

That Requests supplies so many 'additions' gives us some measure by which to compare the conciliar courts emerging in this period, and to ascertain whether Requests was *the* 'poor man's court', even if only relatively. Haskett's survey of around 8,000 casefiles from the late-medieval Court of Chancery confirmed the prevalence there of what he referred to as the 'middling' sorts. 'Lay rank' individuals of the gentry, especially esquires, knights, and gentlemen, were among the most common petitioners, at a substantial 48 per cent of the total identified, with clergymen trailing behind at 28 per cent, and 'Trades', particularly merchants and mercers (as in Requests), at 21 per cent.[68] Guy's analysis of Star Chamber plaintiffs and defendants in the years of Wolsey's tenure as Lord Chancellor (1515–29) found that the largest groups of petitioners were of the rank of 'gentleman and above', at 28.7 per cent of the total, followed closely by yeomen and husbandmen at 25 per cent combined. The clergy were also quite prominent, coming in at 17 per cent of petitioners in Wolsey's Star Chamber. This is slightly higher than the number in Requests for the longer period (15 per cent), though Guy implied that the ecclesiastics in Star Chamber were higher ranking. Guy concluded of Star Chamber that 'the principals to litigation were almost invariably gentlemen, beneficed clergy, officials, merchants, or prosperous yeomen and husbandmen'; indeed, the same ranks appeared in near identical proportions as defendants, too, giving the impression of this as a court where the gentle and middling classes sued one another.[69] Meanwhile, Haskett observed that Chancery largely served 'esquires, knights, merchants, clerks, mayors and bailiffs ... the middle ranks of English society'.[70] On another note, Guy's analysis did not touch on gender, but Haskett found that widows made up 'fully 95 percent' of women given social description, reflecting the similar dominance of that label in Requests and in society at large.[71]

The overall impression, then, is that these three tribunals entertained a similar spread of litigants, men and women, but in different proportions. Comparatively speaking, Requests *did* offer a forum through which those at the lower end of the social spectrum might sue their equals or their betters. Even before its clientele was properly regulated, it lacked the kind of 'upper echelon' of elite plaintiffs so evident in Chancery and Star Chamber. Moreover, its litigant base trended towards the humbler end of most of the categories it shared with these fellow royal courts.

---

[68] Haskett, 'The Medieval English Court of Chancery', 290–1.
[69] Guy, *The Cardinal's Court*, 109.
[70] Haskett, 'The Medieval English Court of Chancery', 290–1.   [71] Ibid., 289.

Conclusion

This social and geographical analysis of the early Tudor Requests tells us a few things about royal justice that we may have presumed but could not hitherto prove. The most obvious conclusion is that this provision reflected the sort of diversity appropriate for a 'national' system of courts. Requests, at least, received complaints from all over England and from other territories governed by the English Crown. It entertained litigation from the country's 'porest prior' as from the king's own mother, but in general it served a humbler sort of litigant than its fellow conciliar and central courts – even if the very *poorest* members of society are visible in only a handful of cases. Having used the Court's rich archive to establish its social reach in a statistical sense, the same material can help us to reconstruct how it worked, whom it benefitted, and what sort of justice it instituted. Moreover, the general impression of its early Tudor clientele set out here must now be qualified with more specific, qualitative readings of petitioners' pleadings. In particular, with more information about the costs and resources required to access Requests in hand, we will see that the precise make-up of its litigant base changed over the course of the early sixteenth century, particularly as the Court settled down. And so, in the remaining two chapters of Part II, we will investigate the full breadth of Requests procedures and litigants' experiences as a case was pursued, from the eruption of dispute to the creation of a petition.

CHAPTER 5

Disputes and Dispute Resolution

If petitioning for justice functioned as a means by which 'the governed played a role in their own governance', we must ask what sort of governance the diverse array of supplicants to the early Tudor kings wanted.[1] Investigating how and why litigants ended up seeking royal justice starts from a recognition of near-universal proficiency with the law, its personnel, and its mechanisms in late medieval England. Research has shown that 'women and poorer villagers' were involved in processes of information gathering for manorial courts; that husbandmen, labourers, merchants, and craftsmen routinely served as presentment jurors in all kinds of local tribunals; and that a considerable cross-section of early modern society – right down to those relying on charity to get by – were called in as witnesses to ecclesiastical and civil courts.[2] Elsewhere, records of litigation reveal the more subtle means by which 'law-mindedness' was inculcated in the intimate environs of the local community, where dispute resolution was undertaken in the 'shadow of the law' even if in a non-curial setting.[3] With all of this in mind, the consensus of much recent social, anthropological, and gender-studies work in this field is that the larger part of society did not simply *experience* law as a force imposed from on high. Rather, they *engaged* and even *negotiated* with legal and extra-legal structures – and the governors who ran them – on

[1] Shagan, *Popular Politics and the English Reformation*, 19.
[2] Johnson, *Law in Common*, 29; M. K. McIntosh, 'Finding a Language for Misconduct: Jurors in Fifteenth Century Local Courts', in B. A. Hanawalt and D. Wallace eds., *Bodies and Disciplines: Intersections of Literature and History in Fifteenth-Century England* (University of Minnesota Press, 1996); Shepard, *Accounting for Oneself*.
[3] J. Walter, '"Law-Mindedness": Crowds, Courts and Popular Knowledge of the Law in Early Modern England', in M. Lobban, J. Begiato, and A. Green eds., *Law, Lawyers and Litigants in Early Modern England* (Cambridge University Press, 2019), 171–8; A. Musson and E. Powell eds., *Crime, Law and Society in the Later Middle Ages* (Manchester University Press, 2009), 53–66; D. Birch, 'Legal Pluralism in Early Modern England and Colonial Virginia', *Revista Estudos Institucionais* 5:2 (2019), 717–46.

118   Seeking and Requesting Justice

a regular basis.[4] For many of the litigants described in the previous chapter, seeking justice was therefore a habitual and calculated activity.

This chapter bridges the gap between the localities in which disputes erupted and the royal palaces in which they were presented. With no limit on the length of petitions under the generous English bill procedure, plaintiffs had ample space to narrativise their cases. The subject of any given suit – 'the specific thing at the centre of the matter', like a parcel of land – was always indicated within the first few sentences of a petition.[5] Yet petitioners framed such specific demands with a whole host of actions and circumstances that constituted a general call for Crown intervention into their lives. Here breaches in harmonious relations between neighbours, friends, family members, and business partners took centre stage, rather than specific transgressions of law. Moreover, in justifying their recourse to the king for aid, many litigants provided lengthy descriptions of earlier attempts at dispute resolution in various local, rural, and urban courts, and in a mixture of informal and institutionalised forums. Echoing contemporary grievances about the inaccessibility of justice, as observed in Chapter 1, petitions to Requests emphasised the barriers to gaining a fair trial against strong opponents and the need for the unblemished and impartial justice of their sovereign lord. A survey of the business entertained in Requests continues our study of its jurisdictional parameters (or lack thereof). The broader narratives of injustice expressed here also encourage us to envisage royal litigation as just one part of a reflexive process within the lives of ordinary subjects – one that neither started nor ended with the king.

Subjects in Variance

What sorts of disputes were pressing enough to push people towards royal justice? The most serious issues raised by Requests' petitioners were those involving outright acts of violence that had infringed upon health and livelihood. This was an age in which swords, bows, and all manner of armaments for war were stored locally for the training of a community's

---

[4] See the introductions to E. W. Ives and A. H. Manchester eds., *Law, Litigants and the Legal Profession* (Royal Historical Society, 1983); B. Kane and F. Williamson eds., *Women, Agency, and the Law, 1300–1700* (Pickering & Chatto, 2013); A. Shepard and T. Stretton, 'Women Negotiating the Boundaries of Justice in Britain, 1300–1700: An Introduction', *JBS* 58:4 (2019), 677–83. We might also think of litigants as 'consumers': see D. L. Smail, *The Consumption of Justice: Emotions, Publicity and Legal Culture in Marseille, 1264–1423* (Cornell University Press, 2013).

[5] Haskett, 'The Medieval English Court of Chancery', 291–2.

Disputes and Dispute Resolution 119

young men, while tools for agricultural work in the countryside – staves, staffs, axes, and pitchforks – could be fashioned as weapons. It may surprise us, then, that physical injuries ranging from assault, rape, and imprisonment to armed riots were the principal issue in only around 2 per cent of Requests' early Tudor cases. They certainly make for some of the more colourful and urgent cases in this archive, nevertheless. For example, in the very early years of Henry VIII's reign, it was claimed before the Requests committee that Robert Worsley, a yeoman, had met with a labourer called Roger Heritage as he was coming home from ploughing his fields in Kineton, Warwickshire, when Roger 'sodenly caste an hachate [hatchet] at yor said orator [Robert] and with the same hym felled to the grownde', leaving him for dead.[6] This account reads as an entirely random act of violence, which was certainly true in some cases: for instance, in Agnes Hatfield's claim that her young son, Thomas, had his arm accidentally broken during a fight between two other men while he sat behind one of them on horseback.[7] Sometimes, however, pre-existing animosity between warring parties are hinted at within pleadings. When called to answer to Robert Worsley's allegation, Roger Heritage did not deny that an assault had taken place, but claimed that Robert himself had started it by saying 'thowe fals harlott thowe artt evur a yenst me in evury mater', implying a much older grudge between the pair.[8] Such a grudge only deepened when an adult man was injured or maimed in such a way that it prevented them from working for a living, their petitions demanding recompense to make up for lost income.[9]

Notwithstanding the potential for evoking royal pity here, the rate that cases predicated purely upon acts of interpersonal violence ended up before the king and Council in Requests was much lower than in its fellow conciliar tribunal – in Star Chamber. That Court saw 20 per cent of its caseload taken up by accusations of violence in this period, and would go on to be defined by its jurisdiction over riot cases as the sixteenth century went on.[10] The divergence in the figures here is partly explained by the exclusion from the Requests data of accusations that large groups of unnamed individuals had assembled with 'jakkes bowes and arrows swords buklers billes glayves and other defensible wepons' and destroyed or commandeered livestock, crops, goods, or the entirety of the petitioner's

---

[6] REQ2/8/50. For similar cases see REQ2/2/66, 2/12/99.   [7] REQ2/4/169.   [8] REQ2/8/50.
[9] E.g., REQ3/21 *Tailor v Woodward*.
[10] For these and all other figures from Star Chamber and Chancery cited in this chapter, see Haskett, 'The Medieval English Court of Chancery', 300; Lehmberg, 'Star Chamber: 1485–1509', 202; Guy, *The Cardinal's Court*, 16, 52–3.

property, sometimes throwing them out in the process.[11] Usually such allegations were formulated to force a determination on the title to certain lands and properties, with the element of violence being exaggerated if not entirely fabricated. The legal fiction of 'force and arms' ('*vi et armis*'), in which riot and expulsion may have symbolised a less dramatic dispossession, was a particular feature of Star Chamber business and appeared frequently in Requests too. Yet whereas in Star Chamber these riot cases were typically levelled by landlords against their rebellious tenants, in Requests they were more often brought by neighbours against other, more powerful neighbours, accused of using their 'extort power' to seize lands and profits. We will explore the fuller range of land cases below; otherwise, Requests' entertainment of disputes alleging serious, interpersonal violence and assault declined in the early sixteenth century.

The possession of moveable goods was central to the social status attributed to individuals and households, and so comprised the main subject of around 9 per cent of petitions to the early Tudor Requests. In such cases, complainants usually sought the return of goods and chattels that most often included household wares, jewellery, and livestock. Many of these objects pertained to bequests made in last wills and testaments, for which the petitioner might be an executor or an expectant beneficiary. Widows and sons were especially likely to bring such suits, claiming to stand in line to an inheritance including goods and chattels worth anything from a few shillings for some clothes and furniture up to an entire estate valued at over a thousand marks.[12] Others alleged outright theft; for example, in the late 1510s, the widow Agnes Reling petitioned the king to claim that her servant, Robert Bull, had sought to 'robbe and spoyle' her by obtaining the keys to the house adjoining her 'mancion place' in Ivy Lane, London, and breaking down a wall to steal a chest containing £80 in gold and £20 in groats, along with other household stuff.[13] Otherwise, of those included in the demography set out in the previous chapter, merchants and tradespeople were the most common complainants about the possession of moveable goods – usually the wares that they traded for their respective crafts. The value of goods and property argued over by these men frequently ascended into double or triple figures: a clothmaker and a draper from Kent came to Requests in 1522 to dispute the possession of £130 worth of broad cloth, to give just one example.[14]

---

[11] Such as we see in REQ2/6/80. [12] E.g., REQ2/2/32, 2/7/153. [13] REQ2/5/300.
[14] REQ2/3/124.

Disputes and Dispute Resolution 121

Other supplicants of this sort argued over the rights to goods lost and seized at sea, matters that fell under the Crown's admiralty jurisdiction.[15] One of the earliest surviving Requests casefiles, dating to 1495, contains the petition of Herve Morvan of the port town of 'Gelvynek' in France, complaining that John Whale of Winchelsea had seized his ship and freight of a hundred tuns of Gascon wine, contrary to a licence granted by Henry VII.[16] Later, in 1519, John Rastell famously reported to Requests that his journey 'unto the new found land' on the *Barbara* was thwarted when his purser 'compellyd hym to gyff up his viage' and then robbed the ship of all its wares and goods, stranding Rastell in Ireland.[17] This case accords with the general connection between those litigants from further afield – from Ireland, the Channel Islands, and Calais – and maritime disputes, which alone make up 0.4 per cent of Requests' cases here. Closer to home, many more run-of-the-mill goods cases involved complex transactions gone wrong, including the requisitioning of horses and dogs for the use of the king's officers or cows and oxen impounded by neighbours and landlords as distraint for monetary debts.[18] Incidentally, suits about goods were brought to Requests at a much higher rate than in Chancery or in Star Chamber, where this type of dispute barely features among the case-type data previously collected. This discrepancy speaks to the broader variety of subjects and actions allowable in the king's attendant conciliar court, perhaps.

Even before the culture of credit truly took hold in early modern England, debt weighed in terms of physical pounds sterling or figured as part of broken promises was a major part of the economy. Consequently, 13 per cent of Requests' cases in our period pertained to debts of money owed, as defaults in payment for lands, goods, and other property. Where these outstanding payments had outlived the debtor, their executor – very often their widow – was in charge of chasing them up. It was in this role that the widow Margaret Hyde of London pursued the merchant John Bonyfaunt of Exeter across several local jury panels and central common-law courts and finally to Requests in *c.* 1501, with his many delays much to

---

[15] For a fuller analysis of Requests' admiralty jurisdiction in later years, see E. Kadens, 'The Admiralty Jurisdiction of the Court of Requests', in J. Witte, S. McDougall, and A. di Robilant eds., *Texts and Contexts in Legal History* (Robbins Collection, 2016), 349–66.

[16] REQ2/2/146. This case was determined at Sheen in April 1495, where the Council decided that Whale should have the rights to the goods he had seized: REQ1/1 fol. 39v.

[17] REQ2/3/192. See W. Reed, *Early Tudor Drama: Medwall, the Rastells, Heywood, and the More Circle* (Methuen & Co., 1926), 11–12, 187–201; J. A. Williamson, *The Voyages of the Cabots and the Discovery of North America under Henry VII and Henry VIII* (The Argonaut Press, 1929), 86–8.

[18] REQ2/4/226; REQ3/18 *Dickenson and Byrde v Austen*.

her 'extreme and irrecup[er]able costes'.[19] Widows also frequently suffered from the administration of their late husband's estates by his sons (her stepsons), alleging especially that bequeathed annuities had gone unpaid.[20] Other familial debt cases pertained to dowries, with men suing their fathers-in-law over their failure to hold up settlements agreed upon at the time of their marriages. Elsewhere, the high number of members of the mercantile and labouring classes in Requests reflects the frequency with which they pursued outstanding payments following bargains and sales for materials, goods, and animals, or the repayments of substantial loans within established terms. Often the matter came down to the documents (or 'instruments') recording debts, and especially faults in their production or failure to meet their terms. Though written records were the cornerstone of transactions by this time, there was enough of a lingering role for oral or gestural agreements that both debtors and debtees could find themselves without the requisite paperwork to confirm what they had agreed. The consequences are no more apparent than in the suit brought to Requests by Laurence Orell, a cleric who petitioned the king in 1530 to complain that he had let his parsonage of Luckington in Wiltshire to Sir Henry Long, a knight, 'thinking the promese by mouth of the said Sir Henry to have been sufficient and substanciall', but that Long had since defaulted on the payment of £20 for its rent. With 'no maner of specialtie wherby he might charge the said Sir Henry', Orell could not try the suit at common law.[21]

The foundation of local 'Courts of Requests' specifically to handle debt cases in later centuries may lead us to assume that their national predecessor was similarly predisposed.[22] Certainly, across all of these different types of debt case, whether predicated upon wills, sales, or obligations, Requests dealt in values ranging from annuities of only a few shillings per year right up to parcels of £100 or more owed from land deals. Yet, while defaults on documents in particular were quickly becoming standard fare for a jurisdiction grounded in conscience, already by the early Tudor period such matters lay more clearly in the remit of Chancery than elsewhere. For reasons of convenience the provincial councils were the exception to this general rule. The Council in the Marches appears to have been routinely appealed to in debt cases, while the same matters formed 'the greater part of the civil business' of the Council in the North, which was popular with merchants

---

[19] REQ2/10/15. For other examples, see REQ2/7/130, 2/8/119.
[20] For example, REQ2/2/106; see also REQ2/4/314, 393. [21] REQ2/7/107.
[22] For details of these tribunals see Tidd Pratt, *An Abstract of all the printed Acts of Parliament for the establishment of Courts of Requests*.

Disputes and Dispute Resolution 123

and traders.[23] Otherwise, the take-up of any kind of debt case in the central conciliar courts was relatively low in the broader picture, at just 13 per cent of cases in Requests and 10 per cent in Star Chamber compared to 46 per cent of cases in Chancery arising from some form of debt or obligation.

In fact, Requests was much more preoccupied with different assets altogether. This was an age in which moveable possessions and ready money were just one metric of wealth. Another measure, common in contemporary social stratifications, was the volume of lands that an individual owned (their immoveable property) and the value yielded in rents and profits per year. Bitter disputes over the title to and occupation of lands and properties for dwelling, for working, and for money-making predominated in many jurisdictions across the realm and lay at the heart of changes in law and legal practice in the early Tudor period. Possession of lands and estates, no matter what other action was alleged, was therefore the principal subject of almost 70 per cent of the casefiles from Requests in the period under investigation. This represents a much higher proportion for this business than in Star Chamber, where land was central to (at most) 50 per cent of cases, and in Chancery, of 25 per cent. Property in question in Requests comprised anything from single tenements and small messuages, mills, and fish weirs up to whole manors and lucrative estates comprising hundreds of acres of arable lands, pastures, meadows, and woods; from the occasional use of one room in an almshouse or chapel to lordship over a conglomeration of manors, upon which entire livelihoods were said to depend. This was a period in which the ability to freely transfer or divide lands within families was increasingly of concern to those with holdings. The Crown's own interest in keeping a check on landholdings was reflected in legislative efforts to restrict novel mechanisms like the enfeoffment to use, protecting the king's revenues and profits in the process.[24]

A substantial subsection of Requests' caseload in these matters raised another timely issue of concern to central government: the use of common lands and highways. On the rise in early Tudor England was the enclosure of vast swathes of the countryside by landlords and fellow tenants, a late phase in the transition away from open-field farming with the intention of turning arable lands or common pasture into lands for keeping sheep. The tenantry of the well-populated midland counties of England was deeply affected by (and associated enclosure directly with) reduced capacity for tilling and grazing on lands previously held in common, and they appealed directly to the Crown

---

[23] *LP* I. 956, 3289; Skeel, *The Council in the Marches of Wales*, 32–3; Hereford, Herefordshire Archives and Records Centre BG11/29, 1513 fols 1, 2, 1520 fols. 6, 7, 9, 11, 1521 fol. 1; Reid, *The King's Council in the North*, 298, 305.

[24] E.g., 27 Hen. VIII c. 10.

124   Seeking and Requesting Justice

for aid.[25] Commissioners appointed by Requests to investigate one such case in the late 1510s reported that an enclosure of arable land in Ascot had caused four ploughs to be laid down and the tenantry to 'avoyde theyr fermes'.[26] Another group from the mid-1520s compiled an account of the bushels of barley and oats lost by every person affected when the commons of Lyneham Down and Norbury Hill in Oxfordshire were enclosed.[27] Perhaps in response to supplications on these matters, the early Tudor government issued numerous proclamations and Acts condemning this 'greatist abuse and disordre of the naturall soile of the grounde' and the detriment caused to tillers, husbandmen, chapmen, and victuallers in the villages, borough towns, and cities of the realm.[28] In their complaint to Henry VII in 1503, the inhabitants of Bosworth in Leicestershire – where that first Tudor king had won his crown – reminded him of a proclamation he had made a couple of years earlier in Coventry that 'alle suche enclosures shold be cast downe'. They even recounted having 'presented a bille to your highness of the … unlawefull enclosure' made of their parcels of land by the Abbot of Leicester during that same visit of the king to their region.[29]

On the back of more complaints like this, in 1517 a large-scale royal commission to investigate enclosures in various counties across the midlands was established by Thomas Wolsey. Held in the summer months, these sessions were overseen by Dr John Veysey, the Dean of the Chapel Royal who was also the leading judge in Requests at this time.[30] While any pressing business that he discovered was channelled into Chancery, and not Veysey's own court, this personnel overlap might nevertheless have bolstered Requests' reputation as being sympathetic to this offence, which clearly pertained to the king's peace, too.[31] An indicative case is that

---

[25] For a summary, see J. Thirsk, *Tudor Enclosures* (Historical Association, 1958); and Thirsk ed., *The Agrarian History of England and Wales, Volume IV: 1500–1640* (Cambridge University Press, 1967), 200–55.

[26] REQ2/8/256.   [27] REQ3/15 *Beckingham v Horne*.

[28] Henry VIII made at least three proclamations on the subject, ordering that enclosures be pulled down or else proven to be 'benificiall for the com[m]on welth of this realme' in Chancery: Hughes and Larkin eds., *Tudor Royal Proclamations*, vol. I, 122, 154, 186; SP1/17 fol. 43; 6 Hen. VIII c. 5, 27 Hen. VIII c. 22.

[29] REQ2/2/97. This proclamation presumably sought to ameliorate the series of riots against enclosures that had occurred in Coventry across the 1490s, although it indicates something of a turnaround from Henry's previous stance that the commonality should simply obey their civic rulers: Liddy, 'Urban Enclosure Riots', 41.

[30] *LP* II. 3297; I. S. Leadam ed., *The Domesday of Inclosures 1517–1518* (Longmans, 1897), vol I., 81–6. There are no order-book entries between 20 Jul. 1517 and 23 Jan. 1518 – the gap in between is marked by three blank folios and the new run of entries is headed with the title '*Termino Hillarij a[nn]o ix H. R. Octavi Nono*': REQ1/4 fols. 78–83.

[31] Only one case is known to have been heard in the commissions and, apparently, sued to Requests – that of the Constable of Ascot, Nicholas Eustace, against Sir Robert Dormer: REQ2/8/256; Leadam ed., *The Domesday of Inclosures*, vol. I, 343.

Disputes and Dispute Resolution

brought by the parishioners of Nether Shuckburgh in Warwickshire, again in 1517. These inhabitants complained that their lord, Thomas Shuckburgh, had interrupted their customary Rogation day procession around their parish by blocking their main path, 'whiche hath been a wey ever for the said parishe', accompanied by several armed servants – an escalation of an ongoing dispute about Shuckburgh's digging up of common pastures.[32] In the end, the investigations of this period found that in just ten English counties tens of thousands of acres of land had been enclosed, and thousands of people displaced.[33] At least some of these people turned to the Crown for help.

In more day-to-day litigation, land title and possession were thrown into dispute between parties of more equal stature, in many different ways. Feuds arose from claims that relevant deeds, evidences, charters, and/or muniments were held by adversaries or third parties, precluding suits at common law; from accusations of the 'withholding' of lands and all their profits, despite existing agreements or payments for transfer; and from narratives of more sudden and forcible expulsion from lands already occupied. Otherwise, many complainants vaguely stated that they had realised their right to certain lands but that an opponent would not 'allow' or 'suffer' them to 'enjoy' their lands. Either way, any of these disputes could turn out to be very complex indeed. Many came down to the validity of inheritance through the petitioner's descendants as opposed to a more recent bargain or sale, lease for term of years, enfeoffment to use, or other agreed transfer of the same lands said to have been made to the defendant. They threw into question a plethora of seigneurial rights and customs, including the practices of different manors and regional variations in land law. The ultimate consequence was that king and Council entertained complaints and arguments from both sides of these fallouts: from long-term tenants who were suddenly dispossessed *and* those who sought to dispossess long holders of lands. It is hardly surprising, then, that across the early Tudor period land cases of all kinds dominated the business of the conciliar courts.

Relationships at Risk

No matter the legality of the case at hand, however, petitioners to the king hardly ever used terms like 'trespass', 'disseisin', 'detinue', or any other common-law action that we might employ as a frame of reference for their

---

[32] REQ2/8/339. [33] Thirsk ed., *The Agrarian History of England and Wales, Volume IV*, 241.

126   Seeking and Requesting Justice

accusations.[34] They preferred to highlight their own personal loss, disinheritance, and impoverishment as a result of opponents' greed than to denounce specific legal transgressions. Most overtly, many plaintiffs framed claims to land and property with allegations of serious and prolonged persecution by lords and landlords – going far beyond any simple, categorisable legal action, and for which the only solution was royal intervention. A particularly extreme example from Henry VII's reign alleged that Sir Walter Herbert, brother to the late earl of Huntingdon, had imprisoned a poor man called John Nicholas in Chepstow Castle in Monmouthshire for nine weeks, so as to extort him out of lands and goods worth £40. Having surrendered all his worldly possessions and been released, Nicholas had already complained to the king, who had written to Herbert on four occasions asking him to make restitution, 'the which lettres [Herbert] little regarded, but made a peir of new galos [gallows] at yor besechers owne dorre thretenyng hym to be hanged there [so] . . . yor suppliante should not complayne to yor highness no more'.[35] Elsewhere, another plaintiff, Thomas Bower of Newent in Gloucestershire, ended his petition with the plea that 'yf itt wher knowyn that I shewed this unto your good grace I schuld be kyld for itt I schyld never [e]skape'.[36] The reality or even simply the fear of such unjust behaviour made for a strong case to the king's extraordinary remedies.

Other fallouts were more private but no less heated. Seemingly appropriate for royal mediation were arguments between family members: between siblings, parents and children, and sometimes even spouses. In terms of subject matter these cases were more variable than seigneurial disputes, concerning all manner of perceived debts or detaining of lands, goods, and money, often from controversial or poorly managed bequests. One such case from Kent in 1543–4 saw John Catlyn sue his brother, Hugh, for entering into all the lands that had been inherited by them and by their late brother, Richard, contrary to the provision for the equal division of lands between all heirs required under the county's custom of gavelkind. This was presented as a straightforward case of one 'greatlye ffrendyd & allyed' brother acting to 'vexe & trouble' another, but other family cases – especially those between

---

[34] See Guy's discussion of disseisin being moulded to the equity-court bill procedure: *The Cardinal's Court*, 54.

[35] REQ2/6/76. The same case has a petition in the Star Chamber archive: TNA STAC2/34/162. Sir Walter eventually did appear before Requests in this case, on two occasions in 1504, though with no clear end reached: REQ1/3 fols. 125v, 145v. He was also summoned to the tribunal for two other cases, both concerning tenants in his lordship: REQ1/3 fols. 109v, 168v.

[36] REQ2/2/153.

Disputes and Dispute Resolution

parents and children – leant much more heavily on the immorality of breaking bonds of kinship.[37] A particularly vivid example is the grievance of Jeffrey Symonds junior of Wymondham, Norfolk, against his father, also Jeffrey Symonds. The son told of how he had been quite happily retained in the service of a master in Kent when his father had requested that he return home, seeing that his newly acquired literacy made him 'expedyent for suche busynes & affayers as he [the father] had to do'. The son, 'accordyng unto hys naturall obedyence' to his father, did as he was told. Yet soon his stepmother, Amy, 'p[er]seyvyng that the seid Jeffery the ffather was mynded to p[re]ffere your orator' and to lend him money, devised of her 'malicious & delvyshe [devilish] mynde . . . one ffalce & untrew s[ur]myse' to her husband, causing him to be 'sodenly browght in suche dyspleasure furie & rage' against his son. The nature of the 'surmise' is unspecified, but it was enough to bring Jeffrey senior to assault Jeffrey junior in the stables, beating him with staffs and forcing him to eat manure. The 'good favor' and 'resonable wagis and lyvyng' provided by the master in Kent formed a stark contrast with the conduct of the father.[38] In a different case, the widow Katherine Bassingborne told in her petition how her son, John, had of his 'cruell & evyll disposicion . . . wrongefully & without cause or color of right' come into her manor house and 'beyten wounded & evyll entreated' her and the women servants in her employ. Katherine begged the Council that since 'the said John is now present affor your lordshipps', presumably for some other business, they might remind him to 'bear the kynges peace agaynst yor said pore oratrice'.[39] In all, the high emotional stakes involved in unnatural family feuds seem to have made them especially suitable for extraordinary royal tribunals such as Requests.[40]

While arguments between spouses were typically reserved for the church courts, Stretton's work has proven marital litigation to have been a particular interest of the Elizabethan Court of Requests.[41] There is some evidence for this earlier, too: at least twelve petitions to the early Tudor tribunal were on this subject. In one of the more emotive examples, Margaret Coke described how she had married Robert Coke in 1528 at the church of St Sepulchre in London, but that in the years since, 'meny and divers tymes w[ith]ought any occasyon . . . [he] hath soor and greveously beten yowre said poor hooratryse'. While she 'wold [go] uppon handes and

---

[37] REQ3/18 *Catlyn* v *Catlyn*.   [38] REQ3/2 *Symonds* v *Symonds*.   [39] REQ2/13/84.

[40] Stretton found the same emphasis on kinship links in petitions to the Elizabethan Court of Requests: *Women Waging Law*, 203–7.

[41] T. Stretton ed., *Marital Litigation in the Court of Requests 1542–1642*, Camden Fifth Series 32 (Cambridge University Press, 2008).

128 Seeking and Requesting Justice

knees togett his love', Robert had deserted her for another woman in Bristol and had tried to pay Margaret to dissolve their union. Given that, 'fereyng the daynger off god', she was 'loth to be deforsed ffrom her husband', she seemingly sought reconciliation – though she also alleged that Robert had threatened her life and had told others that 'yor poore hooratryse shuld waight in the nyght with a knyfe to kill him in hyse bede'.[42] Less common were husbands suing their wives for similar abandonment and neglect. One such case from the early Tudor period saw Richard Friday, a sherman of London, petitioning Henry VII in the mid-1490s to complain that his wife, Agnes, had left him and returned to her parents in St Giles Field, and that she was having an affair with William Aylove, a lawyer of Lincoln's Inn, with whom she had borne a child.[43] Friday seemed more concerned with the punishment of Aylove and Agnes's parents for maintenance than with any reunion with his estranged wife. Indeed, Aylove, Agnes, and Agnes's mother, Margaret Hall, were each eventually hauled before the Requests committee by a serjeant-at-arms.[44] With no precise subject matter stated, marital litigation reveals a reading of the royal jurisdiction that placed more emphasis on mediation of relations than on any straightforward award of property.

The most extreme social breaches brought before the king were complex, multifaceted, and cross-generational feuds between neighbours. To better understand such long-running and vitriolic disputes, Requests allowed the submission of a single complaint against many different people, or against one person for a multitude of different offences. It allowed, for example, the widow Eleanor Vernon to petition in the early years of Henry VIII's reign for rights to various lands and tenements in Kent against twelve different men and women, allegedly occupying many of these properties (though only one appears to have been called in to make answer).[45] In 1521, it also accepted the single petition of John Jones, a ropemaker from Somerset, against Thomas Lane for putting him out of a tenement *and* against Stephen Gardener for failing to repay him for hiring a surgeon seven years earlier – two entirely unrelated events, for which both parties would have to be summoned separately.[46] It was also possible to use the unlimited petitions of the English bill procedure to narrate a long series of offences by one opponent. The ultimate example from the Requests archive is the petition of Hugh Litheley, a tenant of the

---

[42] REQ2/3/369. See also REQ2/8/120.   [43] REQ3/16/1 *Friday v Hall and Aylove.*
[44] REQ1/1 fols. 155, 156v. It appears that Aylove was licensed to marry another woman in 1508, though he named several illegitimate children in his will: *CPR 1494–1509*, 563, 565; TNA PROB11/19/7.
[45] REQ3/2 *Varnon v Foule et al.*   [46] REQ2/9/57.

Forest of Galtres in Yorkshire, against his neighbour, Robert Frost, submitted in 1523. Within one lengthy bill of complaint, Litheley accused Frost of withholding lands from him, entering his woods and killing his cattle, threatening his children as they played in the forest, conniving with another man to detain household goods, selling his calves even though they 'were but a ffortenyght old', ignoring a writ of *subpoena* already issued by the Council, lying in wait to slay him at night, slandering him as a 'heretyke & a lowler' (a Lollard), and of generally being a promoter of other troublesome locals. The real animosity between the two men was hinted at in Litheley's claim that Frost had said to him 'God forbid that ever thou schuld reste in Cristen mannys berialls'; although Litheley was also independently reported to have been a 'lyght person' ever trying to 'putt this part of ye contre [Yorkshire] to gret vexacion'.[47] This case lays bare the extent to which arguments over clashing claims to real property could be framed by a series of more serious actions which had escalated to litigation before the king. Such openness in its petitioning and its jurisdiction surely increased Requests' popularity with litigants.

No less complicated were the significant number of cases that involved furious and costly disagreements between complete strangers. The mapping out of origins of petitioners or the locale of their disputes in Figure 4.2 belies the extent to which Requests entertained suits that crossed county lines. Of the 5,133 surviving early Tudor casefiles, around 6 per cent or so in fact name several different counties in which properties and parties lay. Although such cases often arose from wealthy families contesting ancestral lands far from their main mansion, they could also come about when principal parties happened to live in different parts of the country altogether. One especially vivid example was the lament of Richard Ereton, a draper from Wheatley in Nottinghamshire, presented to the king in 1536. His petition described how, during his journey back home from Wiltshire, his packhorse and the wool it was laden down with had become mired in the mud at Scampton in Lincolnshire. When he '[a]lighted of[f] his horse wheron he rode to socour his said packhorse', leaving his saddlebag and its contents of at least £40 and other goods unattended for a moment, his riding horse did 'brake from hym with the said baget money and stuf'. The horse was eventually caught and kept by William Edlington of Scampton, who refused to return anything – essentially

---

[47] REQ2/13/111; this latter claim appears in a letter from Thomas Dalby, Archdeacon of Richmond, to the Dean of the Chapel Royal (perhaps Clerk), referring to many commissions Litheley had summoned in Yorkshire: REQ3/30 *Litheley* v *Unknown*.

130 Seeking and Requesting Justice

bringing him into the purview of Requests for the unconscionable, though not illegal, adage of 'finders, keepers'.[48] In such instances, both petitioners and defendants were hindered in gaining justice by the absence of an impartial or convenient jurisdiction in which to try their case. Cases like this epitomise how far the proclaimed subject matter of a given case often forms only one part of the story. The narrative petitions allowable in the royal conciliar tribunals tell us that various moral and social obligations, to neighbours and kin as well as to passing acquaintances, were also at stake.[49]

The Absence of Justice

As the more complex cases brought into Requests demonstrate, petitioners' woes were regularly compounded by the problems or barriers to seeking justice by other means. Well before the late fifteenth century, the more densely populated areas of the country were served by a blanket of often-overlapping tribunals and jurisdictions, including manorial, leet, borough, guild, mayoral, and market courts, along with the regional quarter sessions and assizes, each with their own rhythm and routine.[50] Meanwhile, a parallel set of church courts, from the archiepiscopal forums (such as the Court of Arches, for the Canterbury province) and the bishops' consistory courts down to the administration of rural deaneries, served spiritual and moral needs. There were often specific jurisdictional parameters that might predetermine the selection of any one of these authorities over another as a source for appeal. For example, whether a litigant wished to see monetary restitution from a breach of contract or public punishment for a breach of faith might determine their decision to seek out either their borough or civic authorities or the instance side of their nearest ecclesiastical court, respectively.[51] Recollections about earlier attempts to resolve disputes featured within many petitions to the conciliar courts. They supply further examples for what historians, anthropologists, and legal

---

[48] REQ2/6/166. For a similar case, see REQ3/9 *Dale* v *Spencer and Newman*.

[49] For analysis of Elizabethan Requests pleadings along the same lines, see Stretton, *Women Waging Law*, 191–215.

[50] Johnson, *Law in Common*, Part I; D. J. Guth, 'Enforcing Late-Medieval Law: Patterns in Litigation during Henry VII's Reign', in J. H. Baker ed., *Legal Records and the Historian* (Royal Historical Society, 1978), 80–96.

[51] P. Cavill, 'Perjury in Early Tudor England', in R. McKitterick, C. Methuen, and A. Spicer eds., *The Church and the Law*, Studies in Church History 56 (Cambridge University Press, 2020), 182–209; Johnson, *Law in Common*, 29–30. For more on strategising across jurisdictions see J. McComish, 'Defining Boundaries: Law, Justice and Community in Sixteenth-Century England', in F. Pirie and J. Scheele eds., *Legalism: Community and Justice* (Oxford University Press, 2014), 125–49.

Disputes and Dispute Resolution

scholars have referred to as 'legal pluralism' in medieval and early modern England, with the duties of dispute resolution moving between the local and the central authorities in the realm.[52] Yet, for the most part, any commentary on other judicial experiences in this context emphasised what had gone and could go wrong.

As we saw in Chapter 1, it was largely expected that neighbours would see 'evene assise' done between themselves in the first instance.[53] This faith in friendliness was optimistic; the warm embrace of neighbourliness could be quickly withdrawn if a member failed to properly govern themselves and their household. Questions of moral probity arising from marital disputes appear to have prompted particularly proactive neighbourly intervention. Reflecting on the breakdown of his marriage to his wife Agnes, Richard Aylove recalled how 'alle the honest neghbors duelling [dwelling] in the parish where yor seid orator duelled [dwelled] were not content with her rule Wherof they complayned thaim to the same yor orator and willed hym to see the reformacion of the same yf he intended to abide stille in the paryssh'.[54] In especially convoluted feuds, certain individuals with a strong relationship to the parties might be asked to step in as an umpire. For example, a curious aside in the Catesby litigation narrative mentions how, in an earlier phase of the dispute, John Hugford 'desired and p[ray]ed John Spens[er] of Hodenhill' in Warwickshire, who 'hadde ben acqueynted with the seid Nich Catesby [since] chyldehode to labor hym to be agreable to a tretys and a lovyng ende to be taken bytwen them'.[55] In this instance, a careful choice was made about who might be best placed to talk the parties round.

The presumed duty of any friends and acquaintances called on for this purpose was not to establish legal right but to reach an agreeable compromise. Spenser was said to have spoken 'many gode & kynde wordes' to Catesby, convincing him to release his interest in some of the lands in variance with Hugford, and also to meet with Hugford in person at his home in Princethorpe to discuss the matter further.[56] Usually these arrangements went awry when one party simply refused to agree, or went back on any terms reached later on. A particularly detailed answer provided to Requests by the clerk John Hodgkin later in Henry VIII's reign described his labours in seeking some 'ende and quietnes' between the

---

[52] For a recent summary see Birch, 'Legal Pluralism in Early Modern England and Colonial Virginia'.
[53] Kail ed., *Twenty-Six Political and Other Poems*, 6.
[54] REQ3/16/1 *Friday* v *Hall and Aylove*. For another marital case mediated by friends, following a ruling by the 'ecclesyastycall iudges', see REQ3/3 *Thornell* v *Tenant*.
[55] TNA E163/29/11 m. 10.   [56] Ibid m. 10.

132   Seeking and Requesting Justice

'very poore' William and Mary Steward and the 'sore woman' Lady Cornwallis over leases for a house in Dartford, Kent. The Lady, Hodgkin recalled, had been intent to be 'revenged' on her opponents, especially because they could no longer find their written lease. He and her neighbours together convinced her to 'be contented and deale charytable-[y] with these folkes [since] they can make you no recompence bycause they be pore ... and that whiche is paste to forgive it for gods sake'.[57] Amid all this talk of reconciliation, none of the cases just described suggest any kind of officially enforced peace, particularly since the individuals acting as mediators had no authority other than as third parties. Here, as Wood has pointed out, law (or the 'shadow' of it) 'was not so much a forum within which conflict could be perpetuated as a means of binding local society together, settling feuds and reasserting basic social norms'.[58] When things went right, mediation probably prevented many feuds from reaching formal litigation. But this was not a universal experience.

A marginally more structured means of dispute resolution was the appeal to a local powerholder for arbitration. This umpire was no friend or fellow, but someone who had the requisite social cachet to receive due deference from disputants. According to Edmund Dudley, it was the duty of the realm's 'chivalry' – by which he meant dukes, earls, barons, knights, esquires, and gentlemen – to 'be the maker of endes and lovedaies ... bytwene neighbors and neighbors, frindes and frindes'.[59] Their help, like the king's, was sought through a written petition, and procedures that followed involved summonses to appear at hearings held in churches or taverns.[60] Sometimes the result was a recorded determination or indenture to which the arbiters and the parties set their signatures and seals. More usually, though, the purpose of even this more organised arbitration was to come to a compromise instead of a firm award of possession or title in either direction. To give a standard example, sometime in the later reign of Henry VII it was said that one Nicholas Specott had 'made complaint unto my Lord [Willoughby de] Broke he being then att Bereferys [Bere Ferrers]' in Devon, resulting in his opponent, John Fry, and all of his chosen witnesses being summoned before the Lord and asked to give testimony. Finding 'that the matier was nott good', the Lord 'advysyd the said Nicholas Specott ... to make entretie' with Fry.[61] In an altogether different

---

[57] REQ3/4 *Steward* v *Hodgkin*.   [58] Wood, *Faith, Hope and Charity*, 45.

[59] Dudley, *The Tree of Commonwealth*, 44.

[60] For examples, see REQ2/13/43, REQ3/7 *Olyff* v *Monk*; Catesby's case was heard first at 'the Church of Seynt Jones' (possibly St John's) in Warwick, followed by a second 'day of co[mmun]icacion' at the Greyfriars in Coventry: TNA E163/29/11 m. 4.

[61] REQ2/6/240. For more on arbitrations like this, see Rawcliffe, 'The Great Lord as Peacekeeper'.

Disputes and Dispute Resolution 133

sort of case, when Thomas Combe and John Underwood of Bucklersbury in Berkshire fell out over the ownership of two sheep and their wool, Sir Humphrey Foster determined that each man should keep one sheep and one fleece.[62]

This sort of even-handed arbitration was being done by a much broader spectrum of society, temporal and ecclesiastical, than Dudley had implied. The general vexations ongoing between Thomas Balle and Edward Compton of Warwickshire were first put to the 'mediacion of their friends' before being 'putt in the arbitrement of the parson of Oxshelf [Oxhill] & the viker of Honyton [Honington]' – two clergymen, along with two other men of unspecified background – who eventually produced an award that was written up, engrossed, and sealed.[63] That this responsibility was becoming more common even among the wealthier merchants and craftsmen of the cities by the early Tudor period is indicated by the inclusion of a 'Fourme of Award geven out by Arbytroment' in the chronicle of the London merchant Richard Arnold, based on one that he, 'R. A. hab[erdasher]', and other tradesmen of the city had overseen – a document that he presumably thought especially fitting for his readership.[64] While most arbiters mentioned in accounts of previous resolution efforts were men, there are a few examples in Requests and elsewhere of prominent women being approached for this task. One petitioner in 1520 mentioned having 'sued for his remedie to the priores[s] of the Monastery of Blackladye of Browde' – Brewood Priory, in Staffordshire – she 'being chief lady of the said manor' of Broome, over 20 miles away in Worcestershire.[65] Elsewhere, an aside in Catesby's narrative of litigation related how 'it fortuned that Maister John Ebrall [Eborall]' had visited Robert Catesby's hometown of Newenham, Northamptonshire, to preach to the congregation. It turned out that Eborall was then in royal favour, 'by cause he maried Kynge Edward and Quene Elizabeth [Woodville] toged[er]' in secret, in 1464. Eborall suggested that Robert 'make a bill of the seid mater and putt it up to the seid Quene', and to Earl Rivers and 'my lady of Bedforde than moder to the seid Quene'.[66] All manner of figures with the right social cachet could be approached for justice-giving, then. Yet they could just as easily refuse to

---

[62] REQ3/6 *Combe* v *Underwood*.   [63] REQ2/5/377.

[64] Richard Arnold, *The customs of London, otherwise called Arnold's Chronicle*, ed. Francis Douce (London, 1811), 118–19. One case in which merchant tailors acted as arbiters and produced a written award is REQ3/16/2 *Heyton* v *Orell*.

[65] REQ3/16/1 *Smyth* v *Simkins*.

[66] TNA E163/29/11 m. 5. The petition that Robert Catesby wrote to Elizabeth Woodville is copied into this document too.

134 Seeking and Requesting Justice

help. The Prioress of Brewood, it was said, 'hath alwayes denyed' her supplicant's rights, causing him to seek remedy in Star Chamber; and Elizabeth Woodville apparently declined to help Catesby for fear that 'hit myght cause a gruge bytwen hir & the seid Erle of Warwyke', who happened to be master to Catesby's opponent.[67]

Depending on a complainant's locale, another port of call for the commencement of litigation might be the manor court. Sitting several times a year in rural villages and market towns, these tribunals were concerned with general governance in their immediate surroundings. In this business they required the cooperation of tenantry; the more substantial inhabitants in their remit worked as presentment jurors, providing information to the lord and steward about a whole range of offences that ranged from the overtly unlawful to simply disruptive.[68] The outrage expressed in one petition to Requests against Sir John Audley, lord of Pickenham in Norfolk, for convening a manorial court 'secretly' on a Monday morning so that 'at the same court [there] were but v tenauntes present' demonstrates the expectation that these gatherings were to be public, regular, and well-advertised.[69] This communal forum was the place to witness and contest inheritance disputes, tenantry arrangements, and the rights to homage and other liberties on the basis of the local custom.[70] Its officials could also be more proactive on these matters. An especially detailed account of a court session, included in a petition to Requests in the late 1510s, described how Sir Roger Lewkenor had ordered his steward, Richard Sutton, to hold a court at Barcombe in Sussex with the express charge to 'inquyre of the dyyng seased [seised] of ev[er]y ten[au]nte and who was nexte heyre unto them', bringing all the tenantry together to make presentment on behalf of themselves and their neighbours.[71] Reflective of the manor court's role in preserving the memory and customs of the surrounding landscape is the frequency with which plaintiffs appealing to the king pressed their rights according to 'copy of court roll' – that is, their possession of the copy of the title that had been enrolled and kept within the lordship.

Given that Requests was so dominated by private land disputes, it is no surprise that the manor was cited so often as the initial locus for dispute

---

[67] REQ3/16/1 *Smyth* v *Simkins*; TNA E163/29/11 m 6.
[68] McIntosh, 'Finding a Language for Misconduct'; Christopher Harrison, 'Manor Courts and the Governance of Tudor England', in C. Brooks and M. Lobban eds., *Communities and Courts in Britain 1150–1900* (Hambledon Press, 1997), 43–59.
[69] REQ2/3/127.   [70] See, for example, REQ2/4/38, REQ3/9 *Walton* v *Hammond*.
[71] REQ2/9/142.

Disputes and Dispute Resolution 135

resolution, albeit with mixed results. Outsiders were particularly troubled by the inherent authority of the manorial court over the division of lands within its remit. When William Lewyn, a tailor of London, wished to acquire various lands in Buckinghamshire that had belonged to his late brother, but which were now occupied by his widowed sister-in-law, Anne, he initially sought out 'the steward of the lordes court' to dispossess her. This was not a successful strategy; presumably Anne was protected by her neighbours and by the will of the manorial lord, as the ultimate legitimiser in this sphere.[72] Even less tranquil relations within the manor are illuminated by the depositions taken from the inhabitants of Kingford, Worcestershire, in 1530. They reported how their neighbour William Byrd had attended on their lord, William Tracy, in court to ask that his copy for some pastures in the area be amended to name Byrd's wife as co-tenant. Tracy allegedly met this request with 'opprobryouse wordes[,] seyeng that the lyvyng of his wyfe was nought and that no suche myslyvyng woman shuld have no land of his'.[73] Elsewhere, the 'powre' William Unthanke complained that the new lord of the manor of Stretton in Derbyshire, the gentleman Robert Revell, had taken his copy of court roll for lands in the area, 'red it over & ... then ymmedyatly in the presens of all the tenauntes of the said manor ... cast [it] in to the ffyre & ther brend [burned] it', leaving Unthanke dispossessed and remediless.[74] It was this sort of butting of heads between tenants and lords that often brought litigants to higher jurisdictions; in fact, Requests' *c.* 1543 ordinances specified defaults by lords and stewards as exceptions to a general preclusion of copyhold cases.[75]

The people of the realm's towns and cities were faced with 'institutional density' that facilitated a greater range of options for litigation but also placed them at the discretion of a range of different authorities.[76] Elected urban officials routinely received directives from king and Council to investigate seditious speech and riotous outbursts, along with letters missives and privy seals pertaining to ongoing suits in the conciliar courts, which they were tasked with communicating onwards to their citizens.[77] Day to day, they were also expected to administer justice in civil disputes,

---

[72] REQ2/12/180.
[73] REQ3/4 *Byrde* v *Goodman.* Requests determined in Byrds's favour: REQ1/5 fol. 103.
[74] REQ3/16/1 *Unthanke* v *Revell.* [75] BL Add. MS 25248 fol. 32v.
[76] Johnson, *Law in Common*, 55–85.
[77] C. D. Liddy, '"Sir ye be not kyng": Citizenship and Speech in Late Medieval and Early Modern England', *The Historical Journal* 60:3 (2016), 571–96. See, for example, one Requests case in which the Mayor of Sandwich called two parties before him and 'causyd [the king's] moost drad lettres to be red': REQ2/5/372.

136 Seeking and Requesting Justice

which they did with varying regularity and formality. Surviving civic records give us an impression of the judicial activities of civic authorities when acting as a 'city court'. The ordinances of late-medieval Chester stated that once four or five neighbours had tried to mediate a disagreement it was down to the mayor alone to arbitrate – implying some loose hierarchy for dispute resolution in this context – while the mayor and aldermen of late medieval and early modern London sat in numerous configurations and settings to hear different kinds of business.[78] In most instances, parties appeared before the mayor personally at the guildhall or some other civic space to rehearse their actions and grievances verbally, though they were sometimes written up into books.[79] In one case eventually tried in Requests, two founders from London 'by recognisaunce were bounden to [each] other before the Maire of yor said Citie in the summe of xx li to abide thawarde of certain persones indifferently chosen' to arbitrate. When this failed, the city authorities had ordered the defendant to pay damages to the plaintiff.[80]

The authority vested in the occupant of the mayoralty, even beyond their term in office, comes through in petitioners' stories of seeking civic justice. Particularly vivid is Margaret Rede's description of how she had 'complayned her unto the ryght worshippfull Syr John Shaa knyght than beyng Maire of the saide Cite' of London. Shaa was said to have called the plaintiff, her opponents, and their witnesses before him in order to have 'the p[er]fyght knowledge of the ryght and title of the seide Margeret'. His judgment was that Margaret could keep the lands in question, a situation that had remained in place after Shaa's tenure and until his death in c. 1503.[81] It is unclear in what capacity Shaa had been acting here, though contemporary chronicles tell us that he established a civil tribunal for poor suitors, incidentally by 'soom namyd court of Requestis'.[82] Many were likely reliant upon the personal sort of justice offered by local worthies such as Shaa, even if just for their short term in office. John Joseph of Deal in Kent had hoped that the mayor of Sandwich, who had 'jurisdiction of the

---

[78] As cited in J. Laughton, *Life in a Late Medieval City: Chester 1275–1520* (Oxbow Books, 2008), 126–7; Tucker, *Law Courts and Lawyers in the City of London*, 89.

[79] Attreed ed., *The York House Books*; Dormer Harris ed., *The Coventry Leet Book*.

[80] REQ2/3/18.   [81] REQ3/3 *Rede* v *Dychehand*.

[82] Thomas and Thornley eds., *The Great Chronicle of London*, 320. There is no reference to this court in the London records covering Shaa's tenure as mayor: LMA COL/AD/01/012. It is likely a separate entity altogether from the 'Court of Requests' (perhaps also known as a/the court of conscience) established in the city to hear small debt cases in c. 1518: LMA COL/CA/01/01/010 fols. 137, 158v, 162v; William Bohun, *Privilegia Londini: or, the laws, customs, and priviledges of the city of London* (London, 1702), 398–9. I am grateful to Penny Tucker for sharing her thoughts on this subject.

Disputes and Dispute Resolution

pece' in Deal as well, would aid him in evicting opponents after a successful indictment before the county Justices of the Peace (JPs). He was forced to sue to the king, he said, because the 'mayre hath refused to do his office'.[83] In c. 1519, another Requests complainant lamented that his opponent had 'reviled and rebuked' him in front of the mayor and the aldermen of London as they passed over the 'brigge of Westminster', ruining his good credence – and, he no doubt intended to imply, his likelihood of getting justice in the city.[84] In the close quarters of the city, where the mayor was as easily intercepted in the street as in the courthouse, reputation and relationships mattered.

Eventual petitioners to the Crown had sometimes also come from other 'courts in the city': those tribunals and officials sitting within city walls but presiding over the wider region.[85] The sheriffs of the counties and cities received regular citation within Requests' petitions, often in relation to their duties in presiding over city courts of pleas, county courts, and tourns.[86] Numerous suits for possession that ended up in Requests had at some point been heard in the shrieval system, when a plaintiff approached the sheriff at the county court for a writ of *replevin* for the return of impounded cattle or a precept to the bailiffs for recovery of a debt.[87] This process was not always to the benefit of plaintiffs, and could be abused to good effect by their opponents. One of Henry VII's gentlemen ushers complained that the sheriff of Cornwall had effectively facilitated his adversaries' vexatious litigation by dutifully returning a *nihil habet* (a writ declaring that the defendant had not been served process because they lacked property on which they might be attached) upon a *novel disseisin* assize that had been empanelled in the locality of the case at his adversaries' request. This was surely the intention of this process in the first place, the gentleman implied; given that he was away in service to the king, he could not be expected to reside or own sufficient property in that area.[88]

Whereas the shrieval county courts and tourns were generally in decline by the early Tudor period, other regional commissions were in ascension.[89] Accusations of riotous entries into disputed lands were particularly well suited to the quarter sessions presided over by the JPs of each county and county borough, which came to handle both general administration in the

---

[83] REQ2/6/51. [84] REQ2/12/50.
[85] This is to use a distinction made in Tucker, *Law Courts and Lawyers in the City of London*, 84–9.
[86] Summarised in J. McGovern, 'The Sheriffs of York and Yorkshire in the Tudor Period', *Northern History* 57:1 (2020), 60–76.
[87] REQ2/2/80, 2/2/161, 2/4/356. [88] REQ2/5/215. [89] Gunn, *Early Tudor England*, 74.

138   Seeking and Requesting Justice

region alongside more serious misdemeanours.[90] Again, though, these authorities sometimes proved fallible. One Requests plaintiff told how he had 'labored at dyvers sessions' in Lincolnshire 'to have hadde ... iiij riotours founde [guilty]', but was barred from this route when the maintainer of those same rioters turned out to be the JP himself.[91] Otherwise, since Requests largely received civil complaints over title to land, most citations were to earlier hearings under the authority of the biannual assize courts held by the king's common-law justices. This included, predominantly, sessions of *nisi prius* or *novel disseisin* – possessory assizes, determining titles to land – though a few cases concerning wrongful entries had been entertained in *oyer and terminer* assizes instead.[92] Of great importance to supplicants, no doubt, was the element of publicity pertaining to these tribunals, compared to the more closed-off nature of manorial courts, overseen by an individual lord and attended only by their tenants. Indeed, after her manor house was invaded by a long-term local opponent and his cronies in 1502, the widow Elizabeth Letton reported in her petition to Requests that the offenders were 'twis indited at the next comen and quarter sessions by ij enquestes be cawse hit was so oppenlie known' by the locals.[93] The result of such trials, if successful, could be a positive common-law judgment and a writ of restitution to be executed by the sheriff. That said, one beneficiary of this process bemoaned that the suit had 'cost yor seid supplyant more money then the londes be worth'.[94] And so this supplicant, like many others, laid claim to the extraordinary aid of the king's council courts instead.

Even an impressionistic survey of the range of previous litigation routes related by petitioners to Requests tells us that reasons for turning from the localities to the Crown are not easily generalised. Intimidation and inefficient administration seem the obvious explanation for supplicants to abandon the manor, the borough, or the county authorities. There were also economic considerations in play in some cases: most notably, the fact that the manorial and shrieval systems technically only heard cases worth

---

[90] Riot cases sued at quarter sessions and then at Requests include REQ2/2/168, 2/3/122, 2/6/39, 2/11/97; REQ3/3 *Bele* v *Bate*; REQ3/15 *Goore* v *Goore*.

[91] REQ2/6/39.

[92] REQ2/5/215, 2/9/75; REQ3/3 *Norres* v *Horthorne*; REQ3/3 *Bate* v *Bele*; REQ3/4 *Tanner* v *Crasse*.

[93] REQ2/11/97. Further details of this case emerge from Star Chamber pleas back and forth between the Lettons and the Bates, in which both parties are accused of breaking into the manor house: TNA STAC1/1/12, 25; discussed in D. Youngs, '"In to the Sterre Chambre": Female Plaintiffs before the King's Council in the Reign of Henry VII', in L. Clark ed., *Fifteenth Century XVII: Finding Individuality* (Boydell & Brewer, 2020), 140.

[94] REQ2/3/6; REQ2/9/75.

Disputes and Dispute Resolution

below the threshold of 40s, meaning that larger estates and debts had to be tried elsewhere.[95] Otherwise, the choice of a forum for resolution came down to simple practicalities. For example, in the lengthy narrative compiled by one Robert Pilkington, detailing his litigation against various opponents for lands in Mellor, Derbyshire, in the late fifteenth century, a meeting at Manchester with 'ayther ij. frends' of Pilkington and his adversary was set up in 1494 simply because the sheriffs of Derbyshire were too 'labured' – that is, too busy – to assist personally.[96] In the similar account of Catesby's conciliar litigation, it was suggested that he had appealed to Requests only because 'my seid Lorde Chaunceler and other lordes of the kynges Counsell wer so bysied ^with^ mat[er]s for the kynge & also for other gret p[ar]ticler mat[er]s whech the kynges g[ra]ce were spedde so that fewe other p[ar]ticler maters p[ro]ceded that t[er]me in the Sterre Chamb[er]'. Of course, we might, like Catesby's opponents, suspect that any such parallel litigation was really designed to cause 'gret troble vexacion & cost' to all involved.[97]

Indeed, this overview of early modern England's complex legal 'system', 'network', or 'patchwork' told through the eyes of Requests' petitioners should not lead us to assume that the path of litigation moved in a straight line upwards.[98] This was not always a trajectory that began with the 'rough' justice of the village and ascended to an 'official' ruling by the Crown – not least because, as we will see in Part III, royal justice itself was neither formal nor final. From the very start many litigants did not restrict themselves to one lawsuit or jurisdiction at a time. Limited searching of English manorial court rolls, for example, suggests that at least some eventual Requests suitors were active in pursuing their rights before their local lords even while their causes pended with the king. To provide just one example, Thomas Pycher senior of Thornbury in Gloucestershire, who successfully pursued possession of various lands, meadows, and pastures in the lordship of Hawksbury through Requests in 1529, can be found exhibiting his copies for several of those properties in the manor court that same year.[99] In this

---

[95] C. Muldrew, *The Economy of Obligation: The Culture of Credit and Social Relations in Early Modern England* (Palgrave Macmillan, 1998), 204–5.

[96] *The Narrative of Robert Pilkington*, 34. The original document, entitled 'The tytyll of pylkynton to anesworth landys', is not fully legible: Northallerton, North Yorkshire County Record Office, ZDV X 1.

[97] TNA E163/29/11 m. 16. For a similar tale of multi-jurisdictional litigation, see L. R. Poos, *Love, Hate and the Law in Tudor England: The Three Wives of Ralph Rishton* (Oxford University Press, 2022).

[98] McComish, 'Defining Boundaries', 126.

[99] Specifically, the pastures called 'the Inhooke' and the right to graze 300 sheep were mentioned in both the Requests decree and the manorial court-roll entry: REQ1/5 fol. 61; TNA SC2/175/59 fols. 3–4.

140 Seeking and Requesting Justice

instance, at least, the manorial court was not a precursor to litigation to the Crown but a parallel forum for pressing rights. Hence the expansion of conciliar justice at the centre and in the provinces was not at the expense of other local and regional tribunals, which generally followed the same upturn in business levels that other jurisdictions experienced with the economic growth and population boom of the 1520s onwards.[100] That eventual Crown litigants were so frequently able to traverse this range of different courts, authorities, and jurisdictions means they do not easily fit the mould of the 'poor' suitor, whatever descriptors they might have applied to themselves before their king.

Conclusion

In accordance with the multifaceted and contentious definitions of justice explored in Part I, this chapter has shown that petitioners conceptualised *royal* justice not as an established forum for particular areas of case law but as a mechanism for remedying tangled feuds that could not be so simply defined nor easily remedied elsewhere. In the first instance this has implications for our conceptualisations of Requests' own jurisdiction. Historians have traditionally labelled Chancery as serving victims of legal technicalities, Star Chamber as punishing riots and corrupt officials, Requests as helping poor suitors with 'trivial civil suits', and the provincial councils as primarily administrative entities.[101] Where comparison of the subject matter of cases from a statistical standpoint has been possible, this seems to be a largely accurate categorisation. Yet this analysis has indicated that despite its long-standing characterisation as the 'poor man's *Chancery*', Requests' business in fact appears to have more closely resembled that of its fellow conciliar courts. Whereas Chancery was becoming increasingly clogged with suits that were narrowly framed around instruments and documentary evidence, Star Chamber and Requests heard a wider range of interpersonal disputes over real property and goods – although, as we have seen, the statuses of the parties that they treated generally differed.[102]

---

[100] On manor courts, see J. Whittle, *The Development of Agrarian Capitalism: Land and Labour in Norfolk, 1440–1580* (Oxford University Press, 2000), 46–64; Muldrew, *The Economy of Obligation*, 238; Harrison, 'Manor Courts and the Governance of Tudor England'; H. Garrett-Goodyear, 'Common Law and Manor Courts: Lords, Copyholders and Doing Justice in Early Tudor England', in J. Whittle ed., *Landlords and Tenants in Britain, 1440–1660: Tawney's 'Agrarian Problem' Revisited* (Boydell & Brewer, 2013), 35–51.

[101] Guy, *The Cardinal's Court*, 71.

[102] Haskett, 'The Medieval English Court of Chancery', 296–7, 301.

Disputes and Dispute Resolution 141

Furthermore, the narrative qualities of Requests' petitions enable us to move beyond such a narrowly legal reading of disputes and their resolution. As we will see in the next chapter, petitioning to the king required a combination of jurisdictionally appropriate frameworks and heartstring-tugging rhetoric. Issues experienced within other elements of the legal system were another part of the general set of circumstances through which petitioners hoped to call on the royal Council to judge the subject matter and the breaches in the peace that were in variance. As such, we must resist the temptation to isolate a petition to the king and the burgeoning conciliar courts from what had come before. With this wider picture in view, we are also reminded 'not to overdraw the boundary between legal culture and local culture', nor that between 'local' and 'national'.[103] In turn, and in the absence of many definitive contemporary statements on the jurisdiction of the early Requests, these narratives of shopping for justice give us some insight into how the king's jurisdiction was perceived as part of the wider system of law and justice, too. It could certainly be treated as a kind of release valve for failing, outdated, or corruptible legal processes in the lower courts. Yet it might also be figured as just one more force – albeit an especially powerful one – in the collaborative creation of justice.

[103] Wood, *Faith, Hope, and Charity*, 133.

CHAPTER 6

'Your Poor Orator': Petitioning the King

As one eighty-year-old widow claimed in her plea for royal justice, many disadvantaged people felt that they had no means to 'contende agaynst a lorde for [t]here ryght oy[er] wyse then by peticion'.[1] The petition was a distinctively emotive form of supplication, part of a wider culture of complaint and bill-making as much as of the legal world of the courtroom. By the early Tudor period, the written vernacular complaint was an established mechanism for communicating personal grievances to authorities. And so, for sociolegal histories, the petition has been the fundamental object of study, whether to elucidate the course of individual cases or to survey the work of entire jurisdictions – though interpretive problems remain either way.[2] Most obviously, we are faced with the challenge of whether to take the stories contained in petitions at face value or to dismiss them as pure rhetoric; to act either as the willing 'storyteller' in litigants' stead or as 'translator', reading between the lines. In truth, supplications for any kind of justice had inherently 'fictional' qualities, and the means and form of their construction tells us as much as any perceptible or provable 'truth'.[3] In Requests, the rhetoric framing disputes is overt. A recurring feature in its documents is the notion of the 'poor orator',

---

[1] REQ3/1/1 *Causefield v Rich.*

[2] Key works include Ormrod, Dodd, and Musson eds., *Medieval Petitions: Grace and Grievance*; Dodd, *Justice and Grace*; H. Killick and T. W. Smith eds., *Petitions and Strategies of Persuasion in the Middle Ages: The English Crown and the Church, c.1200–1550* (Boydell & Brewer, 2018). Recent and current research projects continue to improve access to petitions and provide further interpretation: 'The Power of Petitioning in Seventeenth Century England' (2019), www.petitioning.history.ac.uk (accessed Jan. 2023); 'Civil War Petitions: Conflict, Welfare and Memory during and after the English Civil Wars, 1642–1710' (2017), www.civilwarpetitions.ac.uk (accessed Jan. 2023).

[3] The central thesis in the influential work by N. Zemon Davis, *Fiction in the Archives: Pardon Tales and Their Tellers in Sixteenth-Century France* (Polity, 1987); for more recent discussions see Bailey, 'Voices in Court: Lawyers' or Litigants'?', 406–7; Beattie, 'Your Oratrice: Women's Petitions to the Late Medieval Court of Chancery'; T. Stretton, 'Women, Legal Records, and the Problem of the Lawyer's Hand', *JBS* 58:4 (2019), 684–700.

142

'Your Poor Orator': Petitioning the King 143

a phrase common to deferential supplications but carrying particular weight in this supposed 'poor man's court'.

Having established *who* sued to the king's Council in Requests and their reasons for doing so, this chapter sets out the formulae and lexicon involved in petitioning to the king. Where possible, it also brings together the evidence for the logistics behind this process. In the broader arc of the so-called 'legal revolution' of early modernity, the 'monetary and emotional investment of ordinary users of the law' has been seen as a principal motivator.[4] Yet, although we have plenty of evidence for the phraseology that moved requests for royal justice, we have far fewer traces of how, exactly, petitions were produced and submitted.[5] Requests' archive contains bills of litigants' costs and a range of ephemeral memoranda – all revealing something of the resources, knowledge, and actions required to commence a suit before the king. This gives us a basis from which we can further scrutinise litigant identities and self-identification. We have seen the array of possessions and relationships at stake in the disputes that made it this far, and the emotions and values that animated them. Now we examine how litigants put their money, knowledge, and narrative potential to good use.

Knowledge of the Law

As we saw in the previous chapter, the pursuit of a grievance often began long before a suit to the king and Council became an option. Indeed, for many of the king's subjects an entire cultural framework for complaint was learned outside of legal contexts. The very ideal of justice and identification of its dissidents was inculcated by the rumour mill churning in the alehouse, the parish church, and the manor court, where everything from local drama to national scandal was subject to communal adjudication. Many eventual litigants would also have been exposed to the world of bill-casting, where complaints against neighbours and authorities were written down and widely circulated. Wendy Scase identified two essential features of this 'discursive practice'. Firstly, these scurrilous bills, libels, and schedules were produced in secret, and their authors and narrators remained largely anonymous. Secondly, and paradoxically, the mode of dissemination for these documents was deliberately public, posted up on doors and windows, in market squares, guildhalls, and courtrooms. Their texts, often

---

[4] Kagan, *Lawsuits and Litigants in Castile, 1500–1700*, xx–xxi; Smail, *The Consumption of Justice*, 17.
[5] An exception being Dabhoiwala, 'Writing Petitions in Early Modern England'.

144   Seeking and Requesting Justice

formed as rhymes and songs, claimed to speak on behalf of all the 'commons' and their rights.[6] And so, while partly reliant on networks of literate readers, the criticisms and cajoling contained in bills could easily pass into oral culture. Late-medieval governors frequently expressed concern about the dangers of escalating 'bill-casting campaigns' for the reputation and legitimacy of governments, both local and national.[7]

In short, then, Tudor subjects encountered a whole corpus of complaint, with implications for the relationship between Crown and society. The various genres it contained – letters, bills, schedules, broadsides, prophesies, ballads, libels, pamphlets, plaints, petitions, and clamour more generally – shared certain linguistic features, particularly the expression of outward loyalty to the Crown and to the community under the banner of the 'true commons'.[8] There was no clear line of delineation between formal and informal acts of claim-making; judicial formulae bled into non-judicial texts and vice versa. The rhetoric of honest 'supplication' was the guise for grievance-making in statements made by the rioters and rebels across our period, their 'petitionary gestures' borrowing the format, while knowingly eschewing the proper procedure, of judicial petitioning.[9] At the same time, bill-casting against neighbours and governors was influenced by judicial procedures. Some surviving bills from the fifteenth century take material forms similar to petitions, while others satirised the language of legal bills and royal proclamations; indeed, Scase has speculated that it was an earlier phase of improved accessibility to royal justice in the reign of Edward I that formulated the patterns for bill-casting in the first place.[10] In practice and format, then, complaints as diverse as posted bills, rebel supplications, and legal petitions 'imagine[d] the whole of the realm as a council-chamber or parliament in which complaints may be freely expressed to the king and justice achieved'.[11]

Contact with a multitude of judicial forums further inculcated an awareness of the formulae specific to the legal petition or plea in most

---

[6] Scase, 'Strange and Wonderful Bills'.

[7] Liddy, *Contesting the City*, 63–5, 161–4; see also C. Ross, 'Rumour, Propaganda and Public Opinion during the Wars of the Roses', in R. A. Griffiths ed., *Patronage, the Crown and the Provinces in Later Medieval England* (Gloucester, 1981); S. Justice, *Writing and Rebellion: England in 1381* (Berkeley, 1994).

[8] For some discussion of the terminologies, both modern and contemporary, surrounding these genres, see W. Scase, *Literature and Complaint in England, 1272–1553* (Oxford University Press, 2007), 1–3, 183; Justice distinguishes between petitions and plaints: *Writing and Rebellion*, 60–4.

[9] Scase, *Literature and Complaint*, 86; Justice, *Writing and Rebellion*, 50.

[10] Scase, *Literature and Complaint*, 1–17; Liddy, *Contesting the City*, 150.

[11] Scase, 'Strange and Wonderful Bills', 246.

'Your Poor Orator': Petitioning the King

would-be royal litigants. Even the earliest logical step in resolving a contentious dispute, arbitration in the disputants' locality, was initiated by bill of complaint. This was the case in the long-running land feud pursued by the Catesby family, whose narrative roll preserves a petition to the Duke of Buckingham requesting that he 'make a fynall direccion in thes premisses'.[12] A written supplication was also used to inform the manorial lord of problems in governance of his manor, as extant late-medieval examples demonstrate.[13] When asking for justice the standard tropes were deployed: in one 'bill of peticion' to the Abbot of Stratford incidentally copied into the Requests archive in the early 1520s, we find essentially the same kind of plea as we might find in any petition to a conciliar court, with the 'poor orator and bedeman' requesting to 'have the lawe according to the maner & custom of the ... lordship'.[14] Beyond the lord's court, petitions presented to regional authorities such as JPs told a familiar tale of oppression and 'utter undoing' at the hands of local opponents that left plaintiffs with 'noght now to leve by bot the grace of good [god] and gud pepille' and asking for unspecified 'remedy'.[15] In other words, during the course of any arbitrations and lawsuits arising from neighbourly disputes *before* they came into Requests, litigants would have become familiar with the generic conventions common to all petitions for justice.

Still, these conventions had to be adapted to a specific format required for petitioning to the king – a format of great enough interest and novelty to be noted down and circulated by various late-medieval observers. Among the statutes, poems, and recipes compiled in his commonplace book, the merchant John Colyns copied up two petitions to the king, both for grace. One asked for 'yor gracious letters of presentacyon' of the parsonage of B.', to be directed via the clerk of the Hanaper in the Chancery, and the other purported to be the petition of Sir John Trevelyan of Somerset, asking the king's pardon after he had accidently

---

[12] TNA E163/29/11 m. 2. For more on petitioning for arbitration in a later context, see J. Kelsoe, 'Arbitration in English Law and Society before the Act of 1698' (unpublished PhD thesis, University of Cambridge, 2021), 65–6.

[13] J. F. Nichols, 'An Early Fourteenth Century Petition from the Tenants of Bocking to their Manorial Lord', *The Economic History Review* 2:2 (1930), 305–7.

[14] REQ2/5/279.

[15] See, for example, the petitions to the justice of Lancaster preserved in one Henrician Requests casefile: REQ3/2 *Brathwayte* v *Stanley and the Abbot and Monks of Furness*. For later documents of the same type, see the transcriptions published through the 'Power of Petitioning' project: Sharon Howard ed., *Petitions to the Cheshire Quarter Sessions 1573–1798*, British History Online, www.british -history.ac.uk/petitions/cheshire, accessed Jan. 2023.

146   Seeking and Requesting Justice

given 'a stripe to on[e] Wyll[ia]m Hyller . . . of the which stripe he dyed'.[16] Colyns's fellow Londoner, Richard Arnold, dedicated an entire section of his published chronicle to forms for the 'making of Supplications to the king and to the other Lordis and Estatis'. Some of these were surprisingly personal, including one petition to the Archbishop of Canterbury and the mayor and aldermen of London from 'R. A.' himself, rehearsing an argument he was having with John Foster, Archdeacon of London (afforded no such anonymity) over debts and asking for the case to be heard in the Court of Chancery.[17] Another set of transcriptions comprised a petition, answer, proofs, and witness statements from a case that Arnold had sued to the king and Council directly sometime in Henry VII's reign.[18]

Crucially, amid these examples and others like them there are signs that these petitionary forms were copied not just for interest or for posterity but for later utility, whether for the compiler themselves or for some wider readership. Within many of the legal documents in Colyns's collection full names were replaced with the pseudonym 'J. at Noke', short for 'John-at-Nokes', a stand-in equivalent to 'John Doe' in today's parlance.[19] The example supplications and letters patents in Arnold's chronicle similarly provided initials such as 'A. B.' in the place of all the principal parties.[20] The stripping out of personal detail in the process of compilation, and the provision in other commonplace books of different sentence and language forms too, suggests that these documents were saved as templates for later use.[21] Within the notebook of gentleman Humphrey Newton of Cheshire, compiled in the early sixteenth century, we even find a quire containing standard opening lines to grants and supplications, in a mix of English and Latin and with embellished lettering. One takes the form of a vernacular petition for justice, reading: 'Lamentably shewithe unto your haighnesse youre feithfull subgiet & trewe liegeman John Stathym sone and heire to Thomas &c decesset howe one Thomas Hawardyn by his extort myght & power . . .'. Newton copied out some of the example addresses to a 'Serene and illustrious prince'.[22] It is possible, as Deborah Youngs has suggested, that this represents a parchment booklet of 'model petitions to the king', acquired by Newton in relation to his work as a scribe for his neighbours.[23]

---

[16] The text of the pardon eventually granted by Henry VIII is printed in J. Payne Collier ed., *Trevelyan Papers to A.D. 1558*, Camden Fifth Series 67 (Camden Society, 1857), 103–19.

[17] Arnold, *The customs of London*, 123–6, 129–34.   [18] *Ibid.*, 130–4.

[19] BL Harley MS 2252, fol. 36.   [20] Arnold, *The customs of London*, 123, 129–31.

[21] For other examples see Bodl. Tanner MS 407 fol. 58v; L. T. Smith ed., *A Commonplace Book of the Fifteenth Century* (Trübner and Co., 1886), 131–51.

[22] Bodl. MS Latin Misc. c. 66 fols. 96–119.

[23] D. Youngs, *Humphrey Newton (1466–1536), an Early Tudor Gentleman* (Boydell, 2008), 46–50.

'Your Poor Orator': Petitioning the King

Certainly, for the rural gentry as for the middling men of the city, legal paperwork like this was increasingly common fare. By extension, the route to royal redress was becoming more easily chartable.

The Role of Legal Aid

Whether or not individual complainants possessed these petitionary formulae, they typically did not produce petitions by themselves. Navigating the legal system was facilitated by a growing body of professional and non-professional lawyers and scribes, and seeking their aid was a habitual process by the early Tudor period. Among the legal contents of many of the commonplace books surviving from this time we find 'the forme of making of lettres of attorney': that is, a formal document by which people named an attorney to oversee transactions and agreements in their name.[24] Likewise, the series of entries recording admissions of legal representatives in Requests' order books tell us that parties there employed at least two men: an attorney and legal counsellor. Those named as attorneys had often received some formal training at the inns of Chancery, to the west of the city of London.[25] Education was not a requirement for this role, however. Many of those so admitted left no discernible trace in the registers of the inns, while some are identified in Requests' books according to other associations, such as their place of residence: for instance, Philip Ball 'of Woodstock', Henry Erlesley 'of Bucklersbury', and Thomas Everarde, living at the 'White Friars of Fleet Street' (a relatively wealthy Carmelite priory).[26] Others plainly had different, non-legal occupations altogether. One Requests plaintiff identified a skinner from London and a merchant from Dartmouth as his 'attorneys' in a debt dispute with a local abbot pursued in *c.* 1512; another used a letter of attorney to elect a leather seller and a fuller as representatives.[27] Uniting these individuals, presumably, was some form of legal knowledge and literacy. Whatever their background, surviving bills of litigants' costs tell us that attorneys were paid 20*d* each term to attend on Requests and manage the

---

[24] Oxford, Balliol College MS 354 fols. 106v–107; Cambridge, Trinity College MS O.2.53 fol. 32; Arnold, *The customs of London*, 108. For a longer letter of attorney in Requests, giving several men the power to act in the plaintiff's cause for the titles to lands, tenements, rents, and services in Beverley and Risby (Yorkshire), see REQ2/8/150.

[25] Of those men named in Requests and associated with the inns of Chancery, 16 per cent were acting as counsel and 84 per cent as attorneys, according to cross-checking in J. H. Baker, *The Men of Court 1440 to 1550: A Prosopography of the Inns of Court and Chancery and the Courts of Law*, Selden Society Supplementary Series 18 (Selden Society, 2012). On education in the inns of Chancery, see Brooks, *Pettyfoggers and Vipers*, 159–70.

[26] REQ1/3 fols. 182, 217, 269.   [27] REQ2/13/77; REQ2/8/150.

148   Seeking and Requesting Justice

procedural aspects of their client's suit. Within the order books, attorneys' signatures sometimes appear alone beneath the entries admitting them, even where counsel had been named alongside them, indicating that of the two representatives only attorneys were present at the initial stages of a suit.[28] In other words, attorneys kept suits ticking along as physical proxies for litigants, who presumably could not always be in the Court if it was constantly moving or if it resided far from their homes.

In contrast, the men identified as legal counsel (*consilium*) for Requests' litigants were more likely to appear among the registers of the elite inns of court. In a role equivalent to the advocates or barristers of other jurisdictions, they moved substantive motions and argued in favour of their client's legal rights before Requests' judges.[29] They also contributed directly to the contents and presentation of pleadings. Bills of costs regularly record fees paid to counsel for 'drawing' up bills in conversation with clients and for 'opening the matter at the barr'. Indeed, many of the loose pleadings in the Requests archive are endorsed at the bottom with small signatures and surnames, and cross-checking these with the order-book admissions entries proves that they almost invariably belonged to men appointed as *consilium*.[30] Allocating bills in this way was more common after 1520, when it became standard for Chancery pleadings to be signed by the lawyer taking responsibility over a case.[31] Dacres' ordinances of *c*. 1543 furthered this policy in Requests by declaring that 'all makers of Bills ... subscribe their names, both to answers, Replicacions and Reioynders, and every person omitting the same to repaie the fee by him receaved to the parties thereby hurte and damnified'.[32] Later on in proceedings, counsel might be paid additionally for compiling interrogatories, examining depositions, and calling upon the matter in court each term. Their total termly fee was usually in the region of 3*s* 4*d*, but could increase substantially if they also assisted in the production of further documents or were 'comyng to the barre' multiple times to argue for their clients.[33]

---

[28] E.g., REQ1/4 fol. 104; REQ1/104 fols. 59, 68, 70v, 158v; REQ1/105 fols. 4v, 9v, 10, 10v, 12v, 13, 13v, 15, 17; REQ3/30 fol. 264.

[29] For the same dichotomy in ecclesiastical law, see R. H. Helmholz, *The Profession of Ecclesiastical Lawyers: An Historical Introduction* (Cambridge University Press, 2019), 3–5.

[30] Still, by the end of the sixteenth century the practice of subscribing petitions by counsellors instead of by an 'attourney, solicitor, clarke or scrivenor' was not always observed, according to one critic: BL Add. MS 25248 fols. 2v–3.

[31] Metzger, 'The Last Phase of the Medieval Chancery', 81.

[32] BL Add. MS 25248 fol. 29. For a similar order from Edward VI's reign, see HL Ellesmere MS 2652 fol. 11v.

[33] REQ2/4/101, 2/9/97, 2/10/189, 228, 2/13/25; REQ3/5 *Jerard* v *Brasbryk and Longsdale*; REQ3/6 *Forthe* v *Daldry*; REQ3/9 *Chamber* v *Patrell*; REQ3/30 Chapman; REQ3/14 *Cobley* v *Denys*. See also Knox's

'Your Poor Orator': Petitioning the King 149

All of this tells us little about how lawyers were approached and employed in the first place, questions that pertain to our broader inquiry about the accessibility of royal justice. The presence of two types of representative among Requests' named counsel in particular gives us cause to think that some litigants, at least, employed the 'lower branch' of the legal profession on hand in their home region.[34] Firstly, hundreds of the trained common lawyers engaged occasionally in the early Tudor Requests otherwise worked their trade in King's Bench or Common Pleas – and they *always* acted in cases from the same county or region. For example, John Basset from Buckinghamshire worked as an attorney in Common Pleas for Wiltshire, Buckinghamshire, and Oxfordshire in the 1510s and represented two defendants from Buckinghamshire in Requests around the same time.[35] Lawyers like Basset were not necessarily based in the area they represented – they likely kept rooms at the inns of court – but they may well have been chosen and approached at Westminster on the recommendation of acquaintances and clients back home. Secondly, a smaller country-based group of representatives comprises those men who were *not* generally employed as lawyers, even if they had been trained at one of the inns, but who instead worked in provincial and judicial offices: as sheriffs, mayors, stewards, and, most often, as JPs. Again, these men acted primarily for clients from the regions in which they lived and governed. For instance, while acting as JP for Essex, Peter Barnes was admitted as counsel nine times in Requests, with at least one of these cases originating in Essex and another in the neighbouring county of Hertfordshire. Prospective litigants might have recognised JPs as the 'principal form of local government' in their county, but their local renown for learning and prestige would have made them obvious resources for legal aid, too.[36] Indeed, of all the representatives recorded in the early Tudor Requests, it was these powerful local administrators who likely had the greatest hand in conveying disputes from localities to centre.

Where this sort of expertise was not so readily available to a litigant, a standard form of legal and procedural advice could be found in house. Requests' various clerks and under-clerks sometimes served as attorneys; in fact, this was part of their apprenticeship in the Court. The earliest known beneficiary of this trajectory was Robert Sampson, an occasional attorney

comprehensive list of costs in the Edwardian Requests: 'The Court of Requests in the Reign of Edward VI', 323–4.

[34] Brooks, *Pettyfoggers and Vipers*; T. S. Haskett, 'Country Lawyers? The Composers of English Chancery Bills', in P. Birks ed., *The Law of the Land* (Hambledon Press, 1993), 9–23.

[35] Baker, *The Men of Court*, 277.   [36] Baker, *OHLE*, 265.

150   Seeking and Requesting Justice

in the 1490s and later clerk of the privy seal and Council (also the elder
brother of Richard Sampson, Dean of the Chapel Royal in the 1520s), who
was initially apprenticed to Robert Rydon, a more senior clerk.[37]
Thereafter, the most prevalent attorney-turned-clerk in Requests was
Richard Turnor of the Middle Temple, said to have spent 'threescore
and six years partly as servant and partly as Officer' in the Court.[38] In his
early career he was admitted as an attorney in over 100 cases, taking charge
of the order books by 1515 and ascending to clerkship of the privy seal on
Sampson's death in *c.* 1520.[39] In the years that followed, Turnor was
supported in managing Requests' clients by a series of leading attorneys:
John Patten, between 1493 and 1500; then William Wilkins, who put in
twenty-seven separate appearances between 1502 and 1504; John Radford,
who dominated proceedings in 1518 and 1519, as Requests' business levels
were rising; then Thomas Wetherby of Gray's Inn, who made thirty
appearances between 1517 and 1523, along with Jacob Gerard and Henry
Bury of the Middle Temple, who were admitted around twenty-five times
each in the same period. Admissions of attorneys were barely recorded in
the mid-1520s, but on the Court's return to form at the end of that decade
there was an even clearer predominance of William Dobson of Staple Inn
(fifty-one appearances, 1529–33), Simon Sampson (son of Robert and
nephew of Richard Sampson, who made exactly 100 recorded appearances,
1530–46), and Richard Flower (fifty-four admissions, 1532–45). In other
words, the Court usually had dedicated attorneys and their numbers
increased towards the end of our period.

   An intriguing document discovered among the uncatalogued paperwork
in the Requests archive further illuminates the behind-the-scenes dealings
involved in hiring legal advisors, particularly for disputants already on the
back foot. This is a list of 'Intruccyons for Thomas Bawne of Sckerne',
Yorkshire, a defendant called into Requests in the later years of Henry

---

[37] REQ1/1 fol. 16. He was appointed clerk of the privy seal in Apr. 1497, *CPR 1494–1509*, 112. However,
   the pardon roll of 1509 refers to 'Robert Sampson or Samson, of the Household, clerk of the King's
   Council, clerk of the Privy Seal': *LP* I. 483 (3). Rydon had been appointed as clerk of the Council in
   April 1492 'for that the Councell should not be unserved for the multitude of hard Causes daily
   riseing in the said Councell': TNA C82/92; Bayne and Dunham eds., *Select Cases in the Council of
   Henry VII*, lxxix.

[38] Lambarde, *Archeion*, 229–30. This contradicts Baker's view that there were three separate men called
   Richard Turnor – the 'busiest attorney in Requests', a clerk of the privy seal, and the 'clerk of the
   Court of Requests': *The Men of Court*, 1566. That there was just one Turnor is supported by the
   continuity of his handwriting in the books from 1515 until at least the end of Henry VIII's reign, and
   by a reference to his service to Henry VII, Henry VIII, Edward VI and Mary I for the previous fifty-
   four years in a grant made in 1555: *CPR 1554–1555*, 222–23.

[39] Knox, 'The Court of Requests in the Reign of Edward VI', 253–4, 256; *LP* IV. 1860 (5).

'Your Poor Orator': Petitioning the King 151

VIII's reign. The anonymous author of the note advised Bawne to avoid taking the advice of 'one Turnebull a lernyd man of the spyrytuall law at Yorke' because he was already of counsel with the plaintiff, the widow Ellen Forster.[40] Incidentally, then, this petitioner had found counsel locally and had sought advice *not* from a common lawyer, as was usual in Requests, but from someone learned in ecclesiastical or canon law. Meanwhile, it was recommended that Bawne seek out 'Mr Hedley ... Mr Flower [and] Mr Sampson of the Whyt Halle' – that is, the lawyers regularly on hand to act as attorneys in Requests. Interestingly, Bawne was informed that he could find them at 'a wyttelyng howsse' – a victualling house, or tavern – belonging to a man called John Williams and located within the precinct of the Palace of Westminster. This was surely valuable knowledge for a person forced to quickly put together a case for their own defence (a perspective we will return to in Chapter 8). While this document is rough and hastily written, the handwriting bears a striking resemblance to Turnor's, which appears near ubiquitously across the Court's paperwork in the early Tudor period.[41] Perhaps more of the build-up to petitioning and pleading happened within the Court and its surrounding corridors and streets than we might presume.

Some form of counsel having been found, the process of drafting a petition was distinct from the action of writing it up on parchment or paper for delivery to the Court. This much is clear from the bills of costs, which cite separate fees paid for the 'drawing' of the bill of complaint with the advice of counsel and for its 'engrossing' onto parchment.[42] This second charge was made out not to counselling lawyers but to a 'clerk' – a term that here refers to a person with clerical and administrative skills. This was someone who was literate, who could write, and who, more importantly, understood the form and structure required for royal courts. These scribes leave little trace through which we might identify them. Evidently, educated gentry men such as Humphrey Newton worked casually as scribes for friends and neighbours; elsewhere, vicars, churchwardens, and storekeepers might also be approached for help with document production.[43] Within the legal world, public notaries attached to an array of local courts or apprenticed to

---

[40] REQ3/3 *Forster* v *Bawne*.

[41] It compares quite closely to the memorandum that Turnor scrawled personally on another court document, reading 'M[emoran]d[um] that I Richard Turnor deliv[er]ed this indentur herin specified to Thomas Sharpe the xxij^{ti} daye of Oct a[nn]o xxix': REQ3/6 *Sharpe* v *Sharpe*.

[42] E.g., REQ2/2/97, 2/3/162, REQ3/5 *Jerarde* v *Brasbryk and Longsdale*, REQ3/30 *Winbylston* v *Landlowe*, REQ3/30 *Golder* v *Unknown*.

[43] M. Spufford, 'The Scribes of Villagers' Wills in the Sixteenth and Seventeenth Centuries and their Influence', *Local Population Studies* 7 (1971), 28–43.

152   Seeking and Requesting Justice

lawyers could step in to write up fair copies of complaints initially drafted by counsel, and a professional cadre of scriveners was becoming available for employment by our period.[44]

The range of scribal options available to litigants, depending on convenience and cost, is reflected in the variety in hand, length, style, and neatness of petitions in the early Tudor Requests archive. A small proportion of surviving bills dating from the early reign of Henry VIII are in the same neat secretary hand, such as would suggest that they were produced by (and possibly even within) the Court itself. Indeed, a couple of petitions signed at the bottom by Robert Sampson are in the same handwriting; perhaps he performed scribal work on the side of his duties as clerk of the privy seal.[45] Otherwise, the scant detail provided by the bills of costs tell us that counsel sometimes employed their own clerks, and litigants paid them an additional fee to produce a standard form of bill.[46] At the other end of the spectrum, the presence of very scrappy and non-formulaic petitions – without title or structure, and written in the first person – indicates that some complainants did not have convenient access to particularly professional or knowledgeable scribes. Many of these stand out for their irregular and regionalised spellings: for instance, the Cumberland-based Margaret Coupland's description of herself as a 'pouer wedoo', the tendency for Gloucestershire petitions to use 'y' for 'I' (instead of the more formal 'your orator'), and the unusual opening of the husbandman William Whore's petition, 'Besechyng yor nobull hyghnes to have compacyon apon yor daylye bedman', from that same county.[47] Indeed, although we are almost always told where the plaintiff hailed from within the opening lines of their complaint, we cannot be certain that the dialect of the petition is theirs. It could well be that of the scribe instead, whose origins are unknown and unknowable.[48] Still, the range of styles, idioms, and spellings among Requests' pleadings confirms that there was likely a great number of

---

[44] Youngs, *Humphrey Newton*, 46–50; H. Killick, 'The Scribes of Petitions in Late Medieval England', in Killick and Smith eds., *Petitions and Strategies of Persuasion in the Middle Ages*, 64–87; N. Ramsay, 'Scriveners and Notaries as Legal Intermediaries in Later Medieval England', in J. Kermode ed., *Enterprise and Individuals in Fifteenth-Century England* (Alan Sutton, 1991), 120–2; K. Wrightson, *Ralph Tailor's Summer: A Scrivener, His City, and the Plague* (Yale University Press, 2011), 62–74.

[45] E.g., REQ2/13/84. It has been suggested that an earlier privy-seal clerk, Thomas Hoccleve, also spent time 'moonlighting' as a scribe for petitioners: Killick, 'The Scribes of Petitions in Late Medieval England', 69, 71–3.

[46] REQ3/22/1 *Complay* v *Palmer and Lobbes*.   [47] REQ2/2/153, 2/4/268.

[48] See the introductory discussion of petitions in M. Benskin, M. Laing, V. Karaiskos and K. Williamson eds., 'Index of Sources', *Electronic Linguistic Atlas of Late Mediaeval English* (2013), www.lel.ed.ac.uk/ihd/elalme/elalme.html, accessed Jan. 2023.

'Your Poor Orator': Petitioning the King 153

'country lawyers' and local scribes, of varying degrees of expertise, on hand to turn a grudge into a formal complaint fit for the king.

In most cases, a bill went through several iterations before being worked into a fair copy ready for presentation to the Council, as evidence of some editing suggests. Whereas an initial draft of William Chapell's petition of *c.* 1529 was marked with numerous crossings out and interlineations, including one note adding in another named plaintiff and upgrading their self-designation from 'poure men' to '*very* pore men', a second version appearing within the same casefile in the Requests archive is much neater and more elaborate, with large and emboldened letters to mark new clauses.[49] Clearly Chapell and his new co-petitioner could afford for this extra work to be done on their behalf. Other petitions, in contrast, contain lines squeezed in around holes in the page, or bear the marks of the parchment having been scraped to remove and replace lines of text. On a few occasions the sense is that such editing removed references to the original addressee, presumably the Lord Chancellor, and redirected the same bill to the king.[50] So, while some plaintiffs could spare the expense of drafting and redrafting their bill, others did not wish to waste ink, paper, or the time of their legal aid. In all, as Gwilym Dodd has suggested, petitions for justice were the product neither of the Crown and its agents nor the localities alone; rather, making a supplication involved a range of inter-mediaries along the way, from the village to the Council and household itself.[51]

The Substance of Petitioning

All this knowledge, advice, and money went into petitions which, like other forms of complaint literature, were formulaic but also informationally and rhetorically complex. It should be reiterated that, aside from *always* being addressed to the king, petitions to the quasi-institutionalised early Tudor Requests were near identical to those submitted to Chancery, Star Chamber, and the provincial councils. Following a structure similar to that of the 'Ancient Petitions' of earlier centuries, they contained five rough sections: an opening address from the 'poor orator'; some background to the case and the assets in dispute; a description of the current fallout, containing a narrative of offences committed; a line or so justifying resort to royal justice and the

---

[49] REQ2/8/121 (my emphasis).
[50] E.g., REQ2/2/5, 136, REQ3/10 *Huntley* v *Spermon*, REQ3/13 *Rowsell* v *Mallett*.
[51] G. Dodd, 'The Rise of English, the Decline of French: Supplications to the English Crown, c.1420–1450', *Speculum* 86 (2011), 118–20.

154   Seeking and Requesting Justice

demands being made on this authority; and a final expression of good wishes for the king's prosperity.[52] By way of example, a standard petition to Requests looks something like this:

> To the king our sov[er]ain lord
>   Schewyth unto yor moste g[ra]cious highnes your true and faithfull subgiett Thomas May son and heir of Thomas May late of Sunnynghill decessed / That wher[e] he and his auncet[or]s tyme that no ma[n]nys mynde is to the contrary have ben peasablye possessed and seased in their demeynes as of fee w[ith]out any int[er]upcion of any man[er] p[er]son aswell in & of a crofte called Purycrofte set & lyinge w[ith]in the p[ar]ishe of Wynkefeld as of certain quiet rentes of vj s viij d yerlye goynge out aswell of the said crofte as of a mese & other landes w[ith] thapp[ur]tenaunces called Hullrewe set & lying w[ith]in the said p[ar]iche late appertenyng to oon John Spens[er] decessaid / So it is g[ra]cious sov[er]ain lord that on[e] John Batale gent of his extort power co[n]trary to all right & good co[n]science forsiblye hath entered into the said crofte called Purycrofte & also deteigh-neth from yor said power supliaunt xvj d yerely of his said quiete rent and by his grete myghte the same occupieth & kepeth from your seid supliaunt to his uttre undoyng as by good and sufficient dedes therуppon made mor playnly it doth appere / And to the dyssherynting of yor said suppliaunt w[ith]out yor grace esp[ec]ial her[e]in to him be shewed // It may please y[er]for yor highness in tendr consideracion of the p[re]misses and in asmoche as yor said power suppliaunt ys of non power to sue for his remedye herin agayn the said John Bataile by the cours of yor comyn lawes to co[m] maunde the same John Bataile by yor moste drade co[m]maundeme[n]t to be & p[er]sonally apper before the lordes of yor moste honorable counsaill at a briefe day & und[er] a greyte payne to answer to the p[re]misses and further to be ordered in the same as schall accord with yowr lawes right & good conscience / And yor said orator during his lyffe schall daily p[ra]y to god for the long p[re]s[er]vacion of yor estate royall /[53]

The subject matter of complaints to Requests, which takes up most of the middle part of petitions, was examined in Chapter 4. We now turn instead to the subtle differences in the content and framing of claims made to Requests and other royal tribunals to illuminate how plaintiffs perceived

---

[52] This maps on roughly to the structure of a letter in the *ars dictaminis* tradition, with the *salutatio, exordium, narratio, petitio,* and *conclusio,* appearing in older petitions to the Crown too: G. Dodd, 'Writing Wrongs: The Drafting of Supplications to the Crown in Later Fourteenth-Century England', *Medium Aevum* 80:2 (2011), 224–7. This is more straightforward than Chancery petitions, where Haskett identified as many as eleven distinct sections: T. S. Haskett, 'The Presentation of Cases in Medieval Chancery Bills', in W. M. Gordon and T. D. Fergus eds., *Legal History in the Making* (Hambledon Press, 1991), 12.

[53] REQ2/12/14; for many more examples of standard petitions to Requests, see Leadam ed., *Select Cases in the Court of Requests.*

'Your Poor Orator': Petitioning the King 155

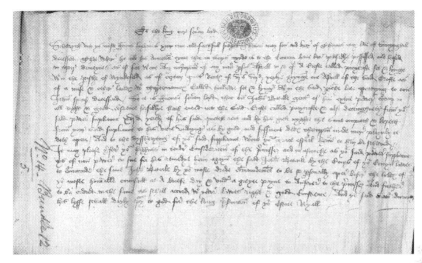

Figure 6.1 Petition of *Thomas May* v. *John Battel*, submitted to the king and Council in the Henrician period. © The National Archives, ref. REQ2/12/14.

the diversification of this judicial provision. Petitions submitted to Requests, Chancery, and Star Chamber were more regular and individualised than collective petitioning or anonymous bill-casting. And yet, despite belonging to a mechanism of speaking to authority that was deferential and 'deeply conservative', these petitions were crucial to moulding more innovative, responsive elements of governance.[54] Their evocations of law, peace, and conscience, mixed with commentary on social disparity and its consequences, were central to the respective cultures of the conciliar courts.

To gauge the range of possibilities open to royal petitioners, it is worth beginning with exceptional cases before building up to the general culture of justice in this context. Although there was a generic documentary canon in place by the early Tudor period, there was considerable leeway for personalisation. It probably suited the most desperate suitors to break from convention. The petition of eighty-year-old Richard Aungern from Southwark, dated to sometime in Henry VIII's reign, is worth quoting at length for its distinctiveness in contrast to standard examples:

> Most noble and excellent prynce and sov[er]aigne lord and yet more noble in the studye of godlynes than in the ornamentes of fortune Forasmoche as

---

[54] Scase, 'Strange and Wonderful Bills', 367. On petitions and agency see Wood, 'Subordination, Solidarity and the Limits of Popular Agency'.

> yor daily orator and pour bedman Rychard Aungern . . . being of the age of lxxx yeres or there abowte vere impotent through the debelite and ffeblenes of old age knowlegyth hym self un worthy to have any words in the p[re]sens of yor excellent hyghnes And that he can not attayne to yor gracis speche when he wold Therfor he humble desyreth you in the way of charyte and for the blessed love of cristes passion to rede ov[er] thys simple byll of complaint . . . Or elles the same yor besecher ys lyke ^to^ dy through hunger and thurst and an impotent woman his wyf for souche thynges as should sustayne old age onles yor grace have now remors upon us / Thys at the rev[er]ence of god and wey of charyte and the same yor pour orator his wyf and pour chyldren shall ev[er]more pray god for the p[ro]sp[er]ous astate of yor noble highness long p[ro]sp[er]ously to contenue and endure /[55]

Here the typical deferential language of the petition is heightened even further than usual through references to 'godlynes' and 'cristes passion' and the implication of the king's care for the very life and death of his subjects. It also gives the impression that some complainants, at least, believed that they could feasibly 'have . . . words in the presens' of their sovereign, but that the written bill of complaint served as a suitable stand-in. The emphasis on physical modes of address combined with written media was contained in orators' claims to prostrate themselves at the feet of the sovereign, and was further encapsulated in the later practice of Masters of Requests kneeling before the monarch while discussing cases, consciously taking the place of petitioners.[56] Similar physicality and reverence comes through in the claim in the exhortation, more elaborate than usual in Aungern's petition, that supplicants prayed every day for the king.

This is an exception that proves the rule; it confirms what was normal for a Requests petition and how far formulae might be adapted and pushed.[57] Another, different approach was taken in the mid-1520s suit of Lucy Atkins, who also abandoned the deferential petitionary canon by submitting her plea in first-person letter form. She began directly, without even an opening address to the king: 'Lucy Atkyns power widow dothe put be fore yor Mastershypp [one of Requests' judges] thys wrytyng for by cause I am an olde woman not having remembrawnce to utter my tale

---

[55] REQ2/8/175.

[56] Kesselring, *Mercy and Authority*, 116–17; Dabhoiwala, 'Writing Petitions in Early Modern England', 132. For the same in other petitionary contexts see W. M. Ormrod, 'Murmur, Clamour and Noise: Voicing Complaint and Remedy in Petitions to the English Crown, *c.*1300–*c.*1460', in Ormrod, Dodd, and Musson eds., *Medieval Petitions: Grace and Grievance*, 135–55.

[57] As was also the case for Gwilym Dodd's analysis of one particularly rhetorical set of fifteenth-century petitions in TNA SC 8: 'Thomas Paunfield, the "heye Court of rightwisnesse" and the Language of Petitioning in the Fifteenth Century', in Ormrod, Dodd, and Musson eds., *Medieval Petitions: Grace and Grievance*, 222–42.

'Your Poor Orator': Petitioning the King

redely in thys audyaunce in the whyche I do yow to wete that I am a power woman & he the sayd John Segar clarke [the defendant] a ryche man.' The rest of her petition recounted previous efforts undertaken by the Bishop of Chichester to mediate the dispute before beseeching the judges 'to be good unto me & consider my ryght for I am not able to sew the law no longer'.[58] Another self-proclaimed 'pore widow' did not even name herself in her simple, seven-line petition, lamenting only that in pursuing a man called William Burwell for debts it 'hathe cost me & hendred me xx^{ti} marke & hathe a most undon me with howt yor noble grace se me remedyd'.[59] A contrasting example is a much less obsequious plea submitted to Wolsey as Chancellor by one 'trewe power cristen Ingleshe man' and his wife, who said that if they received no remedy 'they may make opyn crye and abrode saye that there is right nor Justice in England'. This sentence, and an accompanying allegation that the Chancellor of the London diocese was 'blynd deth and domb' to their plight, was at some point crossed out.[60] We might wonder whether an *ab*normal petition was the consequence of employing cheaper counsel and scribes, or a strategy designed to make a plea stand out in a sea of near-identical bills. In favour of the latter theory is the observation that many of the above examples, far from being scrappy in appearance or idiosyncratic in writing, looked exactly like other, more standard bills. The rejection of formulae could therefore have been a choice in which litigant, lawyer, and clerk collaborated.

The capacity for such collaborations to promote petitioners' voices over scribes' conventions has been debated by sociolegal scholars. But nowhere was the plaintiff's viewpoint clearer than in those instances in which educated men had to record the stories of poor women. Cordelia Beattie has written of the 'petitioning subject' constructed around female litigants, even in bills in which they were named as plaintiffs alongside a spouse.[61] In Requests, while a petition against the sheriff of Bristol, William Skelke, for abusing his position and allowing a debtor to escape judgment was presented in the name of John Wylley and Agnes, his wife, it was Agnes's voice that dominated. She and their legal counsel emphasised not only her own vulnerability but also the trouble she had faced in chasing up debts far from

---

[58] REQ2/13/43.
[59] REQ3/14 *Unknown* v *Burwell*. This plaintiff might be Alice Golding, assuming this is the same case as is filed in REQ2/11/187.
[60] REQ3/25 *Verdon* v *Spencer*.
[61] Beattie, 'Your Oratrice: Women's Petitions to the Late Medieval Court of Chancery'. For a similar study see D. Youngs, 'Reading Ravishment: Gender and "Will" Power in the Early Tudor Star Chamber, 1500–50', in Kesselring and Mears eds., *Star Chamber Matters*, 41–60.

158   Seeking and Requesting Justice

the couple's hometown of London. She reminded the king that 'yor seyd towen of Brystoll ys a countye in hym selff', and argued that 'the seyd William Skelke [was] a grett rycheman gretely ffryndid & borne w[ith]in the same towne' whereas 'yor seyd oratrix is a power woman & abydyng in yor Citie of London & notte able to trie wyth the seid [William] Skelke within yor seyd towne of Bristoll'.[62] Another case saw Elizabeth Redknapp, named as wife of the principal petitioner in a suit over the withholding of lands owing to her as survivor of her late husband, centre her own cause by lamenting having been 'dryven of powre necessite to marey ageyn' to George Redknapp, 'a powre man the whiche ys sore dryven in age havyng no substaunce ne goodes to helpe ne suker hym ne his saide powre wieff'.[63] As we will see further below, a sole female plaintiff in any conciliar tribunal had recourse to a particular set of discourses about women and the law which might heighten their position as a supplicant especially worthy of mercy and aid.

The potential for individuality did not preclude the recurrence of certain sets of expectations surrounding justice itself, however. The most overt norms evoked in petitions, though perhaps also the most surprising given the later characterisation of courts of conscience as extra-legal, were the laws and statutes of the realm. Sometimes references to such frameworks could be quite general, as in the many pleas that simply described opponents' conduct as 'contrarie to yor lawes statutes & peax' or, where there was suspicion that an adversary was being maintained or funded by another, as against an unspecified 'statute of champertie'.[64] A smaller number cited specific legislation, passed in recent memory. Statutes from the 1495 parliament, in which Henry VII had sought to prove his commitment to the commonwealth, were particularly resonant in the years that followed.[65] Hugh Shirley's petition of 1496 requested that a JP be empowered to investigate his rioting tenants, 'accordyng to the Statute made in your last Parliament for such assembles and riotes'.[66] In c. 1501 the inhabitants of Bosworth referred to the 'statute of perjurye' – presumably that introduced in the parliament of 1495 and continued in 1497 – under which they would have tried the Abbot of Leicester for his maintenance of a jury if they were not so poor.[67] Later on, Richard Halswell's petition of c. 1520 evoked the

---

[62] REQ3/5 *Wylley v Skelke*.   [63] REQ3/5 *Redknapp v Gough*.
[64] REQ2/2/73, 2/4/327; REQ3/16/1 *Pedley v Cooke*; REQ3/3 *Ashe v Byrde*. This plaintiff might have been referring to any number of acts against the financial maintenance of litigants passed in the late medieval period: 4 Ed. III c. 11, 20 Ed. III cc. 4–6, 1 Rich. II c. 4.
[65] Cavill, *The English Parliaments of Henry VII*, 16, 74–6.
[66] REQ2/2/81, referring to 11 Hen. VII c. 7.   [67] REQ2/2/97.

'Your Poor Orator': Petitioning the King 159

1514 statute 'concerning dekaye of howses & husbondry'.[68] The growing body of legislation concerning landholding passed in the early sixteenth century provided especially useful to Requests' petitioners. The 1536 Statute of Uses was occasionally cited in bills throughout the following decade to claim properties freed up by 'the extynguysshement of uses' or to explain efforts to make new estates in lands threatened by its terms, perhaps exploiting its initial lack of clarity.[69] In these instances the detailed contents, caveats, and consequences of any cited legislation were largely glossed over. Rather, they were raised as a standard against which opponents had offended – and which the king, as the fount of all law and justice, must defend.

The same argument could be fruitfully employed in the other direction, too, with petitioners' behaviour framed as ultimately loyal and lawful because it aligned with the king's will. The 'poure subiectes habitants and treue liechemen' of Abbotsham in Devon petitioned the king in 1515 to complain about their treatment at the hands of the Abbot of Tavistock, under whose lordship their manor fell. Their bill recalled how they had lately heard 'comandement appon proclamacion by oon Thomas Goodman yor late officer shireff of ... yor said Countie of Devonshere by auctorite of an acte of parliament made the iiijth day of Februarii in the iiijth yere of yor said Reigne That buttes shold be made repaired and kepte in every ... Citie Townes and places'. They felt themselves tasked with installing archery butts to 'excersice them selff with long bowes in showtyng', which they dutifully did, until the abbot ordered the manor's surveyor and clerk to seize the inhabitants' goods, apparently as restitution for some perceived misbehaviour. These petitioners might have provided a deliberately vague account of their dispute; for his part, the abbot claimed that he had tried some of his tenants in the Abbotsham manor court for armed trespasses. What is important, however, is that this group of reportedly poor inhabitants and their scribe had direct access to the text of the 1511–12 Act 'concerning shooting in Longe Bowes', reported to them in 1513 but perhaps also posted up in the nearby market town of Barnstaple if not in their own locality. Their petition rehearsed the Act almost word for word; there is even one spot where the scribe's eye must have slipped down a line and they erroneously copied out 'every of them be compelled to make and [contynewe such butts ...]' before replacing it with the

---

[68] REQ2/3/134; 6 Hen. VIII c. 5.
[69] E.g., REQ3/4 *Sewarde* v *Ilcom and Thomas*; REQ3/7 *Glasyer* v *Symonds*; REQ3/8 *Manning and Manning* v *Beale*.

160 Seeking and Requesting Justice

correct line about 'every Citie Towne and Place' added in.[70] Contrary to any presumption we might hold that the conscience-based jurisdiction of the Council allowed it to undermine the common law, cases like this reveal that many petitioners believed that the king was precisely the person to go to in order to see that law upheld.[71]

Still, any technicalities of legislation or procedures of common law were always secondary in petitions to narratives of individual suffering and some abstract gesturing to the good health of the wider realm. Rarely do we see here the language of 'commons' or 'commonwealth' present in the anonymised libels and in the rebel manifestos of this period, whether in the sense of a political community or in relation to the lower echelons of society.[72] Yet petitioners might insist that their opponents' bad behaviour had disrupted the immediate social harmonies. Victims of serious assaults or verbal abuses described themselves as going about their business 'in God's peace and in yours' – the king's – until their adversary showed up.[73] All armed mobs were characterised as 'riotous riotours and brekers of yor peax', and petitioners asked for help in allowing themselves, their friends and neighbours to 'lyve in yor peace sovereign lord'.[74] Cases between two disputatious neighbours could likewise be subsumed under the suffering of the whole neighbourhood. So, while the widow Joan Tyller had her own grudge against Robert South of Salisbury, it served her interests to add in that he was 'ye greatest suppressor of yor graces pore subjectes within ye cyte'.[75] Resolution in any of these matters was conceived as laying in the king's role as moral exemplar to his subjects. John Nicholas presented Sir Walter Herbert's oppression and extortion of his tenants in Monmouthshire as being to 'the haynouse example of all extorcions & misdoers', while a physical assault on Margaret Lentall by the yeoman John Wyndover in the fields of Mounton, Devonshire, was said to be a 'perillous example of all evill doers in those partes if this shuld be unpunysshed'.[76] So, while there may have been no outright language of broader solidarities in these petitions, the consequences of injustice were nonetheless framed as damaging to social cohesion.

[70] REQ3/1/1 *Lacy* v *Abbot of Tavistock*; 3 Hen VIII. c. 3.
[71] For more on the citation of statutes and charters in petitions, see A. Musson, 'Patterns of Supplication and Litigation Strategies: Petitioning the Crown in the Fourteenth Century', in Killick and Smith eds., *Petitions and Strategies of Persuasion in the Middle Ages*, 90–2.
[72] Watts, 'Public or Plebs: The Changing Meaning of "The Commons"', 242–60.
[73] E.g., REQ2/2/156, 2/4/285, 2/5/104, 2/6/16, 2/7/139, 2/8/50, 2/10/32, 2/11/97, 2/12/4, 229, 2/13/82.
[74] REQ2/2/59, 2/8/272. For a discussion of the 'normative concept' of peace in local contexts, see Johnson, *Law in Common*, 45–7.
[75] REQ3/3 *Tiller* v *South*. See also REQ3/4 *Russell* v *Jolice*.   [76] REQ2/6/76, 2/2/66.

'Your Poor Orator': Petitioning the King

Moreover, uniting all petitions to the king's conciliar justice were the intertwining principles of right, justice, conscience, pity, charity, and mercy that we observed in Chapter 1. Rhetoric-heavy supplications hardly yield firmer definitions of these terms and concepts than do the vague speeches, sermons, and advice literature of the early Tudor period, however. The invocation of 'right and good conscience' was so commonplace in petitions of all kinds that it is difficult to discern what was meant by either term, and even whether they were considered distinct from one another.[77] Perhaps the most functionally important concept in the context of conciliar justice was conscience – but *whose* conscience? First and foremost, it was the defendant's conscience, and their faltering sense of right and wrong, that was on trial. Many plaintiffs did not miss the opportunity to describe their adversaries as 'a man of small conscience', or better yet as being 'without consciens' altogether, with this internal forum triable in the process of making an answer under oath.[78] More typically, 'conscience' was evoked in conjunction with 'right', 'truth', 'reason', and 'justice', as wider virtues violated by the defendant, and so all the events set out in a given complaint – the seizure of lands, distraint of cattle, withholding of wages – might be summarised as being 'against right and good conscience'.[79] Otherwise, in Requests, more than in Chancery or Star Chamber, justice, conscience, and their cognate concepts were framed as characteristics embodied by the king himself. Petitions took him to be naturally possessed of 'abundant' mercy, pity, and charity, and willing to direct his prerogative in favour of his subjects whenever required. The multiple meanings of 'conscience' in Requests are encapsulated by the petition of Richard Bigges, a clothmaker from Kent, who lamented that '[the defendant] lytyll regarding his conscience good truth or equate hath delayed yor said orator in his payment . . . to [Bigges's] utter undoing except he be holpen here by conscience'.[80] Conscience was a standard to which both the adversary and the Court's judges – and, by extension, the king – might be held.

The similar concept of equity was evoked much more rarely at this early date. A few petitioners expressly sought a remedy consonant with the 'equitie of yor [the king's] laws' or that might 'stond wythe equyte & the dexteryte of [the] comen lawe of thys realm'.[81] This wording at least implies an understanding of equity as the mitigation of the rigour of law, acting on

---

[77] For a fuller discussion of the meaning of 'conscience', 'equity', and alike terms in the sixteenth-century Court of Chancery, see N. Jones, '"Equity" in the Court of Chancery, 1529–1615', in D. Foster and C. Mitchell eds., *Essays on the History of Equity* (Hart Publishing, forthcoming, 2023).
[78] REQ2/7/51, 2/12/155. [79] E.g., REQ2/2/136, 2/4/55, 393, 2/7/6, 128. [80] REQ2/3/124.
[81] REQ2/2/154, 2/3/290, 2/4/94, 123; TNA STAC2/28/1.

162   Seeking and Requesting Justice

its spirit even if not its word. Generally, though, this notion was deployed
with much less precision and without a specifically legal meaning. Indeed,
petitions much more often layered up many near-synonymous virtues,
including equity, for maximum effect. Thus in the late 1520s the widow
Edith Roberts asked the king to be 'charitablie moved with pitye &
compassion of yor habundant grace and rightwiseness mercyfully'.[82]
A letter from a man called John Lucas to Thomas Thirlby, Dean of the
Chapel Royal and judge in Requests, is similarly illuminating for its
reminder that Thirlby was tasked with examining 'causes of pytie and
the succour and helpe of poore men in ther causes of Justice, aienste
[against] suche wronge doers as wolde oppresse poor people'.[83] This rare
statement of purpose reminds us, again, that this was a tribunal characterised contemporarily in terms of function rather than law or jurisdiction; as
having a general care for the poor, best figured as pity or mercy, rather than
as operating on any more defined, juridical principle of equity.

This intention was manifested in a more distinctive element of petitions to the king and his Requests Council: the justification by way of
self-fashioning that took up the latter half of the bill. We saw in
Chapter 4 that a significant proportion of petitioners provided some
description of their occupation, trade, or status in life. Yet in thousands
of casefiles – 68 per cent of all the surviving petitions to the early Tudor
Requests, in fact – the plaintiff offered *no* self-identification at all. They
instead levelled general claims to being either chronically poor or in the
process of impoverishment. The opening lines of petitions often feature
descriptions of the plaintiff as a 'poor orator' – a phrase so common to
petitionary vocabulary here and elsewhere that it ought to be taken as
rhetorical rather than as a point of fact. Yet in Requests the final portion
of a bill was frequently used to further qualify and explain this positioning. Petitioners might assert that they were the main breadwinner of their
household or the primary carer of children, that they were homeless or
destitute, or that they were reliant entirely upon the wages of their daily
labours or the 'almeys & giftes of well disposed peple'.[84] Even if petitions
contained a tale of excessive prior litigation like those we encountered in
Chapter 5, this did not cancel out a claim to poverty, since the supplicant
could claim to have been bankrupted, or to have 'consumyd their

---

[82] REQ2/2/116. For another example of mercy and pity complementing justice, see the petition of
Agnes Silkby to the king to acquire the estate of her late husband, who had been condemned as
a Lollard and burnt in 1521–2: P. R. Cavill, 'A Lollard of Coventry: A Source on Robert Silkby',
Midland History 38:2 (2013), 226–31.
[83] REQ3/7 *Wylson* v *Garland*.   [84] REQ3/8 *Marten* v *Yeo*.

'Your Poor Orator': Petitioning the King 163

substaunce', in that pursuit.[85] Combined with allegations of failing legal mechanisms elsewhere, these claims painted plaintiffs as subjects worthy of the king's charity and mercy.

Above all, petitioners to the king and Requests were keen to demonstrate that they were at a disadvantage compared to their opponent. Here, 'poverty' and 'poorness' were *relative* qualities, determined by factors beyond money and property. Certainly, it was not uncommon for petitioners to stress that they were economically worse off than their adversaries. A remarkably specific example is the plea of John Ryce, submitted to Requests in the later years of Henry VIII's reign. Ryce recounted suffering various vexations at law, including in Requests itself, intended to 'make me spende all that I have', while his opponent's family 'hathe xl li in landes and C ponde in goodes left with them' and 'so myche mony to feyd the lawers that thei care nott what they spende'.[86] Much more often these relative subject positions were figured in terms of a wider set of social realities and relationships, however. We have seen already that gender determined the contents of a petition for justice: a sole female plaintiff could describe herself as an 'innocent woman no expert in worldly business', as charged with childcare, or destitute for lack of a living husband; meanwhile, men emphasised their work, stressed that they had 'nothinge but that he gettethe by his daylie labor', and mentioned their responsibilities for wives and children.[87] For exceptionally elderly plaintiffs, age was a mitigating circumstance. Avice Willes of Hothfield in Kent claimed to be 'of thage of iiij score yere & tenne' – over ninety – and described how 'two yong men' of her town had 'perceived the debilitation weyknesse and innocencey of yor said aged pore bedwoman' and had tried to short-change her in the sale of her lands.[88] Such descriptions were sometimes accompanied by reference to physical ailments or disabilities, such as blindness and deafness.[89] Similarly, very young plaintiffs, who usually sued alongside a guardian, alleged that their minority had been taken advantage of by relatives and acquaintances who coveted their inheritances.[90]

Generally speaking, though, plaintiffs and counsel typically left aside specifics in favour of sweeping statements about the consequences of social disparity. These particularly related to the due processes of justice, as per the narratives of previous, failed attempts at litigation explored in

---

[85] E.g., REQ3/10 *Gregory* v *Lawde and Parkyn*.   [86] REQ3/3 *Ryce* v *Ryce*.   [87] REQ2/3/4.

[88] REQ2/13/59; see also REQ2/1/1, 2/3/246, 2/5/383, 2/6/39, REQ3/1 pt 1 *Cause* v *Rich*, REQ3/7 *Olyff* v *Monk*.

[89] REQ2/6/75, 2/7/7; REQ3/6 *Robyns* v *Hall*.

[90] REQ2/12/27; REQ3/5 *Samford* v *Samford*; REQ3/18 *Pulker* v *Pulker and Welsburn*.

164 Seeking and Requesting Justice

Chapter 5. The description of a defendants' unconscionable, unjust, and unlawful behaviour was usually followed in the bill of complaint by the plaintiff's final plea for aid, reading something like this: 'yor seyd Orator be but pore and of small substance in godes and have but fewe frendes & lytell acquytance and the seid [defendant] ys a man of grete substance aswele in land as in godes and hath grete frenshippe alyance favors & acqueytance and ys born by diverse men wherefore yor seyd pore orator[s] canne have no true tryall in the premisses by course of the comen lawe', or some variation of one or all of these claims to disadvantage.[91] This rather profuse example captures the sense that it was not only money, age, or ability that set neighbours apart, but the structural elements of immoveable property, kinship, and favour too. It was for this reason that one petitioner could define himself oxymoronically as a 'pore gentylman', in reference to points of disparity other than wealth and status; and that another 'powre man' could describe himself as a 'jorney laborer' surviving only on his daily work, and his opponent, a husbandman, as 'a man of substaunce'.[92] Set against the shifting set of parallel hierarchies that we observed in Chapter 4, the implication of this emphasis on positionality was that there was no fair justice to be had. This was a balance that only the king might restore with his own 'indifferent justice' – which was, paradoxically, thought to serve the vulnerable most of all.

Closing out their petition, complainants and their counsel did not just ask for resolution in general terms, however; they sought immediate procedural action. Most asked directly that the king send his 'letters of privy seal' – or, more vaguely, his 'wrytt of subpena', 'commandment', or 'letter' – to accused parties, summoning them to make answer. More obstinate defendants might instead be thought to require 'attachments of ther bodyes' by a serjeant-at-arms to bring them into line. A smaller proportion of petitioners, especially those living in locales more distant from the royal household, asked instead that the king initially institute a commission to investigate their disputes: that he send out 'letters of commission', commencing an authorised arbitration right away. To this end, the narrative, allegations, and requests contained in the petition were invariably rounded out with the promise on behalf of the plaintiff to pray for the king's life and rule forevermore.

---

[91] REQ2/4/393. For a fuller discussion of relative poverty in Requests' petitions, see L. Flannigan, 'Litigants in the English "Court of Poor Men's Causes", or Court of Requests, 1515–25', *Law and History Review* 38:2 (2020), 329–37.

[92] REQ3/19 *Dakenfield* v *Sheffield*; REQ3/21 *Yolond* v *Sture*.

Making Complaint

Once a lawyer and his clerk had placed a petition in their client's hands, what came next? That petitioners and their lawyers knew which documentary processes to ask for is unsurprising; these mechanisms were well known by this period and were even becoming notorious, as we will see in Part III. And yet, noticeable in petitions surviving in Requests' archive is the complete absence of reference to any specific institution or court expected to move these procedures. In fact, whereas by this time plaintiffs and counsel might direct their complaint to the 'counsell in the Star Chamber' or the 'honorable Courte of Chauncery', they did not speak directly of any 'Court of Requests' handling their complaints. Rather, petitions that ended up in Requests were those that asked for hearing by the king's 'honourable council', sometimes specifically by the Council 'attendant on your person', and occasionally by the Dean of the Chapel Royal. If Requests remained the unnamed, nebulous part of this system, how did complainants ever reach it? The distinctive qualities setting Requests' petitions apart from other conciliar-court supplications – the emphasis on relative poverty, the connection of mercy to the king's own gift, the general absence of legal technicality – indicate that the counsel and scribes who compiled them *did* understand there to be some discrete channel for justice within this arm of the royal Council. This is apparent right from the very earliest petitions surviving for Requests.

Indeed, widespread awareness of numerous distinct judicial forums by this time becomes even more apparent when examining parallel suits submitted to each of them in turn. A particularly well-recorded example is the long-running land dispute between the Strode and Halswell families from Devon, which first emerged in Requests in the mid-1510s in a case brought by Richard Halswell against Richard Strode.[93] Over the following two decades it was brought to Chancery (in the 1520s), the Council in the West (*c.* 1538–42), Star Chamber (on four separate occasions in 1541–2, *c.* 1543, 1545, and 1546), and again in Requests (in 1543). The petitions that John Halswell and his son, also called John, submitted to Requests stressed their great impoverishment, emphasised that the Strode men were of gentle status and had 'gret londes substans & goodes', and alleged that the Strodes had previously lavished a common-law jury with 'greet gyftes and rewardes'. These petitions appealed directly to the king's 'most abundant

---

[93] The case goes on to involve several Richard Strodes, one of whom died in 1518. It may have involved the namesake of the so-called 'Strode's Act' passed at the 1512 parliament: 4 Hen. VIII c. 8.

166   Seeking and Requesting Justice

pity' and requested 'succour and reformation'. All of this is in keeping with the examination of typical Requests bills undertaken above. In contrast, the petitions presented by the Strodes to Chancery were much shorter and less emotive, making only the formulaic claim that evidence and charters for the lands in variance were in the possession of the Halswells and that no common-law case could be pursued until they knew the certainty of their contents. Later on, in Star Chamber, the Strodes played up to that Court's growing jurisdiction over riots by centring their narrative on a violent assembly in Stokingham, in which the Halswells 'yn ryotose maner with force and of armes came with wepyns & array . . . cry[ed] owt with a lowed voyse kylle the horeson thevys & a downe with them'.[94] This single dispute encapsulates the perceptible distinctions emerging between the main conciliar and conscience courts by the early sixteenth century, each requiring tailored emphases and lines of justification.[95]

Perhaps the vagueness in Requests' petitions related to its conceptualisation as the king's own justice more than anything else. While the drafting of a complaint was a collaborative effort between litigant, counsel, and scribe, it was the petitioner's responsibility to physically seek out this justice – and to do so they went to the household or to Westminster in person. Some supplicants may have gained a reprieve from this labour. In his petition, John Bonyfaunt remarked that because 'yor sayd Orator ys agyd' he was 'nat able to ryde from those partes to com byfor yor grace'.[96] Similarly, the ninety-year-old Avice Willes referred to her son as the 'berer' and 'bringer' of her petition in her stead.[97] These are, again, exceptions that prove the general rule that making supplication was a physical act as much as a written medium; the same can be inferred from Richard Aungern's allusion to the possibility of having 'words in the presens of yor excellent hyghnes'.[98] Sources external to Requests give us more information about the logistics for petitioning in similar contexts. In September 1505, representatives of the borough of Christchurch, Dorset – including their rent collector, Thomas Westbury – rode first to the nearby town of Winton to seek the counsel of 'Master Newport' and then to Canford Magna, where they intercepted Henry VII's Council and presented their supplication (the details of which are left out of Westbury's brief accounts).[99] In the

---

[94] REQ2/3/134, 2/4/394; TNA C1/443/19, 1/570/1, 2; TNA STAC2/20/311, 2/28/1.
[95] For a similar discussion of how the same case might be framed in different courts, see E. Kadens, 'A Marine Insurance Fraud in the Star Chamber', in Kesselring and Mears eds., *Star Chamber Matters*.
[96] REQ2/1/1.   [97] REQ2/13/59.   [98] REQ2/8/175.
[99] Dorset History Centre, DC-CC/C/1/3. They may have been referring to the common lawyer John Newport, of the neighbouring county of Hampshire: Baker, *Men of Court*, 1156–7.

'Your Poor Orator': Petitioning the King 167

same year, the dean and chapter of Hereford Cathedral travelled around 100 miles to Nottingham to plead to the king regarding their dispute with the mayor and citizens of Hereford about rights to certain taxes in the city. Henry VII himself eventually ordered that this matter be considered more fully, and the parties were called to appear before him at Woodstock the following Easter term.[100] These cases, it should be noted, did not fall under the remit of the Requests committee. Neither appeared in the Court's order books, anyway; if they were recorded centrally at all, it was probably in the now-lost main Council registers.

Such accounts do, nonetheless, tell us something of the resources, time, and money required for reaching a roving tribunal. Some of Requests' records give a similar impression. An outstanding example comes from the plaintiffs John and Margaret Hannibal, who used one petition to describe how they had already 'suyde unto your most noble grace at yor manor of Newhall' and were commanded 'to gyve attendance at Wyndesore', before presenting themselves again 'unto yor noble grace at yor manor of Wodstoke & twyse to Hampton Corte & v tymes to Grenewich for ther remedy' in 1518.[101] We can only imagine how much this uncertainty and delay, lasting for as long as seven months, must have put the Hannibals out.[102] For other cases we need not speculate, since many later litigants included expenses for travel and accommodation in their bills of costs. This represented by far the largest single expense for plaintiffs and defendants alike, especially once the Court was more settled at Westminster and litigants were expected to travel to London. Money claimed for this element of litigation ranged between 12d and 20s, depending on distance and number of horses required. One petitioner cited a rate of 14d a day for his two-day journey from Soham in Cambridgeshire to London, while another claimed 16d a day for a four-day, 100-mile trip.[103] Going by these rates, a single day's journey to Requests equated roughly to two days' wages for a skilled tradesman.[104] Since bills of costs seem to have been innovations of the latter half of Henry VIII's reign, we do not possess the same

---

[100] Hereford Cathedral Archive, MS 2971. My thanks to Professor Steven Gunn for pointing me in the direction of these references to justice in the itinerant household.

[101] REQ2/10/235, dating to 1520–1.

[102] This is according to Samman's itinerary, which gives the household as being at Newhall and Windsor in January, Woodstock in April–May, and Greenwich by the late summer of 1518: 'The Henrician Court during Cardinal Wolsey's Ascendancy', 349–50.

[103] REQ2/3/34, 162, 249, 2/9/74; REQ3/6 *Johnson v Johnson*, REQ3/8 *Unknown v Benet*; REQ3/30 *Wynbilston v Landlowe*.

[104] According to The National Archive's online calculator of purchasing power in the early sixteenth century: www.nationalarchives.gov.uk/currency-converter, accessed May 2022.

168 Seeking and Requesting Justice

information for the years when Requests was properly itinerant. Yet we might think the fees in those years not too dissimilar from the 20*d* claimed by Westbury for riding from Christchurch to Canbury, and the further 2*s* 4*d* cited for the materials his delegation needed to present a supplication to Henry VII.[105] This was less expensive, overall, than litigants to Requests in the White Hall claimed later on.

This inference of the cheapness of conciliar justice available locally compared to the expense of travelling to and staying in the capital city should give us pause as to whether the settling of Requests at Westminster altered its core clientele and in any way limited its ability to serve the poor. An impressionistic comparison between the status identifiers for petitioners in the period 1500–3, at the height of Requests' itinerancy on progress, and those attending in 1540–3 at the White Hall sheds some light on the consequences of this move. While the proportions of professionals, groups, civic administrators, and clergy among the clientele remained the same across the period, other social categories were more affected. The most substantial increase in numbers was amid the crafts- and tradesmen, who constituted 10 per cent of petitioners in the earlier years but over 20 per cent towards the end of our period. Presumably, since these individuals might often have passed through or been based in London, they found the settled Court more accessible. Conversely, the proportion of royal servants decreased, more than halving from 20 per cent to 8 per cent, for the opposite reason: Requests was no longer in the household and so out of their immediate reach. Otherwise, settlement at Westminster largely did not affect propertied people of lay rank, who accessed Requests' justice at almost the same rate regardless of its location and who were only just beginning to be turned away consistently by the early 1540s. Similarly, the share of non-gentle yeomen and husbandmen increased only marginally, while widows remained as prevalent at both ends of our period.

Yet, reading between the lines, it appears that the burgeoning Westminster-based Court of the 1540s *did* generally serve litigants positioned closer to the wealthier end of each of these social categories than in years prior. Once all the monasteries had been dissolved, any clergy in Requests were more likely to be among the more upper-ranking, secular ecclesiastics. Taking geographical origin into account too, plaintiffs now had to travel much further to litigate; and so, whereas many widows had approached the attendant household on progress from nearby towns, those recorded in 1540–3 were more often from further afield, as far away as Devon, Worcestershire, and

---

[105] Dorset History Centre, DC-CC/C/1/3.

'Your Poor Orator': Petitioning the King

Lincolnshire. From this evidence we might form only impressionistic conclusions, of course. Yet the picture accumulated across this chapter is that petitioning to the king required time, solid social networks, and considerable expenses. Therefore, it seems plausible that while the itinerant Requests had been able to entertain poorer people in several social categories, these same sorts of people were unlikely to reach Westminster.

Conclusion

In all, given the extent of legal knowledge and strategising observed across this part of the book it is little surprise that some plaintiffs to Requests recalled being on the receiving end of threats that they had to 'wyne . . . by the lawe', that they would be sued no matter the cost, or that their opponents would 'feyd the lawers' as much money as it took to achieve victory.[106] It was also inevitable that a petitioner could describe their opponent as 'a greate baractor' (a barrator, someone given to vexatious litigation) or as a 'wrangler in . . . yor lawes'.[107] People of all social ranks were capable of pursuing rights to lands and properties from the intimate environs of the village to the halls of Westminster, making use of networks of knowledge about justice-giving and its structures, however nascent.[108] In envisaging a route to the king's ear and constructing a petition to present to him, they were informed by a pre-existing culture of political complaint cast in less formal contexts. That everyone involved in making complaint expected royal justice to be applicable to the most mundane of matters – anything from the occupation of a single tenement or ownership of one sheep up to the rights to a whole manor and its rents – and sensitive to social realities as much as legal technicalities comes through in Requests' surviving petitions.

Indeed, in addition to the nuances around status, origins, and case type raised in Chapter 4, the last two chapters have somewhat corroborated the reputation of Requests as the court for poor suitors, albeit with several caveats. Firstly, many litigants treated the king's Council as a court of appeal as much as one of first resort, and so were plainly able to traverse the broader legal landscape. Secondly, 'poverty' was a relative term rather than an economically absolute one, wielded by plaintiffs as a signifier of their

---

[106] REQ3/1 *Causefield* v *Rich*; REQ3/3 *Ryce* v *Ryce*.
[107] REQ3/10 *Corbett* v *Hall and Underhill*; REQ3/19 *Halyday* v *Denham*.
[108] For more on the accessibility of justice, particularly at the common law, see J. McComish, 'The Rhetoric and Reality of Access to Justice in Sixteenth Century England', *Beiträge zur Rechtsgeschichte Österreichs* Band 2 (2013), 494–501.

disadvantages against mightier opponents. Finally, Requests' limited itinerancy by the end of Henry VIII's reign coincided with a narrowing in its litigant demography, in terms of both geographical origin and social status. Nonetheless, against the backdrop of the stop–start institutional evolution ongoing within early Tudor government that we observed in Part I, we may well interpret the steady and increasing stream of petitions to the 'king's honorable counsaill' and eventually to the 'Court of Requests' by name as the true source of this tribunal's growing curial identity. In the movement of arguments from the localities to the centre we might even discern the floating upwards of ideals and expectations of government – principally, that the king was the ultimate lord, as responsible for the stability of the wider realm as he was for his own demesne. And yet, while litigants may have defined the kind of justice they sought, they hardly had the last word. We turn now to a part of the petitionary process often overlooked by historians of courts like Requests: what happened once a bill of complaint landed in the right hands.

PART III

Delivering and Contesting Justice

CHAPTER 7

Before the King's Most Honourable Council

So far, this book's analysis has been trained on the expectations and efforts of Requests' plaintiffs, drawn from a vast cross-section of English society, at whose behest all the procedures of this Court ran. Now we return to the royal Council, to whom the king delegated justice-giving. How best to handle the influx of subjects turning up at court and brandishing petitions was plainly on the minds of early Tudor ministers as the cycle of demand and supply of justice accelerated in the early sixteenth century. As late as 1542, one plaintiff was admonished for making 'clamorous complayntes to the kinges maiestie ... aswell by mowthe' as by 'several billis', and his case was summarily dismissed without further hearing.[1] In this brief entry we are confronted with the potential for pressure to be applied through face-to-face encounters in each Requests suit, as a petitioner lingered in the vicinity of the king and household for the most opportune moment to present their case in words and in writing. Who was on hand to mediate the space between prince and petitioners?

The final part of this book examines what Requests *did*, for better or for worse. The survey of the Court's organisation and reorganisation in Chapter 3 charted its transition from a fluid committee within the itinerant entourage of Henry VII to a more settled court, housed in the White Hall at Westminster, by the end of Henry VIII's reign. Its well-preserved books of orders and decrees confirm the near-continuous receipt of petitions and hearing of cases across the early Tudor period, besides a brief pause at the accession in 1509 and a low point in business levels in the mid-1520s. In the age of the so-called 'revolution in government', slumps in Requests' activity were increasingly met with attempts to reform its judiciary, culminating in the installation of an expanded set of judges in January 1538, after which case levels rose exponentially.[2] Throughout our period and well beyond, this tribunal was much more often referred to as the 'king's honourable

---

[1] REQ1/7 fol. 108.   [2] Caesar, *The Ancient State*, 91.

173

174   Delivering and Contesting Justice

council', or the 'counsaill attendaunt upon [the king's] personne for requestes', than as the 'Court of Requests'.[3] Yet, as we saw in the previous chapter, plaintiffs, counsel, and scribes plainly discerned a distinct route for judicial remedy here, reachable with a petition that was calculatedly vague about its intended destination. In order to better understand the benefits of Requests' indefiniteness, we now pick up where the previous chapter left off: in the halls of royal palaces, where petitions were presented.

Of all the early Tudor conciliar courts, Requests possesses the richest surviving evidence for what royal justice looked like. The main Council's registers now survive only partially in late sixteenth-century transcriptions, the order books for the Court of Star Chamber were lost before 1705, and the scholarly consensus is that Chancery did not enter decrees into rolls until the 1540s.[4] The Council in the North commenced its own registers around the same time, but these too are no longer extant.[5] Requests is one of the few tribunals from this developmental phase in conciliar and conscience-based justice for which a consistent record of procedures and judgments still remains, then. Part III examines this rich seam of evidence, overlaying the administrative structures set out in Part I onto the social picture painted in Part II to examine how individuals interacted with and within this institution. We will explore the careers and duties of the ministers meeting petitioners at the palace gates, the steps that they took to determine civil disputes, and what these same men did to help fulfil the promise of accessible justice in Requests.

Personal Royal Justice?

We start, however, with the king himself – whose aura and surprisingly personal involvement in justice-giving helped it retain an element of the extraordinary. On the rare occasions in which petitions described previous suits to Requests, litigants insinuated that they had made a 'humble' suit by

---

[3] See REQ3/15 *Cokkes* v *Pate*; REQ2/7/101.

[4] Drafts survive for thirty-one decrees from Wolsey's tenure in Star Chamber, according to John Guy, 'Wolsey's Star Chamber: A Study in Archival Reconstruction', *Journal of the Society of Archivists* 5 (1975), 169, 171; Haskett, 'The Medieval English Court of Chancery', 269, 278–9. The Chancery decree rolls are filed under TNA C78 and C79, while its order and decree books, commencing in 1544, can be found under C33. I am grateful to Dr Neil Jones for his insights on the dating of these documents.

[5] Transcriptions of the northern Council's lists of attendant judges made by Thomas Widdrington, the Recorder of York, in the mid seventeenth century suggest that the Council kept books from *c.* 1537 onwards: BL Harley MS 1088 fols. 1–39. Another well-recorded tribunal is the Council/Court of the Duchy Chamber, the archive for which includes a series of order and decree books, starting in 1474: TNA DL5.

Before the King's Most Honourable Council   175

'bill of peticion' to their monarch, who had then seen fit to 'dyrecte the said byll' to one of his councillors. One incidental account in particular gives us reason to believe that this was no fiction: that subjects *did* prostrate themselves before the king to make a verbal complaint in advance of a written petition, as we encountered in theory in the previous chapter. The supplication of William Clerk and his son, Thomas, claimed that in 1522 they had 'knelyd byfore yor nobyll grace wythowt yor gatys of Grenwych wherapon yt pleasyd yor grace to assyn ... that I ye seyd Thomas shuld move a byll unto yor nobyll grace'.[6] A reality of personal monarchy was that humble subjects could gain an audience with their king in certain contexts. The chamber finance books and privy-purse accounts from the early Tudor period record small sums of money paid to poor people who gained access to the court and the attention of the king, including at least one poor woman who appeared 'at Greenwich park gate' in Henry VII's reign and another who 'asked of [Henry VIII] for the love of saint George' for aid.[7] This was an extension of the revived practice of healing the poor in ceremonies held at various royal palaces, which also involved handing out gold angels as tokens (worth about 7s 6d under Henry VIII).[8] One-off payments to the poor might also be made in response to specific complaints, such as the gift of 3s 4d said to have been made 'to a pore man that had his corn etyn [by] the king[es] Deyre besid[es] Okyng' during the progress of 1505.[9] Day to day, then, the early Tudor household was alive with the movement of people – even the very poor – and the paperwork they generated.

Yet it was a general truism of monarchical governance that if it was to be executed efficiently most judicial business had to be delegated, and that extended to the growing burden of civil justice-giving on a more regular basis. Indeed, a noticeably consistent feature of reports about past Requests suits is the characterisation of judicial business being '*comytted* [by] the kynges hyghnes' to 'comyssioners by [his] highness appointed' after the initial petition.[10] Having appeared at the Greenwich gates, Thomas Clerk

---

[6] REQ3/17 *Clerk v Clerk*.

[7] TNA E36/214 fol. 54; N. H. Nicolas, *The Privy Purse Expenses of King Henry VIII from November 1529 to December 1532* (William Pickering, 1827), 93, 145, 150. For more examples of payments made to 'poor' people and children at court, see TNA E101/414/16 fol. 9, 101/415/3 fols. 15, 34v; BL Additional MSS 7099 fol. 83, 59899 fol. 38.

[8] Stephen Brogan, *The Royal Touch in Early Modern England: Politics, Medicine and Sin* (Boydell Press, 2015), 45–66; Nicolas ed., *The Privy Purse Expenses of King Henry VIII*, 16, 20, 37, 46, 77, 93, 150, 156, 160, 161, 163, 164, 170, 173, 203, 213, 217, 221, 225, 237, 243, 249, 253, 264, 265, 272, 278.

[9] BL Additional MS 21480 fol. 23v.

[10] REQ2/3/134, 2/7/40; REQ3/1 *Orgor v Hovill* (my emphasis).

176   Delivering and Contesting Justice

was reportedly told by Henry VIII to submit his case in writing, first to the Lord Chancellor, Wolsey, and then 'unto Master Doctor Stokesley' in Requests.[11] Indeed, litigants typically identified the Dean of the Chapel Royal or another leading judge in Requests as the eventual recipient, and the signatures of those same men on the documents that followed confirm that this delegation took place as described.[12] Further direction of bills post-submission is indicated by the occasional note scribbled on the back of petitions labelling them as going 'to the kyngys highness honorabill councell in ye Whithall' or being 'for the White Hall' – as early as 1521, when the Court was first settled there on a temporary basis.[13] These annotations, subtle as they seem, give the impression of Requests as a royal commission to which bills could be channelled from elsewhere within the central administration.

Requests' archive essentially contains a register of everyone involved in moving its paperwork and making its decisions, with their signatures, handwritten notes, and personal amendments appearing across both the loose documents and the books. This represents a unique mine of information among the early Tudor conciliar courts. Whereas bills of complaint surviving from Star Chamber were typically marked only with a perfunctory statement about the return date for the relevant parties, Requests' pleadings served as a secondary archive for its clerks and judges. They were regularly marked with lengthier memoranda and orders representing the initial stages in a case, and these were, like the book entries, sometimes given a date and location of their writing. On comparing dated petition orders with book entries from the same time, it is often apparent that orders were scrawled onto loose pleadings even while the judges were sitting for hearings with the books in front of them. This was not simply a matter of convenience, then; the judges and clerks consciously maintained two discrete sets of records. The continuum between them – between initial petition and later book entries – is crucial to further reconstructing the procedure of Requests, allowing us to distinguish between the commencement of a case and the phases of its litigation.

Dividing the many autographs and annotations in the archive along these lines confirms that the delegation of royal justice in Requests worked in two concentric circles. A small, inner group received petitions and signed off paperwork and a larger cohort sat as judges and were listed in

[11] REQ3/17 Clerk v Clerk.   [12] See, for example, REQ3/17 Clerk v Clerk; REQ3/7 Seward v Hert.
[13] REQ2/4/183, 2/5/348; REQ3/9 Warley v Willoughby; REQ3/13 Sanger v Hewe and Lewes.

Before the King's Most Honourable Council 177

the books.[14] The full list is provided in the Appendix. We will explore the second group in more detail later; for now, it is the signatories of petitions that concern us, because they represented the first line of response to complaints working their way through the household. Between the first datable petitions filed in Requests' archive, from *c.* 1495, up to the end of Henry VIII's reign, there were as many as fifty-one individual bill signatories. Usually only a very small number were active at any one time; so, while cases were heard by as many as twenty-six different councillors in the regnal year of 1493–4, initial processes were overseen by just a few. In general, the judges of Henry VII's Requests were an ever-shifting, changeable group, many of whom appeared within its records just once or twice, presumably when they happened to be with the attendant, itinerant entourage. On the contrary, the signatories in these early years represented a more consistent and restricted quorum: including Thomas Savage (Bishop of London), Thomas Janne (Dean of the Chapel Royal), and Richard Foxe (Bishop of Durham) in 1497–8, for example, and Geoffrey Symeon (the new Dean of the Chapel), Richard Fitzjames (Bishop of Rochester, later London), and Thomas Hobbes (or Hobbys, Dean of St Stephen's and a royal chaplain) in 1501–2. These two circles did not even necessarily overlap at this time; for instance, the single autograph of Hobbes in *c.* 1501 is the only known time that he engaged with Requests in any capacity.[15]

The growing prominence of Symeon in both elements of the tribunal's work, receiving petitions and hearing cases, between the turn of the century and his death in 1508 marked a turning point in Requests' management. In the couple of decades that followed, the Court's two circles of personnel contracted, and both procedural and judicial business was overseen by a double act of the Dean of the Chapel Royal and the royal almoner: first Symeon and John Ednam (or Edenham); then William Atwater and Thomas Wolsey in the early years of Henry VIII's reign; John Veysey and Richard Rawlins up to 1519; and John Clerk and John Stokesley in the early 1520s. While they handled bills together, they were likely joined for final decision-making by a few other men employed around the household. By 1515, lists of sitting judges were no longer recorded in the books, so the total composition of the Court becomes less clear from then on. Yet anecdotal recollections of the Court's

[14] For a summary of Requests' personnel within these structures, see L. Flannigan, 'Conscience and the King's Household Clergy in the Early Tudor Court of Requests', in McKitterick, Methuen, and Spicer eds., *The Church and the Law*, 210–26.
[15] REQ2/3/347.

178   Delivering and Contesting Justice

composition and autographs on bills suggest that in the 1530s and 1540s the judiciary of the settled Requests evolved once again, with the balance of the two circles flipping. By the end of our period there could be as many as eight men – a mixture of bishops, civil lawyers, and royal servants – working together in larger numbers to process bills, with the smaller quorum reserved for sitting in judgment. This broad change in the handling of petitions maps onto the evolution of Requests from a fluid conciliar entity to a duty of the household clergy and finally to a well-staffed court by the end of Henry VIII's reign. What persisted was the efficiency of the Court in receiving and actioning requests for justice.

Frontline Response

The king's delegates met plaintiffs, defendants, and their counsel face to face; it was their countenances that determined the ethos of Requests; their consciences that were (at least in part) tested in each case; and their connections that were deployed to establish facts and mediate peace. Who were these men, and what qualities made them suitable for handling royal justice? Advice treatises of the early sixteenth century expressed concern that the king should choose individuals of 'good conscience', capable of passing 'without delay a just judgment on anyone requesting it', to be his representatives within his own courts – the emphasis being on their discretion and capacity to take on this work.[16] That every person identified as working within the Requests tribunal in these years was a trusted royal servant is a given. But each member acted with varying levels of dedication to judicial work alone, and with reference to differing education and experience.

The most frequent recipient and signatory of bills at any given time was the man acting as the 'president' of this tribunal. Transcriptions taken from the Henrician Council minutes speak of a 'President of the requestes' at work as early as 1486.[17] Within the recorded Requests tribunal, 'president' was a title most prominently applied to Thomas Savage, Bishop of London, in his role within the attendant Council from 1497 until his accession to the archbishopric of York in 1501, and then to his successor in both the Council and in the see of Rochester, Richard Fitzjames.[18] The title was occasionally revived with regard to the Court of Requests in the

---

[16] Dudley, *The Tree of Commonwealth*, 34; Baron, *De Regimine Principum*, 79.
[17] HL Ellesmere MS 2652 fol. 2v; Lambarde, *Archeion*, 139–40.
[18] REQ1/1 fol. 45v; REQ1/2 fols. 79, 93; REQ1/3 fol. 193; REQ2/11/197; REQ3/3 *Chesilden* v *Chesilden*; REQ3/4 *Selwood* v *Danvers*; REQ3/11/2 *Hygden* v *Knedy*.

Before the King's Most Honourable Council   179

early 1520s, in reference to John Clerk and then John Stokesley.[19] Each of these men was an omnicompetent royal servant in his own right: well-educated and connected in the fields of canon and civil law and theology; councillors and diplomats managing the geopolitics of two eventful reigns; pluralist (and non-resident) clergymen operating at the highest ranks. Notably, though, the title of 'president' was only ever given informally – it was never officially bestowed by the king. Individuals *not* described as 'president' but clearly acting in that capacity were just as diligent and effective in their duties within Requests. John Veysey, for example, was one of the most frequent signatories in the Court's early years, with his autograph appearing on at least 226 pleadings and every account of its hearings during his tenure there, 1514 to 1519, describing him as the leading figure. Still, he was only ever known as the Dean of the Chapel Royal.[20]

It will be apparent from the examples just given that Requests' petition recipients were overwhelmingly men who occupied ecclesiastical and spiritual positions at court and further afield. Of the fifty-one total bill signatories identifiable in Requests between *c.* 1495 and 1547, twenty-nine, roughly 57 per cent, were clergymen of various ranks and roles.[21] All of the figures that we might take as presiding in some fashion in the middle of Henry VII's reign were bishops: first Richard Foxe, who was also Keeper of the Privy Seal, then Savage and Fitzjames, each of whom held large, wealthy dioceses. Even in the very earliest surviving paperwork we consistently see the hands of the deans of the Chapel Royal and of the king's almoners. Effectively, the move from Henry VII's later reign onwards to promote multiple successive deans – Symeon, Atwater, Veysey, Clerk, and then Sampson – to preside over Requests might be interpreted as a growing reliance on lower-ranking churchmen who were more constantly on hand within the household. A position in the Chapel Royal and its orbit was a stepping-stone towards more lucrative ecclesiastical postings anyway. Savage had been the dean and Fitzjames the almoner before they became bishops, and almost all of the men just named moved straight from their household positions to bishoprics of their own (Richard Mayhew from the almonry to Hereford, Atwater to Lincoln, Veysey to Exeter, for example).[22]

---

[19] REQ2/6/207, 2/11/148; REQ3/1 *Orgor* v *Hovill*; REQ3/6 *Martyn* v *Tunsted*; REQ3/11/2 *Herd* v *Estwood and Sone*.

[20] REQ2/4/264, 2/6/207, 2/7/139, 2/10/56, 200, 2/11/196, 2/12/217; REQ3/9 *Cause* v *Abbot*; REQ3/10 *Barney* v *Sturges and Cause*; REQ3/22/1 *Mayor of Exeter* v *Toker*; TNA CP40/1016 m. 539.

[21] See the Appendix for the full list. Short biographies for most of these men were compiled by Leadam and are drawn upon in the following pages of this chapter: *Select Cases in the Court of Requests*, cx–cxxiv.

[22] The exceptions were Symeon, who died in post in 1508, and Ednam, who retained the archdeaconry of Norwich and a deanery at St John's College in Stoke-by-Clare, Suffolk, until his death in 1517.

180 Delivering and Contesting Justice

This connection between the realm's spiritual leaders and the king's most intimate justice tribunal was remarkably long-lived, surviving the Church's many tribulations in the early Tudor period. Although the slowing down of the 1520s saw a pair of lawyers (Wolman and Englefield) handling the remaining trickle of Requests' business, there was something of a return to the pattern of delegating this work to a senior clergyman in the later years of Henry VIII's reign. More than half of the fifteen individuals named in the Court's proposed list of judges in January 1529 were clergymen, with the Bishop of Lincoln (John Longland), Abbot of Westminster (John Islip), and Dean of the Chapel Royal (Richard Sampson) prominently featured.[23] The same was true of the list of six 'commissioners' appointed in January 1538, which included the Bishop of Chichester (Sampson again), Thomas Thirlby (Dean of the Chapel Royal, and then Bishop of Westminster), and Edmund Bonner (a royal chaplain, soon to be made Bishop of Hereford).[24] In the following decades, all three of these men received and signed paperwork in Requests, alongside Nicholas Heath, Bishop of Worcester, and Cuthbert Tunstall, Bishop of Durham, more occasionally. Again, each had risen through the ranks of the household chaplaincy. Furthermore, by this time the position of Dean of the Chapel could be retained alongside a bishopric, as in the case of both Sampson and Thirlby.

What united many of these men was that they had at one point or another been charged with the cure of the king's soul. The Dean of the Chapel led his courtly department of chaplains, gentlemen, and choristers, totalling as many as forty to fifty men and children during major ceremonies and fewer on progress, in a series of weekly rituals at court.[25] The almoner, meanwhile, is frequently depicted in accounts of the royal household and in chronicles of this period at the king's right-hand side, proffering advice and wisdom while also being central to courtly processions and rituals, including by doling out alms to the poor.[26] They and the Court's bishop-ministers were typically members of the Council, too. As such, they were closely trusted and constantly attendant on the king, conveying him to and from chapel and maintaining access to his ear as he listened to mass

[23] REQ1/5 fol. 43v. [24] Caesar, *The Ancient State*, 91.
[25] F. Kisby, 'The Royal Household Chapel in Early Tudor London, 1487–1547' (unpublished PhD thesis, London University, 1996), 73, 75–83; F. Kisby, 'Kingship and the Royal Itinerary: A Study of the Peripatetic Household of the Early Tudor kings 1485–1547', *The Court Historian* 4:1 (1999), 36.
[26] C. M. Woolgar, *The Great Household in Late Medieval England* (Yale University Press, 1999), 163; James Gairdner ed. *Letters and Papers Illustrative of the reigns of Richard III and Henry VII* (Longman and Green, 1861), 392; Hall, *Hall's Chronicle*, 540, 565, 674, 730.

Before the King's Most Honourable Council

each day within his privy closet.[27] We might wonder whether later years saw a preference for men more favourable to the tides of religious reform that were increasingly convenient to Henry VIII's conscience and authority. Certainly, whereas Clerk had openly opposed the king's quest for an annulment and even counselled Catherine of Aragon at Blackfriars in 1529, Thirlby, Heath, and Tunstall were each involved in drafting the more reformist doctrine and vernacular scripture issued in the 1530s and 1540s. This hardly made them fervent supporters of reform, however, and by Edward VI's reign each was viewed as occupying the conservative end of the spectrum.

Prospective litigants to the king's justice were likely less concerned with religious outlook than with the legal expertise that each of these chief judges could offer in Requests. In terms simply of formal education, it is unsurprising that among this cadre of clergymen there was no common-law training – rather, they were educated in the ancient universities of England and the continent. The successive almoners at work in Requests up to the 1520s were all doctors of theology, with the exception of Wolsey, who was educated only to bachelor's level in the subject. The deans and bishops, meanwhile, offered more variation: a mixture of pure divinity (in the case of Symeon, Atwater, Longland, and Heath) and training in civil law (Veysey and Bonner), canon law (Janne and Clerk) or, more commonly, both laws (Nix, Sampson, Thirlby, and Tunstall). Observable here again is a shift over time that may reflect a changing ethos in royal justice. In the middle years of the 1500s and 1510s it had become broadly acceptable for Requests to be almost entirely staffed by theologians. Some were committed, conservative scholastics, in fact; Atwater's surviving library contains handwritten annotations indicating his preference for theology over law, which causes men's faith to 'fall into error'.[28] In the later, busier years of Henry VIII's reign there was a preference again for men with more comprehensive legal backgrounds.

Education is but one metric for appreciating how Requests' bill signatories approached their work; another is prior judicial experience. Some of their earliest involvement in rule enforcement came during years spent at the colleges of Oxford and Cambridge, where many transitioned from students to officers. Prior to his work in Requests, Stokesley spent a spell as standing vice-president at his *alma mater* of Magdalen College, Oxford,

---

[27] F. Kisby, '"When the King Goeth a Procession": Chapel Ceremonies and Services, the Ritual Year, and Religious Reforms at the Early Tudor Court, 1485–1547', *JBS* 40:1 (2001), 51–2.
[28] Oxford, Brasenose College Library UB/S I. 27 fol. 71v; M. Bowker, *The Secular Clergy in the Diocese of Lincoln, 1495–1520* (Cambridge University Press, 1968), 14.

182   Delivering and Contesting Justice

which he had taken up after Richard Mayhew, himself once a judge in Requests, was made Bishop of Hereford in 1507. Abstracts from that college's registers demonstrate the expectations placed on its governors to keep an eye on accounts and to punish offences against regulations committed by fellows. However, a visitation made by the Bishop of Winchester's officials in 1507 informs us that these were tasks in which both Mayhew and Stokesley had been not just unsuccessful but negligent.[29] Elsewhere, Fitzjames had acted as bursar and as warden for Merton College, Oxford, from 1483 onwards, prior to and overlapping with his time in Requests. Part of his job there was to receive and determine bills of complaint from tenants of the college's lands.[30] Civil justice was overseen more regularly by Atwater in his duties as commissary in the Chancellor's Court of Oxford between 1498 and 1503. Surviving registers name him as umpire in disputes within the university and between town and gown, concerning lands, debts, employment contracts, and college privileges, and he often took sureties to stop parties from vexatiously litigating in other courts.[31] Each of these men were here practising a form of civil law, applying their logic and their consciences to manage the worldly goings-on of the institutions that had educated them.

Otherwise, a few of Requests' frontline judges brought experience of administering justice elsewhere within the central administration's growing network of tribunals. Prior to his time in Requests, Thirlby had sat as part of the Council of the North in the aftermath of the Pilgrimage of Grace, tasked with taking oaths from rebels seeking the king's forgiveness but also with dispensing 'common justice' on receipt of 'bills, supplications, and complaints' from subjects in that region.[32] Although Tunstall's later work in Requests was less intensive than many of his fellows there, he too surely conveyed his considerable experience as the president of the Council of the North from 1530 until 1538 (at which point he had excused himself from the role on the basis of his age and supposed ill-repute with

---

[29] W. D. Macray ed., *A Register of the Members of St. Mary Magdalen College, Oxford, from the foundation of the college* (Oxford University Press, 1894), vol. I, 35–61.

[30] See, for example, the complaint of the parishioners of Burmington, Warwickshire, brought to Fitzjames 'to make a concorde ... according to ryght and consciens': H. E. Salter ed., *Registrum Annalium Collegii Mertonensis*, Oxford Historical Society LXXVI (Clarendon Press, 1923), 32–4.

[31] W. T. Mitchell ed., *Registrum Cancellarii 1498–1506*, Oxford Historical Society New Series XXVII (Clarendon Press, 1980), 19–21, 27–56, 89. Fitzjames also served temporarily in the same capacity as 'Cancellarius natus', the oldest doctor of divinity, acting in the term between two chancellors: *Ibid.*, 57, 170. See also H. E. Salter ed., *Records of Medieval Oxford* (Oxford Chronicle Company, 1912), 74–6.

[32] *LP* XII. i. 98, XII. ii. 102 (2).

Before the King's Most Honourable Council 183

the people of that region).[33] Veysey was a renowned legal theorist, with practical experience in several spheres. At Blackfriars in 1515 he was famously called upon by Henry VIII to give his opinion, according to the law of God and his own 'knowledge and conscience', as to whether secular judges might try clergymen; he agreed with Henry Standish that they could.[34] Two years later, he was appointed to head the commissions investigating enclosures, held across seven English counties and returnable to Chancery, a job that kept him so busy as to apparently halt business in Requests in the latter half of that year.[35] In all, then, the predominance of men learned in theology and divinity in this tribunal should not be taken to mean an absence of judicial expertise. Both collegiate and conciliar adjudication would have made these Requests' frontline judges familiar with aspects of law – mostly civil and canon, but also common law where it touched on the administration of lands – and fluent in the art of treating with petitioners.

In any case, Requests' chief judges did not have to rely solely on their own education and experiences. The rest of the bill signatories in this period were royal administrators, knights of the realm, and – the second-largest group, at around 25 per cent of the total signatories in this period – men trained at the inns of court in common law. For the duration of Henry VII's reign and up to the late 1510s, while the dean and the almoner kept court in Requests, there is little evidence of any lawyers handling bills (though they might sit in judgment, as we will see later). The first major exception to this rule was John Gilbert, who signed at least fifty-two bills between 1516 and 1519. He was referred to variously by litigants who encountered Requests at this time as an 'armiger', a 'squyer', and as a royal councillor, but one described him as 'lerned in [the king's] laws'; indeed, he was admitted to the Middle Temple in *c*. 1500, and acted as legal counsel in Requests in 1506.[36] The additional appearance of Thomas More's signature on a few pleadings around the same time might be taken as evidence of some conscious expansion of the small Requests circle to men trained in common law. Neither Gilbert nor More was dedicated to Requests, however. Gilbert was sometimes said to be 'associate[d] with'

---

[33] Reid, *The King's Council in the North*, 502–3; SP1/124 fol. 183.

[34] J. H. Baker ed., *Reports of Cases by John Caryll*, Selden Society 116 and 117 (Selden Society, 1998–9), vol. II, 683–91.

[35] *LP* II. 3297; Leadam ed., *The Domesday of Inclosures*, 81–6. There are no order book entries between 20 Jul. 1517 and 23 Jan. 1518: REQ1/4 fols. 78–83.

[36] REQ1/4 fol. 3; REQ2/3/134, 2/10/200; REQ3/10 *Barney* v *Sturges and Cause*; REQ1/3 fol. 259; Baker, *Men of Court*, 749.

184   Delivering and Contesting Justice

Veysey, and this is substantiated by their occasional signing of Requests' bills together and by Gilbert's role in the enclosure commissions, too.[37] The end of his time working in Requests coincided with Veysey's accession to the see at Exeter, in autumn 1519. Meanwhile, More was a versatile and favoured councillor of Henry VIII, famously combining a legal education and parliamentary career with humanism and private asceticism. His judicial activity was not limited to Requests; we also find him sitting with the main Council and passing decrees in the Court of Star Chamber, and working as a judge in the smaller conciliar committee headed by the Prior of St John's, throughout the late 1510s and 1520s.[38] In other words, Gilbert and More crossed paths with this tribunal because they otherwise operated around the central administration.

Yet across the following decades there *was* a more concerted effort to put Requests' paperwork in the hands of lawyers. Stokesley's dismissal from Requests in early 1523, possibly because he was deemed too unlearned in the law (which we will come on to in the next chapter), commenced a spell in which petitionary business was handled chiefly by Richard Wolman, a canon and civil lawyer trained at Oxford and abroad. He was another ecclesiastic, with enough benefices to be one of those 'fat priests' targeted by Henry VIII for a benevolence in 1536.[39] And yet, unlike his predecessors in Requests, Wolman was never a member of the household clergy, and it was his legal talents that were most exploited at court, especially in the defence of the king's Great Matter. He was highly active in Requests after 1523, signing at least 129 bills in the rest of that decade and through to his death in 1537. In this work he was accompanied more occasionally by Thomas Englefield, a seasoned serjeant-at-law from the Middle Temple who had recently been knighted and who also sat in Star Chamber in the mid-1520s.[40] Englefield was soon superseded by William Sulyard, another prominent common lawyer who went on to become one of the most prolific members of the Court. He had already signed bills in Chancery, and was active in the same capacity in Requests from *c.* 1529 until his death in 1540 while also being involved with the Council in the Marches.[41]

---

[37] REQ2/3/134.

[38] BL Lansdowne MSS 1 fols. 108–108v, 160 fols. 310v–312v, 639, p. 95; HL Ellesmere MSS 2654 fols. 22v, 24v, 2655 fols. 10, 13v, 15v, 16v, 18; TNA STAC10/4/123.

[39] *LP* XI. 834.

[40] There are plenty of references to Englefield hearing cases, but only five known pleadings signed by him: REQ2/12/5; REQ3/1/1 *Manger* v *Arnold and Webbe*; REQ3/5 *Pope* v *Baskerfield*; REQ3/9 *Stower* v *Squire* (and documents for the same case in REQ3/18); REQ3/15 *Beckingham* v *Horne*. For his Star Chamber work see TNA STAC10/4/123.

[41] Baker, *Men of Court*, 1486; Skeel, *The Council in the Marches of Wales*, 68–9, 70, 73.

Before the King's Most Honourable Council 185

As Requests' judiciary became more dedicated and diverse in the later years of Henry VIII's reign, petitioners could be met by any one of a mixed group of legal experts. This included more common lawyers (Robert Bowes, Roger Townsend), but also civil lawyers (Edward Carne, John Tregonwell, William Petre). Broadly speaking, the rise in lawyers coincided with a drop-off in numbers of the other cadre of men that had been prevalent here earlier on: lords and knights holding assorted household offices and seats on the royal Council. A number of Henry VII's courtiers – among them Richard Guildford, Charles Somerset, Henry Wyatt, and Lord Daubeney – appeared in earlier lists of Requests' judges, while Sir John Hussey (the Chief Butler) and Sir William Fitzwilliam (Treasurer of the Household) were named as 'commissioners' in the 1529 list. But their engagement here did not usually extend to receiving bills. The chief exception is Sir Thomas Neville, a common lawyer, former Speaker of the House of Commons, and royal councillor who signed around twenty-four bills in Requests after his appointment on the list in 1529 while also sitting in Star Chamber.[42] Capable men like Neville blur the lines between neat career categories. In reality, most of the men discussed here moved in many different circles and their duties were defined by their close relationship and regular proximity with the king. Nonetheless, by the end of our period most had been squeezed out in favour of a combination of bishops and lawyers with judicial expertise.

Another significant development was the introduction of the Masters of Requests, dedicated judicial officers who blended the qualities of the clerical and legal judges. They quickly became the most active members of Requests' frontline, signing off hundreds of bills combined. Although the name of the office was used quite patchily at first, a list of its occupants begins to emerge from the archive: first Nicholas Hare, active from 1537 and referred to as a 'master of Requests' in 1540, then Robert Southwell and Robert Dacres, all common lawyers.[43] Like the deans and almoners of years past, these men were attendant on the king, working within the household and (Privy) Council. But they were distinct in two important ways from their predecessors in Requests. Firstly, the masters' *entire* duty was to

---

[42] For his other work, see BL Lansdowne MS 1 fols. 108–108v; HL Ellesmere 2655 fols. 9v–15v; TNA STAC10/4/123.

[43] This title was given to Hare by the French ambassador (to whom it may have had different connotations, given its long usage in France) in 1540: *LP* XV. 289. Although, as we have seen already, John Tregonwell was once referred to as a 'master of Requests' in a diplomatic context, but he otherwise acted as commissary general for the Court of Admiralty and as a Master of Chancery throughout the 1540s.

186   Delivering and Contesting Justice

handle petitions within the central administration, for justice and for other matters. The prolific Hare presented various 'affayres of the suttours' before the Privy Council throughout the 1540s, eventually being assigned regular meetings with them on Wednesday afternoons.[44] In the register of matters sent to William Clerk, the aptly named clerk of the Privy Chamber, for authorisation under the king's 'privy stamp' in the last couple of years of Henry VIII's reign, we find reference to petitions for grace – for alms, prebendaries, offices, and pardons – forwarded 'at the request of Mr Hare', too.[45]

Secondly, the service of these legally trained masters was effectively retained by the king through a substantial annuity. This had some precedent in a yearly payment of £150 made to Thomas Englefield, for 'his judgys ro[o]me and his assysys [and] manye other offyces', and then transferred in c. 1537 to Sulyard at the higher rate of a £200 'fee', according to Cromwell's remembrances.[46] Again, later decades saw a regularisation of this practice. In October 1537, shortly before Hare's signature first appears within Requests' paperwork, he was granted a similar £100 annuity 'for good service' – this time through the more formal mechanism of the letters patent under the great seal.[47] When Hare was briefly imprisoned for giving legal advice designed to circumvent the Statute of Uses in 1540, this annuity and its associated 'roome' were regranted by the same means to Southwell.[48] Once Hare was reinstated to his position and to royal favour, Southwell continued to work alongside him; when attending the Privy Council in January 1541, the latter was said to be just 'one of the masters of the Requests'.[49] The cadre of masters expanded again in mid-1541, when Dacres was awarded an equivalent annuity and joined Hare and Southwell in signing and judging cases in the years that followed.[50] Importantly, none of these grants specified appointment as a 'Master of Requests' by name, and delegated no precise task to the recipient equivalent to John Harrington's employment as 'clerk of our council of requests and

---

[44] Dasent et al. eds., *Acts of the Privy Council of England*, vol. I, 240, vol. II, 355, 358, 410.

[45] SP4/1/52–59.

[46] SP1/126 fol. 173 (*LP* XII. ii. 1151). A couple of years later, in 1539, John Tregonwell wrote to Cromwell reminding him of his loyalty and diligence in coercing the surrender of monasteries across England, and asked that he be awarded an annuity of £100 too – though apparently to no avail: SP1/156 fol. 140.

[47] REQ2/2/179 sees Hare signing an interlocutory order in Nov. 1537; TNA C66/675 m. 26, C82/731; *LP* XII. ii. 1008 (38).

[48] C66/690 m. 2 (*LP* XV. 436 (56)). A note on the back of the letters patent for the same states that 'Mr Robert Southwell [is] to be admitted of the Councell in Mr Hare[s] Roome with the ffee of C. li': C82/764.

[49] *LP* XVI. 447 (my emphasis).   [50] TNA C66/708 m. 38, C82/785 (*LP* XVI. 1135 (8)).

Before the King's Most Honourable Council   187

supplications' in 1483.[51] Rather, Hare, Dacres, and Southwell were covered for general 'service' to the king. Still, that they were so frequently and consistently busy in Requests is a sign that their expertise as common lawyers was being retained by these grants. This is not dissimilar to the yearly fees and reimbursements for travel, accommodation, and food offered to provincial councillors while they sat in judgment.[52] By contrast, there is little evidence to suggest that Requests' clerical councillor-judges were officially appointed or paid in any way for this work.

Litigants would also have come into regular contact with Requests' clerks, who handled all elements of its administration throughout our period. In Henry VII's reign and the early years of Henry VIII's, Requests was served by clerks who worked interchangeably for the privy seal and the Council (and some also served as attorneys, as we saw in Chapter 6). The earliest such figure was Robert Rydon, whose handwriting dominates the first order book, followed by Robert Sampson up to his death in 1520. As we have seen, Richard Turnor was the first to be known as the 'clerk of the kynges honorable cort of requestes' and was omnipresent there from 1501, when acting as an attorney, until his death in 1558.[53] Each of these clerks attended hearings, wrote up witnesses' depositions, received and kept hold of evidence, signed off writs and orders, and sometimes even mediated cases themselves. Turnor came to be recognised as the first point of contact for litigants in Requests, perhaps following initial verbal suppli-cation: they wrote to him to request certain dates for their appearances, for example.[54] In addition to their income from scribal work on litigants' behalf, these clerks were also formally appointed to their roles by letters patent and received an annuity worth 40 marks.[55] To a certain extent their role increasingly overlapped with the masters. Occasional annotations indicate that bills could be forwarded to either Turnor or Hare, and in the later order books we find Hare and Dacres acting like clerks, taking recognisances, receiving paperwork, and giving orders to litigants.[56] Plainly, though, the clerks had a particular speciality in producing the

---

[51] *CPR 1476–1485*, 413.   [52] *LP* XIII. i. 1269 (2), 914.

[53] Knox, 'The Court of Requests in the Reign of Edward VI', 252–71. Petitioners also referred to him as 'clerk of the king's council' and 'clerk of the White Hall': REQ2/4/181, 2/10/166.

[54] E.g., REQ3/16/1 *Hayes* v *Hunt*, where the plaintiff wrote to Turnor to say that his wife had died and that he could not attend court.

[55] This was the case for Rydon in April 1492: TNA C82/92.

[56] An annotation on one bill from *c.* 1534 reads 'To Mr Turnor clerc of the White Hall yeve thes ij billes': REQ2/7/95. Later on, Anthony Belassis, clerk of Chancery, redirected poor suitors to Hare: REQ2/5/3; REQ3/17 *Foster* v *Woodward*. See also REQ1/6 fols. 192, 216; REQ1/7 fols. 152, 153, 167.

188   Delivering and Contesting Justice

Court's documentation, and so Turnor could be asked to 'drawe one order' in a case heard by Dacres.[57]

To summarise, what comes through from the various glimpses into the daily life of Requests afforded by scrawled annotations and signatures within its pleadings archive is that litigants came face to face with a range of intermediaries in the process of initiating their suits. The everyday movement of the early Tudor king around and between palaces provided an opportune moment for catching not just his roving retinue but also, if parties were lucky, the man himself. Otherwise, the presence of the principal household clergymen at the 'highly formal ceremonial procession[s]' taking place around the court likely formed another possible route for slipping a bill of complaint into the right hands – perhaps explaining why these frontline personnel sometimes annotated petitions themselves, presumably when put on the spot.[58] Yet the interface of Requests undoubtedly changed in the period under investigation here. The frontline of the Court was increasingly staffed by lawyers who were formally appointed to the job and, as we saw in Chapter 3, who occupied a set space at Westminster. And so, while interactions with a fluid household enterprise dominate earlier accounts, a petition from 1537 has an annotation on the back that reads 'this bille was presented afor the kinges counsaill at Westm[inster] in the White Halle'.[59] Complainants eventually came directly to the White Hall with their complaints, as they might to any of the courts down the hallway.

Commencing Litigation

These shifts in Requests' constitution notwithstanding, a consistent aspect of early Tudor royal justice was the immediacy of its response to petitions. As we saw in Chapter 6, plaintiffs requested two main forms of process and these were authorised by the frontline of Requests' judges, masters, and clerks. The first and most popular option was that named defendants be immediately summoned to attend the Court and submit a formal answer to the complaints raised against them. The Court's personnel put this into motion by writing a short memorandum in Latin to the clerks of the privy

---

[57] REQ2/4/88.
[58] Kisby, 'When the King Goeth a Procession', 52–7. Examples survive with Symeon's handwriting: REQ2/5/372, 2/12/4, 2/13/84; Atwater's: REQ2/5/66, 380; Veysey's: REQ2/2/54, 2/5/378; Rawlins': REQ3/9 *Messetur* v *Sherard*; Gilbert's: REQ2/5/323; Stokesley's: REQ2/4/28, 320, 362, 2/6/217, 2/7/130, 2/10/63, 2/12/65, 80, 88; and Sulyard's: REQ2/12/75.
[59] REQ2/10/234.

Before the King's Most Honourable Council   189

seal to order the production of a writ.[60] They often recorded this decision on the back of the petition, too. The text of the writ, entitled 'By the King' and coming with a large wax seal, commanded the recipient 'all excuses and dilaies utterlye laied apparte [that] ye bee and personallye appere before us and our said counsaille ... wheresoever we then shalbe within this our Realme'.[61] They were also given a set date by which to appear: sometimes 'immediately upon sight' of the document, often within a period of six to ten days, but more regularly by the next return date in the following legal term. Crucially, these writs were executed *sub poena* – under a financial penalty. In this powerful jurisdiction such fines were steep, starting at £100 and increasing to £200 for the second and £300 for the third writ sent out.

Once the writ had been created, signed by the clerk, and sealed, it was conveyed with haste from the royal household to named defendants. Sometimes the plaintiff took this duty upon themselves, but more commonly it was undertaken by an acquaintance or relative, by a bailiff or constable in the locality of the case, or by a messenger of the king's chamber.[62] Whoever acted as bearer, they were dispatched quickly; in one suit in April 1545, the process-server was back in Requests to testify to the delivery of the writ just ten days after it had been issued.[63] Other testimonies to the same effect describe deliveries taking place within the recipient's own 'dwelling house', or within the homes of local authority figures.[64] Yet much more often the summons was handed over in as public a setting as possible. In May 1495, John Franklin swore before the Requests committee that at 4pm on 28 April he had delivered a privy-seal writ to the wife of one William Bush on the busy high street of Dorchester.[65] Other messengers served their targets in the tavern, in the marketplace, or even at a court session – anywhere that they might be in the presence of 'divers[e] and many persons'.[66] By far the most popular location for process-serving was the parish church, particularly on feast days and at matins or vespers, when all the parishioners could be expected to be in attendance.[67] Indeed,

---

[60] Several of the orders survive in the present-day collection of privy-seal material, signed by Wolman at Enfield in July 1527 and by Sampson in summer 1529: TNA PSO2/4, items 98, 109, 112, 114, 118, and item 49 of the 'August 9 Hen. 8 to April 20 Hen. 8' bundle in the same class.

[61] For examples, see REQ2/5/316, 2/8/193, 2/9/61, 2/10/53, 216; REQ3/3 *Wild* v *Shening*.

[62] In the spring of 1505, Roger Barker, 'messenger of the King's Chamber', delivered three privy-seal writs to the same defendant: REQ1/3 fols. 167, 171, 175. See also REQ1/104 fol. 116; REQ1/6 fol. 133 (Nov. 1542, when the messenger was Robert Smyth); REQ1/7 fols. 56, 189v, 190v, 226, 236v. At least one petitioner asked that the king 'send on[e] of your messengers attendyng apon yor court of requestes' with a privy seal: REQ3/21 *Allott* v *Bassett*; REQ3/7 *Cordrey* v *Tull*.

[63] REQ3/7 *Pawlyn* v *Askewe*.   [64] REQ1/1 fols. 61, 75, 108.   [65] REQ1/1 fol. 104v.

[66] E.g., REQ1/1 fols. 111, 148v; REQ3/9 *Worley* v *Willoughby*.

[67] REQ1/1 fols. 151, 157, 158v; REQ1/3 fols. 62, 119v, 134, 140v.

190   Delivering and Contesting Justice

one witness to a Requests case grumbled that when his father had been served process, the messenger 'cam[e] into the churche . . . and there made suche busyness that the people were so troubled w[it]h hym that they couthe not here masse'.[68] When an addressee could not be located, the writ might be posted up somewhere visible instead. Often it was said to have been 'affixed above the doorway of the house' (*affixisse super [h]ostium domus*) of the defendant.[69] Here, as elsewhere in the processes of administering justice in late medieval and early modern England, we get the impression of just how public disputes and their litigation could become.

The communal dimension of dispute *resolution* was invoked in the second main process issued by Requests: a writ founding a local commission. This Court could establish two different types of commission, in fact. The first was for fact-finding, set up to retrieve the defendant's answer under oath, to examine witnesses according to pre-prepared interrogatories, or to investigate the technical aspects of the case, for example by perusing documents and surveying properties in question. This information would be reported back to the Court and would aid its judges in making their own determination. The second and more common type of commission was one in which named arbiters were asked to achieve a 'friendly end' between the parties, preventing them from taking up further litigation in Requests and effectively dismissing the matter from the Council's jurisdiction. Petitioners could request either type of examination right away in their bill of complaint, and it is surprising how often they turned to the king simply to authorise local mediation rather than to initiate centralised litigation. They sometimes went as far as to name a preferred set of commissioners – perhaps men they knew and expected some favour from – and these nominations were typically accepted by Requests' bill signatories.[70] More usually, however, several commissioners were nominated on the part of each litigant and were appointed *ex assensu* of all parties and their counsel. Among the commissioners named in surviving writs and order-book entries we most commonly find knights, esquires, and gentlemen, often accompanied by abbots, bishops, and lower-ranking clergymen – all men of prominent status and social cachet in their localities. Very few commissioners were common lawyers, perhaps because the intention of these authorised interventions was not to determine the finer legal points of disputes but to enforce peace through moral authority at close proximity. Taking on the king's voice – though more likely reflecting the knowledge of Requests'

---

[68] REQ2/4/298.   [69] REQ1/2 fols. 39, 48v, 49, 53v, 110v.

[70] REQ2/2/173, 2/10/32. Others changed their minds and scraped this demand out in favour of a vaguer request for the appointment of 'indifferent persons' in the locality: REQ3/13 *Pyott v Abbot of Dieulacres*.

Before the King's Most Honourable Council 191

judges and masters, conveyed to clerks – covering commission writs ordered recipients to 'determine the same matiers with al convenient celerite according with reason and good justice' so that the parties would have 'no cause reasonable eftsonys to retourne unto us for further remedie'.[71]

A distinctive quality of this second kind of documentary process was that it was, in this period at least, issued under the more personal seal: the smaller signet seal, which was not yet 'out of court'. Another, intriguingly, was that Requests' writs for commission were also signed off by the kings themselves – as in the example depicted in Figure 7.1. In the wider context of the inner workings of Tudor government, this degree of personal royal input may not initially seem very surprising. Both Henry VII and Henry VIII routinely initialled the household account books presented to them by their treasurers during weekly meetings, and authorised grants of lands and offices through signed signet and privy-seal warrants for the great seal.[72] They were also

Figure 7.1 Writ for commission signed by Henry VIII, countersigned by William Atwater, and issued from Woking by the Court of Requests, August 1509. © The National Archives, ref. REQ2/5/379.

---

[71] E.g., the writs in REQ2/2/85, 145, 2/9/36; REQ3/10 *Symmes* v *Beckford*.
[72] Elton, *The Tudor Revolution in Government*, 176, 264, 268, 270–4, 276–7; many of these warrants for the great seal are in TNA C82 and TNA PSO2/4. The king also occasionally signed privy-seal writs to halt legal proceedings, as discussed in G. McKelvie, 'Kingship and Good Lordship in Practice in

involved in the movement of all kinds of petitions and process, for justice and for grace, at court each day. Henry VII is known to have signed off as many as sixteen supplications for grants and patronage in a single day and perhaps one hundred in each year of his reign.[73] As for passing judgment in matters of justice, Henry VII sat with his main Council to hear legal cases, while Henry VIII sent letters to cancel decrees and dismiss causes from Star Chamber.[74] One intriguing note in the margins of a Requests order-book entry moving a case into the Star Chamber, reading '*ad interloquendum Rege*', suggests that this tribunal, too, could run its business by the king, at least when it concerned other elements of his conciliar court system.[75] In short, both monarchs were certainly informed about judicial proceedings running in their name, and were involved in all kinds of decision-making on this front.

Yet they did *not* employ such a regular, personal touch in the procedures of these other tribunals; they did not sign writs resulting from their processes, in the manner observable in Requests. There are enough of the otherwise ephemeral commission writs surviving within Requests' early archive to illustrate that they were largely the product of an active attendant household, under direct supervision of the monarch. The hands-on Henry VII issued writs under his signature on the move, from Greenwich, Woodstock, Salisbury, Reading, and Nottingham, for example.[76] We might speculate that he signed off documents during mass, when he remained in his privy closet and could process paperwork with his closest councillors. After all, the same circle of men who signed off bills in Requests – eventually, the household clergy – also ordered and counter-signed its commission writs. However, since these writs are dated to all days of the week and all times of the year, this work does not seem to have been restricted to fixed meetings. Instead, the impression is that it was under-taken on a more impromptu, and presumably more efficient, basis.

This system continued under Henry VIII, with one notable difference. By the end of 1510 at the latest, this young king's real autograph was

---

Late Medieval England: Henry VII, the Earl of Oxford, and the Case of John Hale, 1487', *Journal of Medieval History* 45:4 (2019), 504–22.

[73] M. Hicks, 'Attainder, Resumption and Coercion 1461–1529', *Parliamentary History* 3 (1984), 16; see M. A. Hicks, 'What Was Personal about Personal Monarchy in the Fifteenth Century?', in S. McGlynn and E. Woodacre eds., *The Image and Perception of Monarchy in Medieval and Early Modern Europe* (Cambridge Scholars, 2014), 11–15. For examples, see W. Campbell ed., *Materials for a History of the Reign of Henry VII*, Rolls Series 60 (Cambridge University Press, 1873–7), vol. I, 118, 156, 172, 273, 282, 314, vol. II, 110–11, 227–8, 241; W. C. Richardson, *Tudor Chamber Administration, 1485–1547* (Louisiana State University Press, 1952), 12.

[74] HL Ellesmere MSS 2654 fols. 1–24, 2655 fols. 3–6, 2652 fol. 11.   [75] REQ1/2 fol. 3.

[76] For examples, see REQ2/2/82, 86, 95, 99, 103, 141, 145, 148, 149, 153, 2/4/74.

replaced by a 'wet stamp', an inky facsimile of his signature, which remained in use for the next several decades (visible in Figure 7.2). For a short time, this same stamp was applied to warrants for the great seal and to circulars ordering preparations for the military campaign in France in 1512.[77] Otherwise it was seemingly reserved for judicial administration within the attendant household, for which it may well have been created in the first place. The rationale for its creation and use likely lies not in the volume of business in Requests, which was apparently quite low after the accession in 1509, but in the simple fact that Henry VIII did not enjoy paperwork. Within the first decade of his reign, he admitted to finding writing 'somewhat tedius and paynefull', and even when he had settled into his kingship he was known to be 'always lothe to signe'.[78] Stamping instead of signing certainly proved efficient, allowing writs to be churned out within a matter of days if not immediately upon receipt of the petition. In one suit presented to the Council in early 1520, an order establishing a commission recorded on the back of the initial petition *and* the resulting stamped signet-seal writ are both dated to the same day and location, 8 February at Greenwich, and countersigned by John Clerk.[79] Hence the

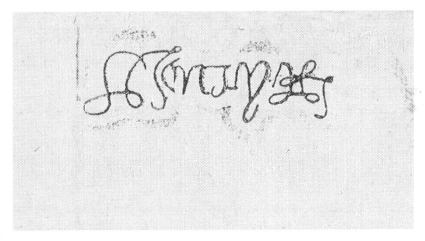

Figure 7.2 The 'wet stamp' of Henry VIII's sign manual on a commission writ issued from the Court of Requests, June 1523. © The National Archives, ref. REQ3/5 *Slack* v *Colinson*.

---

[77] TNA C82/337 no. 3147, 82/378 no. 3193; SP1/229 fol. 114; *LP* I. 1172 (2), 1217.
[78] *LP* III. 1; SP1/101 fols. 50–50v (*LP* X. 76).
[79] REQ2/7/96. See also REQ2/9/42, 57, 94, 2/12/43.

194   Delivering and Contesting Justice

number of surviving stamped writs increases from 1515 onwards, an upwards trend reversed only when Requests settled in the White Hall and switched to the in-house privy seal as the primary mechanism for all its outgoing orders.[80] In the shorter term, application of the stamp to Requests' writs several times at Greenwich in November 1520, while Henry VIII resided at Wanstead, suggests that it also removed the need for direct royal oversight and allowed this business to be fully delegated.[81] In all, the stamp retained the appearance of royal authority behind orders going out to the realm's local governors from the household while streamlining the process at the administrative centre.

At the other end of this process, commissions brought royal justice directly into the intimate communities of England's villages, towns, and cities. On receipt of the king's writ and any existing paperwork for the case at hand, the small group of addressees promptly sent out their orders calling the disputants before them for examination; on occasion, they proved their authority by showing the defendant their royal authorisation.[82] Once everyone was in place, hearings occurred in public spaces like churches, town halls, and (before their dissolution) in local abbeys.[83] Discussions could run for several days, requiring accommodation for the parties, their witnesses, and the commissioners themselves – some bills of costs even record expenses for commissioners' dinners.[84] These gatherings presumably made royal justice tangible to the poor labourers, servants, and farmers who commonly provided depositions. Interrogatories were often designed to draw out their valuable knowledge about the history of landholding in the local area, among other things. Particularly memorable examples from Requests' archive include the questioning of an entire community about the exact age of a potential heir, and whether any remembered his birthday; and the remembrances of a local physician about the dying moments of one of his patients, and whether he had divulged that his round box was full of leases before it was stolen.[85] Whatever their findings, and however successful they had been

---

[80] For a fuller examination of the stamping mechanism in context, see L. Flannigan, 'Signed, Stamped, and Sealed: Delivering Royal Justice in Early Sixteenth-Century England', *Historical Research* 94:264 (2021), 267–81.

[81] REQ2/8/283, 2/9/94, 2/11/148; Samman, 'The Henrician Court during Cardinal Wolsey's Ascendancy', 357.

[82] REQ3/8 *Lappe* v *Revell*; REQ2/7/51.

[83] See, for instance, REQ2/3/345, where the commissioners (two gentlemen) are said to have sat within the church at Easingwold, Yorkshire, to hear witnesses; REQ3/5 *Burton* v *Woode*, REQ3/9 *Stevenson* v *Middleton*.

[84] REQ2/9/97, 2/10/189, 2/13/25.   [85] REQ2/8/317; REQ3/15 *Knight* v *Watts*.

Before the King's Most Honourable Council 195

in any requested mediation, commissioners certified their views to the judges in Requests and returned the casefile to the Court.

Whether writs were signed or stamped, the processes they initiated proceeded quickly and seamlessly, feeding back into decision-making at the administrative centre. One early suit, between John Thacham and his son-in-law Edmund Eyre, was heard by commissioners in Salisbury and certified back to Requests on 8 October 1505, while the king and his retinue were travelling through Hampshire. Just six days later, on 13 October, a signed signet-seal writ was sent from Reading back to the same commissioners, ordering them to use their knowledge of the case 'to sette a liefull ordre and direccion' between the parties. The commissioners duly convened again in Salisbury on 19 October and certified the defendants' obstinacy back to the king two days later; Eyre was then summoned to appear before Requests under a privy-seal writ of *subpoena*, which he did in January 1506.[86] In this example and many others it appears that signet-seal writs could allow for cases to be moved out to the localities, fully examined, and returned to the centre within a few days – and sometimes to be remitted for good. No wonder, then, that writs under the royal seals were so highly sought by plaintiffs. We should not underestimate the 'symbolic power of a royal document when in someone's personal possession', given its power to 'induce awe' and to put sophisticated procedures into motion quickly.[87]

Staying the Course

As effective as royal justice could clearly be, were the procedural steps just described feasible for most prospective petitioners? We have seen already that while Requests' petitioners were drawn from the poorer sort of most social categories, these same people were most adversely affected by the Court's settlement at Westminster. Each stage of investigation and determination, from the supplication onwards, also required considerable costs from plaintiffs and from defendants. Privy-seal writs to summon parties into court cost between 6s 8d and 7s 4d, to be paid to the clerks of that seal, with an additional fee to a messenger if required totalling as much as 6s 8d. As and when a commission was established, the price for 'sealing and writing' the writ was between 5s and 7s 4d, with further fees for drawing up lists of witnesses, for writing up and formally engrossing the

---

[86] REQ2/2/149; REQ1/3 fol. 223.
[87] Musson and Powell eds., *Crime, Law, and Society in the Later Middle Ages*, 43.

196   Delivering and Contesting Justice

interrogatories, and for the examination of each deponent.[88] It was also customary for interim orders in cases to be entered into the Court's books, for which a small fee would be exacted by its clerk. These mounting expenses hardly seem in line with Requests' reputation as a court for the poor. To mitigate these potential barriers, another duty that apparently fell to the members of the king's honourable Council in Requests was to establish who was eligible for their justice in the first place.

An apparent benefit of the concentration of Requests' functions in the hands of theologians and of civil and canon lawyers for much of the early Tudor period was the emergence of admissions of suitors *in forma pauperis* – as a pauper. Although the parliament of 1495 had passed a bill requiring admissions for 'such persons as are poore' in the king's 'Courtes of Recorde' by limiting costs, there is little evidence to suggest that this was applied in the common-law courts for which it was intended.[89] In fact, this principle was much more firmly established by this time in courts following the codes of civil and canon law. Historians of the early Tudor church courts have observed occasional *in forma pauperum* admissions, for example in the act books for London and York in the first decade or so of the sixteenth century.[90] This most likely entailed the provision of counsel and waived fees for the production of documents by the court's clerks. This would have been in alignment with texts like William Lyndwood's *Provinciale*, a manual of the laws for the Province of Canterbury circulated widely among clergymen following its completion in 1430 and printing in 1483, which cited the decretals of Pope Gregory IX as the basis upon which court advocates might be assigned to the poor. As Lyndwood summarised it, 'justice is quickly violated with gold'.[91]

These existing precedents aside, by the outset of Henry VIII's reign admissions *in forma pauperis* had also become in some way associated with the conciliar courts. This is insinuated by the plans set out by the main Council in 1509 to waive fees for legal counsel in the common-law courts at Westminster upon the abolition of certain conciliar 'bye courts' – the implication being not only that the 1495 Act was not being observed at common law, but also that these conciliar tribunals *had* offered such

---

[88] See the bills of costs filed in REQ2/3/162, 2/4/45, 2/6/223, 2/10/189; REQ3/2 *Berde v Berde*; REQ3/4 *Copinger v Wyrall*; REQ3/5 Jerarde, REQ3/30 Chapman.

[89] 11 Hen. VII c. 12. Baker found only a single bill for *in forma pauperis* in King's Bench in 1539: *OHLE*, 97 n. 77; there is another example recorded for a widow from Wiltshire in Common Pleas in 1532: TNA CP40/1075 m. 242.

[90] R. H. Helmholz, *Canon Law and the Law of England* (Hambledon, 1987), 44, 47.

[91] William Lyndwood, *Provinciale seu constitutiones Angliae* (Oxford, 1679), 68c; P. Cavill, 'The First Readers of Lyndwood's *Provinciale*', *Ecclesiastical Law Journal* 24:1 (2021), 2–13.

Before the King's Most Honourable Council   197

provision.[92] In fact, its usage in the conciliar courts became even more widespread after 1509. Wolsey's influence, from his vantage point in Star Chamber and Chancery, is detectable here; the Venetian ambassador, Sebastian Giustinian, reported that Wolsey had a reputation for justness and had encouraged lawyers to waive their fees – to plead *gratis* – for paupers.[93] Going by the annotation of bills and pleadings with the word *'pauper'* or a phrase to that effect, Metzger counted 'two dozen' admissions in the late-medieval Chancery while Guy found a couple made in Star Chamber under Wolsey's chancellorship.[94] There are signs that the provincial councils were undertaking the same practice by this time, too. Instructions sent to the Council in the North in 1538 feature a passage about the judges' 'discression to appoint consalle and other requisites without paying of any money' for 'poure sueters havyng no money', and this was included too in a reissue to Lord Russell and the Council in the West the following year.[95] Meanwhile, one Requests bill bears memoranda from the Council in the Marches at Ludlow from the late 1520s identifying the plaintiff as a *'pauper'*.[96] Of course, admissions could also have been requested and made verbally, so there may have been more in each of these forums for which there is now no tangible evidence.

Going on the evidence we *do* have, of all these comparable institutions Requests appears to have admitted the greatest number of poor suitors with waived fees in the early Tudor period. Across the whole pleadings archive, forty-six of its casefiles are marked with the word *'pauper'* or some variation thereof, either on the back of the petition or on the writ for commission, alongside the signature of the presiding judge. Significantly, at least thirty-five of these admissions were concentrated in the late 1510s and early 1520s, when the household clergy, usually learned in canon and/or civil law, handled all of Requests' business. By comparison, just three survive for the 1530s and six for the 1540s. The tenets of *in forma pauperis* were likely especially familiar to household clergymen; Veysey was even bequeathed a copy of Lyndwood's *Provinciale* a couple of decades before he started working in conciliar justice.[97] Around the time of his tenure in Requests, plaintiffs started to occasionally ask for this process within their petitions.

---

[92] Baker, *OHLE*, 194, 203–4; BL Lansdowne MS 639 fol. 28; HL Ellesmere MS 2655 fols. 7–7v.

[93] Sebastian Giustinian, *Four Years at the Court of Henry VIII*, trans. Rawdon Brown (Smith, Elder & Co., 1854), vol. II, 314.

[94] Metzger, 'The Last Phase of the Medieval Chancery', 82; Guy, *The Court of Star Chamber*, 62.

[95] *LP* XIII. i. 1269 (SP1/133 fols. 211–221v).   [96] REQ3/8 *Plommer* v *Ward*.

[97] A. B. Emden, *A Biographical Register of the University of Oxford to A.D. 1500* (Clarendon Press, 1957–9), vol. III, 1948.

198 Delivering and Contesting Justice

In 1517, the husbandman William Cowper stated that he 'had not money to pay for the [privy seal]' due to his 'extreme povertie', and so he asked 'in consyderacion of hys povertie' for the production costs to be waived.[98] An unusual example from a couple of years later further highlights that openness to the poor was coming to characterise Requests' jurisdiction. When Sir Henry Wyatt sued to Requests it was not only on the basis that he 'in noo wise canne be absent' from the royal court to sue elsewhere, but also because his opponent was 'a pore man and not able to recompence your saide servaunt for suche costes and dammages as he is like to bere'. In other words, he hoped that the Council might step in to cover expenses he expected to win back.[99]

How, exactly, Requests' clerical judges made assessments about poverty and eligibility is less apparent. Household clergymen were presumably used to identifying paupers, since they were engaged in the practice of doling out alms to any such person presenting themselves before the entourage on the road or at palace gates. Lyndwood's commentary collated several definitions of a 'pauper' under canon law: economically speaking, it meant someone who had less than fifty 'gold coins' (*aureos*), but it also applied to people who subsisted on their labour, could not work, were not of sound mind, or lacked dependants (women, orphans, and the disabled).[100] In addition to these identifying features, Requests' frontline might have been influenced by claims to relative poverty made within petitions. While most judges simply wrote '*pauper*' or variations such as '*valde pauper*', '*pauper & misera*' (very poor, poor, and wretched), John Clerk annotated a few bills with notes reading '*pauper ut dicit*' (pauper as he/it says).[101] Throughout much of the legal system, and particularly in the church courts, poverty was a self-attributed status that had to be sworn to under oath.[102] Given that Requests imposed oaths on all other testimonies it gathered, its judges may have done the same to establish the worth of litigants. They could receive further corroboration of a plaintiffs' general self-identification from other sources, too: legal counsel might disclose their client's worth, especially if it exceeded the threshold allowable in Requests; third parties could write into Requests to testify to an

---

[98] REQ3/13 *Cowper v Markley and Willard.* Another petition recalled being 'amitted in forma pauperis' and being granted a commission by the Council in an earlier suit: REQ3/24 *Fishpole v Turner.*

[99] REQ3/15 *Wyatt v Mercer.*   [100] Lyndwood, *Provinciale*, 68c.

[101] E.g., REQ2/7/40; REQ3/18 *Plomer v Oliver*; REQ2/7/127; REQ3/16/2 *Dilcock v Mitton.*

[102] See, for example, the London consistory court records: LMA DL/C/0001 fols. 24, 26, 30v, 42v, 81v, 128v, 178, 210v, 230 (I am grateful to Dr Paul Cavill for providing these references).

Before the King's Most Honourable Council 199

acquaintance's poverty; and commissioners sometimes used their certificates to speak up for vulnerable parties, particularly groups of poor tenants.[103] In any case, the judges' role, Lyndwood had stressed, was not to simply pay for these plaintiffs from a court's purse but rather to provide advocates so that everyone might have legal advice. This suggests that the fees of litigating in a particular court determined where the threshold between paupers and the general body of litigants lay. Certainly, this tailored application of *in forma pauperis* seems apparent in occasional notes on Requests' bills indicating that a lawyer had been appointed '*in cownsel pauperis*'.[104]

Aside from this care for the poorest litigants, Requests' frontline judges sought to appraise the socioeconomic status of *all* those who came into Court. Another intervention that the judges made personally by the later years of Henry VIII's reign was to adjudicate on awards of compensation for court costs to the 'winning' party in a case. Increasingly over our period, litigants produced and submitted their bills of costs, which the judges then signed off with a short statement on how much the 'losing' party had to reimburse ('*taxatur*', followed by the total sum awarded), sometimes crossing out those expenses that they had decided not to grant or silently leaving them out of the totals. They ignored requests to cover losses caused by the 'absence from … husbandry' during litigation, for example.[105] Recipients of any such repayment had to then write up and sign a bill confirming receipt of the money in open court.[106] At the same time as this procedure was becoming more common, the number of recorded *in forma pauperis* admissions appears to have tailed off. It is entirely possible that the latter process continued without being in any way recorded; certainly, by the late sixteenth century it was lamented by commentators that Requests admitted far too many paupers without proper scrutiny.[107] Either way, the crackdown on rich suitors and the institution of controlled fee reimbursements perhaps demonstrates another means of reserving Requests for the king's poorest subjects on the part of its later, secular judges.

Did any of these strategies succeed in keeping Requests accessible? Status identifiers occasionally recorded alongside litigants' names in the later order books (distinct from the descriptors that litigants gave themselves and their opponents within their initial petitions, examined in the previous chapter) can shed some light on who, exactly, made it 'before the king's

---

[103] E.g., REQ2/7/88; REQ3/1/1 *Lacy* v *Abbot of Tavistock*; REQ3/19 *Dakenfield* v *Sheffield*.
[104] REQ2/6/224, 2/10/63; REQ3/10 *Pante* v *Knight*.   [105] REQ2/4/101.   [106] E.g., REQ2/4/181.
[107] BL Add. MS 25248 fols. 7–7v.

200 Delivering and Contesting Justice

honourable Council'. The picture emerging for the early Tudor period as a whole is that the proportions of widows and clergy are consistently higher within the books than in the pleadings. Putting aside the general social ubiquity of those categories of description, especially compared to more transient and overlapping terms like 'gentleman' or 'esquire', their predominance in the books nevertheless reflects the ability and willingness of those so described to pursue suits to later stages of litigation. They either had resources to hand (in the case of well-established clergy and richer widows) or the Court was more likely to take pity on them (in the case of poorer widows, and perhaps many of the judges' fellow ecclesiastics). Otherwise, there is a noticeable drop-off in the numbers of craftsmen between the petitioning and hearing stages (23 per cent of identifiable petitioners versus 6 per cent in the books), perhaps suggesting that they were more likely to use royal justice to force their opponents' hand rather than to initiate full litigation. Even more obvious is the absence of the non-gentle and labouring landed people, including yeomen and husbandmen, in the books when compared to the petitions (12 per cent versus 1 per cent). In fact, the terms 'husbandman' and 'yeoman' hardly appear to have been applied by the clerks within the registers at all, while the Latin terms *vidua*, *generosus*, *miles*, and *clericus* were commonly used throughout the whole period.[108] A social survey of the order books inevitably therefore reflects the clerks' recording habits, particularly when compared with the rawer – albeit rhetorical – petitions.

Nevertheless, the book 'additions' do corroborate the trend towards more limited accessibility as the Court settled down, supporting the findings of the brief comparison of petitioners in 1500–3 and 1540–3 undertaken in Chapter 6. The book entries closer to the end of Henry VIII's reign include a much higher proportion of landed gentleman and upper-ranking clergymen than do those from previous decades, while at the same time indicating an overall decline in all other social categories, and even in the usually ubiquitous widows.[109] We might infer from this evidence that any attempts to expand accessibility down the social scale and exclude the upper echelons from full suit were not especially successful. Moreover, processing times were lengthening by the last decade of Henry VIII's reign. While the average duration between initial bill and a final

---

[108] According to entries in REQ1/1, 2, 3, 4, 5, 6, 8, 104, and 105. REQ1/7 has been excluded from this survey so as to avoid some duplication of entries, because it overlaps entirely with REQ1/6 (1537–46) and REQ1/8 (1546–7) and so contains many of the same cases.

[109] According to a comparison of statuses given in REQ1/3 (1502–8), REQ1/5 (1523–33), and REQ1/6 (1537–46).

Before the King's Most Honourable Council 201

judgment had usually been in the region of six months, Requests was so busy even by the late 1530s that a secondary book had to be commenced solely to keep track of the continuation of cases across several terms.[110] A decade later, endorsements on a number of bills noting that matters therein had been 'expedited' imply a backlog of work that required prioritisation, as opposed to the quick and ad-hoc sign-offs of earlier decades.[111] Dacres had, after all, complained about the 'great hinderaunce and delaie' within the Court in *c.* 1543.[112] This surely affected the Court's ability to offer on-the-spot judicial processes to the truly poor; and so those with fewer resources were likely dropping out sooner than before.

Still, that Requests' judges evinced some desire to act with sensitivity to social disparity, in line with the king's charitable persona, may explain why this Court continued to be seen as a reliever of the poor in spite of all the real caveats set out above. While it was always commonplace – even formulaic – for petitioners to insist that they could not afford common-law suit, in the later years of Henry VIII's reign it became more usual to also suggest that they were 'not of abilitie to bere and meynteyn the chargeable and long sute' of the king's other courts, even Chancery, either.[113] From a purely economic perspective this was truer on some counts than others: attorneys generally worked in Requests for half the price they charged in Chancery and Star Chamber, though a privy-seal summons could cost double the fees required for the original writs used in the other principal conciliar courts.[114] Costs were about equal across the board, then – but the potential provision of justice for the poor may have set Requests apart. And so, by the end of our period, litigants sometimes claimed to be 'so poore that they be not able to sue for their right consernyng the premisses in any other of yor graces Courtes than before yor highnes in yor majesties Courte of Request'.[115]

Conclusion

Even in a court as small and nebulous as the early Tudor Requests, the creation of justice involved the efforts and expertise of a diverse range of people across a wide social spectrum, from centre to localities. The

---

[110] REQ1/6, then REQ1/8.   [111] REQ2/7/83, 108, 2/8/313, 2/10/170.
[112] BL Add. MS 25248 fols. 29–33.   [113] REQ2/10/30, 249; REQ3/15 *Rochford* v *Mondy.*
[114] According to comparison between lists of costs for Chancery and Star Chamber in J. Guy, *The Court of Star Chamber and its Records to the Reign of Elizabeth I* (HMSO, 1985), 63; REQ3/6 *Clerk* v *Thrale.*
[115] REQ3/1/1 *Hallam* v *Goodam.* Similarly, see the replication of William and Thomas Paramore, who insisted that their matter was 'determinable within thys honorable courte forasmoche as the sayde complaynants ar very poore men & not riche': REQ3/22/1 *Paramore and Paramore* v *Dodd.*

202 Delivering and Contesting Justice

moment of initiation could involve a face-to-face meeting between the lowliest subject and the king himself. Indeed, evidence in Requests broadly corroborates contemporary complaints that Henry VIII was presented with private grievances when he was 'passing from place to place' and that he often had to placate petitioners personally.[116] This was not the only place where the rhetoric of royal justice became a reality. The unusual practice of Henry VII and Henry VIII personally viewing and signing procedural documents gives us cause to believe that both were more interested in the goings-on of this part of the household operation than we might otherwise have presumed. But this mediation was facilitated on a more regular basis by a series of committed judges and masters in Requests to whom judicial work was delegated day to day. It was these men who met litigants, accepted their petitions, decided on the first line of process, authorised orders under the king's seals, presented writs to the king for his signature, managed access to their court, and attempted to mitigate its costs.

To our picture of a fluid quasi-institution with a wide clientele, the survey of Requests' personnel and their work in this chapter adds a sense of the interpersonal engagements going on outside of the surviving written record. It also demonstrates the consequences – the benefits, even – of the ad-hoc, informal quality of Requests' work for so much of this period. Precisely *because* it was not set up to act on the same days every week and in one place, its responses to petitioners could be speedy and seamless, reaching quickly into communities across the realm and drawing on the knowledge of the people there. Yet something else that comes through in this analysis is the problem that petitioners presented to the frontline judges, not only in terms of their growing numbers but in the complexity of the cases they brought and the rhetorical nature of their self-presentations. Having explored all the intermediaries who made Requests function we now turn to the other major party that its justice-giving touched: defendants. On taking up their perspective it becomes clear just how much royal justice became more contestable in this period.

---

[116] Nichols ed., *A collection of ordinances and regulations for the government of the royal household*, 159.

CHAPTER 8

Answers and Arguments

The full record of litigants' back-and-forth pleadings in the Court of Requests forces us to confront the assumption that litigation was a largely positive force in early modern society. Examining and resolving a dispute certainly required a great deal of collaboration between suppliants, their neighbours, lawyers, local powerholders, and the central administration. These processes might, in the long term, have legitimised and strengthened governmental authority. Yet, as Hindle recently reminded us, 'defendants did not enjoy being sued and ... plaintiffs did not enjoy having to sue them'.[1] This may seem obvious given that, as we have seen, going to law even in the so-called 'poor man's court' was a costly and time-consuming exercise. Still, while it has long been accepted that accounts contained in petitions were to some extent 'fictive', historians still tend to take plaintiffs' versions of events at face value and the defendant's point of view is rarely considered. In a sense, this is to do what one disgruntled observer claimed of some sixteenth-century lawcourts: that they allowed 'he that told the first tale' to be 'best belevid'.[2]

In fact, defendants' responses often give us cause to question petitioners' narratives, their self-fashioning, and their very right to sue in this arena. In this they followed prevailing opinion in legal commentary of the time that the growing conciliar justice system gave too much precedence to petitioners and did not treat defendants kindly.[3] Without this more critical perspective on the expansion of litigation, we risk creating a simplistic narrative in which state and society, localities and centre, easily co-existed – a picture that hardly helps us to explain why the system of courts facilitating this harmony could be so easily brought down in 1641. This chapter examines how those on the receiving end of Requests' justice and the

---

[1] Hindle, 'The Micro-Spatial Dynamics of Litigation', 142.
[2] Thornley and Thomas ed., *The Great Chronicle of London*, 320.
[3] For another recent study of defendants see Taylor, 'Labourers, Legal Aid and the Limits of Popular Legalism in Star Chamber'.

203

204 Delivering and Contesting Justice

lawyers who represented them problematised definitions of 'poor', questioned the authority of summoning processes, and claimed that this Court operated outside the 'law of the land' – grounds on which conciliar justice, and specifically Requests, could be resisted. In all, it will become apparent that the expansion of litigation under the early Tudors was not warmly received in all quarters. This criticism was, in turn, essential to how justice-giving adapted in the sixteenth century.

Receiving Writs

Defendants' resistance to royal justice could begin as soon as they were summoned to appear before the king's Council. The publicity of process-serving gave it an air of notoriety, and so the arrival of a process-server on one's doorstep could be an unwelcome and upsetting surprise. The messenger John Franklin reported that William Bush's wife had been 'crying and weeping' (*flens & lacrimans*) when she had received the writ in the Dorchester high street on her husband's behalf.[4] The messengers' testimonials before Requests record recipients' various strategies to avoid being served at all. Occasionally there is an inkling within these accounts of some understanding that if a person did not take the writ into their hands it had not been executed. The twenty-four-year-old Ralph Chatterton of Mellor in Derbyshire recounted how, at the parish church of Denton, on Candlemas day and in front of 'all the parisshon[er]s', he had tried to deliver a writ to John Rushton. When Rushton 'wold not receyve [the writ] in his hande', the deponent had 'laied it upon his arme'. This act instigated a fight in the churchyard, where the defendant's servant 'gave many greate wordes and wold have stryken this deponent in the churche yf weldisposed persons' had not intervened.[5] A common phrase appearing in alike accounts was that the defendant had 'taken flight' (*fugam fecit*) on seeing the writ. The extreme inconvenience that this posed to the process-server comes through in William Egerton's testimony of March 1502, in which he recounted searching for Roger Vernon, the addressee of a royal writ, in 'Wrikesworth, Haddon, Ashborne, Duffild, [Nether]sheyle, Tomworth et Derby', to no avail.[6]

Once they had been served, more resourceful defendants engaged in a whole range of delaying tactics to avoid or counteract a writ. In the later

[4] REQ1/1 fol. 104v.
[5] REQ3/4 *Rattcliff and Cotterell* v *Rushton*. For a similar example, see REQ2/4/109.
[6] REQ1/2 fol. 183.

Answers and Arguments

years of Henry VII's reign, a poor husbandman had tried to deliver a summons to the vicar of 'Stodenge' and his servants, but had found himself committed to Oxford prison 'by the space of half a yere[, the king's] said gracious lettres of prive seale being about hym as the same vicar knew well'.[7] A similar tale emerged from Bedfordshire in the mid-1510s, when it was reported by Thomas Russell that the local bailiff, William Jolice, 'understanding and knowledge havyng that yor said por orator had obteyned yor said graciouse lettres of privye seale', moved to have Russell and his associates arrested and imprisoned in Bedford gaol. Jolice promised to release them only if they agreed not to serve the writ; in the meantime, he endeavoured to gain his own writ for surety of the peace from the criminal courts of London, effectively binding Russell to good behaviour against him.[8] These were the judicial remedies that might be employed by defendants to slow the process of extraordinary royal justice and out-manoeuvre their opponents. Others were vaguer about their way out. When the mercer William Hunt was served a writ at his home in London, he simply mounted his horse and rode out of the city, declaring that he was protected by the king from the force of such an order.[9]

Other testimonies recounted outright rejection of the king's orders. Process-servers were not popular figures, often rebuffed with 'unfitting words & language' and with unsheathed weapons.[10] John Cheyney junior, who memorably complained about interruption of the mass in his parish church, did so while being investigated by Requests for his 'evil demeanor against the kynges prevy seale'. He had allegedly threatened the writ-server that he would 'slitte his nose and crop his eares', had thrown him out of the church, and sent servants to hunt him down across the surrounding fields.[11] The plaintiff Martin Bagworth of Tottenham chose to deliver his acquired writ personally to his opponent, Richard Bolday, a clerk of Chancery – who, being of 'rebellious mind', 'cruelly strake' Bagworth for his troubles. In a follow-up petition to the king and Requests, Bagworth begged that the king send a serjeant-at-arms to seize Bolday, saving him the money and personal risk of suing out more writs which Bolday clearly did not 'drede'.[12] Even Westminster Hall was not safe: the merchant tailor Thomas Twynne reported in a petition that when he had tried to serve a writ there he had been beaten and intimidated in front of the seated justices.[13] A more serious

---

[7] REQ3/3 *Hickden* v *Knody and others*.
[8] REQ3/4 *Russell* v *Jolice*. For a similar case of assault and imprisonment of a process-server, albeit in the context of common-law process, see REQ3/7 *Forster* v *Stele, Colle and Castell*.
[9] REQ1/1 fol. 164v.   [10] REQ1/104 fol. 129; REQ1/2 fol. 195.   [11] REQ2/4/298.
[12] REQ2/4/383.   [13] REQ3/12 *Twynne* v *Chamberlain*.

206   Delivering and Contesting Justice

case of communal resistance was raised at the common law in 1504, with a criminal commission established to inquire into allegations that the prior and tenants of Hatfield Regis in Essex had threatened to shear the hair of a process-server, cut off his horse's tail, and put him in the pillory. Eventually the poor messenger was forced to kneel in the marketplace and swear that he 'shall hereafter never bring suche prevy seale nor other the kynges writt unto thys town in hurthyng of o[u]r fraunces', perhaps referring to the franchise of the priory.[14] Here the prior, like William Hunt of London, evoked some understanding that a privilege or liberty protected certain subjects from a peremptory royal summons.

That this case was heard in King's Bench, by some of the most senior legal minds, tells us how much the Crown was concerned by this time with the repudiation of the writ, its wax seal, and the king's authority as justice-giver that they represented. Messengers' testimonies to Requests routinely describe encounters with recipients who 'obstinately toke and then cast [the writ] away', threw it on the ground in the street, or ripped it up – usually before running off.[15] Numerous defendants were said to have tossed the writ aside with 'opprobrious words', with one even supposedly having said 'that [they] caryd not therfor but despitefully defied the same'.[16] In another suit from the early 1520s, commissioners appointed by Requests to investigate a matter locally reported back that the defendant 'little regarded the kinges writing', having once openly declared 'that if the king sent his brode seale and my lord Cardynall his seal' he would still not obey.[17] A more unusual feature of these accounts of process-serving was the regularity with which obstinate defendants forced others to *eat* the seal itself. This was one of the many threats made by the prior and chief inhabitants of Hatfield Regis against the messenger to their town.[18] Likewise, in Requests, William Cartwright complained that when he had sent his maidservant to the home of Sir John Burdett with a privy-seal summons, she had been seized by Burdett's servants and forced to 'ete a pece of the seid wex [seal]', causing her to take to her bed for four days and instigating another suit to Requests for a new writ.[19] This strange act of violence occurred in many legal and judicial contexts. Perhaps it represented something similar to the symbolic refusal to take a writ in hand: an order could not be enacted if its authorising seal was destroyed.

---

[14] TNA KB9/446/41. For a similar communal gathering against a writ-server see REQ2/4/325.
[15] For example, REQ1/1 fol. 112v, 161; REQ1/2 fol. 178.
[16] REQ3/10 *Symmes* v *Beckford*. See also REQ1/1 fols. 142v, 161, 164v; REQ1/2 fols. 50, 178; REQ2/2/123, 2/4/383.
[17] REQ2/7/51.   [18] KB9/446/41.   [19] REQ2/4/337. See also REQ2/4/109.

Answers and Arguments

It is difficult to ascertain on a case-by-case basis how far we might interpret refusal to be summoned as informed disobedience of the royal jurisdiction. In most instances, defendants probably acted impulsively to avoid costly litigation. Still, the Crown and its courts took their renunciations seriously. In Requests, the financial penalty for non-appearance increased quickly to £300 and, failing that, the local sheriff and bailiffs would be ordered to attach – to physically seize – defendants and convey them to the court. Those cases where the defendants fled *again* saw them openly proclaimed as rebels.[20] Moreover, speaking out against the king's summons was so serious that it would eventually be considered seditious, examinable under the Treason Act of 1534. One gentleman from London accordingly found himself arraigned in King's Bench for having publicly declared that he 'set not a pudding by the kynges brode seale'.[21] The royal authority embodied by writs issuing out of the Council and Requests did not engender automatic deference.

Making Answers

Most defendants received the king's letters 'humbly and reverently' and *did* peaceably attend on Requests, however.[22] Their first appearance before the Court was duly recorded in its order books, and there followed a period of a week or so in which they were expected to attend each day. This was their window of opportunity to build a solid defence against the potentially unlimited number of allegations made against them by the petitioner – some of which they may have been hearing for the first time during hearings – and to introduce any facts and circumstances convenient to their own case. These procedures could pose serious problems for a defendant caught off guard by litigation, even if they were well connected and financially resourceful.

The construction of a strong response to a complaint saw defendants turn to the same kind of professional help as their accusers. In fact, since they were usually on the back foot already, professional counsel was at an even greater premium. As his bill of costs reveals, Martin Sedley of Suffolk took proper legal advice so seriously when he was sued in Requests in 1536 that he made numerous expensive trips 10 miles from his home to consult closely with his two counsellors.[23] Another defendant, George Daldry, paid his counsel 6s 8d – about twice the normal rate – for 'comyng to the barre

---

[20] E.g., REQ1/3 fol. 164. [21] TNA KB9/540/26; KB27/1109 REX m. 2.
[22] E.g., REQ3/15 *Elyot* v *Reed and Hesand*. [23] REQ2/12/70.

208   Delivering and Contesting Justice

iiij tymes for the dyssolvyng of [an] injunccion' ordering that he cease his countersuits elsewhere.[24] If it was affordable, defendants might stretch to hiring serjeants-at-law, some of the most senior members of the profession. In 1532, one defendant in Requests took no chances and paid 20*s* per term to retain three serjeants and two 'prenteses' (apprentices-at-law).[25] Securing expert advice also required good connections: in 1546, William Bowham was able to gain the services of Edward Saunders, a serjeant-at-law trained at the Middle Temple, after a letter of introduction was written on his behalf by another lawyer of the same inn.[26] Yet due to the speed of proceedings many defendants had to rely on Requests' in-house lawyers, as we have seen already. This is implied by the recommendation that the defendant Thomas Bawne seek out for his 'lernyd cownsell' John Hadley, Richard Flower, and Simon Sampson, all of whom regularly worked as attorneys in Requests.[27] By the end of Henry VIII's reign, virtually all defendants were represented by these most accessible of legal aids.

Defending against a petition was a multi-part process, each element bearing its own cost. Making an initial appearance and having it recorded in the order books incurred a fee of between 8*d* and 12*d*, given to the Court's clerk. Acquiring a copy of the petition cost somewhere in the region of 2*s*. Making an answer entailed costs to the counsel for 'drawing' or compiling the text, usually in the region of the standard 3*s* 4*d* termly fee. This was separate from the cost to have that answer 'engrossed' on parchment by the lawyer's clerk, also costing around 2*s* to 3*s*.[28] So just this documentary part of the process alone could cost around 10*s* – or about two weeks' worth of wages, enough to buy a cow.[29] Given the lack of limitations on the length of the vernacular pleadings submitted to Requests and the other conciliar courts, answers could be as short as a few lines and as long as several pieces of paper or parchment stitched together. In some instances, it plainly suited defendants to be as exhaustive as possible in stating their case.

This answer was so integral to proceedings that when a defendant was too infirm or unwell to ride into court and to speak in person, Requests would establish a small commission of local men to write it down and bring

---

[24] REQ3/6 *Daldry* v *Forde*.   [25] REQ2/1/74.   [26] REQ3/17 *Clench* v *Bowham*.

[27] REQ3/3 *Foster* v *Bawne*.

[28] For some examples of defendants' costs, see REQ2/1/74, 2/3/52, 64, 2/4/45, 401, 2/7/94, 2/12/70; REQ2/5 *Carter* v *Coraunt, Turnor* v *Sutton*; REQ3/6 *Daldry* v *Forde*; REQ3/8 Bennet; REQ3/30 Harte.

[29] According to The National Archive's online calculator of purchasing power in the early sixteenth century: www.nationalarchives.gov.uk/currency-converter, accessed May 2022.

Answers and Arguments 209

it back. Whether at home or in the courtroom, answers were rehearsed under oath. This was one way in which early 'equity' tribunals instilled an emphasis on morality and conscience besides purely legal considerations.[30] Petitioners often expressed a firm belief that the truth would come out when their adversaries were made to swear before God, a procedure they sometimes took to be especial to this jurisdiction; one plaintiff hoped 'to have the matier of trouthe to appere to this honorable courte of consciens ffor if he have not help in this courte he is uttrely doon in this world'.[31] The consequence for defendants was either self-incrimination or (as many petitioners surely hoped) perjury.[32] Only once the sworn answer was submitted and rehearsed in court before the judges was a defendant licensed to leave, with their attorney attending in their place for any relevant business thereafter.[33] This further work could involve more documentary pleadings, with the plaintiff responding to the answer with a replication and the defendant potentially submitting a further rejoinder. A case might also continue into further commissions to examine the dispute, hear witness testimonies, and certify back to the Council for a final ruling.

The more heated moments of deliberation took place in person, in the presence of the judges, which put even greater financial and time commitments on defendants' shoulders. Indeed, as for plaintiffs, the most substantial totals on defendants' bills of costs were the expenses for hiring horses or boats to reach Westminster, and for acquiring the accommodation required to 'tarry' around or 'wait upon' the Council for as long as a fortnight, waiting to be seen.[34] Little wonder, then, that some defendants opened their answers with the accusation that the suit against them had been 'ymagened for spyte to putt [the defendant] to vexacion & cause hym dayly by ther untrew surmyse to attend uppon your most honorable Councell the Deane of yor Chappell & yor Amenor & other to theym assocyatt'.[35] The same frustration emerges in Pilkington's narrative of his

---

[30] As explored in M. Macnair, 'Equity and Conscience', *Oxford Journal of Legal Studies* 27:4 (2007), 659–81.

[31] REQ3/5 *Wright* v *Parker*.

[32] Macnair, 'Equity and Conscience', 676–7; R. H. Helmholz, 'The Privilege and *Ius Commune*: The Middle Ages to the Seventeenth Century', in R. H. Helmholz, C. M. Gray, J. H. Langbein, E. Moglen, and H. E. Smith eds., *The Privilege Against Self-Incrimination: Its Origins and Development* (University of Chicago Press, 1997), 17–46.

[33] As a note from William Sulyard to Richard Turnor on the back of one bill spells out: REQ2/3/393.

[34] REQ2/3/52, 64, 249, 2/4/45, 101, 2/6/209, 223, 2/7/38, 68; REQ3/5 *Carter* v *Coraunt*; REQ3/6 *Johnson* v *Johnson*; REQ3/8 Benet; REQ3/10 *Fletcher* v *Andrews*; REQ3/11/2 *West* v *Osborn*.

[35] REQ3/20 *Manus* v *Josselyn*.

210 Delivering and Contesting Justice

time as a defendant before the itinerant Council in the 1490s; at one point, while the king ranged between residences at Collyweston, Northampton, Fotheringhay, and Pipewell Abbey on progress, Pilkington had 'folowed the courte viij days and dayle pursewyd to be dismissed'.[36] Elsewhere, lists of costs contain subtle gripes about how defendants had been handled by the Court and the plaintiff. Sir William Perpoint claimed in his list that the privy seal he had received suggested that he should '[ei]ther agree with the seid [plaintiff, Sir Edmund Fletcher] or else appere wheruppon the seid Sir William was constreyned of necessitie to send to my lord Dean of York to knowe the truth of the custome alleged by the seid Sir Edmonde' – a complaint really about the transparency of the summoning process, to which we will return shortly.[37] The tribulations of defending oneself in this most extraordinary of tribunals are starkly demonstrated, here. They are further heightened by the lack of any evidence to suggest much *in forma pauperis* provision for defendants in this Court.[38]

Pilkington's narrative picks up on another line of criticism of conciliar justice which does not normally appear with much colour in the formal documents of the courts themselves: the problem of the arbitrary judge. In the course of proceedings between 1493 and 1495, Pilkington claimed to have faced extreme partiality shown to his opponent, John Ainsworth, by Thomas Savage, then a leading figure in Requests but also a prominent member of the Savage family of Cheshire, public supporters and maintainers of the Ainsworths. In earlier hearings, when Savage was still Bishop of Rochester, the 'grete favor' shown to Ainsworth meant that Pilkington was forced to show his evidence first, even though custom dictated that 'the said John schuld have layde forth furst his evydencez be cause he began the trouble'. On this occasion the more senior judges, including Foxe as Lord Privy Seal, decided that Savage could not reasonably hear this cause and made him 'ryse . . . and goo to the flore tyll thay hade don with that mater'. Things worsened when Savage was promoted to president of the Council and so head judge in its Requests committee. By this time the 'Byschope was so parchall agaynys the said Robert' that he denied Pilkington licence to fetch his evidence and to seek the advice of counsel. At one stage, Pilkington offered the bishop his fourteen-year-old son as ward 'for endyng theis trowbulls and paynys'; at another, Savage read Pilkington's own

[36] The Narrative of Robert Pilkington, 33–9.   [37] REQ2/3/64.
[38] The only possible example of a defendant having fees waived is one suit from the late 1510s, where it was the defendant's name that was annotated with 'pauper' on the reverse side of the bill: REQ2/4/346. For more on defendants' rights to *in forma pauperis* in the later court of Star Chamber, see Taylor, 'Labourers, Legal Aid and the Limits of Popular Legalism in Star Chamber', 125–9.

Answers and Arguments 211

petition to the Council 'privily to him self' and then dismissed it without hearing.[39] This account stands as remarkable evidence for the goings-on behind Requests' suits. It demonstrates how often litigants conversed with the judges directly and how far the personal involvement of these clerical, conciliar, and courtly delegates left room for prejudices to emerge.

The controversy of a poorly placed judge deepened further in the early sixteenth century, with conscience-based justice in the conciliar courts increasingly a cause for concern. In 1526, the common lawyer and future Lord Chancellor Thomas Audley stated in a law reading that a problem with the 'law called "conscience"' was that it 'depends for the greater part on the whim of the judge in conscience'.[40] In the context of the 1520s, the most likely target for much of this criticism was Wolsey, whose apparent contempt 'for lawe canon, or for the lawe common, or for law cyvyll', as the court poet John Skelton quipped, formed some of the complaints raised before his fall in 1529.[41] In Requests a similar figure was cut by John Stokesley, a theologian and royal chaplain-turned-almoner who ended up as the chief, and virtually the *only*, judge at work in this Court between mid-1521 and early 1523. Even in this short timeframe he signed documents in 129 cases and was regularly described as the presiding judge of the Court's hearings. He was prevalent enough in this tribunal to sometimes be called its 'president', particularly once John Clerk, the dean, had left to undertake royal embassies overseas. Yet by January 1523, Stokesley's work had attracted the scrutiny of the main Council, who entered a curious order into their minute books that established a commission of prominent common lawyers to 'review & examine such causes as Mr Stokesley had judged in the White Hall and to report whether they bee allowable or noe'.[42] The composition of the commission and their cited remit suggests that the jurisdiction of Requests, or at least Stokesley's understanding of it, may have been in question.

Putting these comments into the context of its archive suggests that there was a twofold problem in the tribunal at this time. Beyond Stokesley's control was its rapidly rising level of business, no doubt owing to Wolsey's expansion of conciliar justice in the later 1510s and to the cardinal's tendency to remit causes from his courts of Star Chamber and Chancery into Requests. Coinciding with Clerk's absence, this surely left Stokesley very busy with justice-giving, and he responded by keeping

---

[39] The Narrative of Robert Pilkington, 32–3, 36–7.
[40] Baker ed., *The Reports of Sir John Spelman*, vol. II, 198.
[41] Skelton, 'Why Come Ye Not to Court?', in Dyce ed., *The Poetical Works of John Skelton*, 39; *LP* IV. 5749, 5750, 6075.
[42] HL Ellesmere MS 2652 fol. 4v; BL Lansdowne MS 639 fol. 56v.

212   Delivering and Contesting Justice

Requests' business at Westminster, in the White Hall and in St Stephen's Chapel, and sometimes at 'his lodging at Warwykes Inn in the Citie of London', where he met with litigants personally.[43] Nonetheless, disputants reported problematic and difficult experiences with Requests under his remit. One alleged that their cause had pended before Stokesley for 'a yere and iij qwarters', while another claimed that their 'matier hath depended in [Requests] of longe season and noo maner of ende nor Justice doon'.[44] Such delays are corroborated by the evidence that only four of the cases that Stokesley handled seem to have received a final decree. Corners were cut in other cases; untypically for Requests, several entries in the order book from mid-1521 were simply annotated with a brief statement that 'the cause has been determined by Master Stokesley', leaving the details off the record.[45]

It hardly helped that, like Savage, Stokesley reportedly dealt with litigants quite harshly. There are some glimpses of partiality in his treatment of particular cases, too: in December 1521, he wrote personally to Sir William Skeffington, who had been accused of withholding wages as master of the ordnance, warning that he had 'long forborne' delivering an unfavourable judgment against him and suggesting that Skeffington make restitution instead of suffering a court order.[46] At other times he appeared quite forceful with defendants, restricting their right to admit attorneys and compelling them to attend repeatedly in person, presumably in an attempt to hasten proceedings.[47] Another complainant reported to Wolsey that Stokesley had withheld copies of his witness testimonies and would give them up 'neither for money nor request'; yet another said that when he 'putte the charge' of the Court's delays to Stokesley's 'soule and consience', he had threatened to 'laye hym faste by the helys in prison'.[48] That Stokesley himself was part of the problem may be reflected in Edward Hall's description of him as a man that 'had more learning, then discrecion to be a judge'.[49] He may, in fact, have been perceived to lack the necessary level of authority to pass judgment compared to the well-established figure of the dean. After all, one disgruntled defendant argued that a decree was 'oonly the deade & act of that halt prest Stokisley not beyng dean & done withowt auctorite'.[50] While the findings and outcome of the Council's

---

[43] REQ1/104 fol. 132v.   [44] REQ3/1/1 *Orgor* v *Hovill*; REQ3/22/2 *Foster* v *Treherne*.
[45] REQ1/104 fols. 135v, 137v, 143v, 146v.   [46] SP1/25 fol. 212 (*LP* III. 2727).
[47] This was the implication of one complaint made about Stokesley in King's Bench: TNA KB27/1048 m. 75.
[48] REQ3/1/1 *Orgor* v *Hovill*; REQ3/22/2 *Foster* v *Treherne*.   [49] Hall, *Hall's Chronicle*, 585.
[50] REQ3/26 *Langton* v *Revell and Fitzrandall*. It is possible that 'halt' here had its Middle English definition of being in some way physically impaired, or walking with a limp – though there is no other evidence of Stokesley being so described.

Answers and Arguments

commission were never recorded, its ultimate result seems to have been Stokesley's dismissal from conciliar justice. A later petition to Wolsey related that Stokesley had been 'deposid his office' shortly after January 1523.[51] Indeed, he stopped signing Requests' bills in June, and was replaced as royal almoner by the autumn.[52]

From the perspective of plaintiffs and defendants alike, these episodes of conflict with Requests' leading figures demonstrate the worst-case outcome of justice administered freely, informally, and without much regulation.[53] That said, it is unclear how far the Council intended to alter these qualities in the early sixteenth century. The purview of their investigation of Stokesley was not to remove him and all his ilk but rather to 'drawe a forme after which the Deane & his Cort in Whitehall shal be ordered' thereafter – that is, the Dean of the Chapel was to return to his post here, as before.[54] Consequently, though the Council was clearly keeping an eye on things, defendants against the might of royal justice probably continued to be at the mercy of courts with changeable formats, lawyers and clerks with mounting fees, and judges with varying qualities. The continuous intimacy of Requests' justice-giving throughout our period is suggested in several inferences that parties were being entertained in its judges' own quarters – in Veysey's 'place in London', in Dacres's personal 'chambre' – rather than in open court.[55] Yet here as elsewhere, the virtues of the new royal justice system could easily become their pitfalls when viewed from the other side of litigation.

Objecting to Royal Justice

If a defendant persisted, Requests' pleadings process allowed them to voice a series of arguments in their cause – often based on the matter at hand, but sometimes also on this jurisdiction's very authority and legitimacy. Almost by default, every answer contested the truthfulness and validity of the petition, saying that it was 'uncerten and insufficient to be answered'. Especially where Requests was concerned, this was then followed by an opening salvo that declared the case to be answerable 'not in this court' but through the ordinary course of the law, in King's Bench, Common Pleas, or in tribunals at the manorial, mayoral, and shrieval levels. Since this claim

---

[51] REQ3/1/1 *Orgor* v *Hovill.*   [52] *LP* III. 3275.

[53] For a full account of Stokesley's tenure and dismissal, see L. Flannigan, '"Allowable or Not"? John Stokesley, the Court of Requests, and Royal Justice in Sixteenth-Century England', *Historical Research* 93:262 (2020), 621–37.

[54] HL Ellesmere MS 2652 fol. 4.   [55] REQ2/4/88; REQ3/15 *Dolphin* v *Jenyns.*

214 Delivering and Contesting Justice

appears in answers to all of the conciliar tribunals in this period, we might read it as a somewhat empty statement. Yet further social and legal arguments could often be specifically targeted against the authority of Requests itself, informed by a contemporary current of criticism against royal justice.

Particularly distinctive to this special jurisdiction was the personal and social commentary at the heart of many defendants' objections. As we observed in Chapter 6, key to claiming eligibility to petition in this Court was a position of some relative disadvantage – usually economic, though plaintiffs also regularly referred to being 'unfriended' and unsupported, low on moveable *and* immoveable property, or distant from the lands in dispute, compared to their opponents. Moreover, this rhetoric was not necessarily taken at face value by Requests' judges, who actively assessed the wealth of plaintiffs and variably admitted the poor and remitted the rich. A solid ground for counterargument on defendants' parts was therefore that their accusers' self-identification as impoverished was inaccurate; acknowledging the king's care for the poor but implying that opponents were abusing this privilege. For example, in February 1508 a widow called Margaret Hoorne submitted a petition at Richmond Palace alleging that Laurence Trensham of Faversham in Kent had of his 'evill forward disposicion and malice' conveyed away various tiles and timber from her lands there. Appearing before Requests' judges himself, Trensham quibbled that 'Margaret is of such gret substanciall worldly goodes that if she hadd any such matter of trough it should not greve her to sue according to the comen lawe of this lande.'[56] Later, in Henry VIII's early reign, the husbandman John Pond claimed that the complainants against him were 'of fuller gretter substaunce than the said John is & able to sue for ther remedy at the comen law'. Whether or not the judges believed this, they did eventually pass a decree in Pond's favour.[57]

Defendants also commonly asserted that all litigation was designed simply to drain their purses. One answer drawn up for Requests early in Henry VIII's reign suggested in no uncertain terms that the bill of complaint had been 'slanderously ymagened' by 'senystre counsell' to put the defendant and his servants 'to infamye slawndre rebuke busyness trouble & vexacion'.[58] Later, in 1514, Sir Ralph Brereton surmised that a suit brought against him was the 'procurement of suche other persons as be not the

---

[56] REQ2/1/11. See also REQ2/2/76.
[57] REQ2/9/86, REQ1/4 fol. 75. For a similar example see REQ3/7 *Haselrige* v *Neele*.
[58] REQ2/3/23.

Answers and Arguments

lovers of the said Sir Randolph', intended only 'to brynge hym in evill fame and displeasure of the kinges good grace'.[59] More specifically, one self-proclaimed 'marchaunt man' alleged that his opponent's petition was contrived more 'to thentent to bryng hym owt of credence with his creditours than for eny other lawfull cause'.[60] A running theme here is the portrayal of 'poor' plaintiffs as stooges for much greater foes. In 1531, while the widow Anne Kirkby self-described as an 'agyd woman' with 'few ffryndes', the man she accused, John Kirkby, argued back that her 'byll of compleynt was procuryd by oon John Cooke a great adversary of the said [John] Kirkby whiche dothe not only vex and troble the seid defendaunt unlawfully at the comyn lawe but also yn the kynges honorable cort of Chauncery'.[61] At least one petition *was* found to have been brought to the Council 'without consent or knowledge' of the named petitioner, so such corruption was not implausible.[62] These allegations might be layered up with more pointed claims of 'barratry' – the pursuit of multiple court cases simultaneously. For example, in the late 1510s it was said that the grocer John Froston had initially submitted a complaint against the skinner James Leverton to Chancery, but that while it still hung there 'undiscussed' he had 'by force of a fayned and untrew surmised bill' compelled Leverton to 'daily . . . appere before the right worshipfull Doctor Vesy dean of yor most honorable Chapell' – the chief judge in Requests – 'to his grete vexacion and losse of tyme'.[63] When raising this wider context, defendants worked on the assumption that the conciliar courts would not take kindly to being abused or played off against one another.

In characterising their adversaries as troublemakers and litigation as disruptive, we have to wonder how far defendants and their counsel were influenced by those contemporary discourses about the legitimate ends of royal justice that we examined in Chapter 1. By the early sixteenth century, social elites and professional lawyers were decrying the influx of poor litigants invited to petition the king. The first sign of sustained controversy around extraordinary justice with defined criticisms and targets in fact pertained to another tribunal named 'Requests'. According to the Great Chronicle of London, mayor John Shaa's own 'court of Requestis' saw 'moch of the poore people drew unto hym, whom he favoured more somtyme than Justice & good lawe Requyrid'. Consequently, 'the men of myght murmured agayn [Shaa] & said, that he that told the first tale had

---

[59] REQ2/3/126.   [60] REQ2/3/124.   [61] REQ2/3/2.   [62] REQ1/5 fol. 25.

[63] REQ3/16/1 *Leverton v Froston*. For a similar case see REQ3/15 *Bermingham v Bermingham* and Catesby's case: TNA E163/29/11.

216   Delivering and Contesting Justice

avauntage' while 'men of lawe also allowed not his doing for they were hynderid by it, ffor he endyd many maters whiche in the lawe wold have cost moch money'.[64] To powerful men, extraordinary and merciful justice gave petitioners too much benefit of the doubt; while for lawyers, it posed a threat to business, offering an inexpensive and efficient avenue for redress to which their trade was forced to adapt. As another common lawyer, Hall too grumbled that when Wolsey had formulated new conciliar courts 'the poore people perceived that he punished the ryche, [and] then they complayned without number, and he [Wolsey] brought many an honest man to trouble and vexacion'.[65] We can certainly detect a contradiction between the common refrain that the king and his delegates were the fount of 'indifferent justice' and the parallel concept that the king ought to show a *special* care to defend the poor – as well as orphans, widows, and other vulnerable people – against their oppressors, who usually were the rich.

Bolstering this general outcry against the perceived *in*justice of royal justice was a host of more technical arguments leviable directly against the jurisdiction of Requests. Since so many of this Court's cases concerned title to land, its defendants might feasibly argue that there was a more appropriate forum for determination. So, where properties were 'custumarie landes and holden by copy of court rolle', an answer could request remittal instead to 'the court of the said manor', playing into the ambiguity about whether Requests ought to supersede the manorial jurisdiction in such matters (in the early 1540s, the Court seemingly decided that it should not).[66] Although most of Requests' cases came by way of thwarted common-law suits, plaintiffs sometimes alleged that they had been unable to pursue their complaints about testamentary bequests or marital disputes in the spiritual courts due to the 'malicious procurations and compassements' of opponents.[67] In such cases defendants could make a similar appeal to this alternative jurisdiction: for example, in a dispute between two priests about the leasing of the parsonage of St Stephen, on Coleman Street in London, the defendant answered that since these were 'spirituell maters concernyng the right of the seide vicarye' the case was 'only determynable by order of the lawe of holy churche'.[68] Such attempts to have cases dismissed or remitted were generally ineffective, however, with Requests typically examining them regardless.[69]

---

[64] Thomas and Thornley eds., *The Great Chronicle of London*, 320.
[65] Hall, *Hall's Chronicle*, 585.
[66] REQ2/3/127; REQ3/21 *Stere* v *Michelborne*. For discussion of the 1543 order on this subject see Chapter 9, section 3: 'The Limits of Royal Justice'.
[67] REQ2/3/131, 201, 2/6/86.   [68] REQ3/20 *Wentworth* v *Forth*.   [69] REQ1/6 fol. 107v.

Answers and Arguments   217

Otherwise, by invoking the 'law of the land' defendants evoked various customs and norms of common-law litigation to which they expected Requests to adhere. Petitions that had not been properly put together were open to particular rebuke. Against the very flexible remit of Requests, under which petitions might present an array of layered accusations and even cases against multiple defendants, an answer submitted in 1531 by the lawyer Edward Warner emphasised that 'the lawe of this londe is that every man for his perticuler cause shall take his perticuler suit as his cause shall require & not to make of hit oon joynt mater'. This, he argued, nullified the 'doubill & tribull matter comprisyd in the said bill of compleynt' submitted against him.[70] Elsewhere, the royal purveyor William Burwell was especially aggrieved when a petition was submitted against him by an anonymous 'pore wedowe', pursuing a debt for certain 'wyldfolle' to the sum of almost £30; his curt answer demanded that 'the said complaynaunt unnamed in the forsaid fayned and sclaunderouse bille may be so punished as may be example of fere to alle other in like case to make sinister complaint'.[71] Here the informality of Requests' petitionary format was deemed unfair to the defendant's cause, contrary to the clear parameters for bringing suits at common law.

A particularly controversial – and criticisable – type of litigant was the undetermined group of inhabitants. A provably successful objection to cases of this origin was that made by Thomas Shuckburgh against his tenants in Nether Shuckburgh, Warwickshire, who had accused him of restricting their rights to common lands and blocking the way of their Rogation week procession. He insisted that their cause was 'insufficient' because 'it is pursued yn the name of the p[ar]ochyn[er]s & inh[ab]itauntes of Nethershokborough and yeveth them no man[er] of names where yn dede they have no suche corporacion', evoking the notion that an unincorporated body could not litigate. The Court's judges seemingly took this seriously, since a second petition in the name of just one of the inhabitants also appears in the surviving casefile.[72] A similar complication undermined a suit apparently brought by the inhabitants of North Muskham in Nottinghamshire. Entries in Requests' order book give the impression of a straightforward dispute between these villagers and their lord, Richard Skrimshaw, centring on his alleged blockage of a common road needed to pass carts, horses, and cattle between the town and the king's highway.[73] Yet a certificate produced by one of the commissioners appointed to investigate the matter on the ground reveals that many of the villagers

---

[70] REQ2/11/105.   [71] REQ3/14 *Unknown v Burwell.*   [72] REQ2/8/339.   [73] REQ1/4 fol. 44.

218   Delivering and Contesting Justice

considered just one man, Ralph Higden, to be the real 'maynteyner &
berer of this matter' according to his 'own froward mynde' – the rest of
them never desiring him to 'bryng maynteyn or sewe anny privey seale or
anny other writtes or processe in o[u]r names'. Indeed, his elderly neighbours believed that, in truth, 'there is no [common] wey' and the lands in
question could be enclosed at the lord's pleasure.[74] Here, at least, a suit was
not entirely as it appeared.

As we saw in Chapter 1, the perceived problems with justice often lay more
in its practice than in its general principles. And so, aside from the case-
specific objections just described, defendants and their counsel often
deployed well-established arguments against the royal judicial processes.
Much was said in answers and in legal commentaries of the time about the
privy-seal writs used to summon accused parties to attend court. Unlike in
the common-law system, where a particular action and writ form (such as
a writ of trespass) clearly identified the matter in question, privy-seal writs
and royal letters missive were notoriously *not* required to specify the issues or
parties involved. One counter-petition submitted in the mid-1520s by John
Tye, Thomas Newman, and John Hovill of Haverhill against the priest
Roger Orgor duly complained that a messenger had 'by virtue of yor moost
honorable lettres of privy seale comaunded us yor said subjettes personaly to
appere before yor highness wheresoever yor highness were within this yor
realm of ynglond' but 'at non instance [would the petitioner] delyver unto
yor said subjettes the privy seale nor no copy therof [nor] shewe unto us the
cause of our apparaunce'.[75] Copies of writs surviving among Requests'
pleadings confirm that recipients were often warned that they would be
answering complaints 'whiche at yor commyng shalbe laid and objected
against you', and that their accusers did sometimes go unnamed.[76] In this
light we might see why royal writs could be so ill-received.

Crucially, this particular line of resistance was supported by recurring
debates in Council, Parliament, and courtroom about the validity of the
privy-seal writ as a means of moving judicial process. The late-medieval
Parliament had increasingly moved to curb the power of this summons,
against which there was neither appeal nor escape. A series of fourteenth-
century statutes sought to prevent the king's seals being used to 'delay
common right', insisting that the accused had to be properly indicted and
that they should be able to answer by 'due process' under the right seal

---

[74] REQ3/15 *Inhabitants of North Muskham v Richard Skrymshaw.*

[75] REQ3/1 *Tye, Newman and Hovyle v Orgor.* See also REQ2/4/268.

[76] See examples in REQ2/5/316, 2/7/65, 2/8/193, 2/9/61, 2/10/216, 2/12/107. This was also the wording
of some petitions: e.g., REQ2/4/356.

Answers and Arguments   219

(usually meaning the great seal) and before common-law justices.[77] The same concerns were present under the early Tudors, and perhaps even picked up pace in the wake of the expansion of the conciliar courts. A bill presented at the 1495 parliament reportedly proposed that 'no privie seal shold goe against no man, but if the suer therof [the plaintiff] wold find suerty to yeld [to] the parties defendants ther damages'. In other words, its supporters sought to charge petitioners to bind themselves to paying certain costs if the defendant should turn out to be acquitted or dismissed of the cause upon which they had been summoned.[78] A similar bill read at the parliament session of early 1510 addressed the practice of calling subjects 'personally to apere without due originall [writ] be fore diverse persons by privey seall and lettres missives for maters and causes determinabull at the commen lawe'. It suggested that parties so summoned be allowed to pursue an action of debt to recover costs and damages for any 'wrongfull vexacion'.[79] Neither bill was, in the end, successfully passed. The earlier one went unanswered by the king, while the later one moved through both houses only to be vetoed by Henry VIII.[80] They did not need to pass to have some effect, however; the 1495 bill had apparently ensured that the 'lords of the counsell behave themselfe'.[81] Still, as Henry VII's notorious minister Edmund Dudley mused from his cell in the Tower of London at the dawn of Henry VIII's reign, 'though [subjects'] pain or ponysshement should be sorer by the dew order of the law, yet will thei murmur and grudge by cawse thei are callyd by the waie of extraordynarie justice'.[82]

Against the monolith of this justice there was one key piece of legislation that defendants and their counsel could apply to bolster their cause: Magna Carta. Early Tudor people knew this as the 'statute made in the ninth year of the reign of Henry III' (meaning the 1225 reissue), and the freedoms it granted to 'both the learned and to the lewd' were still referenced in sermons by Henry VIII's reign.[83] There were a couple of chapters especially

---

[77] 2 Ed. III c. 8, 25 Ed. III stat. 5 c. 4, 28 Ed. III c. 3, 42 Ed. III c. 3, 11 Ric. II c. 10, 4 Hen. VI c. 23, 15 Hen. VI c. 4.

[78] The bill's contents were reported contemporarily to Sir Robert Plumpton by his attorney, Edwin Barlow: Thomas Stapleton ed., *Plumpton Correspondence: A Series of Letters, Chiefly Domestick, written in the reigns of Edward IV. Richard III. Henry VII. and Henry VIII.*, Camden Old Series 4 (Camden Society, 1839), 114.

[79] Parliamentary Archives, HL/PO/PU/1/1509/1H8 n. 22. I am grateful to Dr Paul Cavill for providing me with a transcription of this document.

[80] See the list of unsuccessful bills from the 1495 parliament: TNA C49/42/2, printed in *PROME* xv, 279; *JHL* I, 5, 6, 7.

[81] Stapleton ed., *Plumpton Correspondence*, 114.   [82] Dudley, *The Tree of Commonwealth*, 36.

[83] J. H. Baker, *The Reinvention of Magna Carta 1216–1616* (Cambridge University Press, 2017), 19–20, 98.

220 Delivering and Contesting Justice

relevant to royal justice-giving and its limits. The most frequently cited was Chapter 29, which declared that no 'free man' could be seized or dispossessed of property except by 'lawful judgment' under the 'law of the land'. The implications of this chapter were raised at the *oyer and terminer* commissions established in July 1509 which, as a 'nation-wide inquiry to redress grievances' of the previous few years, were authorised to investigate any transgressions or offences against Magna Carta in addition to their remit over various treasons, felonies, and riots.[84] Some complaints examined here presented grievances about being summoned before members of the late king's royal Council via privy-seal writs, rehearsing the argument that the 'king should not go upon [any free man] or send upon him' except by 'the law of the land'.[85] Another significant passage, which helped determine where that 'law of the land' lay, was Chapter 11: that 'Common pleas shall not follow our court, but shall be held in some fixed place.' This captured the notion that the processes of royal justice were no longer undertaken in the king's train but had moved 'out of court' and into institutions sitting at Westminster. Clearly, this had implications for the itinerant Requests.

By the early Tudor period the meaning of these chapters had become somewhat warped, it should be noted. Not only had Magna Carta become a 'statute' in general parlance, but it was supposedly a statute 'against the pursuit before the king's Council under the privy seal of causes that touch the common law'.[86] Here we observe a blending, conscious or otherwise, of the liberties enshrined in Magna Carta with the clearer specifications laid out in late-medieval legislation pertaining to due process.[87] Hence the charter could be weaponised in favour of the growing contention that while the common law of the land had been designed to defend the accused against 'false accusers', the conciliar courts advanced the petitioner's cause first and foremost. On this basis, Magna Carta could be put into motion against royal justice by two means. The first and rarer usage was in Requests' own courtroom, in defendants' written answers. The same John Rushton who had been served with process 'laid on his arm' in the parish church of Denton used his answer to point out 'that in the grete charter of the liberties of Englond' – Magna Carta – 'it is graunted to the

---

[84] J. P. Cooper, 'Henry VII's Last Years Reconsidered', *The Historical Journal* 2:2 (1959), 113, 117–18.

[85] Baker, *The Reinvention of Magna Carta*, 32; see, for example, TNA KB9/453/4–7 (all of which name Robert Sheffield as the summoning judge), 26d, 29d, 32d, 41d, 49d, 65d, 68.

[86] TNA KB27/1048 m. 75.

[87] Neither the 1215 nor 1225 versions of Magna Carta made reference to specific processes. These ideas were appropriated from the statutes 2 Ed. III c. 8 and 42 Ed. III c. 3 instead.

Answers and Arguments

kynges subgettes that no common plee shall be sued or followed ayenst theym in the kynges courte but in a place certeyne'. Since 'he is the kynges subgette and enherytt to his lawe and in the seid byll of compleynt is lymytt no place certeyne', he was 'not bounden to answere' in Requests.[88] Here Rushton rehearsed Magna Carta's eleventh chapter, perhaps with reference to the absence of any 'certain place' being named in bills – never 'Requests', only the royal Council – for the determination of a civil matter that might otherwise be heard in Common Pleas. Along similar lines, another answerer begged 'not to be trobled ne vexid contrary to theseid [common] lawe nor contrare to dyvers statutes [passed by the] progenitors & predecessors of our seid soveren lord which prohybytt that none maner of persone within this realme be . . . trobled . . . [but by the] comen lawe of this said realme'.[89]

More jurisdictionally concerning, no doubt, was the growing trend of aggrieved parties approaching common-law authorities under the cover of Magna Carta to scrutinise conciliar procedure. In the first couple of decades of the sixteenth century, a number of defendants who felt themselves wronged by the conciliar courts lodged countersuits in King's Bench. Now plaintiffs themselves, they turned the tables by characterising conciliar process as a trespass against the terms of Magna Carta – similar to the pleas submitted at the 1509 *oyer and terminer* commissions. Specifically, their complaints rehearsed the exact wording from the 1225 version of Chapter 29 regarding the general freedoms of a 'free man' against a peremptory royal summons, and construed suits to the Council as malicious schemes to 'vex, weary, and destroy' opponents through 'intolerable labours and expenses'.[90] Importantly, they very often named Requests' judges – Geoffrey Symeon, William Atwater, John Veysey, and John Stokesley in particular – as the councillors before whom they had been made to appear.[91] It was the procedure rather than the judges themselves that came under fire, however, with pleas reminding the justices that 'every free man ought to implead and be impleaded in common pleas by original writs under the lord king's great seal before the lord king's justices of his Common Bench and not elsewhere'. None of this applied to Requests – which, as they pointed out, involved the hearing of civil matters

---

[88] REQ3/4 *Ratcliff and Cotterell* v *Rushton*.   [89] REQ3/12 *Magar* v *Trewynnard*.

[90] See especially TNA KB27/961 m. 74, translated and transcribed in Baker, *Reinvention of Magna Carta*, 456–8; and KB27/1022 m. 60.

[91] Three cases were brought against proceedings under Geoffrey Symeon as dean: KB27/972 m. 92, 978 m. 28v, 981 m. 104v., 997 m. 75; two against William Atwater as dean: KB27/992, m. 37, TNA CP40/991 m. 529; one against John Veysey: KB27/1022 m. 60.

222 Delivering and Contesting Justice

under the power of the privy seal and before royal councillors, often *not* lawyers, at any available location.[92] Moreover, it was generally implied that Requests did not have a jurisdiction in these specific cases; one plea naming Stokesley as the summoning judge seemed to object to the Council investigating the detinue of household goods as debt for a rent, for example.[93]

We should not overstate the practical implications of these contestations. Those defendants whose answers appealed to Magna Carta and the late-medieval due process statutes still found themselves subject to hearings by Requests. Meanwhile, those few wounded defendants who countersued in King's Bench – there are, it should be said, only sixteen known cases in the early Tudor period – saw little success. Although the justices might summon the disputants and hear their arguments, they do not seem to have ever awarded the restitution called for.[94] Both King's Bench and Common Pleas were, at least for now, as hesitant as the king to do anything to harm this new jurisdiction. Still, these criticisms of conciliar justice and its mechanisms were apparently current enough by the early sixteenth century that legal counsel knew when and how to apply them, even if simply for the purpose of gaining a common-law hearing that could stretch and vex their client's adversaries. Such social, procedural, and legal arguments set the stage for more jurisdictional battles in the later sixteenth century.

Conclusion

The construction of justice was as contested as it was collaborative. Defendants may well have shared a general belief in the principles that undergirded the expansion of royal justice. Indeed, an answer submitted in the early years of Henry VIII's reign provides us with our strongest positive statement from the 'mouth' of any litigant, in its pronouncement that 'in this noble courte It is most convenient that all fauls poulers be presentyd & punysshed . . . for the comyn welthe of the people / And also for the kynges avauntage'.[95] Yet they did have reasonable complaints about the inconvenience, costliness, and unfairness of the royal justice courts. This was grounded in legal theory as well as in reality. It is worth reflecting on the

---

[92] KB27/961 m. 75. For other examples, see KB27/963 m. 22v, 972 m. 92, 978 m. 26v, 981 m. 104v, 991 m. 529, 992 m. 37, 997 m. 75, 1000 m. 37, 1013 m. 40v, 1017 m. 58, 1048 m. 75.
[93] KB27/1048 m. 75, REQ3/6 *Butler* v *Fuller*.
[94] For a full list and summary of each case, see Baker, *The Reinvention of Magna Carta*, 458–62.
[95] REQ2/1/49.

Answers and Arguments 223

place of such actions and arguments in the broader development of royal justice. As this book has so far contended, petitioners to Requests were the driving force of its continuing existence, in the absence of any official order founding or defining this tribunal. They supplied the main narrative of cases, conveyed and kept documents, and had the first word in court. In this Court, as we will see, many decisions appear to have been made in the petitioner's favour just because the defendant had not sufficiently proven their own cause quickly enough. Yet it is possible, indeed likely, that defendants and their objections contributed to a sense of the reasonable limits of justice-giving in this more extraordinary forum. Against the backdrop of recurring, high-profile debates on this topic in Parliament and Council, they may also have informed the eventual destruction of royal conciliar justice.

CHAPTER 9

'A Final Peax': Passing Judgment

Turning to Requests' rich registers of decrees allows us, finally, to better situate this tribunal and the rest of the conciliar justice system within a longer arc of administrative and legal development. In returning to a structural, procedural perspective we need not lose sight of the social dimension to justice and its end results, however. Verdicts, rulings, and judgments made within the legal system were 'meant to *do* something' for both institutions and litigants, whether to record a particular version of events for immediate leverage or for long-term posterity.[1] Yet in almost all early modern jurisdictions, surviving final decrees are vastly outnumbered by pleas and petitions. Indeed, while over 5,000 casefiles survive for the Henrician Requests, there are just 551 recorded decrees. Negative connotations once dominated interpretations of this archival lacuna: courts were slow and costs were high, precluding the pursuit of a full case, it was assumed. But litigation was not necessarily about acquiring a firm judgment. Just as often, it was about invoking a higher authority in the name of peace, about outmanoeuvring and over-awing opponents; and so, a writ of summons, a commission, or an informal arbitration could be enough to achieve a litigant's goals. In all, justice in Requests was as fluid as the tribunal itself.

This chapter examines what Requests *did*, in the end. It begins once again with the circle of judges at work in the Court and the terms upon which they made their decisions, with the input of litigants, counsel, and commissioners. Their decrees are formulaic in such a way that the precise course of discussion and debate remain obscure, but they are nevertheless revealing about the evidence under consideration and the facts deemed most relevant in court. The chapter then explores the impact of decrees: their recording, use in the locality of the case, and enforcement on the ground – as well as episodes in which they were openly reviled and

[1] McSheffrey, 'Detective Fiction in the Archives', 65–6.

224

'A Final Peax': Passing Judgment 225

disobeyed by losing parties. The dispensation of justice was the product of the rhetoric and narratives produced within petitions, the counterarguments and criticisms raised in answers, *and* the learning and discretion of the Court's judges in light of both evidence and circumstance. Yet peacekeeping did not end with Requests, and the contestation of justice continued even after its judges may have felt that a case was closed.

Sitting in Judgment

Decrees were agreed, confirmed, and read out at meetings between litigants, lawyers, and the Court's staff. Some losing parties quibbled that such decisions had been made without their knowledge or presence, but they only prove this rule; according to one gentleman defendant, he had 'loked over the clerkes shulder when the warde was red'.[2] Learned legal counsel helped interpret evidence and determine rights in each case. Some surviving draft decrees include marginal notes detailing their specifications and arguments about certain terms of the text.[3] After all the rhetoric and posturing, it was the king's representatives who held all the power in the courtroom, however. The plaintiff John Ryce described various hearings before 'my lord of Westmester [and] my lorde of Wusceter [Worcester]' (Thomas Thirlby and Nicholas Heath) in which his opponent, his brother, had been openly castigated by the judges. When this defendant claimed that he owed no money from their father's will, Thirlby reportedly argued back that this was 'not so ... ye have the landes yor ffather gave ffor the performans thereoff and have bene before Mr Dakers [Dacres] & Mr Bowys & now beffor me and when ye sawe that Mr Dakers was departed then ye t[h]owght to deceve the pore man for yt hase bene so long in sewyt that the pore man hath spentt all moste so mych for the swytt of it'.[4] Ryce's recollection reveals how important a good rapport with the king's councillors could be.

Lists of names recorded alongside Requests' decrees for much of the early Tudor period illuminate a larger circle of men at work in the task of hearing litigants and passing judgment.[5] We met the presiding figures in the Court in Chapter 7: the clerical presidents of the Council at the close of the fifteenth century, the successive deans of the Chapel Royal in the following two decades, and then a sequence of lawyers and

---

[2] E.g., REQ3/8 *Plommer v Oliver*, REQ3/21 *Coke v Child*; REQ3/9 *Mynton v Salford*.
[3] REQ3/21 *Alston v Alston*.   [4] REQ3/3 *Ryce v Ryce*.
[5] See the Appendix for a full list of the men recorded as attendant judges in the REQ1 order books and mentioned in anecdotal accounts as presiding over Requests' hearings.

226 Delivering and Contesting Justice

Masters of Requests up to the end of Henry VIII's reign. They were usually accompanied when hearing cases by a number of other men who did not handle bills but who no doubt provided supplementary insight and expertise during hearings. So, while we find only fourteen signatories to bills across Henry VII's reign, sixty-five men were recorded as sitting judges in the same period. This 'bench' was at its most capacious in the 1490s, when in terms of numbers, routine, and diversity it was essentially microcosmic of Henry VII's 200-strong main Council.[6] At that time, dozens of bishops, courtiers, and peers on hand within the attendant household could find themselves sitting to hear suits and pass judgment. Their coming and going from the attendant household meant that Requests' sitting 'bench' was transient, sometimes totalling as many as eleven judges at one time or as few as one or two, even within the same month. Because the practice of listing sitting judges in Requests' books declined, the make-up and behaviour of its judicial side become less clear from the 1510s onwards.[7] Still, as we saw in Chapter 7, by the end of our period it had clearly changed in two ways. Firstly, the signatories now made up the larger of the two circles of Court personnel, with a quorum of two or three of them sitting in judgment when required. Secondly, by this time the overall composition of Requests' judiciary was more professional and permanent. There was an increasing prevalence of men with legal training, and they rotated in their roles as judges, masters, and clerks.

Significant to our assessment of how Requests passed judgment throughout this period is the extent and nature of the expertise supplied by its additional judges, especially in law. Unlike the main Council in the Star Chamber, Requests was not normally staffed by the chief justices, justices, and barons of the central common-law courts.[8] The only known exception was William Hussey, the chief justice of King's Bench, who apparently heard cases for the Council alongside the king's solicitor (Andrew Dymmock) and attorney (James Hobart) in the 1490s, according to Pilkington's narrative.[9] Still, the later retaining of common-law experts in the form of the Masters of Requests may have been an advancement on

---

[6] Chrimes, *Henry VII*, 102.
[7] Lists of attending judges are frequent in REQ1/1 but peter out in the books that follow; the last full list dates to December 1505: REQ1/3 fol. 218.
[8] As appears throughout the surviving transcripts of the Council registers: BL Lansdowne MS 160; HL Ellesmere MSS 2654, 2655.
[9] The Narrative of Robert Pilkington, 33. Hussey and Dymmock were also named in the '*iter*' list of 1494: REQ1/1 fol. 1.

'A Final Peax': Passing Judgment

the more ad-hoc involvement of common lawyers like William Greville, Morgan Kidwelly, and particularly Richard Sutton (who appeared as many as thirty-two times between 1498 and 1514) as judges in Henry VII's committee.[10] Additionally, throughout the whole early Tudor period and on a case-by-case basis Requests might call on more senior legal colleagues within the central administration. A few memoranda and incidental recollections of the Court's hearings mention that in combination with their 'owne connyng reason & lernyng' its leading judges had asked 'advice of the kinges justices' or of 'dyvers persons substancially standyd in lawe' in interpreting evidences and titles.[11] Alongside the legal counsel employed by litigants, and the masters present from the 1530s onwards, Requests' leading judges and signatories always had a wealth of common-law knowledge to draw upon in decision-making.

An assortment of household officers, courtiers, and ministers provided occasional input on determinations in the earlier part of this period, too. Some lesser clergy who were also doctors in canon and civil law sat regularly as judges in Henry VII's reign: most prominently Robert Middleton (thirty-nine sittings in Requests, 1493–8), a pluralist who also acted as a diplomat to Scotland and the Holy Roman Empire, and Richard Hatton (twenty-two appearances, 1495–c. 1508), a royal chaplain and councillor who ventured to Scotland, Ireland, and Flanders to represent his king.[12] A series of knights with official positions at court appeared more sporadically over the first few decades. Chief among them were the household treasurer Sir Thomas Lovell, the comptroller Sir Richard Guildford, the vice-chamberlain Sir Charles Somerset, Robert Sherborne as the king's secretary, and the omnipresent Sir Reginald Bray, also chancellor of the Duchy of Lancaster and head of the Council Learned. The peers of the realm who had helped Henry VII to the throne and had settled into management roles within the household were similarly involved in justice-giving; we find Robert, Lord Willoughby

---

[10] Sutton of the Inner Temple appears in lists of judges across the early sixteenth century: REQ1/3 fols. 161, 185, 215, 218, 245, 276; REQ2/6/180, 2/8/114; TNA KB27/978 m. 26d, 981 m. 104d. Greville appeared six times, 1495–9, and Kidwelly on at least nine occasions between 1502 and his death in 1505, according to lists in REQ1/1 and REQ1/2. As the Appendix shows, other common lawyers active on a more limited basis include Robert Rede (four appearances, 1493–4, including on the 'iter' list), John Kingsmill (three times, in the 'iter' list and then in 1498), and Robert Bowring (one appearance, 1498).

[11] REQ1/5 fol. 28; REQ2/3/165, 313.

[12] Emden, *A biographical register of the University of Oxford*, vol. II, 1277–78; A. B. Emden, *A biographical register of the University of Cambridge to 1500* (Cambridge University Press, 1963), 293; *CPR 1494–1509*, 13, 27, 85; TNA E101/414/6 fol. 12, E101/414/16 fol. 77, E101/415/3 fols. 23v, 43.

228 Delivering and Contesting Justice

de Broke, active here in his capacity as steward of the household, and there is evidence too that Giles, Lord Daubeney, was hearing civil causes and making interlocutory orders in cases that otherwise passed through Requests.[13] Most of these men (Lovell excepted) had no legal training to speak of, but they were trusted royal servants, present on a regular basis within the king's orbit and known to have a direct route to speak with him.[14]

Although, as we have seen, the bench ultimately contracted to only a few individuals by the 1540s, proximity to the king continued to be a quality shared by those sitting in judgment in Requests. Indicative of this ongoing preference is the involvement – actual and projected – of several priors of the order of Saint John of Jerusalem in England (the Knights Hospitaller) among the known judges at one time or another. John Kendal's name and title appeared on the '*iter*' list of 1494 and in the margins of several entries later in the same decade; and William Weston, the last prior before the dissolution of the house at Clerkenwell, named in the list of commissioners in Requests in January 1529, was reported to have determined civil cases and signed at least one bill.[15] These men were not ecclesiastics but martial knights, who acted in their old age as lay barons with growing roles as parliamentarians, ambassadors, and commissioners for the Crown.[16] Although their level of engagement with Requests' business hardly matched that of the successive deans and masters, it is certainly telling that at the various junctures at which that Court was reimagined and reinstituted the prior was deemed central to the task. The same could be said for the continual presence of the Dean of the Chapel Royal through to the end of Henry VIII's reign. Overall, this brief survey demonstrates that Requests' decrees were the product of a range of viewpoints and sources of expertise: of arguments conveyed in writing and verbally by lay people, of technical points and objections raised by common lawyers, and of the mixture of legal experience, social cachet, and moral authority represented by the judges.

---

[13] E.g., REQ2/2/156, in which a party asks for hearing before 'My Lord Chamberlain' and others.
[14] For a summary of the household careers of many of these men see S. J. Gunn, *Henry VII's New Men and the Making of Tudor England* (Oxford University Press, 2016).
[15] REQ1/1 fols. 1, 23v, 62v; REQ1/2 fol. 96; REQ 1/5 fol. 43v; REQ2/3/392, 2/8/273. Additionally, the intervening prior, Thomas Docwra (1502–27) was named to the *c.* 1519 committee in the White Hall and is said to have made judgments alongside Sir Thomas Neville, perhaps in the same capacity, around that time: SP1/19 fol. 142; REQ2/11/43. Some of this activity is recorded in BL Lansdowne 160 fols. 310v–311. He was also a sitting member of Star Chamber in 1525: TNA STAC10/4/123.
[16] For a full study with particular attention to Kendal, Docwra, and Weston see S. Phillips, *The Prior of the Knights Hospitaller in Late Medieval England* (Boydell, 2009), 106–9, 120–32.

'A Final Peax': Passing Judgment

Making Decrees

Initially, Requests' recorded decrees were contained to a few brief lines of Latin, including information about the litigants (their names, and sometimes their occupations and hometowns), the matter in variance, and specific orders for them to adhere to going forward: usually an agreed time and place to exchange money, in debt cases, or the terms for transfer of possession in property disputes. In the first few years of the sixteenth century the clerks transitioned to writing their decrees in English, retaining Latin for recording appearances, admissions of attorneys, and continuations. Gradually across the 1530s and 1540s, decrees became longer and more complex, containing greater detail as to the nature of the case, the evidence in question, and the conditions of the Court's award. The decree recorded in a suit between John Mascall and William Blake in 1517 is an illustrative example, of average length and contents for this period as a whole:

Xiiij° die Julij a$^{[nn]o}$ ix°

Wher variaunce ^hath^ byn moeved and had afor the king[es] honorable Counsaill betwene John Mascall of Denham in the Countie of Bukk[e]s sone and heyr to John Mascall & M[ar]garet his wyf dought[er] and heyr of Roger Derby late of Agmonsham complayn[au]nt[es] ayenst Will[a]m Blake of the same defend[ant] / of for and upon the ryght title int[er]est use and possession of a close called Bone crofte conteignyng ij acres & di an half lying and beyng in the p[ar]isshe of Agmonsham aforsaid nowe in the possession of the said William Blake whiche claymeth the same aswell by reason of a divice to hym made by the will of Roger Derby decessed fader to the said Margaret as also by vertue of a feoffament by the said Roger supposed to be made to on[e] John Salcoke and hys heyres in fee to thuse and behof of the said Roger Derby whos estate in the said crofte the same William Blake nowe supposeth to have as in hys aunswer ys alleged Whiche wyll ne feoffament ^he^ hath not yet shewed ne non other mat[er] wherby he shuld be to the said crofte entitled other in lawe or consciens Inconsideracon wherof & forasmoche as the said complaynaunt hath p[ro]ved hym to be cousyn and next heyr to the said Roger Derby by reason wherof he ought to be p[re]ferred to the said crofte aft[er] the course of the comen lawe and not the defend[ant] seyng that he nothyng effectuall hath shewed to the contrary in prouffe or fortyfying of hys p[re]tence made unto the same It ys therefor[e] ordred & by the said Counsaill decreed that the said William Blake shald dep[ar]te out and frome the possession of the said crofte befor[e] the feaste of Saint Michell tharchaungell next co[m]ming aft[er] the date above writon and fromethensforthe peasibly and quietly suffer the said John Marshall [sic] hys heyres and a[ssi]gnes to have and enyoie the same crofte without lete ^or^ impediment of the said William

230   Delivering and Contesting Justice

> Blake or any other p[er]son or p[er]sons by hys p[ro]curyng to the contrarie
> unto such tyme he shewe afor[e] the said Counsaill mat[er] effectuall &
> sufficient in the lawe & consciens for prouff of hys p[re]tence made to the
> said crofte and that upon payne of xl li to be levyed of the land[es] good[es]
> & cattall[es] of the said William Blake to thuse of o[ur] sov[er]ain lorde the
> king if he any thyng attempt or cause to be attempted contrary to the
> teno[ur] of thys decree made by the said Counsaill and subscribed with
> theyr hand[es] the day and yer[e] afor[e] specified /[17]

There are certain observable consistencies in the phrasing of decrees across
our period. One of the most telling is the lack of reference to this tribunal by
name, mirroring the vagueness of petitions. Decrees were almost always said
to have been made by the 'king's honourable council', with the judges and
clerks terming themselves the 'kinges honorable Counsaill in his courte of
requestes' for the first time in 1531 and only sporadically thereafter.[18]
Following this opening statement, the principal disputants and the basic
details of their suit were set out. This information was consistently simplified
here compared to the narrative presented in petitions and pleadings, omitting many of the actions described by the parties in favour of establishing the
right to the true subject of the case (lands, monies, properties). The case
above was relatively straightforward: Mascall had alleged in his petition that
Blake 'by his stronge and might[y] power hath dispossessed and disheritt yor
poor suppliant' since the death of his grandfather, Roger Derby, some time
ago, and so the resulting decree rehearsed the competing claims of Blake's
supposed 'divice' of 'Bone Croft' in Agmonsham (Amersham) through
Derby's will versus Mascall's inheritance as Derby's grandson.[19] Elsewhere
the judges had many more allegations to untangle. For example, whereas the
petition of husbandman William Saunders accused successive abbots of
Buckfast in Devon of withholding a messuage, of contravening previous
bargains made between them, and of driving away his cattle, a subsequent
decree recorded in May 1531 concentrated on the title to the messuage.[20] In
that instance, as in Mascall's case, the decree ended with a clear award of the
property in question to one party, warning them not to 'any thyng attempt
or cause to be attempted contrary to the tenor of thys decree'.

The clearest impression of the Court's decision-making process can be
gleaned from specifications made in decrees about the evidence examined

---

[17] REQ1/4 fols. 76–76v. Similar examples are printed in Bayne and Dunham eds., *Select Cases in the Council of Henry VII*, 117–18; Leadam ed., *Select Cases before the King's Council in the Star Chamber, commonly called the Court of Star Chamber, A.D. 1477–1509*, 188 n. 2.

[18] REQ1/5 fol. 127v, 129, 138v, 140, 141, 142, 163, 193v; REQ1/6 fol. 202.

[19] REQ2/4/80, 145.   [20] REQ2/10/167; REQ1/5 fol. 129.

'A Final Peax': Passing Judgment

in individual cases. Although original proofs were not retained by the Court and so do not survive in the casefiles, we do know that the conscience courts of this period, Requests included, diverged from the common-law system of proofs in two ways. In the first place, they did not require that a specific type of evidence be disclosed in the initial plea and brought in to prove a single, predetermined issue. Furthermore, they abandoned any hierarchy of evidence in which, for example, a written contract would take precedence over spoken testimonies. Accordingly, Requests' decrees refer to a mixture of witness depositions, legal and non-legal documents, and circumstantial reports cited as the grounds for the judges' final decisions, even in a single case, with no overt sense that they automatically preferred one over another. And there is good reason to believe that the conciliar courts took upon themselves an even broader remit for their fact-finding missions than other contemporary tribunals. While many Chancery decrees described considerations made 'by evidence and witnesses', equivalent orders in Requests and Star Chamber were usually said to accord with the 'circumstances of the case'.[21]

Of course, in many suits the primary 'circumstances' confronting the judges were disagreements over lands and the flurry of official, competing paperwork they produced. Requests' judges broadly sought to uphold standard norms of interpretation when examining them. For example, the cases between Patrick and James Bellow was adjudged in 1505 'apon the sight of an endentur writen with the hand of the said Patrike a dede of feoffament made of the same to the forsaid Jamys a letter of attorney for the delyveraunce of possession and season a quietaunce made by the same Patrike to the same James for C marks by the same Patrike received apon the same endentur' as well as 'diverse letters and other writings'.[22] Again, Pilkington's narrative provides unique insight into how closely Requests' judges studied such technical evidence. At a hearing of Requests in August 1493, Pilkington and his opponent, John Ainsworth, personally presented their proofs for estates in Mellor. William Hussey, the chief justice, considered Ainsworth's documents very carefully: he 'lokyd on [them] but a lytyll whyle' but then 'cast thaym away from hym and said thay were enturlynyd, and alowyd thaym not'. In other words, it was suspected that extra words had been added between the lines of Ainsworth's deeds to change their meaning and effect.[23] This rare report

---

[21] Metzger, 'The Last Phase of the Medieval Chancery', 84. See the examples printed in W. Brown and H. B. McCall eds., *Yorkshire Star Chamber Proceedings*, The Yorkshire Archaeological Society XLI, XLV, LI (J. Whitehead and Son, 1908–14), vol. II, 121.
[22] REQ1/3 fol. 191.   [23] The Narrative of Robert Pilkington, 33.

232   Delivering and Contesting Justice

demonstrates the attention paid to documentary conventions, and at least one reason for their voiding in the eyes of royal judges. Generally speaking, the quality of legal proofs is mentioned more frequently in Requests as the early Tudor period went on, according with the increasing presence of common-law expertise there.

That said, examinations were never limited to formal, *legal* deeds and instruments. The decree awarding Mascall the lands to which he laid claim appears to take the right of his inheritance from his grandfather at face value. Elsewhere, in a handful of other cases scattered across the catalogued and uncatalogued Requests pleadings archive, family trees are scrawled onto spare paper, tracking lines of descent and their associated claims to freehold property. Petitioners might also present more personal evidence in court. Pilkington reported how the powerful Savages had '[sent] owte mone dyvers letters to dyvers gentylmen in lancaschyr cheschyr and derbyschyr and also into Mellur chapel and other placys, redde and shewyd on festevall dayes in the pulpyt[,] desyryng and charging all maner of men that wolde doo for thayme to rise agaynys the said Robert', and he showed some of these letters to the judges.[24] A case brought by the Pilbarowe family of London against the Cornish priest Reginald Tregean, concerning the right to the money and possessions of their son, Edward, after his sudden death from plague while trading tin in Cornwall, yielded a set of similarly unusual proofs. Among the surviving paperwork are original letters written by Edward to his parents several years earlier, while he was at school in Rouen. They contain nothing immediately relevant to the case: the adolescent mostly complained of the cost of living and the lack of 'Inglysh mens compeny'. But one witness was asked to confirm the authenticity of Edward's handwriting in these letters, while another swore that the dying man had arranged money for 'hys buryall and charitable dedes' in a hastily prepared last will; the judges presumably sought to compare these two documents and their signatures. When a decree was finally made, awarding £10 to the Pilbarowes, none of this evidence was mentioned, though.[25] This case reminds us how much work went into the short decrees eventually committed to paper, even beyond what was eventually written up. It also shows how the Court might inspect more unique evidence, of a kind not permissible in a common-law tribunal, for creative purposes.

Another benefit of extraordinary, conciliar justice was its capacity to balance documented points of fact with other, more circumstantial details.

[24] *Ibid.*, 32.   [25] REQ2/3/181.

'A Final Peax': Passing Judgment 233

External commissions were particularly crucial for gathering information on the Court's behalf. Most of the interrogatories supplied to commissioners were designed to establish details supplementary to the case at hand, with a community's eldest members commonly asked about their memory of the customs that supported the plaintiff's argument, or witnesses to offences described in the petition asked to confirm or deny the story. Often the purpose was to aid in the Court's interpretation of documents brought in as evidence. For example, in 1531 the complainant Christopher Middleton appealed to Requests to claim £100 worth of household goods from a last will and testament, but witnesses to its proving soon confirmed that 'there is nothing to [Middleton] geven but oonly a cowe'.[26] Verbal testimonies alone could reconstruct the making and terms of unwritten agreements. It was, for instance, the deposition of a sixty-year-old husbandman that helped secure the case of John and Margaret Long, when he recalled 'takyng the ryng off the gate' of certain lands and having 'delyvered astate off all the seyd landes by the delivery of the seyd ryng unto the hands' of a scrivener representing the Longs' relative.[27] Yet just as often the business of question-asking raised matters that were not obviously connected to details in the petition. Rather, it served to draw out further mitigating information for the Court to consider. One case saw the citizens of a London parish asked their view as to how far the defendants could expect 'justice with favor' in the city, while a case from Edward VI's reign included interrogatories inquiring whether the defendant, the unruly vicar of Tathwell in Lincolnshire, was 'a Scotte borne'.[28] These matters were presumably irrelevant to the legality of the cases at hand, but were pertinent to the Court's interest in accessible justice and personal morality.

Whatever their contents, Requests' judges were so reliant on the certificates and testimonies returned by commissioners that some decrees simply rehearsed their contents almost verbatim, or else cited them as the sole basis for their decision. Even the failure of a commission could end up underpinning Requests' rulings. This could happen for a variety of reasons: the sickness of the witnesses and the commissioners, the defendants' failure to attend, or the plaintiff's refusal to serve the necessary writs in the first place.[29] Some commissioners, 'for lake of lawes' and legal training, were eventually forced to admit that their 'lernyng is not sufficient to determyn or fynyshe' the dispute, and so to return the case back to the central administration so

[26] REQ1/5 fol. 137v.   [27] REQ3/22/2 *Long* v *Cockes.*
[28] REQ3/4 *Mone* v *Kyrton*; REQ3/11/1 *Dion* v *Story.*
[29] E.g., REQ3/3 *Faller* v *Inhabitants of Langcote*; REQ3/22/2 *Sergeant and Hole* v *Garrett*; REQ3/24 *Woodward* v *Ferrers.*

234 Delivering and Contesting Justice

that 'men learned therupon may have opon knowlegh and playne instruccion to diffyne ... the same mater according to the law'.[30] Moreover, especially exasperated examiners might use their certificates to report not on the technicalities of the dispute or their own shortcoming but on the parties' respective conduct – in fact, writs sometimes specifically asked examiners to relate the 'demeanure' of the litigants.[31] One unfortunate commissioner, the Prior of Lenton in Nottinghamshire, lamented at the end of his certificate that 'I wolde the mater hade never comyn to my hondes for I have made moch trobull withal at dyverse tymes and no thanke of any parties.' His woes stemmed not only from the failure of the 'lernet men' named to the commission to appear alongside him, but from the conduct of the petitioner, who 'wille always have hys awne wile & jugement' and would not 'be in pease with his neburs'.[32]

Commissioners' impressions of litigants could negatively affect their chances of gaining a ruling in their favour from Requests. When two complainants were reported in 1517 to be 'not mynded to take eny other end or direccion' from the arbiters appointed by Requests to hear their case, preferring to have 'ther title by [the Council] discussed', Veysey and his associate judges immediately remitted them to the common law and dismissed the 'obbedyant' defendant.[33] An even more telling example is the suit brought by Richard and Mary Flint against Robert Hackett, concerning the right to a messuage in Turlington, Leicestershire. The plaintiffs claimed the property by inheritance from John Hackett, Mary's father, while the defendant argued for his part that the same John had bargained and sold the messuage to *his* grandfather some time ago. A commission held in March 1542 heard testimonies confirming that John Hackett had been within age at the time of this sale, so it was lawful, but the returned certificate also reported that the defendant had failed to turn up to five separate days given to him to present his evidence.[34] When the matter was determined in Requests a couple of months later, the judges accepted that Hackett possessed 'wytnes[es] and evidences whereby he clierly myght have had fynalle ende & direccion' – that is, that he should be allowed to keep the lands – but that he had so 'obstynatly disobeyde' the commissioners and vexed the plaintiff by delaying proceedings that he was ordered to pay the plaintiffs forty shillings 'in full satisfaccion for the costes afore assessed and specified'.[35] In this instance, the judges, led at this time by the lawyer

[30] REQ3/3 *Carpenter* v *City of Coventry*; REQ2/2/154.   [31] REQ3/5 *Slack* v *Colisen*.
[32] REQ3/19 *Garnett* v *Alester*.   [33] REQ1/4 fol 56.   [34] REQ3/13 *Flint* v *Hackett*.
[35] REQ1/7 fol 114.

'A Final Peax': Passing Judgment

Robert Dacres, considered the defendant's contempt of their orders to almost outweigh his own evident title to the lands in dispute, creating an unusual situation in which the de facto winner was made to pay damages.

In other cases, commissioners had a more positive effect on a litigant's standing before the Court. As we have glimpsed already, their pleas on behalf of the poor might have encouraged Requests' judges to make procedures more accessible. For example, the two gentlemen deployed in 1519 to investigate the suit of Anthony Complay, a surgeon from Ipswich whose adulterous wife had sold all his possessions while he was on a voyage to Iceland, spoke in favour of Complay's case and noted at the bottom of their certificate that 'the costys of the sewte of the said Antony amountyth to the summe of ... C markes'.[36] Accordingly, Veysey and his fellow Requests judges looked on Complay more mercifully. In the end, and contrary to findings that Complay's wife had no right to sell all of his property, Requests ruled that a local prior who now had possession of Complay's house *did* have the right to it after all, owing to a previous lease made by his predecessor. And yet, perhaps based on pleas made by the commissioners and Complay, they decreed that 'in consideracion only of the povertie and not for noo right nor title on his behalve proved' the prior would pay Complay the sum of four pounds.[37] In these efforts, the on-the-ground perspective of the commissioners was highly valuable. Moreover, for Complay as for Hackett, and under the canonist Veysey just as under the common lawyer Dacres, Requests could put law to one side in the pursuit of justice. As per the Court's general interest in preserving a jurisdiction for the poor, it appears to have been especially susceptible to pleas for charity. This was not the only time that Requests' judges awarded charges to be paid to disputants based only on their 'innocency and poverty'.[38]

These moments of clemency raise the question of how the cognate ideas of conscience (or equity), mercy, and charity were deployed in the dispensation of royal justice, especially in matters supposedly determinable at common law. Contrary to the vagueness with which these associated ideas were evoked in wider culture and in petitionary contexts, its manifestation in procedure was a little more purposeful. In particular, the internal forum of the litigants' own consciences – that of the loyal, truthful petitioner as much as of the 'ill-disposed' defendant – were put on trial by pleadings under oath.[39] Echoing Norman Doe's argument that the 'juridical conscience'

---

[36] REQ2/8/84. [37] REQ1/4 fols. 195v–196. [38] See also REQ1/7 fols. 92, 148.
[39] The significance of this process was explored in Macnair, 'Equity and Conscience'.

236 Delivering and Contesting Justice

resided in a court's 'assessment of damages' and intent to mitigate litigation costs, we might incorporate Requests' canon-law-inspired *in forma pauperis* admissions and awarding of expenses into this procedural framework, too.[40] More generally, though, the judges' conscience was on show in their attempts to mediate fairly, and even to extend charity where required, in their final rulings. Similar to the examples given above, one of the only surviving decrees from the early Council of the North includes the judges' view that a rent 'ought to be apporcyoned in conscyence' between several parties. The same case saw that Council eventually willing to allow the defendant, a very poor man, the chance to surrender his lease to a farm in Yorkshire, with all rent arrears waived and his costs covered by the forgiving petitioner.[41] In other words, sensitivity to social disparity informed judgments eventually passed in the conciliar courts, just as it shaped their procedures beforehand.

An interest in creating fair and largely beneficial rulings meant that many of Requests' cases ended not with a straightforward award of assets in either direction but something more bespoke. Examination of the Court's order books confirms the supposition of some late medievalists that the early modern equity courts essentially represented more formalised versions of the arbitration that had long been available from local powerholders.[42] Certainly Requests borrowed from the existing procedural framework surrounding this form of peacekeeping. Both parties might be voluntarily bound under obligation to observe the award of judges in advance of its making (the *compromissio*, in the canon-law format), and then the arbitration itself would be negotiated and recorded.[43] Late-medieval arbitrations could produce an award of possession in a manner similar to a court verdict, but they more often sought to placate all involved by dividing the assets in question into equal parcels.[44] There are many examples of this even-handedness in Requests, too, particularly where the parties were equally matched in social terms: in decrees which ultimately split lands between the disputants, which confirmed that possession would pass from one party to another at the former's death, or which granted

---

[40] Norman Doe, *Fundamental Authority in Late Medieval English Law* (Cambridge University Press, 1990), 146–7.

[41] REQ3/9 *Fox* v *Vincent*.

[42] Rawcliffe, 'The Great Lord as Peacekeeper', 52–3; Post, 'Equitable Resorts before 1450'.

[43] Edward Powell, 'Arbitration and the Law in England in the Late Middle Ages', *TRHS* 33 (1983), 55. For examples in Requests see REQ1/104 fols. 88v, 132v, 145v, 147; REQ1/5 fols. 134v, 136v. One of these obligations survives in REQ3/17 *Throgmorton* v *Lane*.

[44] See, for an example of the former, the arbitration printed in Rawcliffe, 'The Great Lord as Peacekeeper', 54.

'A Final Peax': Passing Judgment 237

access to growing crops or grazing animals for a limited term.[45] A firmer ruling and a more creative arbitration could go hand in hand. In one instance in the late 1510s, Veysey and his colleagues presided over an arrangement in which a defendant was initially ordered to depart from contested lands to make way for the petitioner, but was allowed to 'retourne and be tenaunte to the complaynaunte' after another hearing six months down the line.[46] Later decrees clearly pronounced the judges' hopes for 'quietnes hereafter to be had amonge the said parties', encouraging even the disputants in whose favour they ordered to put the matter to rest and remit any further grudges or charges.[47]

These agreements did not always end up as formal decrees recorded in the order books, either. In 1495, six of Henry VII's councillors, including Lord Daubeney (the chamberlain), John Dynham (Treasurer of England), the chief justices of both benches and the attorney general were called upon to arbitrate in the dispute of Thomas, Lord Ormond, against Sir Henry Willoughby, Sir Thomas Ferrers, and John Aston for a large estate of lands across the midlands. They eventually ordered that the plaintiff was to have title to all of these properties transferred to him by means of a recovery that he was already pursuing at the assize sessions, but this was on the condition that he agreed to forgive any charges he might gain in that forum and never sue for those damages in the future. This award does not appear in any main Council or Requests register, but was issued as a standalone document, sealed and signed by all the judges and the principal parties, now surviving in the Birmingham archives.[48] Later, in 1502, a case between more humble litigants, the attorneys George Ashby and Thomas Robins, moved through Requests and was eventually resolved by its judges. This decision also went unrecorded in the carefully kept order books of the time; instead, it was detailed in an indenture that remains in the Staffordshire archives. This document, of which both the parties would have received a copy, bound them to 'contynue in love and charite' before explaining how the contested lands were to be divided between them, and was signed at the bottom by the disputants and by Symeon, Mayhew, and Kidwelly.[49] Here the men otherwise working as judges in the Requests committee

---

[45] E.g., REQ1/4 fol. 95; REQ1/5 fols. 28, 102, 228v; REQ1/6 fols. 182–182v; REQ1/7 fols. 46, 51v, 126v, 202v, 238.

[46] REQ1/4 fol. 118v.   [47] REQ1/7 fols. 169v–170.

[48] Birmingham Archives and Collections MSS 3279/11/931 and 3279/11/933.

[49] Stafford, Staffordshire Record Office D938/219. A copy of a similar indenture in another case, made by Richard Sampson, survives in the miscellaneous part of Requests' archive: REQ3/9 *Mynton* v *Salford*.

238   Delivering and Contesting Justice

acted as arbiters and umpires outside of court, technically. Conversely, litigants could also pay to have external arbiters' awards written up into Requests' books, presumably for posterity.[50] These cases remind us that a formal decision made and engrossed centrally was not necessarily feasible or even desirable for all litigants.

Elsewhere, when needed, Requests could make substantial awards. Although its judges were sometimes presented with serious instances of violence that verged on the criminal, they could not impose loss of life or limb. There is no corporal or physical punishment of any kind visible in its order-book pages, nor anything like the public penance and humiliation to which Star Chamber might sentence seditious subjects. Requests did have the power to imprison, it seems. In one instance Stokesley, acting with the authority of the absent John Clerk, sent one John Newman to the Fleet, from whence Chief Justice Fineux had to summon him by a *habeas corpus* for a hearing in King's Bench.[51] This was presumably punishment for Newman's contempt of the Council's orders rather than for his original offences; Stokesley was, after all, known for threatening anyone audacious enough to hassle him about the progress of their case with imprisonment.[52] Otherwise, Requests largely specialised in financial restitution and the award of costs and damages. Orders for the settlement of land ownership were usually framed in terms of one party 'allowing' the other to 'peacefully' possess the property (rather than as something more technical, like a release, surrender, or recovery). Importantly, like Star Chamber, Requests only awarded *possession* – that a party '*gaudeat possessionem*' – rather than the *title* to property, which was typically reserved for the common law. One party might also be ordered to pay any arrears in rents, profits, or tithes, sometimes going back decades.

In more unusual cases, such as violent assaults or marital neglect, Requests facilitated compensation to victims. This could involve substantial amounts of money: the occasional riot case put before the Requests committee in its earliest years could result in fines of £5 for all the known participants, to be paid directly to the king, for example.[53] Later, in 1521, the violent attack committed against Margaret Lentall by John Wyndover, which had left her so 'grievously hurte' that she would 'never recover ... nor can long endure or live in this world', resulted in she and her husband being awarded 20 marks (over £13) paid by Wyndover for her 'hurtes

---

[50] For example, the arrangement reached by arbiters between tradesmen Alex Arnold and William Marley in 1516, which cost each of them 16d: REQ1/4 fol. 28. See also REQ1/3 fol. 1.
[51] Northumberland, Alnwick Castle MS 475 fols. 95–95v.   [52] TNA KB27/1048 m. 75.
[53] REQ1/1 fol. 50.

'A Final Peax': Passing Judgment 239

lechercrafte and other damages'.[54] Married women petitioning about their husbands' negligence were not usually very specific about the remedy they sought. Yet several decrees from the last few years of Henry VIII's reign reveal that Requests' response was typically to order the husband to provide ongoing financial assistance, whether or not the couple reconciled.[55] In other money matters, litigants, lawyers, and judges in the conciliar courts compiled detailed and creative rulings. Debts were to be repaid at precise dates, times, and places: at the north door of St Paul's Cathedral fifteen days after Christmas in Lord Ormond's case of 1495; between 11 and 12 o'clock on the feast of the Purification, next to 'Haxbyes Tombe in York Mynster', as in one Council of the North decree from 1542; and at the parish church of Turlington on a quarterly schedule, according to the order imposed on the disobedient Robert Hackett by Requests in that same year.[56] In one unusual decree from 1541, in which Requests settled a dispute concerning money owed by the father of a bride on her marriage to the plaintiff's son, the defendant agreed that he would 'paye all costes charges & expences' for his new son-in-law's naturalisation as a denizen of England.[57]

All told, weighing up evidence, the type and strength of a particular ruling, and potential punishments involved several stages of hearing and discussion. A decree might go through various drafts and even be manually edited by the judges, often with the effect of adding in additional information about the lands in question or the schedule for repayments.[58] Once finished, the determination was 'published' in open court, read out before the gathered parties and counsel.[59] Having been 'ratefyde confyrmed & decreed', the final order was formally drawn up and, 'in credence hereof [and] entendyng the performance of the same', was 'subscribed with the handes' of the Court's leading judges and sometimes by the disputants too.[60] A couple of decrees endorsed like this, written neatly onto parchment and signed as described, still survive in Requests' archive.[61] These

---

[54] REQ2/2/66; REQ1/104 fol. 124v. This quotation presumably refers to leechcraft, a form of medical treatment for Lentall's injuries.

[55] REQ1/7 fols. 136, 178.

[56] Birmingham MS 3279/11/933; REQ3/9 *Fox* v *Vincent*; REQ1/7 fol. 114v.   [57] REQ1/7 fol. 67.

[58] For example, REQ2/6/240 (said to be '*Per mandatum Ricardi Sutton*'), REQ2/10/188 (signed by John Gilbert), REQ3/6 *Butler* v *Fuller* (numerous drafts, signed by John Stokesley). A draft filed in REQ3/10 *Mitchcroft* v *Hungerford* has the handwriting of at least two judges.

[59] Depositions in one case recalled how a decree had been 'publysshed and shewyd openly in the Whyte Hall by the seyd Deane', John Veysey: REQ3/19 *Stafford* v *Butler*.

[60] This seems to have become standard practice by the 1520s: e.g., REQ1/5 *passim*; REQ2/10/216, 2/11/109.

[61] REQ1/5 fols. 190, 227; REQ1/7 fol. 67.

240 Delivering and Contesting Justice

versions were otherwise typically given to the litigants, while the text of the decree was copied into the books, for a fee of somewhere in the region of 3s payable to the clerk of the Council. These final costs might explain why some decrees appear to survive only in draft versions among the pleadings, never having been fully entered.[62] With a royal ruling residing in litigants' hands and in the central archives, their negotiations before the king's Council were preserved for posterity.

Yet even after all of this work, Requests' decrees were not necessarily the final word in any given dispute. As one set of counter-petitioners insisted, 'all decrees made in the kynges most honorabull councell be condicionell' – that is, 'if the partie defend can hereafter shewe better evidence then the plaintif to the same landes then [they could] be restored agayn'.[63] The judges and clerks certainly understood that cases could be reopened in this way. As in the *Mascall* v *Blake* order, printed above, the standard closing line of decrees by the 1520s asserted that a determination only stood until the other disputant 'have afor the kings counsaill sufficiently and lawfully proved theffecte' of the claims made in their pleadings or could show 'mater effectual . . . that may be thought sufficient to dissolve and make frustrate the order and decree'. This open-endedness presumably served to alleviate the problems that the Requests' peremptory summons and speedy procedures could inflict upon defendants. It is apparent that in many cases the failure of the defendant to prove their case resulted automatically in an award in their opponent's favour. Hence in 1540 the defendant John Rockold successfully reopened a case already determined against him when he was able to produce a composition showing that rents supposedly owed to the vicars of Lewknor in Buckinghamshire pertained to different lands and tenants altogether, and not to him.[64] By technically leaving the way open for further hearings, Requests preserved a sense of dispute resolution as an ongoing process – so pre-empting certain lines of criticism against its jurisdiction.

The Limits of Royal Justice

Critical discourse about conciliar judicial procedures influenced the development and delineation of this jurisdiction too, then. As we observed of petitioners' appeals to statutes in Chapter 6, while Requests operated under

---

[62] As confirmed by the bills of costs in REQ2/10/228; REQ3/6 *Daldry* v *Forde*; REQ3/30 Golder. For draft decrees see REQ2/2/103, 2/3/135, 2/5/154, 2/6/240, 2/9/48, 2/10/12, 24, 188, 2/11/80, 123, 178, 2/12/167; REQ3/5 *Pope* v *Baskerville*; REQ3/6 *Butler* v *Fuller*.
[63] REQ3/21 *Coke* v *Child*.   [64] REQ3/13 *Rockold* v *Richardson*.

'A Final Peax': Passing Judgment
241

the extraordinary prerogative of the king it did *not* operate without reference to the standards of English law. Particularly illuminating on this point are those instances in which this Court declined to take up a petitioner's cause. If either disputant was found to have commenced litigation in a different court while their matter was already pending before Requests, they would be enjoined under penalty to cease this activity immediately and wait for the Council's determination. Conversely, where a matter was found to have been litigated elsewhere *before* being brought into Requests, the latter Court would simply not hear it. So, throughout this period, matters already in process in Chancery, Star Chamber, the provincial councils, and at the common law (sometimes specifically its courts at Westminster) were summarily dismissed upon first hearing by Requests' judges.[65] Stronger sanctions were issued against petitioners who were characterised as vexatious. In 1533, when it was discovered that John Clement's case against John Minsterchamber 'hathe byne prosecuted ... afor the Lorde Chauncellor in the k[ing]es Chauncery', Requests' judges perceived its presentation before them to be 'done more for veaxacion then otherwise'. Their response was to dismiss Minsterchamber and award him 5s for his costs, to be paid by Clement.[66] A memorandum from 1545 saw the judges employ even harsher language, speaking of the 'wilfull and crafty demeanor' of the petitioner, 'myndyng only the vexacion of the defendaunte & continuall suete frome on[e] courte to a nother'. On this occasion, the price to pay was 10s to the frustrated defendant.[67] Such measures served to protect the purview of individual jurisdictions, while addressing complaints that conciliar justice facilitated never-ending litigation.

On a case-by-case basis, Requests also consistently demonstrated respect for rulings made by other legal authorities and courts. Some decrees simply repeated and reinforced decisions already made in the matter at hand, whether in church courts, mayoral tribunals, or under prior arbitrations – essentially, anywhere that litigants might have tried their suits more locally, especially if there was some documented determination that Requests might peruse and copy.[68] The Court's default position was to accept common-law verdicts and compel litigants to obey them, whatever petitioners might have hoped. And so, notwithstanding the evocative tale

---

[65] E.g., REQ1/2 fols. 53v, 55v, 120v, 178v, 184v; REQ1/3 fol 62v, 147v, 188, 210, 294v, 307v; REQ1/5 fol. 186v; REQ1/6 fols. 130, 157.

[66] REQ3/17 *Clement v Minsterchamber*. See also REQ3/24 *Glawen v Watts and Smith*.

[67] REQ1/6 fol. 190v. For similar examples see REQ1/5 fols. 5, 129.

[68] E.g., REQ1/2 fol. 60, 104v, 179v, 183v; REQ1/3 fol. 323v; REQ1/105 fols. 190–4.

242 Delivering and Contesting Justice

presented by the widow Elizabeth Letton detailing a night-time attack on her Lincolnshire manor house, Symeon and his fellow judges awarded the title and possession of lands – the manor of Welbourne, the real matter of the case – to Robert Bate, the leader of the riot. This was expressly 'according to the award thereupon made by Thomas Tremaill knight oon of the kings justices of plees … and John Moore gent', presumably referring to one of the many common-law assize sessions that had been impanelled in this matter, which had also been heard in Star Chamber and by Margaret Beaufort's council at Collyweston.[69] This deferential behaviour seems to have set Requests apart from the better-established Court of Chancery, which could at least compel parties to put aside certain terms of common-law verdicts in the pursuit of a peaceful ending.[70] So, while petitioners believed that royal justice could function as a means of appealing against the rest of the legal system, its personnel were not obliged to act on this expectation.

By the same measure, people finding themselves on the receiving end of a Requests decree could appeal it in another court, with some success. The following note was made in the case between John Mascall and William Blake, immediately following the decree printed above:

> Afterwarde the xviij[th] day of May the xj[th] yere of regne of king Henry the viij[th] the forsaid Consaill upon the sight of the triall of xij men had upon the freeholde of the said landes ~~th have~~ founde to be ryght of the defend have dismissed ~~then~~ and ~~eler~~ clerely discharged hym of any further apperaunce ~~hym~~ herafter to be made and so remitted hym to folowe his proffe aft[er] thorder of the common lawe this decree and order made by the said Consaill notwithstandyng /[71]

In other words, Blake had taken advantage of the open-ended nature of Requests' initial decision. He had successfully impanelled a common-law jury to determine the freehold element of his case, and upon bringing that new finding before Veysey and his fellow councillors had found them prepared to overturn their existing ruling. This was not the only attempt to annul this particular determination. Later on, after William Blake's death, it was decided that since it was his wife Margery who laid claim to the lands in question they would allow the widow to have her evidence 'openly declared' and make their earlier decree 'voide & frustrat'.[72] Margery did

---

[69] REQ1/3 fol. 93; REQ2/11/97; REQ3/3 *Bate v Bele*. See also REQ1/2 fol. 35; REQ1/3 fols. 107, 129, 172–172v.

[70] It was, for example, possible for Chancery to ask parties to 'remit release and clerely forgive' damages 'recovered by order of the common law': e.g., TNA C78/2 m. 1.

[71] REQ1/4 fol. 76v.   [72] REQ3/11/2 *Mascall v Blake*.

'A Final Peax': Passing Judgment

not receive an updated decree, but other counter-petitioners did. A judgment passed in 1533 in a matter between William Coke and Richard Wilkins, awarding possession of a tenement in Newnham, Gloucestershire, was reconsidered after Wilkins secured a commission of *melius inquirendum* to have his evidence examined by the new mayor and burgesses of the town, who in turn contradicted a previous report that lands there were not devisable by will. On this occasion, the judges annulled their previous decree and issued a new one, admitting that this new hearing had the effect of 'falsifying the forsaid certificate returned by the [previous] mayor' and re-awarding possession.[73] Common-law and local legal processes could therefore revise royal justice, rather than the other way around. Indeed, Requests' judges seemed to have expected the suits they had determined to be tried elsewhere in due course: sometimes, their more informal orders were expressly in place only until a matter could 'be determined in the spirituall courte', by the manorial authorities, or at the common law.[74]

All of this might make Requests' rulings seem rather ineffectual, yet they were clearly taken seriously by other judges and jurisdictions. A decree made by Symeon and the lawyers Kidwelly and Sutton in February 1504 concerning an annuity payable from a tenement in Frampton, Lincolnshire, was moved in favour of the defendant, the Prior of Newstead, on the basis of certain 'books and accompts' he had been able to show for his house's 'contynaunce of possession' of that tenement.[75] In the following Trinity term, the prior appealed to the Council Learned in the Law, headed by Richard Empson, to complain about the contempt of the plaintiff, Nicholas Upton, in the face of this ruling. That Council ultimately repeated the findings of the 'K[ing]es Counsel of Requestes that the said Upton shuld pay [the] said rent' and, when he could produce no evidence to the contrary, they committed him to the Fleet prison until he had paid up.[76] Around the same time, Upton himself submitted a plea to King's Bench, framing the prior's initial suit to Requests as a trespass against Magna Carta and its principles that a free man could not be seized other than by the common law of the land and that matters could only be pleaded in Common Pleas under the great seal.[77] Again, Requests' proced-ures and determinations withstood scrutiny, since the matter does not seem to have proceeded in King's Bench beyond the initial complaint. Upton was later enjoined by Requests to be examined personally by

---

[73] REQ1/5 fols. 217, 237v–238v.   [74] REQ1/3 fol. 152v; REQ1/5 fol. 68.   [75] REQ1/3 fol. 104.
[76] TNA DL5/2 fols. 77, 80.   [77] TNA KB27/972 m. 92.

244 Delivering and Contesting Justice

Richard Foxe (Bishop of Winchester), Thomas Lovell, and other royal councillors – perhaps meaning some quorum of the Council in the Star Chamber.[78] This unusually well-recorded piece of back-and-forth litigation illustrates the collaborative relationship between the conciliar courts, and reminds us again that justice-seeking at this level was not undertaken linearly.

Underpinning a largely smooth relationship with the wider system was the development over time of some consistent principles about the sorts of people and cases Requests would and would not entertain. Not only did its judges increasingly remit rich and vexatious litigants, solidifying their purview over the poor and vulnerable suitor. Towards the end of our period, they also more often adhered to traditional norms about *who* could rightfully sue at law in the first place. We have seen already that the judges occasionally compelled groups of 'inhabitants' to name a leading plaintiff where the defendant complained about incorporated bodies in litigation. Elsewhere, they seemed more concerned than before about upholding the doctrine of coverture: in one instance in 1545, it was felt that 'the wife of the complain[an]te of longe tyme obstinatly & wilfully hathe prosecuted the mater in hyr owne person hyr husband never apperyng' and so she ought to be dismissed.[79] Other dismissals pertained to case type. As early as the 1520s, some matters were ended simply to relieve Requests of 'mat[ers] det[er]minable at the comen lawe', echoing defendants' answers, though without much elaboration. Sometimes the rationale for dismissal was more explicitly that a case 'concernythe the right and title of lande' or was 'upon a specialte of obligacion' – confusingly, since for the most part Requests heard these sorts of cases without comment.[80]

This jurisdictional caution was further reflected in the general safeguards built into the examination and determination of matters under the nebulous rules of conscience. In some dismissed cases, the judges appeared to admit that they lacked the expertise or full knowledge to provide remedy at all. For example, one suit brought to Requests in the early 1530s alleged that two men of supposedly 'good credens & very good substans' had been sent to purchase leather from the plaintiff, but that it had since transpired that the elaborate claims of their good credit, endorsed by the defendant as surety, were false; the plaintiff had received only partial payment and the two abettors had fled, one to 'Westminster in to Seyntware [sanctuary]'

---

[78] REQ1/3 fol. 232v. Both Foxe and Lovell were named to the main Council around this time: HL Ellesmere MS 2655 fols. 4–6; *CPR 1494–1509*, 388–9.
[79] REQ1/6 fol. 198.   [80] REQ1/5 fol 11v; REQ3/22/1 *Wilson* v *Reynold*.

'A Final Peax': Passing Judgment 245

and the other 'into Walis'.[81] Having heard contrary witness testimonies from both disputants, Requests' judges – together representing canon-law, civil-law, and common-law training – recognised that this was essentially an 'an accion of discepte' of the kind they might normally hear. Yet they decided in this instance that they did not have enough firm evidence in 'ryght or consciens to adiuge' and that the plaintiff should seek remedy at the common law.[82] So, even issues seemingly well suited to the conciliar jurisdiction – complex and pertaining to conscience as much as to law – might be declined by Requests if its personnel felt uninformed. It was perhaps for the same reason that the scope of most of the Court's decrees in land disputes was consciously restricted. Like those made in Chancery and Star Chamber, determinations applied *in personam*, touching only the relevant parties, and drafts occasionally show amendments made to emphasise that parties might bring further evidence only to advance the same case ('*eadem causa*'). In these ways, royal justice proved increasingly sensitive to complaints about its potential abuse, keeping its procedures socially accessible while developing various checks on the use of its awards.

What these self-restrictions amounted to by the end of our period and beyond was greater definition of this more routinised, and therefore more challengeable, jurisdiction. In the early 1540s, Dacres indicated the implementation of two significant limits on the sort of land cases Requests would entertain. Firstly, his reforms required that if neither 'the plaintif nor his auncestors have not bene possessed of such landes, as are in the complaint specified' for a long duration of time then 'the same parties and the matter by them brought [was] to be remytted to the common law'.[83] The number of years required is left blank in the surviving manuscripts of Dacres' orders, but that there was a minimum term in mind at all suggests that Requests' judges worked more in line with the canon law's prescription of forty years to establish right than the common law's preference for 'immemorial usage'.[84] Indeed, as early as 1520 a land dispute was dismissed from Requests' purview because the plaintiff was a gentleman *and* because 'the grauntfader and fader of the said ... defend have contynued ther estate and possession in the [lands] by the space of xl yeres and more'.[85] Some litigants seem to have been aware of some sort of temporal threshold for land ownership even before 1543. One defendant quibbled in his 'exceptions' against a decree that he '& his aunce[s]tors have contynued in pesible

---

[81] REQ2/2/136.   [82] REQ1/5 fol. 219.
[83] Leadam ed., *Select Cases in the Court of Requests*, lxxxvi.
[84] R. H. Helmholz, *The Ius Commune in England: Four Studies* (Oxford University Press, 2001), 184.
[85] REQ3/7 *Bracebridge* v *Swynerton*.

246   Delivering and Contesting Justice

possession of the seid landes by the space of a C yeres & more'.[86] Later on,
another insisted that 'thorder of this court hath byn that where hath ben
such possession by the space of xxx^{ti} yeres the seid Court hath dysmyssed
the partie defendaunt'.[87]

Secondly, Dacres specified that 'all bills concerning Copie hold landes' –
that is, those lands held by copy of manorial court roll – 'be alwayes
remitted to the Lords officers of the mannour, wherof the landes are
holden'. Again, the Court's judges had probably operated on this principle
for some time, since at least a decade earlier their predecessors sometimes
restricted themselves to freehold elements of a dispute while stating that 'as
to the copy hold of any suche be the p[ar]ties to trie ther title afor the lorde
of whom the same landes are holden'.[88] The same principle perhaps
explains the willingness of the judges in the late 1510s to allow William
Blake to have the freehold part of his estates disputed with John Mascall
heard at common law. Requests may even have been taking the lead from
common-law members and colleagues in this regard. A draft decree in one
case repeated the terms of an arbitration made by Anthony Fitzherbert,
justice of Common Pleas, and the lawyer Anthony Babington as to the
occupation of certain lands in Uttoxeter, Staffordshire: particularly the
caveat that 'the same awarde aforsaid be not to the prejudice and hurte of
the lorde of the lordeshipe of Uttoceter touchyng the copy holde landes . . .
but the said lord and his stywardes have therupon reformacion after the
custome theyr used if any thyng therin be don or made by the said a warde
in derrogacion of the liberties of the said lorde'.[89] This loose rule to protect
manorial custom (excepting cases in which the lord or steward was at fault)
incidentally undermines the long-standing perception of Requests as
a court that championed poor copyholders against their landlords.[90]

The manorial lord was not the only beneficiary of these regulations.
These rules paint a picture of a tribunal responsive to the needs of its
litigants, the criticism of its opponents, and the smooth workings of its
personnel, even if this meant ultimately representing a less radical force for
the lower echelons of society than historians have sometimes presumed.
Dacres's orders restored some protections to the defendant which had been
hard-won in late-medieval statutes but arguably undone by the powerful
procedures of royal justice. Plaintiffs were to be examined under oath
about their substance and remitted to the common law automatically if

---

[86] REQ3/8 *Plommer* v *Oliver*.   [87] REQ3/9 *Rawson* v *Abbot of Dale*.
[88] REQ3/14 *Cobley* v *Denys and Kyrton*.   [89] REQ3/5 *Hogeson* v *Hogeson*.
[90] Leadam ed., *Select Cases in the Court of Requests*, liv–lxviii; Gunn, *Early Tudor Government*, 84.

'A Final Peax': Passing Judgment 247

found to be rich. Otherwise, all parties were liable to a fine if they failed to bring in their pleadings in person by a set date, petitioners were given one term in which to prosecute their cause before being summarily dismissed, and parties were liable to a charge for the production of writs upon which they proceeded to default.[91] This last order is reminiscent of earlier parliamentary efforts to control the use of the privy-seal writ of summons; the effectiveness of such guidelines at this later date can be observed in the issuing of these exact production charges across the 1540s.[92] In all, Requests' staff were working to limit disobedience and vexation in one fell swoop by the end of our period, shoring up the credibility of their jurisdiction and ensuring that where straightforward decrees *were* made they could be robust enough for litigants' needs.

The Afterlife of Decrees

Beyond the procedures of the courtroom, royal decrees had afterlives that can tell us something about how such extraordinary justice was received and dispersed across the realm. Copies of orders bought by litigants were quickly returned to local communities and given immediate utility. A secondary petition submitted by Thomas Sere and his wife Isabell incidentally explained how their previous decree had been deployed: while the text of the order was 'remeanyng in thys honorable Court', in its books, at home they had gathered some neighbouring husbandmen 'to goo with theym peasably towarde the seyde landes & tenements' in variance and 'toke the decre with theym', having it read out in the nearby highway as they 'peasably entryd' into these awarded lands.[93] Royal decrees fitted seamlessly into the rituals of land exchange and transfer so often glimpsed in these accounts, then. Yet many of the simpler land disputes determined in this forum created clear winners and losers. Orders and decrees were therefore not always positively received.

To smooth over any resulting problems with decree enforcement, the Council had a contempt jurisdiction: litigants could return and petition again if decrees had been ignored or defied, in 'contempt of our seid sovereign lord the king' or 'in most open contempt of this court'.[94] The disrespect of Requests' determination levelled by the gentleman William Salford in 1531 was reported in detail, and so is worth discussing at length. After the case brought against him by Richard Mynton, disputing the

---

[91] For Dacres's orders, see BL Add. MS 25248 fols. 29–33.   [92] E.g., REQ 1/6 fols. 222, 205, 171.
[93] REQ3/8 *Sere and Beldon* v *Otteley*.   [94] E.g., REQ2/4/387, 2/10/200.

248 Delivering and Contesting Justice

occupation and rent of a house in London, was resolved in Mynton's favour in an indenture made by Richard Sampson, then Dean of the Chapel Royal, this frustrated defendant made his feelings known to all who would listen. One of Salford's companions, Thomas Browne, informed on him in a long deposition submitted to the Court. He said that he had asked Salford 'howe the matter stode bitwene oon Richard Mynton mercer and the saide Salford the whiche was dependyng in the Whytte Halle ... And than the seid Salford saide that he was at apoyntte with alle / and saide he sette not a strawe thereby.' When asked about the dean's ruling, Salford 'lawft and made answere and saide / That it was past the Deanes handes', and that he had so far avoided being served the decree by the king's pursuivants – again, suggesting that by dodging the document itself he was relieved of its orders. Crucially, he argued, 'the Deane nor none other shuld never have hym at the poynt that they have hadd never whiles he lyved nor that he will pay to the said Mynton never a peny'.[95]

This remarkably detailed episode of disobedience reveals some of the ways in which losing parties might claim that royal justice was ultimately unjust. Salford was not the only person to claim that a matter was not properly within the Dean of the Chapel Royal's capabilities. A few years earlier, the dispute waged between Humphrey Stafford and John Butler over eight lucrative salt vats in the productive pits at Droitwich, Worcestershire, had gone similarly awry, despite being clearly determined by Veysey and his colleagues in Stafford's favour in early 1517.[96] One man who had been present when the decree was proclaimed at the Droitwich Exchequer House testified how, when Butler was asked if he would obey the ruling, he had answered that 'nay he wold not obey it ... [because] it is made by favor of Mr Deane apon a fals surmyse made unto hym'. Later on, Richard Dyne, one of the queen's messengers, gave testimony about the moment he had delivered a new privy-seal summons in the meadows around Droitwich – where Butler had reasserted his opinion that 'this matier [is] passed Mr Deanes lernyng and that it were a mete mater to have in the comon lawe'.[97] It is not clear if Butler ever sought a common-law verdict, but since Stafford had produced evidence for his recovery of the vats under a successful writ of right this matter had presumably been pursued through the central courts under Droitwich's ancient demesne rights already.[98] In any case, reflexive allusions to the lack of legal expertise in conciliar justice

[95] REQ3/9 *Mynton v Salford.*   [96] REQ1/4 fol. 45v.   [97] REQ3/19 *Stafford v Butler.*
[98] On this process see Marjorie McIntosh, *Autonomy and Community: The Royal Manor of Havering, 1200–1500* (Cambridge University Press, 2002), 32–4.

'A Final Peax': Passing Judgment 249

may have been informed by contemporary discourse, particularly among conservative common lawyers, about the arbitrariness of conscience-based justice when dispensed by men without full knowledge of English law. That certainly seems to be the meaning of one defendant's complaint that since a decree had been made only by 'that halt prest [John] Stokisley not beyng dean & done withowt auctorite' it did not bear listening to.[99] Instances of contempt on these grounds indicate that the same scrutiny of judicial learning may have filtered down into wider society.

Such discord sometimes required a further wave of response from Requests. In the first instance, the Court issued a writ or an injunction to the offending party, ordering them either to obey the ruling or appear before the judges to explain themselves, under the same financial penalties as used in initial summonses. Otherwise, Requests generally relied upon local governors to supervise the implementation of its rulings. Hence the decree against John Butler was read out by the bailiffs of Droitwich, who were also expected to 'record [Butler's] demeanor' in response.[100] When things continued to go wrong it was to these same local figureheads that Requests' judges looked for longer-term enforcement. In November 1538, they had ordered that the defendant William Warren should immediately depart from certain lands contested by Arthur Allen and Fulk Barker, but it soon became apparent that he had not done so. A letter in the format of a writ was duly issued to the sheriffs of Northamptonshire, describing Warren as a 'rebell and disobedient subjecte' and ordering them to put aside 'all maner of affeccion' and 'repaire to the saide tenement and landes and thereunto quietly restore the saide Alen to the possession . . . amoeving the gooddes and catalles of the saide Waren'.[101] Likewise, sheriffs' powers of attachment and ability to make 'opyn and solempne proclamacion' naming certain parties as rebels were deployed by Requests for especially contemptuous subjects.[102] Curiously, the remit of these officers might be expected to continue even after the initial matter was settled. They were sometimes called upon to assist the winning party in keeping their possession 'at all tymes hereafter', too, and to send anyone trying to undermine the Court's award down to the White Hall for examination.[103] This suggests that in extreme cases Requests' judges might be willing to abandon

---

[99] REQ3/26 *Langton* v *Revell and Fitzrandall.*
[100] REQ3/19 *Stafford* v *Butler.* Similarly, the enforcement of one decree passed in Chancery was undertaken by the relevant manor court: REQ3/9 *Smith* v *Knight.*
[101] REQ3/27 *Allen and Barker* v *Warren.*
[102] REQ1/1 fol. 144v; REQ1/3 fols. 164, 184; REQ3/25 *Newport* v *Newport.*
[103] REQ3/27 *Allen and Barker* v *Warren*; REQ3/2 *Wyrall* v *Copinger.*

250   Delivering and Contesting Justice

the usual restriction of their orders to the parties named in the original suit. Not all local governors were so pliable to royal commands for constant oversight of such affairs, however. Following another judgment passed under Stokesley's tenure in 1522, it was reported to the Court that the defendants, the local bailiffs, *and* the constables had simply refused to put it in execution, because they suspected that the decree had been 'made deseitfully under a busshe for money'.[104]

That there was so much opportunity for Requests' decrees to get lost in communication raises the question of how enforceable they were, ultimately. As we have seen, the Court oversaw the exchange of money for any costs and charges they awarded and compelled the recipient to make an acquittance too. Otherwise, in theory a losing party in a decree was bound to its performance by a fine, usually said to be 'upon payne of xl li to be levyed of the land[es] good[es] & cattall[es] of the said [party] to thuse of o[ur] sov[er]ain lorde the king if he any thyng attempt or cause to be attempted contrary to the tenor of thys decree', as in the example of *Mascall* v *Blake*, printed above. A forfeit of £40 was the standard, but it could be as little as 20*s* or as much as £300 or even 400 marks on occasion – generally speaking, threatened penalties increased across this period. The agreed total may have depended on an individual party's substance or conduct, or on the value of assets in dispute. Very rarely was this fine said to be owed to the winning litigant, though; much more often it was explicitly for the king's use, and by the mid-1520s decrees specified that any levied money would be directed into the Exchequer. Justice-giving would therefore appear to have been an opportunity for money-making on the part of the central administration, in addition to fees gained through the production of documents by the clerks of the Council and the privy seal. However, as was reported by a bailiff who tried and failed to execute a Requests' decree in the early 1520s, rebellious parties simply behaved as they liked, 'not regarding yor decree nor fearing the penaltye therin by you lymyted'.[105]

Indeed, there is little sign in the Requests' archive that the Court was much interested in pursuing this potential line of profit. What *did* happen is that some dissatisfied and disobedient parties would be called back into the Court on the basis of a recognisance they had been entered into at the time of the decree's making. There they would have to acknowledge before the judges that they now owed the king money by a certain return date – though

---

[104] REQ3/6 *Palmer* v *Cliff*; REQ3/26 *Ellis and Hacche* v *Stepneth*.

[105] REQ3/6 *Palmer* v *Cliff*. A brief search of some of the fines and recorda sections of the Exchequer memoranda rolls (TNA E159) has not turned up any references to fines paid from Requests' litigants anyway. My thanks go to Dr Daniel Gosling for his advice on where to look for these records.

'A Final Peax': Passing Judgment 251

the whole recognisance would be voided if they ceased their vexation in the meantime.[106] It is possible that any such recognisance had a limited term, anyway. The inquiring Thomas Browne put to the disobedient Salford 'howe he dyd with the obligacion that he was bounde yn to the kyng to abide the awarde of the Deane', to which Salford reasoned that since 'the saide Deane made awarde when the date of the obligacion was exspired . . . the saide awarde was to none effect'.[107] Nonetheless, Salford, like other litigants called in on these terms, appears to have escaped fines in the end. Presumably peacekeeping then fell once again to neighbours and local authorities, or to other elements of the legal system.

In the end, where a final peace and remedy *was* successfully achieved thanks to Requests' rulings, the resultant decrees no doubt long remained in the possession of the parties, stored in their locked boxes and chests with other deeds, indentures, and charters that were increasingly in circulation. That cherishing of royal determinations in the short term is glimpsed in follow-up petitions that quoted from them verbatim, whether coming back to Requests or to other tribunals. An even longer afterlife of one judgment is revealed in an incidental marginal note scribbled alongside it in the order book. Next to the decree made in May 1517 for the matter between Isabelle Eyre and Sir Thomas Rockley, a clerk of the Elizabethan Requests, Richard Oseley, wrote the following: 'This decree was exemplified under the pryvie seale and signed by the hande of King Henry the viij[th] & ys in the custodie of Bosseville esq[uier] and ys his evidence for this lande. I did see yt, & yt was shewed by Mr Thomas Seckford to the Quenes Ma[jes]tie Quene Elizabeth.'[108] The engrossed version of this ruling, apparently sent out with a privy seal signed by Henry VIII, still survived in the possession of one of Eyre's descendants all these decades later, and had lost none of its initial authority in confirming right. It also remained among the Court's own records, accessible to its personnel. Notwithstanding the flexibility of Requests' rulings, this tailored justice had social and institutional legacies, both in the immediate heat of a dispute and the longer span of landholding.

Conclusion

The result of all the behind-the-scenes supplicating and negotiating was a form of justice that balanced litigants' demands for a wide-ranging and sensitive jurisdiction with some practical limitations. As the survey

---

[106] E.g., REQ1/5 fols. 96v, 205v, 215v, 237.   [107] REQ3/9 *Mynton* v *Salford*.
[108] REQ1/4 fol. 60v. Seckford was another Master of Requests.

of Requests' bill signatories and sitting judges in the last few chapters has shown, the culture of royal justice had many ideological foundations that ebbed and flowed over time: the common law and its norms, of course, but also civil and canon law, theology, and overarching notions of reason and righteousness. On these grounds, Thomas More once praised fellow judge and royal councillor Thomas Wolsey for 'the prudence and the authority which enable you to administer justice', meaning that 'when disputants engage in intricate quarrels, to the amazement of ordinary people, you sort everything out so well that even the loser cannot complain'.[109] With his own judicial experiences in Requests and the wider Council in mind, More may well have been correct that something much more personal and innate than codified law determined the provision of royal justice in individual cases. But he was surely *less* accurate in assuming that everyone left Chancery or the conciliar courts contented.

There seems to have been little doubt in the minds of Requests' suitors that this was truly justice issued from the monarch's hand – and the role of both the early Tudor kings as recipient and signatory of process, even as endorser of decrees, corroborates this impression. A benefit of continuous attachment to the royal administration was flexibility and efficiency. Indeed, on a practical level, Requests' early history turns on its head the presumption in traditional Tudor historiography that bureaucracy meant better organisation. This tribunal was seemingly *most* effective in determining cases, in caring for the poor, and in manifesting truly royal justice when ensconced in the household. The best evidence for this is its impressively consistent and concise record-keeping, which – if anything – became more sprawling at exactly the time that the Court was 'reinstitutionalised' with a more permanent judiciary and space, in the late 1530s.[110] Otherwise, Requests' final decisions probably defied contemporary expectations surrounding its remit. They were more by-the-book and less directly interventionist than petitioners wanted them to be, and more collaborative and deferential than corrective in their engagement with the rest of the legal system. Even an ideal as universal as royal justice had its limits. Indeed, throughout the early sixteenth century there appears to have been a shift from generalised notions of what this justice *ought* to do towards a more codified vision of what it *could* do.

---

[109] More, *Latin Poems*, ed. Clarence H. Miller et al., 269.
[110] The Court kept two books from around Nov. 1538 onwards – one for main orders, and one for notices of continuations and appearances – and in many instances ran out of space for entries: REQ1/7 fols. 56, 75, 107v, 108v.

'A Final Peax': Passing Judgment 253

No matter how popular and powerful royal justice became, it could not make itself unassailable. Further revisions of Requests' remit came in the later sixteenth century, especially from outside the Court. They began with Edward VI's order of 1551 that Star Chamber, Chancery, and Requests, taken as a single jurisdiction, should no longer hear 'pleas to the derogacion of the commen law' – perhaps designed in part to curtail the authority of the fickle Richard Rich, then Lord Chancellor, suspected of disloyalty to Protector Somerset.[111] More delineations came with the various orders of Elizabethan chancellors and judges that Requests was for suitors too poor for Chancery.[112] Challenges to conscience-based remedies picked up pace towards the end of the sixteenth century, with growing numbers of prohibitions issued to stop proceedings in conciliar tribunals and several test cases at common law questioning their jurisdiction.[113] By that point, the amorphous nature of this form of justice and its lack of firm foundation in statute or ordinance counted against Requests. Yet this chapter has shown that criticism was evoked and received earlier and internally, too. Indeed, from its very beginnings, royal justice was responsive to petitioners *and* to defendants, in case-specific rulings and in the shaping of its jurisdiction.

---

[111] HL Ellesmere MS 2652 fol. 17.
[112] George Williams Sanders ed., *Orders of the High Court of Chancery* (A. Maxwell & Son, 1845), vol. I, 61, 122; Lincoln's Inn, Maynard MS 66 fol. 154v; G. R. Elton, *The Tudor Constitution: Documents and Commentary* (Cambridge University Press, 1968), 108–9.
[113] For a recent summary, see Baker, *The Reinvention of Magna Carta*, 277–83, 484–7.

CONCLUSION

Justice and the Tudor Commonwealth

Royal justice was a constant, and constantly controversial, element of English government into the later sixteenth century and beyond. The conciliar courts where it was best manifested continued to grow and formalise after the death of Henry VIII, eventually becoming the 'prerogative' equity courts of Westminster with which historians of the early modern state are so familiar. Yet the qualities ascribed to these institutions in their formative years remained central to their respective identities. A set of ordinances for 'her Majesties Counsell at Whitehall', or the Court of Requests, written in 1597 gives the impression of a tribunal remarkably similar to that of a hundred years earlier. Bills were only to be accepted if they had been 'first exhibited either to her Majesties person or to the Right honorable Lords of her highnes privie Counsell'; 'thexpedicion' of 'poore mens causes' was still paramount, and the 'immoderate and needlesse prolixitie' of pleadings 'fownde untrue' still problematic.[1] Some 'observations' on the Court's work written down within the first decade of the seventeenth century reiterated the complaints of old, depicting a tribunal that was slow, full of 'unseemly' clamour, and possessing a judiciary too 'interchangeable' to provide stable remedies.[2] Still, however serious these problems were taken to be, the inclination was for reform rather than abolition; for the Court to act 'as in former ages', according to 'all auncyent precedentes in the practize & proceedinges'.[3] Following Caesar's example, it was to the 'ancient' past of the early Tudor age that believers in royal justice looked for justification.

While some felt the Crown *had* gained authority and legitimacy through its accumulation of judicial powers, such ideological appeals could only hold out for so long. At the height of deliberations in the summer of 1641, the Long Parliament passed an Act that drastically curtailed this system of royal justice. The capacity for the Crown and

---

[1] HL Ellesmere 2916 fols. 1–3.   [2] BL Add MS 25248 fols. 2v–8.   [3] Ellesmere MS 2916 fol. 3.

254

Justice and the Tudor Commonwealth 255

its ministers to investigate all manner of interpersonal disputes had become an 'intollerable burthen to the Subjects and the meanes to introduce Arbitrary Power and Government', the Act argued. At a single stroke, it abolished virtually all the royal judicial forums that had come into being over the past couple of centuries: Star Chamber, the provincial councils, the court of the Duchy of Lancaster, and the palatinate court of Chester. It decreed that 'neither his Majestie nor his Privie Counsell have or ought to have any Jurisdiction power or authority by English Bill Petition'.[4] This ruling impinged on matters as heady as the relationship between Crown and justice, the long-established rights of subjects under the legal system, and the ideals and individuals that could make (and unmake) institutions of governance – all of which had been in flux for the previous 150 years, if not longer.

Intriguingly, Requests was not included in this Act, even though it was open to criticism on similar grounds. A separate bill read during the same sitting of the Commons in June 1641 called specifically for the 'Suppressing and Abolishing' of this Court, too, but it disappeared from the parliamentary agenda thereafter.[5] Five months later, Requests was discussed again, while the Commons was engaged in refining the precise terms and language of their 'Declaration on the State of the Kingdom', or Grand Remonstrance, to be put before Charles I. On 22 November 1641, during the final set of debates before the document was approved, members voted on whether a clause 'concerning the Court of Requests, shall be left out of this Declaration'. By some margin they voted that it should, and so the final text of the Remonstrance contained criticism of Chancery, Wards, the provincial councils, and other prerogative jurisdictions, but not of Requests.[6] The Court seemingly retained enough good will among the realm's governors to escape sweeping abolition. Yet it survived only a couple of years beyond this point, fizzling out when Charles I relocated to Oxford in 1643 and took the authorising mechanism of the privy seal with him.[7] This episode represents one last oddity in Requests' history as a court, but not its end as a governmental function. The erstwhile Masters of Requests outlived their namesake institution, continuing to mediate between princes and petitioners for the protectorate and for the restored Stuart line. Principle won out over practice; royal justice as the root of the commonwealth survived the demise of its formalised system.

---

[4] 16 Charles I c. 10.   [5] *JHC* II, 184.   [6] *Ibid.* II, 308, 322.
[7] Knox, 'The Court of Requests in the Reign of Edward VI', 8–17. An attempt was made by Parliament to remove its records from rooms 'near the House of Peers' in 1645: *JHC* IV, 273; *JHL* VIII, 283.

256   Delivering and Contesting Justice

In charting the emergence of this judicial system under the early Tudors, this book has addressed three interconnected themes inherent to scholarship old and new: sixteenth-century governmental institutionalisation as a process with many factors, including subjects' demand; early modern litigation as a forum for sociopolitical relations and popular politics; and the existence and importance of criticism in the relationship between monarchy, society, and law. This book has, first and foremost, reconstructed the activity and evolution of the Court of Requests in its formative years, based on analysis of its entire early Tudor archive and examination of all its component people. Most straightforwardly, this analysis reveals more about what monarchs and their ministers *did* day to day, outside the spectacle and pageantry of rule. Its records provide precious insight into how subjects encountered central government and what resulted from these meetings. The evidence of protracted institutionalisation here exemplifies the preference for continuity with late-medieval traditions, given greater routinisation, as opposed to outright innovation or revolution. Together these observations revise our assumptions about the main preoccupations of Tudor government, almost seventy-five years since this subject was given firm parameters in Elton's work. The ruthless efficiency emphasised under his 'revolution in government' thesis seems at odds with the relatively informal and flexible manner in which king and Council dispensed justice to ordinary subjects in everyday disputes.[8] This was a more paperwork-laden, outward-facing, and morally conscious mode of governance than old administrative-history models have led us to envisage. So, while Requests serves here as another case study to add to our growing corpus of work on litigation and lawcourts, it is also one especially revealing about the potential ordering force of monarchical government.

After all, why – if not to legitimise itself – did the royal administration expend so much time and energy to justice-giving? It is tempting to take the 'centralising trend in the constitution [and] ... constitutionalising trend at the centre' so characteristic of early Tudor government as meaning that in Requests and its fellow courts was a new and authoritarian mechanism by which the Crown could learn about, and exert control over, the localities and their governors.[9] At the very least, one by-product of the formalisation of royal justice was an increasingly perceptible distinction between *legitimate* and *illegitimate* channels for raising complaint. Rebels' self-fashioning as the

---

[8] Elton, *The Tudor Revolution in Government*.

[9] J. L. Watts, '"A Newe Ffundacion of is Crowne": Monarchy in the Age of Henry VII' in B. Thompson ed., *The Reign of Henry VII: Proceedings of the 1993 Harlaxton Symposium* (Paul Watkins, 1995), 53.

Justice and the Tudor Commonwealth 257

king's 'true petitioners' was open to refutation on these grounds by the 1530s: Henry VIII himself declared to the northern rebels of 1536 that he took their insurrection 'm[ar]velous unkindeley' since he had proven himself 'ever most prone and ready bothe to here all his subjectes of all degrees reasorting with peticions or complaintes unto him and ... to see redresse made in all thinges according to justice'.[10] In the longer term, the 'incorporative force' of judicial procedures, moved at the centre and then delegated to local authorities, may also have helped with 'embedding the state' in communities across the realm.[11] Yet, in the absence of any founding statute or proclamation, justice-giving initially seems not to have represented some intentional augmentation of Crown authority, but was rather a consequence of the royal household being accessible. Nor does it appear that monarchs or ministers much exploited this opportunity to undermine local authority, to put plaintiffs in their power, or to fill their own coffers. The protracted and unconscious expansion of Requests set out in Part I of this book should caution us against imposing too deterministic or unidirectional a model on *any* governmental (r)evolution.

This is not to say that the intention of this book has been to offer any new, singular model of curialisation, however. The distinctiveness of this relatively small and fluid tribunal's lifespan should instead encourage us to acknowledge the uniqueness of each court and jurisdiction and their individual evolutionary trajectories. That Requests handled a different sort of matter to Star Chamber, was less technically specialised than Chancery, and was similar in civil jurisdiction if not in geographical remit to the provincial tribunals, was obvious to contemporaries. But it has not been so apparent to historians, seemingly, since evidence for Requests has been applied without question to Chancery, and Star Chamber has been taken as the poor suitor's last resort.[12] This may seem a trivial quibble, but it exposes the need for a more discerning and less generalising approach to lawcourts as subjects of study. Not only is it essential that we understand the structures and routines of any court in question. Plainly our very choice of lawcourt for study, and our awareness of its place in wider systems of law, administration, and statecraft, determines the potential conclusions of our sociolegal analyses. After all, no two courts were the same. Even within one jurisdiction each individual tribunal was the product of different cultures, contexts, and clients; was variably

[10] TNA E36/121 fol. 4v.
[11] Braddick, *State Formation*, 165–6; Hindle, *The State and Social Change*, 87–93.
[12] Gray, 'The Boundaries of the Equitable Function'; Hindle, *The State and Social Change*, 70.

258 Delivering and Contesting Justice

routinised, formalised, and recorded; and prioritised a particular facet of justice, ultimately.[13] It is the absence of this nuance, and particularly of comparative work along these lines, that has left a blind spot in sociolegal history with regard to the practical dimensions involved in going to law and the results of doing so.

With an institutional foundation in place, one of this book's central arguments has been that the primary motivation for the expansion of royal justice lay with litigants themselves. Two reconceptualisations have been intrinsic to this revised account. Firstly, near-contemporary notions of 'use and custom' as the primary justification for court creation come closer to reality than the emphasis placed on ordinances, proclamations, and statutes by common lawyers of the age and by administrative historians writing since.[14] Secondly, royal justice-giving was not simply a point of passive 'pressure', 'participation', or 'engagement' for subjects with complaints, to adopt language used by both late medievalists and early modernists.[15] It was, in fact, the product of *demand* – often very precisely phrased and rhetorically framed. These revisions are especially critical if we intend to further explore how relations between the central administration and wider society in Tudor England were smoothed out in 'points of contact'. We cannot hope to grasp the benefits of these exchanges, or why anyone would stake their money and time on them, without understanding how forums for contact were expected to (and did) work. The adversarial back-and-forth inherent to the conciliar justice courts admittedly sets them apart from other 'points of contact' already brought to light; from Parliament and its service of the political nation (at least, that part which could lobby it), or from the commissions that brought Reformation policies into local communities.[16] And even within this specific judicial sphere, Requests was one relatively small and specialised component. Still, the nature of its personalised exchanges, the social breadth of its clientele, and the variety of voices within its surviving records gives us the chance to explore a wider range of interactions between subjects and sovereign – and their results. Taken together, these features mean that in this central institution a 'negotiative nature' is hardly 'all but invisible'.[17]

---

[13] As demonstrated across various local contexts by Johnson, *Law in Common*.

[14] BL Lansdowne MS 125, fols. 184v–185.

[15] Harriss, 'Political Society'; Watts, 'The Pressure of the Public'; Braddick, *State Formation*; K. Bowie and T. Munck, 'Early Modern Political Petitioning and Public Engagement in Scotland, Britain and Scandinavia, c.1550–1795', *Parliaments, Estates and Representation* 38:3 (2018), 271–8.

[16] Elton, 'Tudor Government: The Points of Contact'; Cavill, *The English Parliaments of Henry VII*; Duffy, *Voices of Morebath*, 87, 120–7; Shagan, *Popular Politics and the English Reformation*, Part II.

[17] Hindle, *The State and Social Change*, 10.

Justice and the Tudor Commonwealth

Although this book joins the critical voices gathering against the potential for any 'negotiation' in which the Crown was party, it has nonetheless sought to deepen our appreciation of supplicants' agency and know-how in these exchanges.[18] Certainly, subjects worked around the rhythms of the royal entourage and put forward cases within defined parameters of deference. Yet in seeing the primary long-term outcome of all of these 'negotiations' as the institution itself, greater emphasis is placed on popular legalism – knowledge of law, justice, and its processes – as a driving developmental force. That said, where contemporary conceptualisations of Requests have been concerned, this book has repeatedly encountered one quite telling interpretive problem: how to assess awareness of a court when so few who sought it out or worked within it gave it any name. Nowhere is this paradox clearer than in a set of witness testimonies given by a clutch of sexagenarian gentlemen and esquires from Droitwich in the summer of 1541. Asked by commissioners to recall an earlier suit before the royal Council, their answers varied. Some remembered with some detail having been called 'before the Deane of the Kynges Chappell', John Veysey, and examined at Windsor upon a 'bill of complaint'; others recalled having 'herde seye' that their neighbours had been summoned before the 'kynges Counsell . . . in the Whyte Hall' by 'sub pena or by privy sealle'.[19] To none of these men was this definitively the 'Court of Requests', notably, even though all the hallmarks of that tribunal emerge from their reminiscences. Such colloquialisms epitomise the continuing fluidity of this forum, as an *event* and *function* of governance as much as an institution of government. Moreover, they remind us that the absence of clear curial identity denoted neither non-existence nor inefficiency to contemporaries, and so it should not for historians either. An on-the-ground perspective reveals Tudor government to have been reactive and nebulous, rather than fully proactive and bureaucratic.

While this framework calls attention to the potential reach and impact of that government on society at large, it also illuminates the flow of ideas, arguments, and expectations upwards. It is to that end that the analysis of this book has followed the course of litigation from initial dispute to final decree. In the first place, litigants' prior experiences and understandings of law are manifest in the details of forum shopping emerging from Requests' pleadings, and informed conceptualisations of the king as justice-giver. Throughout the process of litigating, supplicants worked through their connections to men who could draft and write up bills of complaint; drew

---

[18] E.g., Kesselring, *Mercy and Authority*, 200–8.   [19] REQ3/13 *Stafford* v *Butler*.

260   Delivering and Contesting Justice

on existing formulae for petitioning to lords and judges at the local level; and, in the end, echoed the rhetoric of the king as the fount of all justice that they commonly received through proclamations, statutes, and court charges. The absence of treatises, law reports, or any published statements on Requests, at least, leaves the origins of more practical knowledge about how and where to submit supplications somewhat obscure. Yet the Droitwich depositions quoted above remind us of how many people in one community were drawn into their neighbours' litigation, and suggest one way by which that information might have been embedded and reused. Thus, the social element of 'law-in-society' scholarship is taken further than before – beyond a single case or court and even beyond the courtroom altogether, to broader cultures of law and justice that informed, but were not exclusive to, formal judicial procedures. Here going to law has been characterised not as an extraordinary, rare experience – reflective more of present-day familiarity with the judicial system – but as a routine form of engagement for many people living under Tudor rule. This reality better accords with a view of litigation as a means by which 'the governed played a role in their own governance', pursuing personal and communal interests.[20]

The perception of mutual exchange between subjects and sovereign seems to strengthen the argument that litigation was a cohesive force in the longer span of early modern state formation. Certainly, the ideological connections forged by Crown-centric justice, and especially its capacity for 'incorporating local communities into a national political culture', are manifest in a tribunal with as much social and geographical range as Requests.[21] This union of interests is even more apparent when royal justice is contextualised in the realm of state*craft*. This refers not only to the efficiency of government structures and procedures but to the art of projecting monarchical charisma and sacrality in meaningful ways. As an element of the king's attendant household, it is no coincidence that Requests' initial phase of formulation coincided with the revival of other rituals of the royal court that were designed to improve access to the awe-inspiring presence of the monarch: more regular progresses, refined rituals for alms-giving, and reinstituted ceremonies for dispensing the royal touch.[22] The physical location of this tribunal in the most intimate spaces of power was reflected in the overtures of reciprocity and responsibility

---

[20] Shagan, *Popular Politics and the English Reformation*, 19.
[21] Hindle, *The State and Social Change*, 93.
[22] Brogan, *The Royal Touch in Early Modern England*, 45–66; Kisby, 'When the King Goeth a Procession'.

Justice and the Tudor Commonwealth 261

within the monarchical 'commonwealth' that were aired in this 'common discursive space'.[23] This was not just an institution of government or a court of law but also part of the same arm of government as the provision of royal pardons to felons and the continuing availability of sanctuary to those fleeing arrest. In other words, conciliar justice served as another, more regular means by which the regime dispensed Christian mercy, potentially offsetting some of its harsher legal policies.[24] This context only heightens our visions of law and justice as points of consensus and collaboration in wider sociopolitical relations, and of litigation as an 'important social resource' for all involved.

This book raises several critical caveats to this otherwise positive account, however. Of course, nowhere was the principle of bountiful, accessible royal justice put into clearer practice than in the Court of Requests – the 'poor man's court'. Its archive has much to tell us about what poverty meant contemporarily, how it was measured, and how it might have been mitigated in the hopes of meeting ideals of indifferent justice. As such, the evidence of mounting costs for litigation and lengthening case durations in our period must be weighed against the discovery here that 'paupers' still approached Requests, especially while it was itinerant. Moreover, the Court's judges evidently worked to protect this charitable quality, by offering waived fees to the poor and remitting the rich to other jurisdictions. This intended social sensitivity perhaps even explains *why* Requests retained some good favour – why it was removed from the Grand Remonstrance, for example – despite its evident utility for vexing opponents. That said, the socioeconomic practicalities observed across this book undeniably contribute to recent scrutiny about how far petitioning could have represented a 'safety valve' for early modern European societies. As Martin Almbjär has provocatively argued, the limited representation of the 'lower strata' in most centralised petitioning processes as a result of regulations and expenses designed to exclude them undermines the acceptance of petitioning as a demotic and politically influential medium. Almbjär was speaking rather generally about all kinds of complaint across a range of contexts, but he has nonetheless suggested some important qualifications to our narratives of 'legal revolution' that have yet to be applied to the English litigation boom.[25]

---

[23] Watts, 'The Pressure of the Public', 161.
[24] Kesselring, *Mercy and Authority*; McSheffrey, *Seeking Sanctuary*.
[25] Almbjär, 'The Problem with Early-Modern Petitions'. A similar reassessment was mounted in Vermeesch, 'Reflections on the Relative Accessibility of Law Courts in Early Modern Europe'.

262   Delivering and Contesting Justice

Indeed, when we extend our reconstruction of litigation beyond the petitioning stage it becomes evident that royal justice and the legalism surrounding it contained critical and dissenting voices, too. All involving themselves in this system might agree – or purport to agree – that the 'commonwealth' was connected by, and rooted in, justice and the king's personal supervision of its administration. Yet they did not concur about how it should be put into practice: who for, who by, and to what end. Taking up defendants' perspectives on Crown justice is manifestly feasible, given the ample survival of answers and exceptions in most of its bill-procedure courts. Yet this task is only now coming on to the agenda of sociolegal studies, following recent recognition that without knowing how 'individuals such as defendants judged their engagement with the law, claims about law-mindedness and legitimacy are best kept modest and circumspect'.[26] Even in the king's own Court of Requests, defendants and their counsel raised objections about mechanisms used to summon them into court, about their opponents' claims to disadvantage, and about the very remit of the Crown's civil jurisdiction. These lines of attack were borrowed from debates about how far royal justice accorded with law, ongoing in Parliament, in Council meetings, and in courtrooms. Just as telling about the broader ethos of this justice is the perspective of the Court itself. Requests' judges exhibited more caution in their judgments than we might have presumed; they eventually conceded to the view that this forum offered succour to petitioners but not a safeguard to defendants. Where these concessions qualified the fixity, scope, and longevity of any resulting decrees, obvious ramifications emerge as to how useful or effectual even this most authoritative kind of justice could be.

These questions return us to our readings of litigation before the Crown as either 'popular' or 'political'.[27] Although micro-studies of early modern communities have often envisaged such litigation as an expression of class conflict tried before the realm's greatest authorities, evidence for the results and reception of Requests' rulings should caution us to be more circumspect. Firstly, royal justice was not the be all and end all in dispute resolution. Although written decrees had a utility in affirming agreements between parties, feuds and fighting did not necessarily end here; sometimes

---

[26] D. Sugarman, 'Law, Law-Consciousness and Lawyers as Constitutive of Early Modern England: Christopher W. Brooks's Singular Journey', in Lobban, Begiato, and Green eds., *Law, Lawyers and Litigants in Early Modern England*, 54. See also Hindle, 'The Micro-Spatial Dynamics of Litigation', 142; Taylor, 'Labourers, Legal Aid and the Limits of Popular Legalism in Star Chamber'.

[27] In line with recent commentary on this terminology in Kesselring and Mears eds., *Star Chamber Matters*, 5–15.

Justice and the Tudor Commonwealth

they were relitigated at the common law, and sometimes litigants appealed to the Council again to investigate contempt of its initial determination. Secondly, Requests' remedies may have been wide-reaching, but they were not often particularly world changing. This conclusion somewhat dampens old conceptions of this tribunal as the defender of the realm's poor copyholders against landlords – as indicative of the Tudor Crown's policy of 'relying on the people against the aristocracy'.[28] Not only did it quickly refuse to intervene in manorial copyholding; it also largely answered litigants' calls for return to the *status quo* through the restoration or continuation of existing rights, rather than facilitating some large-scale, upwards social mobility. Lastly, its orders and rulings were not always blithely accepted, either by subjects or by local authorities. The disbelief, scepticism, and frustration expressed by those on the receiving end of writs and decrees displaying the royal endorsement tells us that such interventions could be unwelcome. In all, attention to small-scale disruptions across the realm certainly upheld one of the most important responsibilities of monarchical government at this time – to maintain order through justice – while also helping to publicise and legitimise a new dynasty. But putting justice into practice caused as many problems as it solved. Due recognition of limitations and criticisms moderates the conception of litigation in this sphere as an overwhelmingly positive and harmonious means of social cohesion into the early modern age. The development and the impact of Crown justice appears much more ambiguous when we move beyond the perspective of determined supplicants and a benevolent king to that of everyone caught in the middle.

To summarise, this book locates the beginnings of an English judicial revolution around the Crown within the crucible of early Tudor governance. With regard to the broader chronology of the brink between the late medieval and early modern worlds, this might be taken simply as an argument for relocating the emergence of litigation as a pillar of the participatory 'state' in earlier decades; as another attempt to shake up our chronologies by bringing one explanatory concept to bear on a different period. Certainly, this book *has* sought to properly explore the formative years, and thus the formative impulses, of Crown litigation in the early sixteenth century. This is, after all, still a liminal period, implicitly cast by late medievalists in terms of continuity with what came before while characterised by early modernists in terms of decline, darkness, and dimness before a golden age for state and society beginning *c.* 1550.

---

[28] Leadam ed., *Select Cases in the Court of Requests*, lv.

264 Delivering and Contesting Justice

Offered here is a renewed emphasis on centralisation and formalisation of existing processes under early Tudor rule. By balancing overview with micro-study, and context with reconstruction, this study has sought a more comprehensive vision of how justice-seeking and justice-giving worked together in practice throughout a turbulent and transitional age. In so doing, it adds a much-needed practical dimension to often-theoretical discussions of law in society, taking advantage of the most compact and manageable archive available to put aside sampling and selective studies in favour of something more total. On a broader scale still, we gain some inkling here of the causes and course of the 'legal revolution' as it occurred in England; its pre-eminent jurisdiction, the system of royal justice instituted under the early Tudor kings is studied here through just one of its components, the Court of Requests.

While returning to the well-known centralised vantage point on this period, this study urges us to see governmental institutions not as a constricted space but as a nexus for many different interests and voices. Indeed, the wider enquiry informing this book's central line of research concerned petitioning and justice-seeking as a form of communication between Tudor England's poorest subjects and highest authorities, and as a means for disseminating ideas and expectations about power in regular, real-world settings – outside the flashpoints of elite treatises or popular rebellions. There is no doubt that justice was an element of governance done *with* people and not just *to* them, day to day. The rich seam of information supplied by Requests' archives makes previous conceptions about the 'pressure' of society on government and of 'participation' in judicial processes seem overly passive, neutral, and anonymised – a result often of detachment from institutional realities. The targeted and tailored nature of litigation uncovered in this book allows us to strengthen our language and speak instead of *demand*, leviable in lawcourts, readable in petitions, and identifiable in the process of pleading. The institution is integral to these expressions; even, perhaps, created by them. Yet it is reckoned here as a set of events, discussions, and documents designed to manage fluctuating business, rather than as a set of static procedures and routines imposed from on high. Such reconceptualisations, even if they underline the more negative effects of royal justice, ultimately provide us with a greater appreciation of litigants' choice and use of this jurisdiction over others. This study therefore advocates a more nuanced conception of the possibilities and problems that royal, 'prerogative' justice presented, rather than an outright rejection of its significance in the long run.

Justice and the Tudor Commonwealth 265

In all, justice may not have been gone from the commonwealth, as so many feared by the end of the fifteenth century, but nor was its enactment particularly straightforward. Putting this nebulous ideal into regular practice was especially expedient to rulers and convenient for unceasing waves of petitioners at the dawn of the Tudor regime. Justice could never be one-size-fits-all; consequently, a balancing act was required. On the one hand, the sheer variety of matters brought to the king signifies a virtually unlimited remit for royal justice. On the other hand, the emphasis on relative poverty between petitioners and their opponents underlines that the king's abundant mercy was felt to be best reserved for the most vulnerable in society. Owing to these obvious contradictions, as royal justice-giving became more routinised across the sixteenth century it also became more contestable. It may, nevertheless, surprise us that at the heart of the better-known, high-political developments of the early Tudor years was the hitherto overlooked maintenance of such a socially sensitive arm of governance, *in spite* of the criticism already gathering against it. The continuation and expansion of this system into the booming Elizabethan age was achieved only by folding both demand and dissent into its evolution. In the end, this system of royal justice would be remembered favourably, well beyond its dissolution, for stilling the passions of feuding neighbours, adjudicating disputes across all social levels, and extending charity to the truly poor.[29] The many paradoxes contained within the ideal of royal justice were soon forgotten in its absence.

---

[29] Hutton, *Courts of requests*, 17–18.

APPENDIX

Personnel in the Court of Requests, 1493–1547

Regnal Year	Sitting Judges (listed in REQ1 order books and other sources where specified)	Signatories of Paperwork (appearing in REQ2 and REQ3 pleadings)
8 Hen VII, Aug. 1492–3	Richard Foxe, Bishop of Bath and Lord Keeper of the Privy Seal; Thomas Savage, Bishop of Rochester elect; Thomas Janne, Dean of the Chapel Royal; John Bayley (Bailey), royal chaplain; Robert Middleton; Robert Rede; Geoffrey Blythe, Keeper of the Rolls; William Warham; Thomas Lovell; Giles Daubeney, Lord Daubeney; John Arundell; Richard Guildford, knight; William Hussey, Chief Justice; Oliver King, Bishop of Exeter; William Smith, Bishop of Chester; James Hobart, the King's Attorney; Andrew Dymmock, the King's Solicitor[1]	
9 Hen VII, 1493–4	R. Foxe; T. Janne; G. Daubeney, Lord Daubeney; Reginald Bray, knight; W. Warham, Keeper of the Rolls; Richard Empson; John Blythe, Bishop of Salisbury; John Ratcliffe, Lord Seneschal; T. Lovell; R. Rede; T. Savage; Dr William Sheffield; Dr Richard Mayhew; John Mordaunt; Mr Robert Sherborne, secretary; Dr R. Middleton; Robert Willoughby, Baron Willoughby de Broke; A. Dymmock	

[1] These last five were present at a hearing on 12 August 1493, according to The Narrative of Robert Pilkington, 33.

266

Appendix   267

(*cont.*)

Regnal Year	Sitting Judges (listed in REQ1 order books and other sources where specified)	Signatories of Paperwork (appearing in REQ2 and REQ3 pleadings)
	Additionally: Oliver King, Bishop of Exeter; John Kendal, Prior of St John's; W. Hussey, Chief Justice; John Kingsmill; Richard Guildford; Henry Ainsworth[2]	
10 Hen VII, 1494–5	R. Foxe; T. Savage; T. Janne; R. Mayhew, President of Magdalen College, Oxford; R. Bray; T. Lovell; Henry Wyatt; Richard Redman, Bishop of St Asaph; W. Warham; Dr Richard Hatton; G. Daubeney, Lord Daubeney; Edmund Martyn, Dean of St Stephen's; Thomas Stanley, Lord Derby; Richard Guildford; John Turberville, knight; Richard Fitzjames; John Riseley, knight; Charles Somerset, vice-chamberlain; J. Blythe, Bishop of Salisbury; John Morgan, Dean of Windsor; R. Middleton; William Greville; John Welles, Viscount Welles; Cuthbert Tunstall	
11 Hen VII, 1495–9	John, Viscount Welles; R. Fitzjames; T. Janne, Dean of the Chapel Royal; Mr Sherborne; John Digby, Keeper of the Privy Seal (standing in for R. Foxe); T. Stanley, Lord Derby; C. Tunstall; John Vavasour; 'Pennok';[3] T. Savage, Bishop of Rochester; Dr John Morgan, Dean of Windsor; Dr R. Middleton; Mr William Greville[4]	
12 Hen VII, 1496–7	Mr E. Martyn; T. Janne; Charles Somerset; R. Middleton; T. Savage, Bishop of London; J. Kendal, Prior of St John's; R. Fitzjames, Bishop of Rochester elect; Richard Hatton	T. Janne

[2] All named to the '*iter*' of 1494: REQ1/1 fol. 1.
[3] 'Pennok' appears only once, in December 1495: REQ1/1 fol. 155v. He cannot be identified from surviving registers from the Council, the inns of court, or the household.
[4] Savage, Morgan, Middleton, and Greville were named as sitting at Leicester in late 1495: The Narrative of Robert Pilkington, 36.

268 *Appendix*

(*cont.*)

Regnal Year	Sitting Judges (listed in REQ1 order books and other sources where specified)	Signatories of Paperwork (appearing in REQ2 and REQ3 pleadings)
13 Hen VII, 1497–8	T. Savage, 'President of the King's Council'; T. Janne; R. Mayhew, Almoner; John, Viscount Welles; Thomas Fiennes, Lord Dacre (of the South); Richard Pole, knight; Henry Deane, Bishop of Bangor; Dr Richard Nix; Richard Sutton, 'jurisperitus' (lawyer); (Robert?) Bowring; R. Middleton; R. Sherborne; Richard Hatton; J. Kendal; C. Somerset; O. King, Bishop of Bath and Wells; R. Guildford; R. Bray[5]	T. Janne; T. Savage; R. Foxe, Bishop of Bath and Wells
14 Hen VII, 1498–9	R. Mayhew; R. Middleton, cleric; R. Sutton; J. Kingsmill, lawyer; T. Savage; R. Fitzjames; T. Janne; R. Nix; Christopher Bainbridge; James Tyrell, knight; E. Martyn; T. Lovell; C. Somerset; R. Hatton	R. Bray; T. Lovell; T. Savage
15 Hen VII, 1499–1500	T. Savage; Richard Fitzjames; T. Janne; R. Nix, Dean of the Chapel Royal; Christopher Bainbridge; R. Sutton; R. Mayhew; Geoffrey Blythe, Dean of York; J. Kendal, Prior of St John's	T. Savage; R. Nix
16 Hen VII, 1500–1	R. Nix; T. Savage; R. Mayhew; John Watts, cleric; R. Fitzjames	
17 Hen VII, 1501–2	George Neville, Lord Bergavenny; Geoffrey Symeon, Dean of the Chapel Royal; R. Mayhew; R. Hatton; Morgan Kidwelly, lawyer; R. Sutton; J. Watts; R. Fitzjames, President of the Council and Bishop of Rochester	G. Symeon, R. Fitzjames; Thomas Hobbes
18 Hen VII, 1502–3	R. Guildford, Comptroller of the Household; G. Symeon; R. Fitzjames; G. Daubeney, Lord Chamberlain; R. Bray; T. Lovell[6]	R. Fitzjames, Bishop of Rochester; J. Mordaunt; R. Nix

[5] These last three are said to have sat for a hearing on 16 April this year: REQ2/5/319.

[6] One petitioner specifically requested a hearing before these last three men in this year: REQ2/2/156.

Appendix

269

(cont.)

Regnal Year	Sitting Judges (listed in REQ1 order books and other sources where specified)	Signatories of Paperwork (appearing in REQ2 and REQ3 pleadings)
19 Hen VII, 1503–4	G. Symeon; M. Kidwelly; G. Neville, Lord Burgavenny; John Sutton (*possibly an error for R. Sutton*)	G. Symeon; R. Mayhew; J. Mordaunt; M. Kidwelly
20 Hen VII, 1504–5	G. Symeon; John Ednam, Almoner; Edward Vaughan, 'doctor in decrees'; R. Sutton	G. Symeon
21 Hen VII, 1505–6	G. Symeon; E. Vaughan; R. Hatton; Robert Drury, knight; R. Sutton, 'ar[miger]'; R. Foxe, Bishop of Winchester; T. Lovell[7]	G. Symeon; J. Ednam
22 Hen VII, 1506–7	G. Symeon; R. Empson; R. Foxe, Bishop of Winchester;[8] R. Hatton; R. Sutton[9]	G. Symeon; J. Ednam; John Oxenbridge, canon of Windsor; William Atwater
23 Hen VII, 1507–8	Thomas Dalby; Marmaduke Constable; Thomas Magnus;[10] G. Symeon; R. Hatton	G. Symeon; T. Savage; J. Ednam
24 Hen VII, 1508–9	W. Atwater, Dean of the Chapel Royal; Thomas Hatton (*possibly an error for R. Hatton*)[11]	W. Atwater; J. Ednam
1 Hen VIII, Apr. 1509–10	W. Atwater; Thomas Wolsey, Almoner	W. Atwater; T. Wolsey (as 'Wulcy'); James Denton, royal chaplain

[7] In addition to their names being recorded in the order books, the pleading of *Bartram* v *Barowe* at King's Bench in 1507 describes a hearing in Requests before Symeon, Sutton, Hatton, and others: TNA KB27/981 m. 104d.

[8] One petition in the Requests casefiles is addressed to Foxe as Bishop of Winchester and Keeper of the Privy Seal: REQ2/5/285.

[9] A later petition refers to a decree made on 15 December 1506 by 'Mr Doctor Symeon dean of yor moost honorabill chapel, Mr Doctor Hatton and Mr Richard Sutton': REQ2/8/114.

[10] These three men signed a memorandum dated 11 February 1508, but do not appear otherwise: REQ1/3 fol. 327.

[11] There is no surviving order book for the period between July 1508 and October 1515. This reference comes instead from the King's Bench plea of *Belton* v *Dregge* in Easter term 1509, which mentions a hearing this year involving the Dean of the Chapel Royal, Thomas Hatton, and other unnamed councillors: KB27/992 m. 37.

270 Appendix

(cont.)

Regnal Year	Sitting Judges (listed in REQ1 order books and other sources where specified)	Signatories of Paperwork (appearing in REQ2 and REQ3 pleadings)
2 Hen VIII, 1510–11		W. Atwater; T. Wolsey; J. Denton
3 Hen VIII, 1511–12		W. Atwater; J. Denton; T. Wolsey; T. Dalby
4 Hen VIII, 1512–13	W. Atwater[12]	W. Atwater; T. Dalby
5 Hen VIII, 1513–14	W. Atwater[13]	
6 Hen VIII, 1514–15	John Veysey, Dean of the Chapel Royal; R. Sutton; Richard Rawlins, Almoner; T. Magnus	W. Atwater; J. Denton; Edward Higgons, clerk; R. Sutton; R. Rawlins; T. Magnus
7 Hen VIII, 1515–16	J. Veysey; R. Rawlins; John Gilbert, 'armiger'; T. Dalby[14]	J. Veysey; T. Magnus
8 Hen VIII, 1516–17	J. Veysey; J. Gilbert; T. Lovell, Treasurer of the Household;[15] T. Dalby[16]	J. Veysey; J. Gilbert; R. Rawlins; John Longland, Dean of Salisbury; E. Higgons
9 Hen VIII, 1517–18	J. Veysey; J. Longland, clerk; R. Rawlins, clerk and Almoner; Roger Lupton, Provost of Eton; J. Gilbert 'learned in [the] lawes'[17]	J. Longland; J. Veysey; J. Gilbert; R. Rawlins

[12] Mentioned as having heard a case this year in REQ2/2/74.

[13] Mentioned as having heard a case this year in REQ2/3/126.

[14] According to REQ3/9 *Cause* v *Abbot*, Veysey and Thomas Dalby, the Archdeacon of Richmond, ordered a commission in this year.

[15] A letter written by Sir Richard Fitzlewe to the court asked Lovell and Veysey for good order in his case this year: REQ2/11/174.

[16] A later petition described a decree from February 1517 as being made by Veysey, Dalby, and Gilbert: REQ3/13 *Stafford* v *Butler*.

[17] These five together were said to have overseen a decree made in June 1517, according to a later bill: REQ3/10 *Barney* v *Sturges and Cause*.

Appendix

271

(cont.)

Regnal Year	Sitting Judges (listed in REQ1 order books and other sources where specified)	Signatories of Paperwork (appearing in REQ2 and REQ3 pleadings)
10 Hen VIII. 1518–19	J. Veysey; J. Gilbert[18]	J. Veysey; J. Gilbert; Thomas More; J. Longland
11 Hen VIII, 1519–20	John Clerk, Dean of the Chapel Royal	J. Veysey; J. Gilbert; T. More; J. Clerk
12 Hen VIII, 1520–1	J. Clerk; R. Rawlins; Roger Lupton, Provost of Eton	J. Clerk; R. Rawlins; John Stokesley; R. Lupton
13 Hen VIII, 1520–1	J. Stokesley (as 'presidentis');[19] R. Rawlins	J. Clerk; R. Rawlins; J. Stokesley
14 Hen VIII, 1522–3	J. Stokesley	J. Stokesley; R. Rawlins; Thomas Englefield; T. More
15 Hen VIII, 1523–4	J. Stokesley; Richard Wolman, lawyer; T. Englefield	J. Stokesley; R. Wolman; T. Englefield
16 Hen VIII, 1524–5	T. Englefield	J. Longland; T. Englefield; T. More
17 Hen VIII, 1525–6	R. Wolman; T. Englefield	R. Wolman; H. Wyatt
18 Hen VIII, 1526–7	R. Wolman	R. Wolman; T. Englefield
19 Hen VIII, 1527–8	R. Wolman	R. Wolman
20 Hen VIII, 1528–9	Thomas Neville *Additionally:* J. Longland, Bishop of Lincoln; John Islip, Abbot of Westminster; Richard Sampson, Dean of the Chapel Royal; Henry Standish, Bishop of St Asaph; R. Wolman; William Weston, Prior of St John's;	R. Wolman; T. Neville; R. Sampson; W. Weston; R. Philipps

---

[18] Several references to hearings undertaken in these years mention only Veysey and Gilbert by name, alongside other unnamed 'comissioners' or councillors: REQ2/10/200, 2/11/196, 2/12/203, 217.

[19] REQ2/11/148.

272 — Appendix

(*cont.*)

Regnal Year	Sitting Judges (listed in REQ1 order books and other sources where specified)	Signatories of Paperwork (appearing in REQ2 and REQ3 pleadings)
	Rowland Philipps, Vicar of Croydon; Sir John Hussey; R. Lupton; Sir William Fitzwilliam; 'Dr Cromer'; Sir Roger Townsend; William Sulyard; (Christopher?) St Jermyne[20]	
21 Hen VIII, 1529–30	T. Neville; W. Fitzwilliam; R. Sampson; T. Neville; W. Sulyard[21]	R. Sampson; T. Neville; W. Fitzwilliam; R. Wolman; W. Sulyard; Roger Lupton
22 Hen VIII, 1530–1	R. Sampson; T. Neville; W. Sulyard	R. Sampson; W. Fitzwilliam; T. Neville; R. Wolman; W. Sulyard; R. Philipps
23 Hen VIII, 1531–2	R. Sampson	R. Sampson; W. Fitzwilliam; W. Sulyard; T. Neville; R. Wolman
24 Hen VIII, 1532–3	R. Sampson; R. Wolman	R. Sampson; W. Fitzwilliam; R. Wolman; W. Sulyard
25 Hen VIII, 1533–4	W. Sulyard; R. Wolman, Dean of Wells.	R. Wolman; W. Sulyard; R. Sampson
26 Hen VIII, 1534–5	R. Wolman; W. Sulyard	R. Wolman; W. Sulyard
27 Hen VIII, 1535–6	R. Wolman; W. Sulyard	R. Wolman; W. Sulyard
28 Hen VIII, 1536–7	R. Wolman; W. Sulyard	R. Wolman; W. Sulyard

[20] REQ1/5 fol. 43v.
[21] These last three were said to have passed a decree dated 28 November 1529: REQ3/27 *West* v *Smith*.

Appendix 273

(*cont.*)

Regnal Year	Sitting Judges (listed in REQ1 order books and other sources where specified)	Signatories of Paperwork (appearing in REQ2 and REQ3 pleadings)
29 Hen VIII, 1537–8	R. Sampson, Bishop of Chichester; Nicholas Hare; Thomas Thirlby; Edmund Bonner; Edward Carne[22]	W. Sulyard; R. Wolman; E. Carne; N. Hare; T. Thirlby; E. Bonner
30 Hen VIII, 1538–9	N. Hare; T. Thirlby	N. Hare; E. Carne; E. Bonner; R. Sampson; W. Sulyard; R. Wolman; T. Thirlby; John Tregonwell; Robert Bowes
31 Hen VIII, 1539–40	T. Thirlby; N. Hare, Master of Requests; R. Sampson; Nicholas Heath, Bishop of Rochester	T. Thirlby; E. Carne; N. Hare; W. Sulyard; R. Sampson; J. Tregonwell
32 Hen VIII, 1540–1	T. Thirlby, Bishop of Westminster; Robert Southwell, Master of Requests; William Petre;[23] N. Heath	T. Thirlby; N. Hare; E. Carne; R. Sampson; J. Tregonwell; R. Southwell; W. Petre; R. Townsend
33 Hen VIII, 1541–2	Robert Dacres, Master of Requests;[24] T. Thirlby; R. Southwell; J. Tregonwell[25]	R. Dacres; J. Tregonwell; R. Southwell; T. Thirlby; R. Sampson;

[22] Along with Neville, all of these men are named in the list of 'Comissioners appointed to sit in the court of Requests' in January 1538: Caesar, *The Ancient State*, 91.

[23] One petition mentions a decree made on 11 February 32 Hen VIII and signed by the Bishop of Westminster, Robert Southwell, and William Petre: REQ2/11/109.

[24] A note written to Richard Turnor, Requests' clerk, in this year mentions hearings taken in Dacres' own chamber: REQ2/4/88.

[25] Caesar describes 'A decree all in latine by Thomas, Bishop of Westminster, Robert Southwell, knight, and John Tregonwell, esquire, all three the kings Counsellors in his court of White-Hall', dated to 10 February 1542: *The Ancient State*, 96.

Appendix

(*cont.*)

Regnal Year	Sitting Judges (listed in REQ1 order books and other sources where specified)	Signatories of Paperwork (appearing in REQ2 and REQ3 pleadings)
		N. Hare; W. Petre; E. Carne; N. Heath, Bishop of Rochester
34 Hen VIII, 1542–3	T. Thirlby; R. Southwell; J. Tregonwell; W. Petre; R. Dacres	R. Southwell; J. Tregonwell; R. Dacres; T. Thirlby; W. Petre; N. Hare; N. Heath; C. Tunstall, Bishop of Durham
35 Hen VIII, 1543–4	R. Bowes; T. Thirlby; W. Petre	R. Dacres; J. Tregonwell; T. Thirlby; R. Bowes; N. Heath; W. Petre; E. Carne
36 Hen VIII, 1544–5	T. Thirlby; R. Bowes	R. Bowes; E. Carne; N. Hare; N. Heath, Bishop of Worcester; T. Thirlby
37 Hen VIII, 1545–6	N. Hare	N. Heath; E. Carne; N. Hare; T. Thirlby
38 Hen VIII, 1546–7	N. Heath; N. Hare; J. Tregonwell; William Mey	N. Hare; N. Heath; R. Southwell; W. Mey; John Lucas

Bibliography

Manuscript Sources

Alnwick Castle, Northumberland

MS 475   Precedent book of Robert Catlyn.

Balliol College, Oxford

MS 354   Commonplace book of Richard Hill, *c.* 1503–36.

Birmingham Archives and Collections, Birmingham

MS 3279/11/931   Copy of a commission in dispute between Lord Ormond and Sir Henry Willoughby and others, *c.* 1494.

MS 3279/11/933   Copy of award made by arbitrators in dispute between Lord Ormond and Sir Henry Willoughby and others, *c.* 1495.

Bodleian Library, Oxford

Latin Misc c. 66   Commonplace book of Humphrey Newton.

Tanner MS 407   Commonplace book of Robert Reynes.

Brasenose College, Oxford

UB/S I. 27   John Duns Scotus, *Super III^{or} Sententiarum* (Venice, 1477), once owned by John Longland and used by William Atwater.

The British Library, London

Additional MS 7099   Extract from royal book of payments, 1492–1509.

Additional MS 21480   Royal household chamber book, 1499–1505.

276   *Bibliography*

Additional MS 25248   Collections relating to the Court of Requests.
Additional MS 48025   Star Chamber papers.
Additional MS 59899   Royal household chamber book, 1502–5.
Harley MS 1088   Heraldic manuscript, containing 'A list of the
                           commissioners' in the Council of the North.
Harley MS 2252   Commonplace book of John Colyns, *c.* 1520s–30s.
Lansdowne MS 1   Papers of William Cecil, Lord Burghley.
Lansdowne MS 125   Julius Caesar's copy of his *The Ancient State* with
                           manuscript additions.
Lansdowne MS 160   Papers relating to the Privy Council, Admiralty,
                           and Star Chamber.
Lansdowne MS 639   Transcriptions from Star Chamber registers.
Lansdowne MS 762   Tudor commonplace book, *c.* 1509–64.

Dorset History Centre, Dorchester

DC-CC/C/1/3   Account of receipts and payments of Thomas Westbury,
                   rent-collector, 1499–1507.

Durham Cathedral Archive, Durham

Registrum Parvum IV   Durham Priory, prior's register, 1484–1519.

Herefordshire Archives and Record Centre, Hereford

BG 11/29   Council of the Marches, letters and petitions, 1512–97.

Hereford Cathedral Archive, Hereford

MS 2971   Record of pleas made at Nottingham between the dean and
               chapter of Hereford and the mayor and citizens of Hereford, *c.*
               1505–6.

The Huntington Library, San Marino, CA

Ellesmere MS 2652   Digest of Henrician Council *Acta*.
Ellesmere MS 2654   Henrician Council *Acta* transcripts.
Ellesmere MS 2655   Henrician Council *Acta* transcripts.
Ellesmere MS 2916   Ordinances touching the Court of Westminster,
                         1597.

Bibliography

277

Lincoln's Inn Archive, London

Maynard MS 66	Reports in King's Bench and Common Pleas, 26 Eliz.–14 Jac.

London Metropolitan Archives, London

COL/AD/01	London Letter Books.
COL/CA/01	Repertories, London Court of Aldermen.
DL/C/0001	Instance Act book, London Consistory Court, 1496–1505.

The National Archives, Kew

C1	Chancery: early proceedings.
C33	Chancery: entry books of decrees and orders.
C49/42/2	List of bills, public and private, 1495 parliament.
C66	Chancery: patent rolls.
C78	Chancery: decree rolls.
C79	Chancery: supplementary decree rolls.
C82	Chancery: warrants for the great seal.
CP40	Common Pleas: plea rolls.
DL5	Court of Duchy Chamber: entry books of decrees and orders.
E30	Exchequer Treasury of Receipt: diplomatic documents.
E36	Exchequer: miscellaneous books.
E101/414/6	Chamber account book, 1495–9.
E101/414/16	Chamber account book, 1497–1500.
E101/415/3	Chamber account book, 1499–1503.
E159	Exchequer: memoranda rolls.
E163/29/11	Litigation narrative of Nicholas and Robert Catesby, c. 1490s.
KB9	King's Bench: indictment files.
KB27	King's Bench: plea rolls.
PROB11	Prerogative Court of Canterbury will registers.
PSO2/4	Warrants for the Privy Seal, 1509–40.
REQ1	Court of Requests: order and decree books.
REQ2	Court of Requests: pleadings.
REQ3	Court of Requests: miscellanea.
SC2/175/59	Manorial rolls of Hawkesbury and others, Gloucestershire, 1528–9.
SC8	Ancient Petitions.
SP1	State Papers, Henry VIII.

278 *Bibliography*

SP4   Register of signatures by stamp, 1545–7.
SP6/13   Fols. 2–10: Cuthbert Tunstal's Oration to Parliament, 1523.
SP12/110   Fols. 34–44: Alexander Fisher, 'A Description of the Cortes of Justice in England' (1576).
SP49/2   Fol. 17: Surrey to Wolsey regarding justice in the North.
STAC1   Court of Star Chamber: proceedings, Henry VII.
STAC2   Court of Star Chamber: proceedings, Henry VIII.
STAC10/4/123   Star Chamber minute book, 1520s.

North Yorkshire Record Office, Northallerton

ZDV X 1   The Narrative of Robert Pilkington.

Parliamentary Archives, London

HL/PO/PU/1   House of Lords, original Acts.

Staffordshire Record Office, Stafford

D938/219   Indenture of award between George Ashby and Thomas Robins, 1503.

Trinity College, Cambridge

MS O.2.53   Commonplace book of the Ramston family of Essex.

Published Primary Sources

Arnold, Richard, *The customs of London, otherwise called Arnold's Chronicle*, ed. Francis Douce (1811).

Attreed, Lorraine C. ed., *The York House Books, 1461–1490* (2 vols., Alan Sutton, 1991).

Baker, J. H. ed., *Reports of Cases by John Caryll* (2 vols., Selden Society 116 and 117, Selden Society, 1998–9).

    Selected Readings and Commentaries on Magna Carta 1400–1604, Selden Society 132 (Selden Society, 2015).

Barclay, Alexander, *The Ship of Fools*, ed. T. H. Jamieson (London, 1874).

Baron, Stephen, *De Regimine Principum (1509)*, ed. P. J. Mroczkowski (Peter Lang Publishing, 1990).

Bayne, C. G. and William Huse Dunham eds., *Select Cases in the Council of Henry VII*, Selden Society 75 (Bernard Quaritch, 1958).

Benham, W. Gurney ed., *The Red Paper Book of Colchester* (Colchester, 1902).

Bibliography

Bohun, William, *Privilegia Londini: or, the laws, customs, and priviledges of the city of London* (London, 1702).

Brewer, J. S., J. Gairdner, and R. H. Brodie eds., *Letters and Papers, Foreign and Domestic, of the Reign of Henry VIII* (21 vols., London, 1862–1932).

Brinklow, Henry, *Complaynt of Roderyk Mors, and the Lamentacyon of a Christen Agaynst the Cyte of London, made by Roderigo Mors*, ed. J. Meadows Cowper, Early English Text Society Extra Series 22 (Trübner & Co., 1874).

Brown, William and H. B. McCall eds., *Yorkshire Star Chamber Proceedings*, The Yorkshire Archaeological Society XLI, XLV, LI (3 vols., J. Whitehead and Son, 1908–14).

Caesar, Sir Julius, *The Ancient State, Authoritie, and Proceedings of the Court of Requests* (London, 1597).

Calendar of the Patent Rolls Preserved in the Public Record Office, 1216–1509 (54 vols., Public Record Office, 1891–1916).

Caley, J. and J. Bayley eds., *Calendar of Proceedings in Chancery in the Reign of Queen Elizabeth; to which are prefixed examples of earlier proceedings in that court* (3 vols., 1827–32).

Campbell, William ed., *Materials for a History of the Reign of Henry VII, from original documents preserved in the Public Record Office*, Rolls Series 60 (2 vols., Cambridge University Press, 1873–7).

Carlson, David R., 'The Latin Writings of John Skelton', *Studies in Philology* 88:4 (1991), 1–125.

Cavell, Emma ed., *The Heralds' Memoir, 1486–1490: Court Ceremony, Royal Progress and Rebellion* (Shaun Tyas, 2009).

Cavendish, George, *The Life and Death of Cardinal Wolsey* (Houghton Mifflin and Company, 1995).

Collier, J. Payne ed., *Trevelyan Papers to A.D. 1558*, Camden Fifth Series 67 (Camden Society, 1857).

Dasent, John Roche, E. G. Atkinson, J. V. Lyle, R. F. Monger, and P. A. Penfold eds., *Acts of the Privy Council of England* (46 vols., HMSO, 1890–1964).

Dormer Harris, Mary ed., *The Coventry Leet Book, or Mayor's Register, containing the records of the city Court Leet or View of Frankpledge, A.D. 1420–1555*, Early English Text Society Original Series 134–5, 138, 146 (4 vols., Trübner & Co., 1907–13).

Dudley, Edmund, *The Tree of Commonwealth*, ed. D. M. Brodie (Cambridge University Press, 1948).

Dugdale, William, *Monasticon Anglicanum* (6 vols., London, 1846).

Dyce, Alexander ed., *The Poetical Works of John Skelton* (2 vols., Little, Brown and Company, 1970).

Edwards, Rhoda, *The Itinerary of King Richard III 1483–1485* (Alan Sutton, 1995).

Elyot, Thomas, *The Book Named the Governor*, ed. S. E. Lehmberg (J. M. Dent & Sons, 1962).

Erasmus, Desiderius, *Praise of Folly*, trans. and ed. Betty Radice (Penguin, 1971).

Farmer, John Stephen ed., *Six Anonymous Plays (Second Series)* (Early English Drama Society, 1906).

Bibliography

Fitzherbert, John, *Here begynneth a ryght frutefull mater: and hath to name the boke of surueyeng and improumentes* (London, 1523).

Fortescue, Sir John, *On the Laws and Governance of England*, ed. Shelley Lockwood (Cambridge University Press, 1997).

Gairdner, James ed., *The Paston Letters A.D. 1422–1509* (6 vols., Cambridge University Press, 1904).

Three Fifteenth-Century Chronicles with Historical Memoranda by John Stowe, Camden New Series *28* (Camden Society, 1880).

Giustinian, Sebastian, *Four Years at the Court of Henry VIII*, trans. Rawdon Brown (2 vols., Smith, Elder & Co., 1854).

Given-Wilson, Chris, Paul Brand, Seymour Phillips, Mark Ormrod, Geoffrey Martin, Anne Currey, and Rosemary Horrox eds., *The Parliament Rolls of Medieval England* (16 vols., Boydell, 2005).

Hall, Edward, *Hall's Chronicle: Containing the History of England, During the Reign of Henry the Fourth and the Succeeding Monarchs to the End of the Reign of Henry the Eighth* (London, 1809).

Halliwell, J. O. ed., *A Chronicle of the first thirteen years of the reign of King Edward the Fourth, by John Warkworth* (Nicholas and Son, 1839).

Hargrave, Francis ed., *Collectanea Juridica: consisting of tracts relative to the law and constitution of England* (2 vols., London, 1791–2).

Hemmant, M. ed., *Select Cases in the Exchequer Chamber 1377–1461*, Selden Society 51 (Selden Society, 1933).

Horrox, Rosemary and P. W. Hammond eds., *British Library Harleian Manuscript 433* (4 vols., Alan Sutton, 1979).

Hoyle, R. W., D. Tankard, and S. R. Neal eds., *Heard before the King: Registers of Petitions to James I, 1603–1616*, List and Index Society Special Series 38–9 (2 vols., List and Index Society, 2006).

Hughes, Paul L. and James F. Larkin eds., *Tudor Royal Proclamations* (3 vols., Yale University Press, 1964–9).

Hutton, William, *Courts of requests: their nature, utility, and powers described, with a variety of cases, determined in that of Birmingham* (Birmingham, 1787).

Jourdan, A. J. L., J. Decrusy, and Francois André Isambert eds., *Recueil general des anciennes lois françaises depuis l'an 420 jusqu'à la révolution de 1789* (Paris, 1824), 224–5.

Journals of the House of Commons, 1547–1699 (12 vols., HMSO, 1802–3).

Journals of the House of Lords, 1509–1793 (39 vols., HMSO, 1767–1830).

Kail, J., *Twenty-Six Political and Other Poems (including 'Petty Job') from the Oxford mss. Digby 102 and Douce 322*, Early English Text Society Original Series 124 (Trübner & Co., 1904).

Kekewich, Margaret Lucille, Colin Richmond, Anne F. Sutton, Livia Visser-Fuchs, and John L. Watts eds., *The Politics of Fifteenth Century England: John Vale's Book* (Alan Sutton, 1995).

Kesselring, K. J. ed., *Star Chamber Reports: BL Harley MS 2143*, List and Index Society Special Series 57 (List and Index Society, 2018).

Bibliography

Lambarde, William, *Archeion or, a Discourse upon the High Courts of Justice in England* (London, 1635).

Leadam, I. S. ed., *The Domesday of Inclosures 1517–1518, being the extant returns to Chancery for Berks, Bucks, Cheshire, Essex, Leicestershire, Lincolnshire, Northants, Oxon, and Warwickshire by the Commissioners of Inclosures in 1517 and for Bedfordshire in 1518. Together with Dugdale's MS Notes of the Warwickshire Inquisitions in 1517, 1518, and 1549* (2 vols., Longmans, 1897).

Select Cases before the King's Council in the Star Chamber, commonly called the Court of Star Chamber, A.D. 1477–1509, Selden Society 16 (Spottiswoode and Co., 1903).

Select Cases in the Court of Requests, A.D. 1496–1569, Selden Society 12 (Bernard Quaritch, 1898).

Legg, L. G. Wickham, *English Coronation Records* (A. Constable & Co. Ltd., 1901).

Louis, Cameron ed., *The Commonplace Book of Robert Reynes of Acle: An Edition of Tanner MS 407* (Garland Publishing, 1980).

Luders, A., T. E. Tomlins, John France, W. E. Taunton, and John Raithby eds., *The Statutes of the Realm* (London, 11 vols., 1810–28).

Lyndwood, William, *Provinciale seu constitutiones Angliae* (Oxford, 1679).

Macray, William Dunn ed., *A Register of the Members of St. Mary Magdalen College, Oxford, From the Foundation of the College* (8 vols., Oxford University Press, 1894–1915).

Mitchell, W. T. ed., *Registrum Cancellarii 1498–1506*, Oxford Historical Society New Series XXVII (Clarendon Press, 1980).

More, Thomas, *Latin Poems*, eds. Clarence H. Miller, Leicester Bradner, Charles A. Lynch, and Revilo P. Oliver, *Complete Works of St Thomas More* vol. 3, pt. II (Yale University Press, 1984).

Utopia, ed. George M. Logan (3rd edn., Cambridge University Press, 2016).

Nicolas, Sir Nicholas Harris ed., *The Privy Purse Expenses of King Henry VIII from November 1529 to December 1532* (William Pickering, 1827).

Proceedings and Ordinances of the Privy Council of England (7 vols., Eyre & Spottiswoode, 1834–7).

Nichols, John ed., *A collection of ordinances and regulations for the government of the royal household* (London, 1790).

Pollard, A. F. ed., *The Reign of Henry VII from Contemporary Sources* (3 vols., AMS Press, 1967).

Raine, Angelo ed., *York Civic Records* (9 vols., Yorkshire Archaeological Society, 1939–78).

Ralph, Elizabeth ed., *The Great White Book of Bristol*, Bristol Record Society XXXII (Bristol Record Society, 1979).

Ridley, Sir Thomas, *A View of the civile and ecclesiastical law and wherein the practise of them is streitned, and may be relieved within this land* (London, 1607).

Robbins, Rossell Hope, *Historical Poems of the XIVth and XVth Centuries* (Columbia University Press, 1959).

282 *Bibliography*

Robinson, Richard, 'A Briefe Collection of the Queenes Most High and Most Honourable Courtes of Recordes', ed. R. L. Rickard, *Camden Miscellany 20*, Camden Third Series 83 (Royal Historical Society, 1953).

Rymer, Thomas ed., *Foedera* (London, 20 vols., 1704–35).

Salter, H. E. ed., *Records of Medieval Oxford* (Oxford Chronicle Company, 1912).

Registrum Annalium Collegii Mertonensis, Oxford Historical Society LXXVI (Clarendon Press, 1923).

Sanders, George Williams ed., *Orders of the High Court of Chancery and Statutes of the Realm relating to Chancery* (2 vols., A. Maxwell & Son, 1845).

Shaw, M. R. B. trans., *Joinville and Villehardouin: Chronicles of the Crusades* (Penguin, 1974).

Sheppard, J. B. ed., *Christ Church Letters: a volume of medieval letters relating to the affairs of the Priory of Christ Church Canterbury*, Camden New Series 19 (Camden Society, 1877).

Smith, L. T. ed., *A Commonplace Book of the Fifteenth Century* (Trübner and Co., 1886).

St German, Christopher, *Doctor and Student*, eds. T. F. T. Plucknett and J. L. Barton, Selden Society 91 (Selden Society, 1974).

Stapleton, Thomas ed., *Plumpton Correspondence: A Series of Letters, Chiefly Domestick, written in the reigns of Edward IV. Richard III. Henry VII. and Henry VIII.*, Camden Old Series 4 (Camden Society, 1839).

Starkey, Thomas, *A Dialogue Between Reginald Pole & Thomas Lupset*, ed. Kathleen M. Burton (Chatto & Windus, 1948).

State Papers, published under the authority of His Majesty's Commission: King Henry the Eighth (11 vols., His Majesty's Commission for State Papers, 1830–52).

Stephenson, C. and F. G. Marcham eds., *Sources of English Constitutional History* (2 vols., Harper Brothers, 1937–8).

Stow, John, *A Survay of London Contayning the originall, antiquity, increase, moderne estate, and description of that citie, written in the yeare 1598* (London, 1598).

Thomas, A. H. and I. D. Thornley eds., *The Great Chronicle of London* (London, 1938).

Tidd Pratt, John, *An Abstract of all the printed Acts of Parliament for the establishment of Courts of Requests in England and Wales with the cases decided thereon* (London, 1824).

Valor Ecclesiasticus Temp. Henr. VIII Auctoritate Regia Institutus (6 vols., London, 1810–34).

Vergil, Polydore, *The Anglica Historia of Polydore Vergil, A.D. 1485–1537*, ed. Denys Hay, Camden Third Series 74 (Royal Historical Society, 1950).

Bibliography

Secondary Sources

Almbjär, M., 'The Problem with Early-Modern Petitions: Safety Valve or Powder Keg?', *European Review of History* 26:6 (2019), 1013–39.

Ashdowne R. K., D. R. Howlett, and R. E. Latham eds., *Dictionary of Medieval Latin from British Sources* (3 vols., The British Academy, 2018).

Bailey, J., 'Voices in Court: Lawyers' or Litigants'?', *Historical Research* 74:186 (2001), 392–408.

Baker, J. H., *John Spelman's Reading on Quo Warranto, Delivered in Gray's Inn (Lent 1519)*, Selden Society 113 (Selden Society, 1997).

'Migrations of Manuscripts', *Journal of Legal History* 9:2 (1988), 254–6.

The Men of Court 1440 to 1550: A Prosopography of the Inns of Court and Chancery and the Courts of Law, Selden Society Supplementary Series 18 (Selden Society, 2012).

The Oxford History of the Laws of England: Volume VI 1483–1558 (Oxford University Press, 2003).

The Reinvention of Magna Carta 1216–1616 (Cambridge University Press, 2017).

The Reports of Sir John Spelman, Selden Society 93–4 (2 vols., Selden Society, 1976–7).

Baldwin, J. F., *The King's Council in England during the Middle Ages* (Clarendon Press, 1913).

Barr, H., *The Digby Poems: A New Edition of the Lyrics* (Liverpool University Press, 2009).

Beattie, C., 'A Piece of the Puzzle: Women and the Law as Viewed from the Late Medieval Court of Chancery', *JBS* 58 (2019), 751–67.

'Your Oratrice: Women's Petitions to the Late Medieval Court of Chancery', in B. Kane and F. Williamson eds., *Women, Agency and the Law, 1300–1700* (Routledge, 2013), 17–29.

Bernard, G. W., *Who Ruled Tudor England: An Essay in the Paradoxes of Power* (Bloomsbury, 2021).

Birch, D., 'Legal Pluralism in Early Modern England and Colonial Virginia', *Revista Estudos Institucionais* 5:2 (2019), 717–46.

Bowie, K. and T. Munck, 'Early Modern Political Petitioning and Public Engagement in Scotland, Britain and Scandinavia, c.1550-1795', *Parliaments, Estates and Representation* 38:3 (2018), 271–8.

Bowker, M., *The Henrician Reformation: The Diocese of Lincoln under John Longland, 1521–1547* (Cambridge University Press, 1981).

The Secular Clergy in the Diocese of Lincoln, 1495–1520 (Cambridge University Press, 1968).

Braddick, M. J., *State Formation in Early Modern England, c.1550–1700* (Cambridge University Press, 2000).

Braddick, M. J. and J. Walter eds., *Negotiating Power in Early Modern Society: Order, Hierarchy and Subordination in Britain and Ireland* (Cambridge University Press, 2001).

284 *Bibliography*

Briggs, C., 'Seigniorial Control of Villagers' Litigation beyond the Manor in Later Medieval England', *Historical Research* 81:213 (2008), 399–422.

Brogan, S., *The Royal Touch in Early Modern England: Politics, Medicine and Sin* (Boydell Press, 2015).

Brooks, C. W., *Law, Politics and Society in Early Modern England* (Cambridge University Press, 2009).

Lawyers, Litigation and English Society Since 1450 (Hambledon Press, 1998).

Pettyfoggers and Vipers of the Commonwealth: The 'Lower Branch' of the Legal Profession in Early Modern England (Cambridge University Press, 1986).

Brooks, F. W., *The Council of the North* (Historical Association, 1966).

Bryson, W. H., 'The Court of Exchequer Comes of Age', in D. J. Guth and J. W. McKenna eds., *Tudor Rule and Revolution: Essays for G.R. Elton* (Cambridge University Press, 1982), 149–58.

Bush, M. L., *The Pilgrims' Complaint: A Study of Popular Thought in the Early Tudor North* (Routledge, 2009).

'Protector Somerset and Requests', *The Historical Journal* 17:3 (1974), 451–64.

Cavill, P. R., *The English Parliaments of Henry VII 1485–1504* (Oxford University Press, 2009).

'The First Readers of Lyndwood's *Provinciale*', *Ecclesiastical Law Journal* 24:1 (2021), 2–13.

'A Lollard of Coventry: A Source on Robert Silkby', *Midland History* 38:2 (2013), 226–31.

'Perjury in Early Tudor England', in R. McKitterick, C. Methuen, and A. Spicer eds., *The Church and the Law*, Studies in Church History 56 (Cambridge University Press, 2020), 189–209.

Chrimes, S. B., *English Constitutional Ideas in the Fifteenth Century* (Cambridge University Press, 1936).

Henry VII (Eyre Methuen, 1972).

Coleman, J., *English Literature in History, 1350–1400: Medieval Readers and Writers* (Hutchinson, 1981).

Condon, M. M., 'An Anachronism with Intent? Henry VII's Council Ordinance of 1491/2', in R. A. Griffiths and J. Sherborne eds., *Kings and Nobles in the Later Middle Ages: A Tribute to Charles Ross* (Alan Sutton, 1986), 228–53.

'Ruling Elites in the Reign of Henry VII', in C. Ross ed., *Patronage, Pedigree and Power in Late Medieval England* (Alan Sutton, 1979), 109–42.

Cooper, J. P., 'Henry VII's Last Years Reconsidered', *The Historical Journal* 2:2 (1959), 103–29.

Cooper, J. P. D., *Propaganda and the Tudor State: Political Culture in the Westcountry* (Oxford University Press, 2003).

Cornwall, J. C. K., *Wealth and Society in Early Sixteenth Century England* (Routledge & Kegan Paul, 1988).

Dabhoiwala, F., 'Writing Petitions in Early Modern England', in M. J. Braddick and J. Innes eds., *Suffering and Happiness in England, 1500–1850: Narratives and Representations* (Oxford Scholarship, 2017), 127–48.

Bibliography

Dodd, G., *Justice and Grace: Private Petitioning and the English Parliament in the Late Middle Ages* (Oxford University Press, 2007).

'The Rise of English, the Decline of French: Supplications to the English Crown, c.1420–1450', *Speculum* 86 (2011), 117–50.

'Thomas Paunfield, the "heye Court of rightwisnesse" and the Language of Petitioning in the Fifteenth Century', in W. M. Ormrod, G. Dodd, and A. Musson eds., *Medieval Petitions: Grace and Grievance* (York Medieval Press, 2009), 222–42.

'Writing Wrongs: The Drafting of Supplications to the Crown in Later Fourteenth-Century England', *Medium Aevum* 80:2 (2011), 217–46.

Dodd, G. and A. K. McHardy eds., *Petitions from Lincolnshire c.1200–c.1500* (Lincoln Record Society, 2020).

Doe, N., *Fundamental Authority in Late Medieval English Law* (Cambridge University Press, 1990).

Dormer Harris, M., 'Laurence Saunders, Citizen of Coventry', *EHR* 9:36 (1894), 633–51.

Duffy, E., *The Voices of Morebath: Reformation and Rebellion in an English Village* (Yale University Press, 2001).

Dunham, W. H., 'The Ellesmere Extracts from the "Act Consilii" of King Henry VIII', *EHR* 58:231 (1943), 301–18.

Dyer, C., *Standards of Living in the Later Middle Ages: Social Change in England c.1200–1520* (Cambridge University Press, 1989).

Ellis, S., *Reform and Revival: English Government in Ireland 1470–1534* (The Boydell Press, 1986).

Elton, G. R., *Policy and Police: The Enforcement of the Reformation in the Age of Thomas Cromwell* (Cambridge University Press, 1972).

'The Problems and Significance of Administrative History in the Tudor Period', in G. R. Elton ed., *Studies in Tudor and Stuart Politics and Government: Papers and Reviews 1946–1972 I: Tudor Politics/Tudor Government* (Cambridge University Press, 1974), 249–59.

Reform and Reformation: England 1509–1558 (Edward Arnold, 1979).

'Review: *The Foundations of Political Economy: Some Early Tudor Views on State and Society* by Neal Wood', *EHR* 111:444 (1996), 1265–6.

The Tudor Constitution: Documents and Commentary (Cambridge University Press, 1968).

'Tudor Government: The Points of Contact', in G. R. Elton ed., *Studies in Tudor and Stuart Politics and Government III: Papers and Reviews 1973–1981* (Cambridge University Press, 1983), 3–57.

The Tudor Revolution in Government: Administrative Change in the Reign of Henry VIII (Cambridge University Press, 1953).

'Why the History of the Early Tudor Council Remains Unwritten', in G. R. Elton ed., *Studies in Tudor and Stuart Politics and Government: Papers and Reviews 1946–1972 I: Tudor Politics/Tudor Government* (Cambridge University Press, 1974), 308–38.

Bibliography

Emden, A. B., *A Biographical Register of the University of Cambridge to 1500* (Cambridge University Press, 1963).

A Biographical Register of the University of Oxford to A.D. 1500 (3 vols., Clarendon Press, 1957–9).

Everett, M., *The Rise of Thomas Cromwell: Power and Politics in the Reign of Henry VIII, 1485–1534* (Yale University Press, 2015).

Flannigan, L., '"Allowable or Not?" John Stokesley, the Court of Requests and Royal Justice in Sixteenth-Century England', *Historical Research* 93:262 (2020), 621–37.

'Conscience and the King's Household Clergy in the Early Tudor Court of Requests', in R. McKitterick, C. Methuen, and A. Spicer eds., *The Church and the Law*, Studies in Church History 56 (2020), 210–26.

'Litigants in the English "Court of Poor Men's Causes", or Court of Requests, 1515–25', *Law and History Review* 38:2 (2020), 303–37.

'New Evidence of Justice-Giving by the Early Tudor Council of the North, 1540–43', *Northern History* 49:2 (2022), 281–92.

'Signed, Stamped, and Sealed: Delivering Royal Justice in Early Sixteenth-Century England', *Historical Research* 94:264 (2021), 267–81.

Fletcher, A. and D. MacCulloch eds., *Tudor Rebellions* (5th ed., Routledge, 2014).

Ford, L. L., 'Conciliar Politics and Administration in the Reign of Henry VII' (unpublished PhD thesis, University of St Andrews, 2001).

Fox, A., *Politics and Literature in the Reigns of Henry VII and Henry VIII* (Basil Blackwell, 1989).

Gairdner, J. ed., *History of the Life and Reign of Richard the Third* (Cambridge University Press, 1898).

Letters and Papers Illustrative of the Reigns of Richard III and Henry VII (Longman and Green, 1861).

Garrett-Goodyear, H., 'Common Law and Manor Courts: Lords, Copyholders and Doing Justice in Early Tudor England', in J. Whittle ed., *Landlords and Tenants in Britain, 1440–1660: Tawney's 'Agrarian Problem' Revisited* (Boydell & Brewer, 2013), 35–51.

Godfrey, A. M. and C. H. Van Rhees eds., *Central Courts in Early Modern Europe and the Americas* (Duncker & Humblot, 2020).

Gosling, D., 'The Records of the Court of Star Chamber at The National Archives and Elsewhere', in K. J. Kesselring and N. Mears eds., *Star Chamber Matters: An Early Modern Court and its Records* (University of London Press, 2021), 19–40.

Gray, C. M., 'The Boundaries of the Equitable Function', *The American Journal of Legal History* 20:3 (1976), 192–226.

Griffiths, P., A. Fox, and S. Hindle eds., *The Experience of Authority in Early Modern England* (Macmillan, 1996).

Gunn, S. J., *Early Tudor Government 1485–1558* (Macmillan, 1995).

'Henry VII in Context: Problems and Possibilities', *History* 92:3 (2007), 301–17.

Henry VII's New Men and the Making of Tudor England (Oxford University Press, 2016).

Bibliography

287

Guth, D. J., 'Enforcing Late-Medieval Law: Patterns in Litigation during Henry VII's Reign', in J. H. Baker ed., *Legal Records and the Historian: Papers Presented to the Cambridge Legal History Conference, 7–10 July 1975* (Royal Historical Society, 1978), 80–96.

Guy, J., *The Cardinal's Court: The Impact of Thomas Wolsey in Star Chamber* (Harvester Press, 1977).

Christopher St German on Chancery and Statute, Selden Society Supplementary Series 6 (Selden Society, 1985).

The Court of Star Chamber and its Records to the Reign of Elizabeth I (HMSO, 1985).

'Law, Equity and Conscience in Henrician Juristic Thought', in A. Fox and J. Guy eds., *Reassessing the Henrician Age: Humanism, Politics, and Reform* (Blackwell, 1986), 179–98.

'The Privy Council: Revolution or Evolution?', in C. Coleman and D. Starkey eds., *Revolution Reassessed: Revisions in the History of Tudor Government and Administration* (Clarendon Press, 1986), 59–86.

'Wolsey and the Parliament of 1523', in C. Cross, D. Loades, and J. J. Scarisbrick eds., *Law and Government under the Tudors: Essays Presented to Sir Geoffrey Elton* (Cambridge University Press, 1988), 1–18.

'Wolsey, the Council, and the Council Courts', *EHR* 91:360 (1976), 481–505.

'Wolsey's Star Chamber: A Study in Archival Reconstruction', *Journal of the Society of Archivists* 5 (1975), 169–80.

Gwyn, P., *The King's Cardinal: The Rise and Fall of Thomas Wolsey* (Barrie and Jenkins, 1990).

Harrison, C. J., 'Manor Courts and the Governance of Tudor England', in C. Brooks and M. Lobban eds., *Communities and Courts in Britain 1150–1900* (Hambledon Press, 1997), 43–60.

'The Petition of Edmund Dudley', *EHR* 87 (1972), 82–99.

Harriss, G., 'Political Society and the Growth of Government in Late Medieval England', *P&P* 138 (1993), 8–39.

Harvey, I. M. W., 'Was There Popular Politics in Fifteenth-Century England?', in R. H. Britnell and A. J. Pollard eds., *The McFarlane Legacy: Studies in Late Medieval Politics and Society* (Alan Sutton, 1995), 155–74.

Haskett, T. S., 'Country Lawyers? The Composers of English Chancery Bills', in P. Birks ed., *The Law of the Land: Proceedings of the Tenth British Legal History Conference, University of Oxford, 1991* (Hambledon Press, 1993), 9–23.

'The Medieval English Court of Chancery', *Law and History Review* 14:2 (1996), 245–313.

'The Presentation of Cases in Medieval Chancery Bills', in W. M. Gordon and T. D. Fergus eds., *Legal History in the Making: Proceedings of the Ninth British Legal History Conference* (Hambledon Press, 1991), 11–28.

Hayward, M., *Rich Apparel: Clothing and the Law in Henry VIII's England* (Ashgate, 2009).

Healey, J., 'The Fray on the Meadow: Violence and a Moment of Government in Early Tudor England', *History Workshop Journal* 85 (2018), 5–25.

288 *Bibliography*

Helmholz, R. H., *Canon Law and the Law of England* (Hambledon, 1987).

The Ius Commune in England: Four Studies (Oxford University Press, 2001).

'The Privilege and *Ius Commune*: The Middle Ages to the Seventeenth Century', in R. H. Helmholz, C. M. Gray, J. H. Langbein, E. Moglen, and H. E. Smith eds., *The Privilege Against Self-Incrimination: Its Origins and Development* (University of Chicago Press, 1997), 17–46.

The Profession of the Ecclesiastical Lawyers: An Historical Introduction (Cambridge University Press, 2019).

Hicks, M. A., 'Attainder, Resumption and Coercion 1461–1529', *Parliamentary History* 3 (1984), 15–31.

'King in Lords and Commons: Three Insights into Late-Fifteenth-Century Parliaments, 1461–85' in K. Dockray and P. Fleming eds., *People, Place, and Perspectives: Essays on Later Medieval and Early Tudor England in Honour of Ralph A. Griffiths* (Nonsuch Publishing, 2005), 131–53.

'Restraint, Mediation and Private Justice: George, Duke of Clarence as "Good Lord"', *The Journal of Legal History* 4:2 (1983), 56–71.

'What Was Personal about Personal Monarchy in the Fifteenth Century?', in S. McGlynn and E. Woodacre eds., *The Image and Perception of Monarchy in Medieval and Early Modern Europe* (Cambridge Scholars, 2014), 8–22.

Hill, L. M. ed., *The Ancient State, Authoritie and Proceedings of the Court of Requests by Sir Julius Caesar* (Cambridge University Press, 1975).

Hindle, S., *On the Parish? The Micro-Politics of Poor Relief in Rural England c.1550–1750* (Oxford University Press, 2004).

'The Micro-Spatial Dynamics of Litigation: The Chilvers Coton Tithe Dispute, *Barrows* vs. *Archer* (1657)', in M. Lobban, J. Begiato, and A. Green eds., *Law, Lawyers and Litigants in Early Modern England: Essays in Memory of Christopher W. Brooks* (Cambridge University Press, 2019), 140–63.

The State and Social Change in Early Modern England, c.1550–1640 (Palgrave Macmillan, 2000).

Hodgett, G. A. J., *Tudor Lincolnshire* (History of Lincolnshire Committee, 1975).

Hunt, A., *The Drama of Coronation: Medieval Ceremony in Early Modern England* (Cambridge University Press, 2009).

Ives, E. W., 'The Reputation of the Common Lawyers in English Society, 1450–1550', *University of Birmingham Historical Journal* 7 (1961), 130–61.

Ives, E. W. and A. H. Manchester eds., *Law, Litigants and the Legal Profession: Papers Presented to the Fourth British Legal History Conference at the University of Birmingham* (Royal Historical Society, 1983).

James, S. E., 'Against Them All for to Fight: Friar John Pickering and the Pilgrimage of Grace', *Bulletin of the John Rylands University Library of Manchester* 85:1 (2003), 37–64.

Jansen, S. L., *Political Protest and Prophecy Under Henry VIII* (Boydell, 1991).

Johnson, T., *Law in Common: Legal Cultures in Late Medieval England* (Oxford University Press, 2019).

Bibliography

'Legal Ephemera in the Ecclesiastical Courts of Late Medieval England', *Open Library of Humanities* 5:1 (2019), 1–27.

Jones, M. K. and M. G. Underwood, *The King's Mother: Lady Margaret Beaufort, Countess of Richmond and Derby* (Cambridge University Press, 1992).

Jones, N., '"Equity" in the Court of Chancery, 1529–1615', in D. Foster and C. Mitchell eds., *Essays on the History of Equity* (Hart Publishing, forthcoming, 2023).

Jones, W. R., 'The Court of the Verge: The Jurisdiction of the Steward and Marshal of the Household in Later Medieval England', *JBS* 10:1 (1970), 1–29.

Justice, S., *Writing and Rebellion: England in 1381* (Berkeley, 1994).

Kadens, E., 'The Admiralty Jurisdiction of the Court of Requests', in J. Witte, S. McDougall, and A. di Robilant eds., *Text and Contexts in Legal History: Essays in Honour of Charles Donahue* (Robbins Collection, 2016), 349–66.

'A Marine Insurance Fraud in the Star Chamber', in K. J. Kesselring and N. Mears eds., *Star Chamber Matters: An Early Modern Court and Its Records* (University of London Press, 2021), 155–74.

Kagan, R., *Lawsuits and Litigants in Castile, 1500–1700* (University of North Carolina Press, 1981).

Kane, B. and F. Williamson eds., *Women, Agency, and the Law, 1300–1700* (Pickering & Chatto, 2013).

Kellogg, S., *Law and the Transformation of Aztec Culture, 1500–1700* (University of Oklahoma Press, 1995).

Kelsoe, J., 'Arbitration in English Law and Society before the Act of 1698' (unpublished PhD thesis, University of Cambridge, 2021).

Kesselring, K. J., *Mercy and Authority in the Tudor State* (Cambridge University Press, 2003).

Kesselring, K. J. and N. Mears eds., *Star Chamber Matters: An Early Modern Court and Its Records* (University of London Press, 2021).

Killick, H. and T. W. Smith eds., *Petitions and Strategies of Persuasion in the Middle Ages: The English Crown and the Church, c.1200–c.1550* (Boydell & Brewer, 2018).

'The Scribes of Petitions in Late Medieval England', in H. Killick and T. W. Smith eds., *Petitions and Strategies of Persuasion in the Middle Ages: The English Crown and the Church, c.1200–1550* (Boydell & Brewer, 2018), 64–87.

Kisby, F., 'Kingship and the Royal Itinerary: A Study of the Peripatetic Household of the Early Tudor Kings 1485–1547', *The Court Historian* 4:1 (1999), 29–39.

'The Royal Household Chapel in Early Tudor London, 1487–1547' (unpublished PhD thesis, London University, 1996).

'"When the King Goeth a Procession": Chapel Ceremonies and Services, the Ritual Year, and Religious Reforms at the Early Tudor Court, 1485-1547', *JBS* 40:1 (2001), 44–75.

Kleineke, H., 'Richard III and the Origins of the Court of Requests', *The Ricardian* 11 (2007), 22–32.

Bibliography

Knox, D. A., 'The Court of Requests in the Reign of Edward VI, 1547–1553' (unpublished PhD thesis, University of Cambridge, 1974).

Lander, J. R., *Government and Community: England, 1450–1509* (Harvard University Press, 1980).

Latham, R. E. ed., *Revised Medieval Latin Word List from British and Irish Sources* (The British Academy, 1965).

Laughton, J., *Life in a Late Medieval City: Chester 1275–1520* (Oxbow Books, 2008).

Lehmberg, S. E., 'Star Chamber: 1485–1509', *Huntington Library Quarterly* 24:3 (1961), 189–214.

Leonard, H., 'Knights and Knighthood in Tudor England' (unpublished PhD thesis, Queen Mary University of London, 1970).

Liddy, C. D., *Contesting the City: The Politics of Citizenship in English Towns, 1250–1530* (Oxford University Press, 2017).

"'Sir ye be not kyng": Citizenship and Speech in Late Medieval and Early Modern England', *The Historical Journal* 60:3 (2016), 571–96.

'Urban Enclosure Riots: Risings of the Commons in English Towns, 1480–1525', *P&P* 226:1 (2015), 41–77.

Macnair, M., 'Equity and Conscience', *Oxford Journal of Legal Studies* 27:4 (2007), 659–81.

McComish, J., 'Defining Boundaries: Law, Justice and Community in Sixteenth-Century England', in F. Pirie and J. Scheele eds., *Legalism: Community and Justice* (Oxford University Press, 2014), 125–49.

'The Rhetoric and Reality of Access to Justice in Sixteenth Century England', *Beiträge zur Rechtsgeschichte Österreichs* Band 2 (2013), 494–501.

McCune, P., 'Order and Justice in Early Tudor Drama', *Renaissance Drama* 25 (1994), 171–96.

McCutchan, J. W., 'Justice and Equity in the English Morality Play', *Journal of the History of Ideas* 19:3 (1958), 405–10.

McGlynn, M., 'From Written Record to Bureaucratic Mind: Imagining a Criminal Record', *P&P* 250:1 (2021), 55–86.

'Idiots, Lunatics and the Royal Prerogative in Early Tudor England', *The Journal of Legal History* 26:1 (2005), 1–24.

McGovern, J., 'The Sheriffs of York and Yorkshire in the Tudor Period', *Northern History* 57:1 (2020), 60–76.

The Tudor Sheriff: A Study in Early Modern Administration (Oxford University Press, 2022).

McIntosh, M. K., *Autonomy and Community: The Royal Manor of Havering, 1200–1500* (Cambridge University Press, 2002).

'Finding a Language for Misconduct: Jurors in Fifteenth Century Local Courts', in B. A. Hanawalt and D. Wallace eds., *Bodies and Disciplines: Intersections of Literature and History in Fifteenth-Century England* (University of Minnesota Press, 1996), 87–122.

McKelvie, G., 'Kingship and Good Lordship in Practice in Late Medieval England: Henry VII, the Earl of Oxford, and the Case of John Hale, 1487', *Journal of Medieval History* 45:4 (2019), 504–22.

Bibliography

McSheffrey, S., 'Detective Fiction in the Archives: Court Records and the Uses of the Law in Late Medieval England', *History Workshop Journal* 65 (2008), 65–78.

Seeking Sanctuary: Crime, Mercy, and Politics in English Courts, 1400–1500 (Oxford University Press, 2017).

Metzger, F., 'The Last Phase of the Medieval Chancery', in A. Harding ed., *Law-Making and Law-Makers in British History: Papers Presented to the Edinburgh Legal History Conference, 1977* (Royal Historical Society, 1980), 79–89.

Meyer, L. J., '"Humblewise": Deference and Complaint in the Court of Requests', *Journal of Early Modern Studies* 4 (2015), 261–85.

Muldrew, C., *The Economy of Obligation: The Culture of Credit and Social Relations in Early Modern England* (Palgrave Macmillan, 1998).

Murray, L. P., 'Archbishop Cromer's Register', *Journal of the County Louth Archaeological Society* 8:4 (1936), 516–24.

Musson, A., 'Patterns of Supplication and Litigation Strategies: Petitioning the Crown in the Fourteenth Century', in H. Killick and T. W. Smith eds., *Petitions and Strategies of Persuasion in the Middle Ages: The English Crown and the Church, c.1200–c.1550* (Boydell & Brewer, 2018), 88–109.

Musson, A. and E. Powell eds., *Crime, Law and Society in the Later Middle Ages* (Manchester University Press, 2009).

Nichols, J. F., 'An Early Fourteenth Century Petition from the Tenants of Bocking to their Manorial Lord', *The Economic History Review* 2:2 (1930), 300–7.

Ormrod, W. M., 'Introduction: Medieval Petitions in Context', in W. M. Ormrod, G. Dodd, and A. Musson eds., *Medieval Petitions: Grace and Grievance* (York Medieval Press, 2009), 1–11.

'Murmur, Clamour and Noise: Voicing Complaint and Remedy in Petitions to the English Crown, c.1300–c.1460', in W. M. Ormrod, G. Dodd, and A. Musson eds., *Medieval Petitions: Grace and Grievance* (York Medieval Press, 2009), 135–55.

Ormrod, W. M., G. Dodd, and A. Musson eds., *Medieval Petitions: Grace and Grievance* (York Medieval Press, 2009).

Phillips, S., *The Prior of the Knights Hospitaller in Late Medieval England* (Boydell, 2009).

Pollard, A. F., 'The Growth of the Court of Requests', *EHR* 56:222 (1941), 300–3.

Poos, L. R., *Love, Hate and the Law in Tudor England: The Three Wives of Ralph Rishton* (Oxford University Press, 2022).

Post, J. B., 'Courts, Councils and Arbitrators in the Ladbroke Manor Dispute', in R. F. Hunnisett and J. B. Post eds., *Medieval Legal Records Edited in Memory of C. A. F. Meekings* (HMSO, 1978), 289–339.

'Equitable Resorts before 1450', in E. W. Ives and A. H. Manchester eds., *Law, Litigants and the Legal Profession: Papers Presented to the Fourth British Legal History Conference at the University of Birmingham 10–13 July 1979* (Royal Historical Society, 1983), 68–79.

Powell, E., 'Arbitration and the Law in England in the Late Middle Ages', *TRHS* 33 (1983), 49–67.

292 *Bibliography*

Kingship, Law, and Society: Criminal Justice in the Reign of Henry V (Clarendon Press, 1989).

'Law and Justice', in R. Horrox ed., *Fifteenth-Century Attitudes: Perceptions of Society in Late Medieval England* (Cambridge University Press, 1994), 29–41.

Pronay, N., 'The Chancellor, the Chancery, and the Council at the End of the 15th Century', in H. Hearder and H. R. Lyon eds., *British Government and Administration: Studies Presented to S. B. Chrimes* (University of Wales Press, 1974), 87–103.

Ramsay, N., 'Scriveners and Notaries as Legal Intermediaries in Later Medieval England', in J. Kermode ed., *Enterprise and Individuals in Fifteenth-Century England* (Alan Sutton, 1991), 118–31.

Rawcliffe, C., 'Baronial Councils in the Later Middle Ages', in C. Ross ed., *Patronage, Pedigree and Power in Later Medieval England* (Alan Sutton, 1979), 87–108.

'The Great Lord as Peacekeeper: Arbitration by English Noblemen and their Councils in the Later Middle Ages', in J. A. Guy and H. G. Beale eds., *Law and Social Change in British History: Papers Presented to the Bristol Legal History Conference, 14–17 July 1981* (Royal Historical Society, 1984), 34–54.

Reed, A. W., *Early Tudor Drama: Medwall, the Rastells, Heywood, and the More Circle* (Methuen & Co., 1926).

Reid, R. R., *The King's Council in the North* (Longmans, Green and Co., 1921).

Richardson, W. C., *Tudor Chamber Administration, 1485–1547* (Louisiana State University Press, 1952).

Roberts, P., 'The English Crown, the Principality of Wales and the Council in the Marches, 1534–1641', in B. Bradshaw and J. Morrill eds., *The British Problem, c.1534–1707: State Formation in the Atlantic Archipelago* (Macmillan Press, 1996), 118–47.

Rose, J. ed., *The Politics of Counsel in England and Scotland 1286–1707* (Oxford University Press, 2016).

Ross, C., *Richard III* (Eyre Methuen, 1981).

'Rumour, Propaganda and Public Opinion during the Wars of the Roses', in R. A. Griffiths ed., *Patronage, the Crown and the Provinces in Later Medieval England* (Gloucester, 1981), 15–32.

Samman, N., 'The Henrician Court during Cardinal Wolsey's Ascendancy, c.1514–1529' (unpublished PhD thesis, University of Wales, Bangor, 1988).

'The Progresses of Henry VIII, 1509–1529', in D. MacCulloch ed., *The Reign of Henry VIII: Politics, Policy, and Piety* (Macmillan, 1995), 59–74.

Scase, W., *Literature and Complaint in England, 1272–1553* (Oxford University Press, 2007).

'"Strange and Wonderful Bills": Bill-Casting and Political Discourse in Late Medieval England', in R. Copeland, D. Lawton, and W. Scase eds., *New Medieval Literature 2* (Clarendon Press, 1998), 225–47.

Bibliography

Seaward, P., 'Why the History of Parliament Is Not Written', in D. Hayton and L. Clark eds., *Historians and Parliament, Parliamentary History* Special Issue 40:1 (2021), 5–24.

Seward, D. E., 'Bishop John Alcock and the Roman Invasion of Parliament: Introducing Renaissance Civic Humanism to Tudor Parliamentary Proceedings', in L. Clark ed., *The Fifteenth Century XV: Writing, Records and Rhetoric* (Boydell & Brewer, 2017), 145–68.

Shagan, E. H., *Popular Politics and the English Reformation* (Cambridge University Press, 2003).

'Protector Somerset and the 1549 Rebellions: New Sources and New Perspectives', *EHR* 115:455 (1999), 34–63.

Shannon, W. D., '"On the left hand above the staire": Accessing, Understanding and Using the Archives of the Early-Modern Court of Duchy Chamber', *Archives* 123 (2010), 19–36.

Shepard, A., *Accounting for Oneself: Worth, Status and the Social Order in Early Modern England* (Oxford University Press, 2015).

Shepard, A. and T. Stretton, 'Women Negotiating the Boundaries of Justice in Britain, 1300–1700: An Introduction', *JBS* 58:4 (2019), 677–83.

Skeel, C. A. J., *The Council in the Marches: a study in local government during the sixteenth and seventeenth centuries* (Hugh Rees Ltd., 1904).

'The Council of the West', *TRHS* Fourth Series 4 (1921), 62–80.

Smail, D. L., *The Consumption of Justice: Emotions, Publicity and Legal Culture in Marseille, 1264–1423* (Cornell University Press, 2013).

Somerville, R., 'Ordinances for the Duchy of Lancaster', *Camden Miscellany 26*, Camden Fourth Series 14 (Royal Historical Society, 1975).

Spufford, M., 'The Scribes of Villagers' Wills in the Sixteenth and Seventeenth Centuries and Their Influence', *Local Population Studies* 7 (1971), 28–43.

Starkey, D., 'Intimacy and Innovation: The Rise of the Privy Chamber, 1485–1547', in D. Starkey, D. A. L. Morgan, J. Murphy, P. Wright, N. Cuddy, and K. Sharpe eds., *The English Court: From the Wars of the Roses to the Civil War* (Longman, 1987), 71–118.

Stretton, T., ed., *Marital Litigation in the Court of Requests 1542–1642*, Camden Fifth Series 32 (Cambridge University Press, 2008).

'Women, Legal Records, and the Problem of the Lawyer's Hand', *JBS* 58: 4 (2019), 684–700.

Women Waging Law in Elizabethan England (Cambridge University Press, 1998).

Sugarman, D., 'Law, Law-Consciousness and Lawyers as Constitutive of Early Modern England: Christopher W. Brooks's Singular Journey', in M. Lobban, J. Begiato, and A. Green eds., *Law, Lawyers and Litigants in Early Modern England: Essays in Memory of Christopher W. Brooks* (Cambridge University Press, 2019), 32–57.

Sutton, A., 'The Administration of Justice Whereunto We Be Professed', *The Ricardian* 4:53 (1976), 4–15.

294 *Bibliography*

Taylor, H., 'Labourers, Legal Aid and the Limits of Popular Legalism in Star Chamber', in K. J. Kesselring and N. Mears eds., *Star Chamber Matters: An Early Modern Court and Its Records* (University of London Press, 2021), 115–34.

Thirsk, J., ed., *The Agrarian History of England and Wales, Volume IV: 1500–1640* (Cambridge University Press, 1967).

Thornton, T., *The Channel Islands, 1370–1640: Between England and Normandy* (Boydell & Brewer, 2012).

'Local Equity Jurisdictions in the Territories of the English Crown: The Palatinate of Chester, 1450–1540', in D. E. S. Dunn ed., *Courts, Counties and the Capital* (Sutton Publishing, 1996), 27–52.

Tudor Enclosures (Historical Association, 1958).

Tout, T. F., *Chapters in the Administrative History of Medieval England: The Wardrobe, the Chamber, and the Small Seals* (6 vols., Manchester University Press, 1920–33).

Tucker, P., *Law Courts and Lawyers in the City of London 1300–1550* (Cambridge University Press, 2007).

Vermeesch, G., 'Reflections on the Relative Accessibility of Law Courts in Early Modern Europe', *Crime, Histoire & Sociétés* 19:2 (2015), 53–76.

Walter, J. ed., *Crowds and Popular Politics in Early Modern England* (Manchester University Press, 2006)

'"Law-Mindedness": Crowds, Courts and Popular Knowledge of the Law in Early Modern England', in M. Lobban, J. Begiato, and A. Green eds., *Law, Lawyers and Litigants in Early Modern England: Essays in Memory of Christopher W. Brooks* (Cambridge University Press, 2019), 164–84.

Watts, J. L., 'Counsel and the King's Council, *c.*1340–1540', in J. Rose ed., *The Politics of Counsel in England and Scotland 1286–1707* (Oxford University Press, 2016), 63–86.

'Ideas, Principles and Politics', in A. J. Pollard ed., *The Wars of the Roses* (Macmillan, 1995), 110–34.

'"A New Ffundacion of is Crowne": Monarchy in the Age of Henry VII', in B. Thompson ed., *The Reign of Henry VII: Proceedings of the 1993 Harlaxton Symposium* (Paul Watkins, 1995), 31–53.

'*The Policie in Christen Remes*: Bishop Russell's Parliamentary Sermons of 1483–84', in G. W. Bernard and S. J. Gunn eds., *Authority and Consent in Tudor England: Essays Presented to C. S. L. Davies* (Ashgate, 2002), 33–59.

'The Pressure of the Public on Later Medieval Politics', in L. Clark and C. Carpenter eds., *The Fifteenth Century IV: Political Culture in Late Medieval Britain* (Boydell, 2004), 159–80.

'Public or Plebs: The Changing Meaning of "The Commons", 1381–1549', in H. Pryce and J. Watts eds., *Power and Identity in the Middle Ages: Essays in Memory of Rees Davies* (Oxford University Press, 2007), 242–60.

Whittle, J., *The Development of Agrarian Capitalism: Land and Labour in Norfolk, 1440–1580* (Oxford University Press, 2000).

Bibliography

Williamson, J. A., *The Voyages of the Cabots and the Discovery of North America under Henry VII and Henry VIII* (The Argonaut Press, 1929).

Wood, A., *The 1549 Rebellions and the Making of Early Modern England* (Cambridge University Press, 2007).

Faith, Hope and Charity: English Neighbourhoods, 1500–1640 (Cambridge University Press, 2020).

The Politics of Social Conflict: The Peak Country, 1520–1770 (Cambridge University Press, 2009).

'Subordination, Solidarity and the Limits of Popular Agency in a Yorkshire Valley, c.1596–1615', *P&P* 193:1 (2006), 41–72.

Woolgar, C. M., *The Great Household in Late Medieval England* (Yale University Press, 1999).

Wrightson, K., *Ralph Tailor's Summer: A Scrivener, His City, and the Plague* (Yale University Press, 2011).

Youings, J. A., 'The Council of the West', *TRHS* 10 (1960), 41–59.

Youngs, D., '"A Besy Woman . . . and Full of Lawe": Female Litigants in Early Tudor Star Chamber', *JBS* 58:4 (2019), 735–50.

Humphrey Newton (1466–1536), an Early Tudor Gentleman (Boydell, 2008).

'"In to the Sterre Chambre": Female Plaintiffs before the King's Council in the Reign of Henry VII', in L. Clark ed., *Fifteenth Century XVII: Finding Individuality* (Boydell & Brewer, 2020), 120–44.

'Reading Ravishment: Gender and "Will" Power in the Early Tudor Star Chamber, 1500–50', in K. J. Kesselring and N. Mears eds., *Star Chamber Matters: An Early Modern Court and Its Records* (University of London Press, 2021), 41–60.

Zemon Davis, N., *Fiction in the Archives: Pardon Tales and Their Tellers in Sixteenth-Century France* (Polity, 1987).

Websites

Baker, J. H., 'Hare, Sir Nicholas (c.1495–1557), Lawyer and Speaker of the House of Commons', *ODNB*, Oxford University Press, January 2008, www.doi.org/10.1093/ref:odnb/12305, accessed January 2023.

Benskin, M., M. Laing, V. Karaiskos, and K. Williamson 'Civil War Petitions: Conflict, Welfare and Memory during and after the English Civil Wars, 1642–1710' (2017), www.civilwarpetitions.ac.uk, accessed January 2023.

eds., 'Index of Sources', *Electronic Linguistic Atlas of Late Mediaeval English* (2013), www.lel.ed.ac.uk/ihd/elalme/elalme.html, accessed January 2023.

Cooper, J. P. D., 'Philipps, Rowland (1467/8–1538?), College Head', *ODNB*, Oxford University Press, September 2004, www.doi.org/10.1093/ref:odnb/22132, accessed January 2023.

Howard, S. ed., *Petitions to the Cheshire Quarter Sessions 1573–1798*, British History Online, www.british-history.ac.uk/petitions/cheshire, accessed January 2023.

'The Power of Petitioning in Seventeenth Century England' (2019), www
.petitioning.history.ac.uk/, accessed January 2023.
'Recovering Europe's Parliamentary Culture, 1500–1700: A New Approach to
Representative Institutions', Oxford University, https://earlymodern
.web.ox.ac.uk/recovering-europes-parliamentary-culture-1500-1700-new-
approach-representative-institutions, accessed January 2023.
*Tudor Chamber Books: Kingship, Court and Society: The Chamber Books of Henry VII
and Henry VIII, 1485–1521* (2017), www.tudorchamberbooks.org, accessed
January 2023.

Index

Abingdon Abbey, 79
Ainsworth, Henry, 73 n. 51, n. 52, 267
Albion, Knight interlude, 31, 34, 37
Alcock, John, Bishop of Worcester, 26 n. 9
Almoner, 177, 179, 180–1, 183, 185, 209, 213
Ampthill, 79–80
arbitration, 32, 132–4, 136, 145, 164, 224, 236–7, 241, 246
  by magnates' councils, 52
Arnold, Richard, 133, 146
Arthur, Prince of Wales, 50, 54, 57, 76
Arundell, John, 74 n. 53, 266
assize courts, 64, 130, 137, 138, 237, 242
Attorney General, 237
Atwater, William, Dean of the Chapel Royal, 177, 179, 181–2, 188 n. 58, 191, 221, 269–70
Audley, Thomas, Lord Chancellor, 211

Bailey, John, royal chaplain, 71, 74 n. 53, 266
bailiffs, 53, 111, 115, 137, 189, 205, 207, 249, 250
Bainbridge, Christopher, 266–8
Barclay, Alexander, 31, 35, 39
Baron, Stephen, 47
Beale, Robert, clerk of the council, 77
Beaufort, Margaret, Countess of Richmond, 58, 76, 109, 242
Beaulieu Palace (New Hall), Essex, 79, 167
Bedford, 205
Bedfordshire, 80
  cases from, 100, 205
Belassis, Anthony, clerk of Chancery, 187 n. 56
Berkshire, 76
  cases from, 124
bill-casting, 30, 143–4
Blackfriars Priory, London, 27, 181, 183
Blythe, Geoffrey, Keeper of the Rolls and Dean of York, 73 n. 51, 266, 268
Blythe, John, Bishop of Salisbury, 74 n. 53, 266–7
body politic, 25, 27, 28, 103
Boleyn, Anne, Queen of England, 36

Bonner, Edmund, royal chaplain and Bishop of London, 88–9, 108, 180, 181, 273
Booth, Charles, Bishop of Hereford, 82 n. 87
Bowes, Robert, lawyer, 185, 225, 273–4
Bowring, Robert, lawyer, 227 n. 10, 268
Bray, Sir Reginald, Chancellor of the Duchy of Lancaster, 73 n. 51, 227, 266–8
Brewood Priory, 133
Bridewell Palace, 78–9
Bristol, 29, 46, 54, 128, 157, 158
Buckinghamshire
  cases from, 135, 149, 229, 240
Bury St Edmunds Abbey, 31
Bury, Henry, attorney, 150

Caesar, Sir Julius, Master of Requests, 14, 63, 71, 88, 90 n. 121, 91, 254
Calais
  hearings in, 75
Cambridge, 76
Cambridgeshire
  cases from, 167
canon law, 32, 34, 51, 151, 179, 181, 183, 196, 198, 211, 236, 245
Canterbury, 72
Carisbrooke Castle, 75
Carne, Edward, 88, 89, 185, 273–4
Catesby, Nicholas, 45, 65, 71 n. 44, 131, 133, 139, 145
Catesby, Robert, 133 n. 66, 145
Catherine of Aragon, Queen of England, 112, 181
Chancery, court of, 3, 11, 43, 50, 80, 82, 92, 165, 183, 211
  as court of conscience, 51, 54, 161
  costs, 201
  criticism, 40, 51, 252, 255
  decrees, 174, 231, 242, 245, 249 n. 100
  judges, 34, 197
  jurisdiction, 51, 63–4, 101, 121, 122–3, 124, 140, 241, 253, 257
  litigants, 95, 105, 108, 115

Index

Chancery, court of (cont.)
  petitions/bills, 146, 148, 153, 154 n. 52, 155,
    165, 184
  poor suitors, 197, 253
  procedures, 50–1, 52, 56, 60
  routine, 60, 77
  vexatious litigation, 215
  workload, 82
Channel Islands
  cases from, 100–1, 121
Chapuys, Eustace, 67
Charles I, King of England, 67 n. 30, 255
Chepstow Castle, 126
Chertsey Abbey, 79
Cheshire, 54, 146
  cases from, 210
Chester, 101, 136
Chester, county palatinate
  exchequer, 98, 255
Christ Church (Cardinal College), Oxford, 108
church courts, 32, 117, 130, 196, 198, 241
  jurisdiction, 216
civil law, 32, 34, 51, 179, 181, 182–3, 196, 211, 245
Civil War, 17
clergy, 107–9, 113, 133, 168, 179, 200
Clerk, John, Dean of the Chapel Royal, 82 n. 87,
    n. 88, 83, 129 n. 47, 177, 179, 181, 193, 198,
    211, 238, 271
Clerk, William, 186
Colet, John, Dean of St Paul's Cathedral, 82
    n. 87, n. 88
Collyweston Palace, 58, 75–6, 210, 242
Colyns, John, 31 n. 33, 145–6
common law, 34, 211
  commissions, 243
  courts, 121, 196, *See* King's Bench, court of,
    Common Pleas, court of
  criticism of conciliar justice, 217, 248–9, 253
  expensiveness, 40, 214, 247
  expertise, 183, 227, 245, *See* lawyers
  jurisdiction, 48, 56, 100, 110, 122, 125, 234, 235,
    238, 241, 245–6
  praise of, 32–3, 44
  procedures, 102, 218
  proofs, 231, 232
  relationship with conscience/equity courts, 14,
    17, 37–8, 43, 51, 160, 220, 241–3, 244, 263
Common Pleas, court of, 43, 221, 222, 243
  criticism, 40, 51
  jurisdiction, 213
  justices, 36
  lawyers, 149
commonplace books, 25, 31 n. 33, 39, 40, 145–7
commonwealth, 1, 23, 25, 26, 27, 30–1, 32, 103,
    160, 261, 262

conscience, 36–7, 39, 51, 155, 244
  courts of, 54, 122, 158, 160, 166, 231
  of judges, 38, 178, 182, 211, 212, 235–6
  of the defendant, 51, 161, 209
  of the king, 41, 161
Constable, Sir Marmaduke, 57, 269
Cornwall
  cases from, 98, 137, 232
Cornwallis, Lady, 132
coronation oaths, 24–5, 28, 38, 39, 41
Council in the Marches of Wales, 1, 44, 57, 62,
    64
  abolition, 255
  criticism, 255
  expenses, 58
  jurisdiction, 81, 99, 122, 140, 241
  ordinances, 54–5, 62
  personnel, 184
  petitions, 153
  poor suitors, 197
Council in the West, 58, 81, 165, 197
Council Learned in the Law, 49, 53, 227, 243
Council of the North, 1, 44, 57, 62, 64
  abolition, 255
  criticism, 255
  decrees, 236, 239
  expenses, 58
  jurisdiction, 81, 122, 140, 241
  ordinances, 55–6
  personnel, 182
  petitions, 153
  poor suitors, 197
  registers, 174
Coventry, 56, 124, 132 n. 60
coverture, 105, 244
craftsmen, 106–7, 111, 117, 168, 200
Cromer, George, Archbishop of Armagh, 86, 272
Cromwell, Thomas, 23, 27, 37, 88, 186
Croydon, 79
Cumberland
  cases from, 98, 152
custom, 32, 101, 125, 126, 134, 233, 246

Dacres, Robert, Master of Requests, 90–1, 110,
    148, 185, 186–7, 201, 213, 225, 234–5,
    245–6, 273–4
Dalby, Thomas, Archdeacon of Richmond, 57,
    129 n. 47, 269–70
Daubeney, Giles, Baron
Daubeney, 73 n. 51, 185, 228, 237, 266–8
de Joinville, Jean, 25, 67
de la Pole, Edmund, Earl of Suffolk, 75
de la Pole, Elizabeth, Duchess of Suffolk, 109
de la Pole, John, Earl of Lincoln, 55–6
de Marillac, Charles, 67

Index

Dean of the Chapel Royal, 82, 85, 165, 176, 177, 179, 180, 183, 185, 209, 213, 225, 228, 248–9
Deane, Henry, Bishop of Bangor, 268
debt litigation, 101, 121–3, 157, 222, 239
Denton, James, royal chaplain, 269–70
depositions, 52, 79, 135, 148, 187, 194, 231, 233, 248, 259, 260
Derbyshire
cases from, 135, 139, 204, 220, 231
Devonshire, 168
cases from, 99, 114, 121, 132, 159, 160, 165, 230
Digby, John, Keeper of the Privy Seal, 267
Dobson, William, attorney, 150
Docwra, Thomas, Prior of St John's, 82 n. 88, 83, 184, 228 n. 15
Dorchester, 204
Dorset
cases from, 166
Dover, 79
Dover Castle, 79
Drury, Sir Robert, 269
Duchy of Lancaster, 53, 227
council or court of, 53–4, 64, 71 n. 44
abolition, 255
expenses, 58
jurisdiction, 61, 81, 98
Dudley, Edmund, 24, 28, 47, 132–3, 219
due process, 17, 218–22
Durham, 56
cases from, 98
Durham, county palatinate
exchequer, 98
Dymmock, Andrew, king's solicitor, 73 n. 51, 226, 266–7
Dynham, John, Treasurer, 237

East Hampstead, 76
Ednam, John, Almoner, 177, 179 n. 22, 269
Edward I, King of England, 25 n. 6, 144
Edward IV, King of England, 26, 33, 35, 45, 54, 55, 70, 133
Edward VI, King of England, 12, 89, 91
Edward, Prince of Wales, 56
Egerton, Thomas, Baron Ellesmere and Lord Chancellor, 59 n. 62, 69–70
Elizabeth I, Queen of England, 3
Elizabeth of York, Queen of England, 76
Elizabeth Woodville, Queen of England, 133 n. 66, 133, 134
Eltham Ordinances, 47, 84, 86
Elyot, Thomas, 24
Empson, Richard, Chancellor of the Duchy of Lancaster, 47, 53, 74 n. 53, 243, 266, 269
enclosure, 123–5, 183
Enfield, 79

Englefield, Thomas, lawyer, 85, 180, 184, 186, 271
equity, 17, 28, 36–8, 39, 41, 48, 51, 58, 63, 105, 161–2, 209, 235–6, 254
Erasmus, Desiderius, 33
Essex, 149
cases from, 98, 206
Exchequer, 250
court of, 43, 49, 64
Exeter, 121

Fabyan, Robert, chronicler, 40
Fiennes, Thomas, Lord Dacres (of the South), 268
Fineux, John, Chief Justice, 60, 238
FitzGerald, Gerald, Earl of Kildare, 101
Fitzherbert, Anthony, justice, 36 n. 62, 246
Fitzjames, Richard, Bishop of Rochester and London, 177, 178–9, 182, 267–8
Fitzroy, Henry, Duke of Richmond, 55, 56 n. 51
Fitzwilliam, Sir William, 86, 87, 185, 271–2
Fleet prison, 238, 243
Flower, Richard, attorney, 150–1, 208
Fortescue, Sir Adrian, 41
Fortescue, Sir John, Chief Justice, 25, 32
Fotheringhay Castle, 210
Foxe, Richard, Keeper of the Privy Seal and Bishop of Bath and Wells, Durham, and Winchester, 71, 73 n. 51, 177, 179, 182, 210, 244, 266–9
France, 121
cases from, 101, 121
hearings in, 74
military campaigns, 44, 50, 105, 193
royal justice, 25, 66–8
Francis I, King of France, 67
freehold, 232, 242

gavelkind inheritance, 126
George, Duke of Clarence, 30
Gerard, Jacob, attorney, 150
Gilbert, John, lawyer, 183–4, 188 n. 58, 239 n. 58, 270–1
Giustinian, Sebastian, Venetian ambassador, 197
Gloucester, 76
Gloucestershire, 54
cases from, 126, 139, 152, 243
hearings in, 76
Goldwell, James, Dean of Salisbury, 67
Grafton, 79
Gray's Inn, 32, 150
Greenwich Palace, 78, 167, 175, 192–4
Greville, William, lawyer, 227, 267
Guildford, 79
Guildford, Sir Richard, 73 n. 51, 185, 227, 266–8
Guisnes Castle, 75, 101

300   *Index*

Hadley, John, attorney, 151, 208
Hall, Edward, chronicler, 24, 39, 84, 216
Hampshire, 76, 195
Hampton Court Palace, 167
Hare, Nicholas, Master of Requests, 88, 89, 185–7, 273–4
Harrington, John, clerk of the council, 66, 69, 85, 186
Hatton, Richard, royal chaplain, 227, 267–9
Heath, Nicholas, Bishop of Rochester and Worcester, 90, 180–1, 225, 273–4
Henry IV, King of England, 53
Henry V, King of England, 44
Henry VI, King of England, 48
Henry VII, King of England
    governmental developments, 3, 44, 49
    praise of, 35
    progresses, 29, 38, 46, 72–3, 74–6, 210
    signature, 191–2, 202
Henry VIII, King of England
    advice to, 26 n. 12, 28, 47
    death, 91
    governmental developments, 3, 44
    granting pardons, 38
    imprisonment of complainants, 41
    minority kingship, 78, 91
    progresses, 47, 74–5
    religious policies, 33, 108, 181
    signature, 1, 191, 202, 251
    stamp, 186, 194
Herbert, Sir Walter, 126, 160
Hereford Cathedral, 167
Herefordshire, 54
    cases from, 99
Hertfordshire, 149
Higgons, Edward, 270
Hobart, James, king's attorney, 226, 266
Hobbes, Thomas, 177, 268
Howard, Thomas, 1st Earl of Surrey and 2nd Duke of Norfolk, 57
Howard, Thomas, 2nd Earl of Surrey and 3rd Duke of Norfolk, 56 n. 51, 58
humanism, 23, 33
Huntingdonshire
    cases from, 98
husbandmen, 110–11, 113, 117, 124, 168, 200, 205, 214, 233, 247
Hussey, Sir John, 86, 185, 272
Hussey, Sir William, Chief Justice, 73 n. 51, n. 52, 226, 231, 266, 267
Hutton, William, 2

in forma pauperis, 196–9, 210, 236
indifferent justice, 35–6, 216
interrogatories, 16, 148, 190, 194, 196, 233

Ipswich, 235
Ireland
    cases from, 102, 121
    legal system, 101
Isle of Wight
    hearings in, 75
Islip, John, Abbot of Westminster, 82–3, 86, 180, 271

Jack Cade, 51
Jacquetta, Duchess of Bedford and Countess Rivers, 133
Janne, Thomas, Dean of the Chapel Royal, 71, 73 n. 51, 177, 181, 266–8
justices of the peace, 137, 138, 145, 149

Keeper of the Privy Seal, 48
    jurisdiction, 50
Kendal, John, Prior of St John's, 73 n. 51, n. 52, 73, 266–8
Kent, 127
    cases from, 70, 98, 120, 126, 128, 132, 136, 161, 163, 214
Kidwelly, Sir Morgan, lawyer, 113, 227, 237, 243, 268–9
King, Oliver, Bishop of Exeter, 73 n. 51, n. 52, 266–7
King's Bench, court of, 26, 43, 64, 71, 206, 207, 221–2, 238, 243
    criticism, 40, 51
    jurisdiction, 213
    justices, 36
    lawyers, 149
Kingsmill, John, lawyer, 73 n. 51, n. 52, 227 n. 10, 266–8
Kingston, William, 36

labourers, 113, 117, 122, 164, 194
Lambarde, William, 14, 62, 70
Lambert Simnel, 72
Lancashire, 53, 64
    cases from, 108
landholding
    concepts of, 28
    litigation about, 101, 123–5, 244, 245–6
Langley Palace, 72, 76, 79
Langton, Thomas, Bishop of St David's, 65
law readings, 25, 211
lawyers, 18, 41, 43, 46, 52, 99, 109, 111, 187, 190, 203, 211, 225
    attorneys, 147–8, 237
    costs, 151–2, 208
    criticism of conciliar justice, 211, 215–16
    legal counsel, 148, 207–8, 225, 239
Leicestershire, 53, 124
    cases from, 234

Index

Lincoln's Inn, 63 n. 4, 128
Lincolnshire, 53, 169
    cases from, 99, 129, 138, 233, 242, 243
livestock, 119, 120, 121–2, 129, 137, 161, 217,
    230
London, 99, 146, 147, 167, 212, 213
    cases from, 96, 120, 121, 127, 128, 135, 158, 168,
    205–6, 207, 216, 232, 233, 248
    court of requests, 92, 136, 215–16
    courts, 40, 136, 157, 205
Longland, John, Dean of Salisbury and Bishop of
    Lincoln, 86–7, 180, 181, 270–1
Lord Chancellor, 45, 47
    jurisdiction, 50
Lord Treasurer, 47
    jurisdiction, 50
Louis IX, King of France, 25, 67
Lovell, Sir Thomas, 73 n. 51, 227–8, 244, 266–70
Lucas, John, 274
Ludlow Castle, 54, 55–6, 60, 197
Lupton, Roger, Provost of Eton, 86, 270–2
Lyndwood, William, 196, 197–9

Magdalen College, Oxford, 181
Magna Carta, 63 n. 4, 219–22, 243
Magnus, Thomas, Archdeacon of the East Riding
    of Yorkshire, 57, 269–70
Manchester, 139
manorial courts, 117, 130, 134–5, 138, 139, 143,
    145, 213
    copyhold, 135, 216, 246, 263
marital litigation, 127–8, 131, 216, 238–9
Martyn, Edmund, Dean of St Stephen's, 267–8
Mary I, Queen of England, 54
Masters of Requests, 66–8, 89, 156, 185–7, 202,
    225–6, 255
Mayhew, Richard, Almoner and President of
    Magdalen College, Oxford, 74 n. 53, 179,
    182, 237, 266–9
mayoral courts, 130, 135–7, 213, 241
mediation, 131–2, *See* arbitration
merchants, 101, 107, 111, 115, 117, 120, 122–3, 147
mercy, 25, 35, 38–9, 41, 45, 61, 158, 161–3, 165, 216,
    235, 261
Merton College, Oxford, 182
Mey, William, 274
Middle Temple, 150, 183–4, 208
Middleham Castle, 55
Middlesex
    cases from, 96, 98, 205
Middleton, Robert, lawyer, 71, 74 n. 53, 74, 227,
    266–8
Mordaunt, John, 266–9
More, Sir Thomas, 24, 33–4, 37, 183–4, 252, 271

Morgan, John, Dean of Windsor, 267
Morton, John, Archbishop of Canterbury, 26, 28,
    34, 60, 61

Neville, George, Baron Burgavenny, 268–9
Neville, Richard, Earl of Warwick, 30, 134
Neville, Sir Thomas, 82 n. 87, n. 88, 86, 87, 185,
    228 n. 15, 271–2
Newton, Humphrey, 146–7
Nix, Richard, Bishop of Norwich, 107, 181, 268
Norfolk
    cases from, 99, 127, 134
North, Edward, 31
Northampton, 72, 210
Northamptonshire, 58
Northumberland
    cases from, 98
Norwich, 99
Nottingham, 65, 75, 167, 192
Nottinghamshire, 53, 74
    cases from, 129, 217, 234

Oseley, Richard, clerk of Requests, 251
Oxenbridge, John, canon of Windsor, 269
Oxford, 182, 205, 255
Oxfordshire, 149
    cases from, 124
oyer and terminer commissions, 47, 138, 220, 221

Parliament, 18, 26, 34, 35, 41, 48
    acts, 28, 29, 36, 124, 158–60, 196, 254
    bills, 3, 68–9, 218–19, 255
    committees, 72
    petitions to, 43, 45
    sermons in, 26, 27, 30
Paston, John, 61
Patten, John, attorney, 150
perjury, 158, 209
Perkin Warbeck, 72
Petre, Sir William, 89, 90, 185, 273–4
Philip, Archduke of Burgundy, 75
Philipps, Rowland, Vicar of Croydon, 86–7,
    271–2
Pilgrimage of Grace. *See* rebellions
Pilkington, Robert, 139, 209–11, 226, 231–2
Pipewell Abbey, 210
poetry, 25, 29–32, 33, 40
Pole, Margaret, Countess of Salisbury, 109
Pole, Sir Richard, 268
Portsmouth, 106
Prince of Wales, 54
Privy Chamber, 186
Privy Council, 77, 89, 186, 255
    emergence in 1530s, 48, 90

302   *Index*

quarter sessions, 130, 137–8

Radford, John, attorney, 150
Raglan Castle, 76
Rastell, John, 121
Ratcliffe, John, Lord Steward, 74 n. 53, 266
Rawlins, Richard, Almoner, 177, 188 n. 58, 270–1
Reading, 192
Reading Abbey, 79
rebel petitions, 25, 33, 144
rebellions
    1450 Jack Cade's rebellion, 51
    1469 Yorkshire rebellion, 33
    1483 Buckingham's rebellion, 65 n. 12
    1486 Stafford and Lovell rebellion, 38
    1497 Cornish rebellion, 75
    1497 Perkin Warbeck rebellion, 33, 72
    1536 Pilgrimage of Grace, 33, 37, 39, 58, 182, 257
recognisances, 34, 187, 250–1
Rede, Robert, lawyer, 71, 73 n. 51, 227 n. 10, 266–7
Redman, Richard, Bishop of St Asaph, 65–6, 267
Reformation, The, 11, 33, 108, 109
Requests, court of
    as the 'poor man's court', 96, 113–15, 143, 162–4, 169–70, 197–9, 214, 235, 254, 261
    attempts to abolish, 68–9, 255
    clerks, 66, 89, 149–50, 187–8, 196, 226
    commissions, 164, 190–1, 195, 199, 209, 218, 233–5
    common-law expertise, 226–7
    costs, 168, 195–6, 199, 208, 240
    lawyers. *See* lawyers
    name, 63–4, 66, 70–1, 80, 92, 165, 173–4, 230, 259
    president, 179, 211
    record-keeping, 71, 73, 77, 176, 200, 224
    routine, 76–7
Reynes, Robert of Acle, 31
Rich, Richard, Lord Chancellor, 253
Richard II, King of England, 48
Richard III, King of England, 45, 55, 57, 65–6, 69, 70
Richard, Duke of York, 32
Richmond Palace, 72, 74, 214
riots, 119, 120, 135, 137, 158, 160, 166
Riseley, John, 267
Robin of Redesdale, 33
Roper, William, 82 n. 87, n. 88
royal council
    bifurcation into courts, 43, 59
    committees, 82–4, 211
    investigation of sedition, 33
    membership, 47–8, 185, 226
    ordinances, 48–50
    registers, 174

royal household, 185, 226
    accounts, 4, 175, 191
    clergy, 48, 71, 78, 178, 179–81, 184, 188, 192, 197–9
    itinerancy, 72, 74–5
    messengers, 189
    reforms, 84
    servants and officers, 112, 168, 227–8
royal proclamations, 24, 29, 124
Russell, John, Bishop of Lincoln, 26 n. 9, 27 n. 17
Russell, John, Earl of Bedford, 58, 197
Rutland
    cases from, 98
Rydon, Robert, clerk of the council, 150, 187

Salisbury, 192, 195
Sampson, Richard, Dean of the Chapel Royal and Bishop of Chichester, 85–6, 87–9, 107, 150, 179–80, 181, 189 n. 60, 237 n. 49, 248, 271–4
Sampson, Robert, clerk of the privy seal and council, 149, 152, 187
Sampson, Simon, attorney, 150–1, 208
Saunders, Laurence of Coventry, 56, 60
Savage, Thomas, Bishop of Rochester and London, Archbishop of York, and president of the attendant council, 57, 60, 71, 73 n. 51, 75, 177, 178, 179, 210–11, 212, 266–9
Scottish marches, 98
seals, 202
    great seal, 191, 221, 243
    privy seal, 46, 79, 189, 195, 201, 206, 210, 218, 220, 222, 247, 248, 251, 255
    signet seal, 191, 193, 195
Seckford, Thomas, master of Requests, 251
serjeants-at-arms, 128, 164, 205
Seymour, Edward, Duke of Somerset, 12, 92, 253
Shaa, Sir John, mayor of London, 136–7, 215
Sheen Palace, 72, 74, 121 n. 16
Sheffield, William, 74 n. 53, 266
Sherborne, Robert, King's Secretary and Bishop of Chichester, 157, 227, 266–8
sheriffs, 137, 138, 149, 157, 159, 207, 249
    courts and tourns, 137, 138, 213
Shropshire, 54
    cases from, 99
Sittingbourne, 79
Skelton, John, poet laureate, 34, 211
Smith, William, Bishop of Chester, 266
Somerset
    cases from, 128, 145
Somerset, Sir Charles, 185, 227, 267–8
Southwell, Robert, Master of Requests, 68 n. 31, 89 n. 117, 90, 185, 186, 187, 273–4

Index

303

Spelman, John, 32
St German, Christopher, lawyer, 38, 51, 86, 87, 272
St Paul's Cathedral, 239
Stafford, Humphrey, Duke of Buckingham, 145
Staffordshire, 133
    cases from, 108, 237, 246
Standish, Henry, Bishop of St Asaph, 86, 183, 271
Stanley, Thomas, Earl of Derby, 267
Staple Inn, 150
Star Chamber
    1487 act of, 50
    council in, 59, 70, 72, 226, 244
    court of, 1, 3, 9, 11, 59, 62, 68, 71, 80–1, 134, 161, 165, 192, 211, 242
        abolition, 255
        costs, 201
        decrees, 231, 238, 245
        judges, 34, 184, 185, 197, 228 n. 15
        jurisdiction, 35, 73, 101, 120, 121, 123, 140, 241, 253, 257
        litigants, 95, 104, 115
        name, 92
        petitions, 83, 153, 155, 165, 166, 176
        poor suitors, 84, 197
        procedures, 60
        registers, 174
        routine, 61
        workload, 82, 84, 139
    rooms at Westminster, 59
Starkey, Thomas, 24
Stillington, Robert, Bishop of Bath and Wells and Lord Chancellor, 26, 30, 51 n. 31
Stokesley, John, Almoner and Bishop of London, 81, 83, 84 n. 96, n. 99, 87, 176, 177, 179, 181, 182, 188 n. 58, 221, 222, 238, 239 n. 58, 250, 271
    dismissal from the Court of Requests, 184, 211–13, 249
Stratford Langthorne Abbey, 145
Suffolk
    cases from, 207, 218, 235
Sulyard, William, lawyer, 79, 85–6, 87, 184, 186, 188 n. 58, 271–3
Surrey
    cases from, 98
Sussex
    cases from, 98, 108, 121, 134
Sutton, Richard, lawyer, 112, 227, 239 n. 58, 243, 268–70
Symeon, Geoffrey, Dean of the Chapel Royal, 177, 179 n. 22, 179, 181, 188 n. 58, 221, 237, 242, 243, 268–9

Tempest, Sir Thomas, 39
Thirlby, Thomas, Dean of the Chapel Royal and Bishop of Westminster, 68 n. 32, 88, 89–90, 162, 180–1, 182, 225
Thomas, Earl of Surrey, 57
Thornbury, 79
Toneys, Robert, 82 n. 87
Tower of London, 36, 74, 219
Townsend, Roger, lawyer, 86, 185, 271–3
Tregonwell, John, Master of Requests, 67–8, 185 n. 43, 185, 186 n. 46, 273–4
Tunstall, Cuthbert, Bishop of Durham, 27, 28, 180, 181, 182, 267, 274
Turberville, Sir John, 267
Turnor, Richard, clerk of Requests and the privy seal, 85, 150, 151, 187–8
Tyrell, Sir James, 75, 101, 268

Vale, John, 45
Valor Ecclesiasticus 1534–35, 108
Vaughan, Edward, 269
Vavasour, John, Chief Justice, 267
Veysey, John, Dean of the Chapel Royal, 124, 177, 179, 181, 183, 184, 188 n. 58, 197, 213, 221, 234, 235, 237, 239 n. 59, 242, 248, 259, 270–1
villeins, 114
violence
    litigation about, 118–20, 206, 238

Wales, 53, 245
    1536 Act of Union, 54, 100
    cases from, 98, 100, 126, 160
    hearings in, 74
    marcher lordships, 100
Walsingham, 76
Waltham Abbey, 79
Wanstead, 194
Wards and Liveries, court of, 49, 255
Warham, William, Archbishop of Canterbury and Lord Chancellor, 26, 27, 73 n. 51, 266–7
Wars of the Roses, 17, 33
Warwick, 132 n. 60
Warwick Castle, 65
Warwickshire, 53
    cases from, 45, 114, 119, 125, 131, 133, 182 n. 30, 217
Watts, John, 268
Welles, John, Viscount Welles, 267–8
Westminster, 137, 209, 244
    cases from, 105
    Palace, 40, 44, 48, 58, 64, 72–3, 74, 76, 78–9, 80, 96, 112, 149, 151, 167–9, 195, 220, 241

Index

Westminster (cont.)
  Exchequer chamber, 82
  Hall, 43, 54, 205
  Lord Treasurer's chamber, 82, 83
  St Stephen's Chapel, 212
  White Hall, 79, 80, 82, 88, 90, 98, 168, 173, 176, 188, 194, 211, 212, 213, 249, 259
Westmorland
  cases from, 98, 99
Weston, Sir Richard, 82 n. 88
Weston, William, Prior of St John's, 86, 228, 271
Wetherby, Thomas, attorney, 150
widows, 36, 104, 105–6, 109, 112–13, 115, 120, 121–2, 127, 128, 138, 142, 151, 157, 160, 162, 168, 200, 214, 215, 216, 242
Wilkins, William, attorney, 150
Willoughby, Robert, Baron Willoughby de Broke, 73 n. 51, n. 52, 132, 228, 266
Wiltshire, 129, 149
  cases from, 114, 122, 160, 196 n. 89
Winchester, 106
Windsor Castle, 72, 74, 76, 78, 167, 259
Windsor, Sir Andrew, 82 n. 87, n. 88
Woking, 79, 175, 191
Wolman, Richard, Dean of Wells, 79, 85–6, 87, 180, 184, 189 n. 60
Wolsey, Thomas
  as Almoner, 88, 177, 269–70
  as Lord Chancellor, 24, 34, 56 n. 51, 58, 77, 86
  criticism of, 31, 34, 206, 216
  education, 181

expansion of conciliar justice, 78, 82, 84, 86, 197, 211
foundation of colleges, 108
petitions to, 83, 157, 176, 211–13
praise of, 252
views on justice, 27, 34
Woodstock Palace, 72, 76, 78, 167, 192
Woodville, Anthony, Earl Rivers, 133
Worcester, 77
Worcestershire, 38, 54, 133, 168
  cases from, 135, 248, 259
writs, 16, 45, 100, 249, *See* seals
  contents, 102
  for commissions, 79, 204–7
    contents, 234
  of nihil habet, 137
  of *replevin*, 137
  of restitution, 138
  production, 50, 77, 79, 187, 201, 202
  receipt, 135, 204–7, 263
  subpoena, 164, 189, 195
    criticism, 218–19, 247
Wyatt, Sir Henry, 74 n. 53, 82 n. 87, 112, 185, 198, 267, 271

yeomen, 110–11, 113, 115, 168, 200
York, 55, 58, 66, 69
York Minster, 239
Yorkshire, 53, 55–6
  cases from, 81 n. 83, 98–100, 107, 129, 150, 194 n. 83, 236, 239

Printed in the United States
by Baker & Taylor Publisher Services